EAT MY WORDS

EAT MY WORDS

Reading Women's Lives through the Cookbooks They Wrote

JANET THEOPHANO

palgrave

EAT MY WORDS

© Janet Theophano, 2002

First published 2002 by PALGRAVE™
175 Fifth Avenue, New York, N.Y.10010 and
Houndmills, Basingstoke, Hampshire RG21 6XS.
Companies and representatives throughout the world.

PALGRAVE is the new global publishing imprint of St. Martin's Press LLC Scholarly and Reference Division and Palgrave Publishers Ltd. (formerly Macmillan Press Ltd.).

ISBN 0–312–23378–7 hardback

Library of Congress Cataloging-in-Publication Data
Theophano, Janet.
Eat my words : reading women's lives through the cookbooks they wrote / Janet Theophano.
     p.   cm.
Includes bibliographical references and index.
ISBN 0–312–23378–7
     1. Food writing—History.   2. Women food writers—History.
I. Title.

808'.06641—dc21

2001036834

A catalogue record for this book is available from the British Library.

Design by Letra Libre, Inc.

First edition: February 2002
10 9 8 7 6 5 4 3 2 1

Printed in the United States of America.

For my family
Jeff, Damien, Julia, and Omi
and
in loving memory of
Colin Gilmore, Ralph Ginsberg,
and David M. Smith

Contents

List of Illustrations

I savor each simple gesture in this kitchen, filling the tea kettle, lighting the stove, click of the cup in the saucer. They've all been here, are here, the family of women, nursing one another with teas—de canela, hierbabuena, gordolobo. Straight and erect in their good health or bent with age and arthritis, sacramental acts for another woman, or a husband, father, or child, steeping an old cure that began underground. "It is strange to be so many women," as Adrienne Rich says.

—*Pat Mora,* House of Houses
(Boston: Beacon Press, 1997)

Acknowledgments

During the years I have worked on this project the support, encouragement, and general goodwill of many friends and strangers have exhilarated me.

I owe a debt to Michael Ryan and Daniel Traister of the Annenberg Rare Book and Manuscript Library, University of Pennsylvania, for inviting me to curate the Esther B. Aresty Collection of Rare Books on the Culinary Arts. Nancy Shawcross, Lynne Farrington, and John Pollack of the Annenberg Library graciously guided me through mounting my first exhibition. They and Margaret Kruesi have continued to be an ever-present source of helpfulness, intelligence, and bibliographical advice. Jerry Drew, Jennifer Lindner, Dana Plansky, Rebecca Smith, and Karoline Wallace provided much appreciated research support and the benefit of their own perspectives on the material. Patricia Smith, then of the University of Pennsylvania Press, encouraged me to write this book.

I wish to thank Sherrie Inness for her support and editorial advice as I wrote chapter 7, a version of which first appeared in her edited volume, *Kitchen Culture in America,* published by University of Pennsylvania Press. I thank the Press for allowing me to reprint it here. The excerpt from *House of Houses* is reprinted by permission of Beacon Press, Boston.

I took several leaves from the College of General Studies at Penn to complete the research and writing. I am deeply grateful to Richard Hendrix, director, and to my colleagues for their patience during my absences. In particular, I would like to thank Susan Gill, Denise Miller, and Kristine Rabberman who tended to student affairs while I was away.

A research grant from the University of Pennsylvania Research Foundation enabled me to travel to England to the archives in Lincoln and London.

Staff at the Lincolnshire Archives, Deborah Thornton especially, and the Public Records Offices in London answered a myriad of questions and helped to guide my searches.

Librarians and archivists at the Historical Society of Pennsylvania, the Library Company of Philadelphia, and the Schlesinger Library at Radcliffe helped me locate documents. Stephen Tabor at the Huntington Library, San Marino, California, was especially helpful, as was Ian Argall of the Huntingdonshire Family History Society, England.

At the Library Company of Philadelphia I found librarian Wendy Woloson, an extraordinarily enthusiastic supporter. I am indebted to her for locating letters, manuscripts, and books useful for my study. Excited by the topic, she went above and beyond the call of duty and read the manuscript. Her comments and insights were valuable additions. I would also like to thank James Green of the Library Company for taking the time to talk with me about printing in seventeenth- and eighteenth-century America.

A National Endowment of the Humanities Fellowship at Winterthur Library led me to a new collection of documents and the incomparable association of librarians, fellows, and staff assembled there in the summer and fall of 1999. In seminar discussions, in the archives, and at lunch, I benefited from conversations and guidance from Gretchen Buggeln, Lori Finkelstein, Maggie Lidz, Cindy Lobel, Richard McKinstry, Nicola Shilliam, and Susan Stabile. Their companionship and conversation were invaluable during long days in Winterthur's sanctuary of rare books and manuscripts. I am especially grateful to Jeanne Solensky and Neville Thompson for their inestimable and generous assistance over the past two years.

There are many who read and commented on the chapters. Monique Bourque, Janet Golden, Janet Tighe, and Elizabeth Toone of my writing group read earlier drafts of some chapters and, along with their critiques, encouraged me to keep writing. Regina Bendix read a draft of the manuscript; her gentle editorial comments helped me to develop some of my arguments more completely. Her friendship has been a comfort and an inspiration. Peter Parolin's subtle and thoughtful reading of chapter 6 enriched my ideas about women's reading and writing. I hope he finds the integration he suggested. Peter also introduced me to Susan Frye, whose work on women's literacy enhanced my own understandings. Barbara and Burt Abrams read chapter 2 for accuracy. Masterful writer and friend Gayle Samuels's enthusiasm for the topic supported me through moments of doubt. In addition, she transformed some awkward phrases into elegant prose. Kimberly Lau read a draft of the manuscript and offered countless helpful suggestions and encouragement.

I have benefited from colleagues whose historical perspective has enriched the book: Marc Miller read and commented on every chapter with a historian's eye. His editorial advice evinced clarity from muddy passages. David Traxel read an early draft of chapter 7. Russ Kazal offered suggestions for sources for chapter 2. Janet Golden and Eric Schneider cheered me on as I struggled through the process of completing the manuscript. Kevin Scott Wong shared his knowledge of the Chao family with me. Susan Florio-Ruane provided sources and encouragement. Rita Berger Morra assured me that the book was enjoyable, and Jonathan Shaw's graceful editorial advice helped me to prepare the manuscript for publication. In some of my darkest moments, Tina Phipps gave me her writer's insights and the solace of friendship.

I am grateful to friends and family whose contributions were indirect but sustaining: Stephanie Applebaum, Shellie Bailkin, Deborah Burnham, Peggy and Mark Curchak, Jane Erickson, Lois Ginsberg, Melissa Goldstein, Mary Harris, Harriet Izenberg and Nick Sparozic, Demie Kurz, Max, Melissa, Rachel, and Sterling Mayer, Margaret Mills, Kathy and Lou Pollak, Elisabeth Rozin, and Ann Shultz. Yael and Eviatar Zerubavel urged me to get the book "into and out of the oven before it burned." Barbara Rice listened to the progress of my work on summer walks, fed our family bread and scones, and counseled me to find a sound and sensible pace for my life. Perry Gilmore assigned portions of my work to her class in feminist studies at the University of Alaska, Fairbanks, and indulged us all with a conference call discussion that occasioned enough enthusiasm to keep me going. As surrogate sisters, we have shared the joys of generating families, and from her strength, tenderness, and courage I have learned about enduring inconsolable losses.

My agent Lynn Whittaker's editorial comments, enthusiasm, encouragement, and vision of this book were signposts to guide me along the way. My editor, Michael Flamini of Palgrave, is an author's dream. He cared deeply about the project and supported it wholeheartedly. Alan Bradshaw, Amanda Johnson, and Erin Chan at Palgrave were always there to answer my questions and guide me through the process of production.

Many friends, students, and colleagues donated cookbooks to my collection of ephemera: Malcolm Campbell, Brian Du Bois, Marie Gallagher, Charlie Groth, Amanda Holmes, and Norman Johnston among them. The notable contributions of Roger Abrahams, a "virtuoso" (a gentleman and a scholar), and Rosemary Ranck have been included in this book. I also thank Rosemary for conversations about Lizzie's recipe book. To my mother-in-law, Dina Shultz, I am grateful both for her collection of recipes, which documents her talents as a cook and her—now my—family's history and the welcome I have always received in her kitchen. I am grateful to my mother, Greta Longo, a German Jewish refugee who learned English while in London working in other women's kitchens during World War II. Although she never enjoyed domestic work, she taught me that this labor was one means of survival. She has never recorded her recipes, but I acquired the knowledge of a few of her culinary specialties: pflaumenkuchen (plum cake), saurbraten, and stöllen. More than cooking, however, it is my mother's courage and love of life that have been inspirational.

My son Damien Theophano, a masterful chef in his own right, and stepdaughter Julia Shultz, a gifted writer, listened and waited while their (step) mother worried and wrote. Both taught me how important it was to remember the past and tell its stories, especially at dinner.

Finally, to the two people without whom this book would not have been written I owe something beyond gratitude. Kristine Rabberman, colleague and friend, helped me to shape the book with her brilliance and breadth of knowledge as a reader, thinker, and writer. Kris spent countless hours searching for sources, reading drafts, editing, discussing, and encouraging me. Her grace, humility, and generosity are unparalleled.

My husband, Jeff Shultz, read every word—more than once—and still pretended to be surprised and delighted by what I wrote. He was a jack of all trades for the years I worked on this project. He fixed computers, cooked meals, and negotiated family crises. His patience was unfaltering; his encouragement was unending. For all of his support and love there are no words.

Introduction

Without writing a word, Mrs. Buwei Yang Chao authored a cookbook. Mrs. Chao, a physician, wife, mother, and cook, emigrated from China to the United States in the mid-twentieth century, and the cookbook she composed was written out for her by her daughter and husband. "You know," she tells her readers, "I speak little English and write less." Despite her own lack of fluency in English, Mrs. Chao's *How to Cook and Eat in Chinese* is a double act of translation, for it interprets the techniques of Chinese cooking and the etiquette of eating Chinese meals for an American audience. And between the lines of her recipes, Mrs. Chao also mirrors the act of translation required of immigrants adjusting to their adopted countries. As we, the readers, are taught how to cook and eat in Chinese, we also travel with Mrs. Chao on this more personal journey as she succinctly narrates her affectionate, sometimes tense, relationships with her family and the life experiences that compelled her to author this book. *How to Cook and Eat in Chinese* is thus much more than a cookbook: It is the stage on which Mrs. Chao unfolds a personal, family, and cultural drama.

An exceptional story told by an extraordinary woman, Mrs. Chao's cookbook does not stand alone. For hundreds of years, women of diverse backgrounds have found the homely cookbook a suitable place to record their stories and thoughts as well as their recipes.

Over the past ten years I have been researching manuscript and printed cookery books from the United States and England from the seventeenth to the mid-twentieth centuries and finding myself constantly amazed by the richness of these sources. Few of these materials are readily available to readers today: Some have been kept in families as purely private documents, while others have languished in archives, often in manuscript form. Even those that were published are no longer widely known and now are generally available only in historical collections. My purpose, therefore, is twofold: first, to make some of these materials known to both scholars and general readers; and second, to open a window into the lives of women of distinct classes, cultures, and historical periods who would otherwise be unknown to us.

Beginning particularly in the 1970s, historians and others focused more attention on women's lives and experiences in the past. Before then, many historians had not considered women's domestic sphere to be an important or interesting realm for study and had neglected it in their reconstructions of the past. A lack of sources, caused by two factors, has fostered this omission. First, most women have been included in the written record only if they were engaged in civic affairs or linked with famous men. In addition, while accounts of significant public events were recorded in newspapers, journals, diaries, manuscripts, biographies, autobiographies, and memoirs, information about common folk, particularly women, is more difficult to find. Second, before the twentieth century, fewer women than men were able to write their own accounts of domestic life, for on the whole fewer women were able to read and write than men and, if they were literate, they perhaps did not consider their experiences worthy of recording. As a consequence, attempts at recovering and characterizing women's everyday affairs have been difficult. More recently, especially in the last thirty years, feminist historians and others have attempted to redress the neglect of women's household contributions and roles by using women's private writings and artifacts as well as published books and other documents to reconstruct women's lives in various historical periods. As useful as those sources are, however, they are largely the work of white, middle-class, literate, and often literary women and consequently offer a somewhat skewed historical portrait.

This book contributes to the knowledge we are building of women's actual, everyday domestic lives by focusing on some of the only available documents that women, many of them barely literate, have written themselves. Long overlooked as primary documents that women have written about their own lives and work, these intimate stories reveal individual women telling their own life stories, their versions of their communities, and the visions they have of society and culture. In *A Midwife's Tale,* Laurel Thatcher Ulrich used an obscure seventeenth-century New England midwife's diary to demonstrate that sources many found too cryptic and too trivial to illuminate history could provide a fuller understanding of life in Colonial America. Similarly, the cookbooks studied for this project dramatically expand and enrich our understanding of women's lives. Ulrich's research presents a rich portrait of the life and times of one midwife, Martha Ballard, who earned a living with her skills; by contrast, the cookbooks presented here range from those written by professional and semiprofessional cooks to those written by women for whom cooking was life and work.

My interest in old cookbooks began with a chance discovery over a decade ago when I was browsing in an antique shop and stumbled across a book of writings. When I opened it, I realized I had discovered a manuscript. At first glance, the handwritten book reminded me of a journal or a volume of poetry. When I looked more closely, I discovered that it was a collection of household advice: recipes for Lady Cake and Parker House Rolls, for instance, and folk remedies for flushing the colon and dyeing hair. Inserted between the pages were newspaper clippings of other recipes as well as a poem and a letter dated August 3, 1894, and addressed *"My dear"* and signed *"Kiss the babies for me. John."* (See Figure I.1) The volume also contained a section of clipped recipes pasted onto the pages of an early telephone directory. But what was most intriguing to me about the book was the absence of the writer's name.

After I bought the book for a dollar—from a shop owner reluctant to ask for even that much money—I returned home and searched my new treasure for clues to its author's identity. I was struck not only by this book's recipes with their titles and ingredients but by the other information contained between its covers. There were letters, poems, loose recipes on scraps of paper, devotional texts, and a list of books and rhymes. I also discovered several pages of names and addresses of people in unspecified relationships to the writer. But although I could conjecture something about this woman's life—her social network, that most likely she had children and a husband, her participation in some religious or church-related activity—I still did not know her name. I wondered how many books like

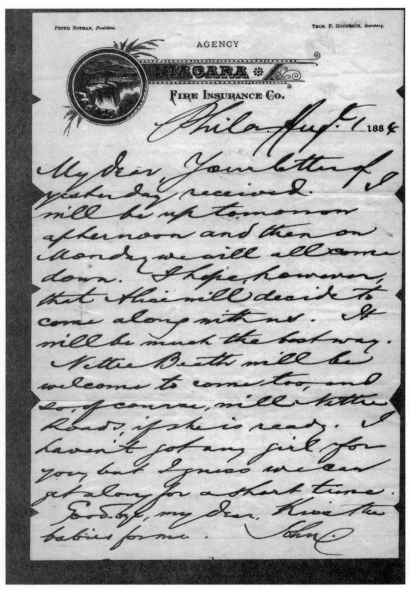

Figure I.1   Letter found in a nineteenth-century manuscript receipt book

this were anonymous and how many had been discarded, lost, or destroyed because they were considered unimportant. How many were intended for publication? Or were they meant to be kept in families and given as legacies to children? Did women compile and keep these books as symbols of wifely and maternal devotion? Or as a way to give themselves identities apart from those roles? Were these books read? If so, by whom? What role did such writing play in women's lives?

Since that time, in conjunction with my archival research, I have searched for and bought a few nineteenth- and early twentieth-century published cookery and household books. But I have not acquired them with a rare book collector's eye or purpose. Rather, I wanted to see how the printed books had been altered or fiddled with, how they had been marked by the reader's sensibilities. I especially wanted books crammed with printed clippings and handwritten notes. Some of these books had been written out in longhand by named or anonymous women; in others, the creative process reflected more of a collage, with women creating their books out of bits and pieces assembled from various sources. Either way, it was clear that these women were carefully constructing books of their own and that we could learn a great deal by studying them.

This recognition led to the writing of this book. First, I want to recapture some of these women's previously undiscovered stories and the sensibilities of women whose lives would otherwise remain obscure—for some of the women who kept these books were only partially literate—and to demonstrate the richness and complexity of their experiences. Second, I want to expand the significance we usually ascribe to cookbooks by considering them as worthy objects of serious textual analysis. We ordinarily focus on contemporary cookbooks for their utilitarian or aesthetic purposes, but I would like to shift our attention to their expressive potential.

As a folklorist trained in an appreciation of aesthetic forms, I look for the continuities in cookbooks as well as the transformations. For despite the political, economic, and social constraints and freedoms that women have experienced in different time periods, despite the changes in food fashions and tastes, the uses to which women have put their cookbooks are remarkably similar over time.

The themes found in cookbooks are timeless: life and death, youth and age, faithfulness and betrayal, memory and forgetfulness. Yet cookbooks also tell us how to make beauty and meaning in the midst of the mundane—a concept especially important for women, whose lives often are punctuated by the demands of feeding others. Despite or perhaps because of their ordinariness, because cooking is so basic to and so entangled in daily life, cookbooks have thus served women as meditations, memoirs, diaries, journals, scrapbooks, and guides.

There is much to be learned from reading a cookbook besides how to prepare food—discovering the stories told in the spaces between the recipes or within the recipes themselves. For me, leafing through a cookbook is like peering through a kitchen window. The cookbook, like the diary and journal, evokes a universe inhabited by women both in harmony and in tension with their families, their communities, and the larger social world. In the seventeenth century, women had begun writing their own household books for publication, previously a male domain; and by the nineteenth century, women dominated the field of household literature as authors, audience, and subjects. Yet most readers will be surprised by the range of subject matter included in these books, for it was in domestic literature such as cookery books that women could develop both their concepts of the feminine ideal and their opinions on social and political issues ranging from women's education to temperance to religion.

The accounts of women's lives recaptured in these previously undiscovered stories will also help us to understand the appeal of cookbooks over time. For some, cookbooks are utilitarian references; for others, they are art objects especially if they are rare documents. Yet the allure of the cookbook is both its mystery and its concreteness. It requires of us, its readers, an imaginative leap. We must cross divides of time, space, and self. For many of us, reading a cookbook is like following a sensate trail to another world remote in space and time. The combination of ingredients, sometimes familiar, sometimes exotic, transformed by culinary acts akin to magic arouses the mind's sensory palate.

As cooks, we must first taste a dish in our imaginations, see it on the table, share it with guests—sometimes more fanciful than real—and then actually reproduce it from a text. A longing for the pleasures of the table reflects a concern for balance and harmony and an integration of the physical and spiritual nature of our existence. In this way, cookbooks are a meditation. Preparing a dish or a meal is not merely an effort to satisfy physical hunger but often a quest for the good life.

As readers, we seek the reveries that cookbooks elicit. Whether about sumptuous dining or frugal making-do, cookbooks open doors into the details of the kitchen, an oddly evocative place to understand other ways of living. It is the details that are important. Anthropologist Clifford Geertz calls for writing in densely packed details—what he calls thick description—when recording the customs of different cultures. On a more popular level, novelist Rebecca Wells in *Divine Secrets of the Ya-Ya Sisterhood* wonders, "If God hides in details, then maybe so do we."

Women today are hungry for such details from other women's stories. Sitting in a doctor's office one afternoon, I left my books as a placeholder on my seat. When I returned to my chair, I found the woman beside me leafing through my volumes on the lives of seventeenth-century women. "I always wondered," she said, "how they coped." So have I. My momentary companion and I shared a need to look behind the scenes of public life to the personal dramas of marriage, pregnancy and childbirth, raising children and caring for elders, youth and age, health and illness, self-sacrifice and desire.

Our brief exchange reminded me of the time I first paged through a seventeenth-century cookery manuscript belonging to an English family and found maternal commentary about children's development written in the margins of the text. I was struck by how different my own notations might have been. Yet the presence of the commentary bespoke a common bond. How deep are the connections between us—a seventeenth-century mother and myself—despite the three hundred years that have elapsed?

The stories that follow will help readers to bridge the gap between the past and the present, between women then and now, and between America and other places. The chapters are arranged thematically and not chronologically. Rather than a history of cookbooks, this book is an exploration of women's lives in their own words from the documents they have left behind.

In chapter 1, I begin with the ways in which women develop and sustain communities through their recipe collections. From at least the seventeenth century, women have exchanged and shared recipes (also called receipts until the late nineteenth century) that they recorded in their cookery manuscripts. The cookbook was a way to demonstrate the wealth, prominence, and status of their social network. Many of the earliest manuscripts and even some early printed books are the work of several hands, a tradition of women's collaborative writing that continued into the twentieth century. The collective nature of cookery manuscripts of the seventeenth and eighteenth centuries in England and America may, in fact, have been the basis for the easy transition to the printed compilations of the nineteenth and twentieth centuries. At that time, groups of women began to gather their recipes into a single volume and sell them to generate funds for charitable activities.

Chapter 2 explores one of these community cookbooks as well as other types of recipe compilations to demonstrate the ways in which these communal documents preserve their communities' histories and memories. Likewise, cookbooks are celebrations of identity. Connections to people, places, and the past are embedded in the recipes women kept and exchanged, transformed, and adapted to their changing world. Often cookbooks have served as a place for readers to remember a way of life no longer in existence or to enter a nostalgic re-creation of a past culture that persists mostly in memory.

In chapter 3, I show that although the knowledge in cookbooks reflects a collective enterprise, a cookbook also represents the individual woman who created it. When the book's subsequent reader is a daughter or other descendant, the heir not only has inherited a domain of cultural knowledge about cooking and household recipes but has received a token of her female kin. The bond created by possessing this physical artifact is the means by which members of different generations become entwined with one another.

As women pass on the recipes that they have gathered from among their social and cultural peers, they create idiosyncratic documents that provide intimate glimpses of their work and aspects of their lives. In chapter 4, I show how these books become the archives of women's domestic lives and perform an autobiographical function. With the addition of marginalia, letters, poetry, and other forms of writing, women divulge their beliefs, dreams, hopes, and fears. Women whose lives were absorbed by the welfare of others found it difficult, if not impossible, to write about themselves in the more usual genres of memoir and journal. As a consequence, some found their cookbooks—companions to their kitchen responsibilities, whether onerous or beloved—opportunities to write themselves into being. Women who thought their lives too everyday, too ordinary to be of interest to others often used their cooking skills and prized recipes as a vehicle for making themselves visible.

Essential to keeping these culinary documents is the ability to read and write. In chapter 5, I discuss the kitchen, food, cooking, and recipe collections as occasions for self-education and the development of literacy. Until the nineteenth century, women's levels of literacy varied widely in England and America, and with the exception of the upper class, women's education tended to be brief and pragmatic. Women used their cookbooks as opportunities to develop reading, writing, and editorial skills. Because recipe collections are collaborative endeavors, men and other women with diverse literacy proficiencies may have provided assistance to women as they deliberately or unintentionally improved their own abilities to read and write. While women used the kitchen and cooking to enhance their own education, children discovered that their mother's cookbook was a handy place to practice writing too. In these ways, kitchen writing helped broaden literacy among women as domestic writings were both the most necessary and permissible for them to read.

The broadening of women's literacy in the eighteenth century coincided with the rise of women's authorship of household literature. In chapter 6, I describe how authoring cookbooks also became a way for women, even those without formal education or training, to gain economic independence and authority. In the seventeenth century, men—and on occasion, women—began to write for ladies and gentlewomen. Starting in the eighteenth century, more books written by women were directed toward the ordinary housewife and household servants. Here was an instance of women entering the professional domain of culinary writing and transforming that domain for domestic life. Some of these successful authors set the stage for aspiring writers; others established models of housewifely decorum to emulate. Some women achieved prominence and renown as authors and became household names through the publication of their cookbooks.

Chapter 7 explores how cookbooks have served as a forum for women to voice concerns about a wide range of political and social issues related to gender, race, religion, and class. Within these writings supposedly focused on the home, women expressed their opinions on topics often considered outside the realm of women's concerns, and their published books had a potential to reach a wide readership. Women's social commentary appears in seventeenth-century English manuscripts, nineteenth-century American community fund-raising cookbooks, and commercially published books. Cookery literature, which expresses a range of perspectives from conservative to progressive, reaches millions of homes and offers women both support for their opinions and voices of dissent. Using food as a metaphor, some authors argue for women's rights, education, and suffrage, child welfare, abolition of slavery, eradication of poverty, and improved social welfare.

Food and cooking reveal what is common to us all and what idiosyncratic historical, economic, social, and local circumstances shape women's accomplishments and interests in this arena. Through the kitchen, we are given glimpses into the constraints and freedoms women encounter in their lives and the people, places, and activities that they value. The stories cookbooks tell are about life and its sustenance in different eras and in different places; they are about enjoyment and desire, family and friendships, stability and change, and the contentment and longings of lives lived in worlds remote from our own.

ONE

Cookbooks as Communities[1]

Bibi . . . began at once to prepare for conjugal life . . . Neglecting the new shipments delivered to the storage room, she began hounding us for recipes, for vermicelli pudding and papaya stew, and inscribed them in crooked letters in the pages of her inventory ledger.

—*Jhumpa Lahiri*, Interpreter of Maladies[2]

Years ago, when beginning my hunt for old cookery manuscripts and books, I discovered an early nineteenth-century American handwritten slender volume that belonged to Jane Janviers.[3] I was struck immediately by the number of different handwritings within the book. It was one of the first volumes of cookery that I would scrutinize in my search so I had yet to learn that many of the manuscripts were either attributed to or actually penned by many people other than the person named on the cover. I was baffled by the proprietary claim of Jane Janviers for a book written by many hands. After years of scouring archives, libraries, and personal collections, I have come to realize that although we think of cookbooks as the product of a single author, surprisingly, a cookbook is a communal affair.

Jane Janviers's recipe collection is a perfect example of women's collective writing. The date when Janviers began compiling her recipe book is unknown, but it appears to have been completed by 1837.[4] Perhaps she began gathering her recipe collection as a young and inexperienced housekeeper, eager to develop her domestic skills. She may have continued adding to the book throughout the busy years of adult life. Most likely family, friends, and neighbors brought her their cooking experience, culinary innovations, and inspiration. As these sources wrote their personal recipes onto the pages of Janviers's cookery book in their own hands, the young woman began to experiment with their formulas, altering some proportions, deleting ingredients, and frequently commenting on their contributions as if it were an ongoing conversation among friends.

Across the recipe "*To Preserve Citron Melon*" Janviers drew a black *X*. Next to it she wrote "*not as good as J. Bare's recipe.*" Later in the book I found "*Mrs. Bare's Recipe for Citron Melon*"—and Janviers's remark that it was "*the best that can be adopted.*" A recipe for "*Tea Cakes*" calls for "*6 large spoonsful of melted lard, 6 of sugar, 6 eggs, flour sufficient to make them stiff and close [—] like doughnuts.*" At the bottom of the recipe, in a different script, the writer editorializes, " . . . *a little brandy and nutmeg is an improvement.*" Janviers may have been the modifier and critic, or it may have been another member of her household. It might have been her daughter who years after its penning decided that the old-fashioned recipe needed updating.

Such modifications and modernizations of old recipes and the invention of new dishes in a woman's cookbook represent the combined efforts of many people. Contributions may come from past generations and from individuals living side by side in small communities, connected to larger social circles, sometimes from one or more cultures, and they also can come to the cookbook from an array of print media. And while we tend to think of cooking as a delight to our senses, the relationships formed through the creation of these culinary compositions are social, cultural, and economic.

This is as true today as it was in earlier historical periods. In fact, the antecedents of the ubiquitous community fund-raising cookbook with which we are all familiar reach back into the early modern period at least to the 1600s. Women then as now were exchanging recipes for food and medicines. Over centuries, in the domestic sphere, the activities related to food and cooking have been primarily in the woman's domain. In the course of day-to-day life, by exchanging recipes and other household advice, women generated their culinary knowledge collaboratively and wrote their cook-books cooperatively. Thus they learned how to prepare foods, medicines, and other domestic necessities for their families' survival. Beyond this pragmatic function, women used food-related activities as opportunities for socializing and creating friendships with women and men.

Cookbooks, then, besides describing foods, are records of women's social interactions and exchanges. In her nineteenth-century recipe book, Ellen Markoe Emlen noted carefully Elizabeth Camac's technique for preparing gingerbread. Emlen wrote, "*Eliza melts the butter in the Molasses, then beats the eggs and milk in last.*"[5] Imagine a friend stopping by for tea carrying a gift of her own freshly baked gingerbread. Her hostess remarks on how delicious the gingerbread is and asks for the recipe. The visitor might inscribe the recipe directly into her friend's recipe book or explain how to make it while they sip tea together. Or perhaps the husband of a newly married couple enjoys a dish at a dinner party. His wife asks for the recipe, which duly arrives in a letter that is then tucked into the recipe book for safekeeping, where, if not immediately, eventually it will be inscribed into the book.

From their cookbooks, we can learn about the writer and the social circles in which she traveled. Attributions in a recipe book marked the number and prominence of one's kin and friends, demonstrating the breadth of a social network and one's standing in it. A collection of recipes compiled over the course of a lifetime was emblematic of the social circles through which an adult woman traveled. Theoretically, nearly all individuals a woman met, from passing guests to servants, could inscribe themselves in her book, leaving a threadlike trail of women's interpersonal relationships. Thus the recipe book became a register of the relationships that comprised at least a portion of a woman's social universe. In this way, women kept records of the foods they cooked and either liked or rejected; in addition, the recipe book became a record of the individuals to whom they were connected through kinship and through other alliances.

Consequently, women's cookbooks can be maps of the social and cultural worlds they inhabit. In the stories of each of the cookbooks that follow, I discovered something about the social networks that gave birth to these culinary inscriptions. Yet deciphering a woman's social network from the names written in her cookbook is fraught with difficulties. I soon learned that the presence of a donor's name did not necessarily indicate a personal relationship between the recipe's giver and its recipient: Women sometimes copied recipes from printed books and other manuscripts. Similarly, the title of a recipe may have pointed to its long-ago origins rather than its most recent transmission. Widening their sphere, cookbook compilers may have corresponded with men and women across the world. It is difficult to know with certainty how broad or narrow a compiler's domain was, how widely read, or how many friends and kin she had. Without the precise information only the writer could provide on how or why a recipe came to be included, a woman's recipe book became a web of social relations to untangle. The women who exchanged recipes with one another did not necessarily live next door, although they often did; they did not have to be kin, although they often were. In truth, they did not have to know one another at all. For the most part, however, at least some of the attributions in women's recipe books were a gesture to those who had entered their domestic lives in one way or another. The names are useful pieces of a puzzle, significant but, by themselves, insufficient shards of information about the people who comprised their social circles.

However, other clues frequently contributed to an overall picture: the compiler's title and name; the size and extravagance of the book; the number of recipes; the lavishness or simplicity of the foods as determined by the number of ingredients, their cost, and the complexity of preparation. By themselves none of these was enough to reveal a cookbook writer's coterie or class. Yet many books also contained more than handwritten recipes, and from these other marginal writings, poetry, and prose, I could make an educated guess. And while no one book could provide a comprehensive view of its historical period, when all of the clues had come together, a picture of an individual and her social world emerged. By comparing and contrasting the body of manuscripts and printed texts of a particular era, I could derive patterns of writing characterizing the period. Individual women created their cookbooks from a common cultural template. In each era, women had shared understandings about what these books would look like, how they would function, and who might contribute to them. The circuitous routes by which these culinary themes traveled to their destinations are complicated to map because despite their similarities, each book was unique. And it was the variations among the books that helped reveal the social, economic, and cultural differences among the women.

Hopestill Brett, Her Booke, 1678[6]

In 1678, perhaps the year she left her natal home for Horncroft, England, Hopestill Brett received a book for keeping recipes.[7] It is an unpretentious, pocket-sized book—small enough to hold in your hand—and bound in unadorned brown leather. No gold initials or ornamentation embellish the cover. It is in keeping with a modest and devout woman.[8]

In some ways, Brett's book varied from other receipt books of the period. For example, Brett wrote nearly all recipes in her own hand, although attributing them to many different people. Was Brett one of the few women in her community who could write?[9] If so, what does this tell us about her community and her role in it?[10] The women who donated their recipes to her book seem to inhabit a world quite unlike that of the aristocratic contributors whose recipes I have found in other seventeenth-century manuscripts.[11] From Brett's rendering of recipes and from her personal revelations, I would learn how distinctive her book was.

At the outset of her small volume, on a loose page, Brett tells us that she ventured to a new place, Horncroft. By writing those words, she acknowledges the significance of the move. We do not know whether Horncroft was a village or town, a manor house, or, perhaps, remotely, a commune of religious women and men. On the same page on which she mentioned Horncroft she wrote, in a clear, well-executed script, all of the possessions she brought with her: "*the Linin [linen], plate [silver] puter [pewter], and goods which I brought to Horncroft.*" (See Figure 1.1) Among them are:

45 payer of sheetts and a od one—15 payer of pillow cots: 11 dosen of napkins 29 table Close: too dosen of towells (and 3) sidbord close . . . 18 dishes of puter: 6 fase basons one porringer: . . . a bras ladle and scommer a payer of [—] hooks, a pyer of grid irons: 3 beds: too bolsters: 3 blankits, one coverlit 9 pillows and two littell ones one chaier: one payer of bras and irons: 5 chests and too trunks one chest of

draers: 3 desks . . . a hanging shelf a littell loocking glass: . . . a Iron boxe . . . and
too baskits: . . . 3 wooden disshes a littell Cheese hoope . . . one brush a littel bras
chafing dish: a sillver porringer: . . . a box Iron a Graye horse.

Brett's worldly goods were not insignificant. In the seventeenth century, owning one bed indicated prosperity. That she brought three beds to her new home indicated a substantial dowry, inheritance, or assets, and she had an unusually large number of linens and many pieces of furniture. Although not fabulously wealthy, she must have been a woman of note.

Still, despite the wealth indicated by her belongings, nothing else suggests that Hopestill Brett was aristocratic. She also recorded in her little book that in "*1683 I had 24 naile of flax and a half: and when it was dresed I had 5 nail of byer: 3 naile of lounrit stuf: one naile and a half of five [—] and 10 nail of cors bow.*" Again in "*1685 I had [—] 4 naile of hemp undresed and a half and half a pound of [—] and 11 pound of [—].*" It is not clear whether Brett worked the flax and hemp herself or had it produced for her. Knowing that Brett had worked the flax herself would provide us with strong evidence that she was not upper class. Although all women, aristocratic and plebian, produced or embroidered textiles—aristocratic ladies were recognized and lauded for exemplary needlework—spinning flax was work for women who needed to supplement their income regardless of their marital status.[12]

Finally Brett tells us that she or someone else either refashioned the goods she brought with her or used the flax and hemp to create more linens: "*woven and cutt out of my linen: too payer of sheets 14 napkins too [—] too pillocotse, one sheete more 14 napkins more worn out : one sheet more: one sheet more: 2 payer of sheets more: a leven napkins one pallebor one sheete more: one payer of sheets more.*" Brett's linen likely may have been handed down from generation to generation, as it was most often through a family's women, and it represented their industriousness. Because of women's intimate connection to cloth, these goods are most likely mentioned in women's rather than men's inventories.[13] It is from such tantalizing snippets in the recipe book, not from Brett's recipes, by themselves not so different from those in other books of the period, that we begin to place Hopestill Brett in the social world of seventeenth-century England.

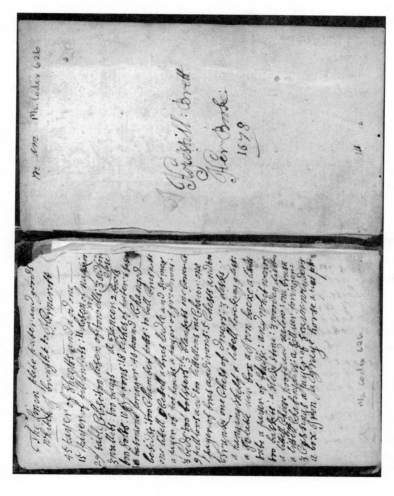

Figure 1.1   Hopestill Brett's list of belongings brought to Horncroft

Did Brett come to Horncroft as a bride, as a widow (called relict in this period) or simply as a single woman coming to live with kinsmen or in an adopted community? The answer is not clear. The unusual number of linens and beds suggest that she may have inherited the chattels of an innkeeper father, uncle, or brother. Moreover, we have little evidence of her marital status or her position in the community. Yet her book offers some clues. Brett's ability to write—by itself a sign of education and perhaps upper-class origins—still does not definitively reveal her social rank. It may suggest that she was reared and educated by parents who believed that literacy was necessary for an individual's spiritual development. Their church urged Protestant women and men of the late seventeenth century to become literate so that they might reflect upon their spiritual condition and read scripture directly, without using priests and clergy as intermediaries. Yet with the exception of her carefully written list of belongings, Brett's manuscript is unpolished. It is not what is called a fair copy, such as those that aristocratic families owned. Rather it is a working document, one used in the course of daily life. Perhaps because of this, her manuscript gives the impression of a person who may have written many of her recipes hastily or had learned to write later in life—when it was difficult to master the pen—or that her penmanship was rusty from lack of use. Although her possessions and ability to write suggest that she came from at least a moderately wealthy family, perhaps the rising middle classes or the gentry, this does not mean that her lineage (her family name) was a noble one.[14] Many middle-class families had abundant wealth and encouraged literacy for their children.

To learn what we can about Brett and the connections she forged with others, we must look at her cookbook and the contributors who left behind their marks or names. Several ordinary Christian housewives, called "goodwives" or "goody" for short, contributed to her collection. According to historian Laurel Thatcher Ulrich, a good wife was "obedient to her husband, loving to her children, kind to her neighbors, dutiful to her servants, and religious in all her words and wayes."[15] Goody Weller gave Brett an ointment and Goody Barber a recipe for rolls. "*Goody Foulers pasty crust*" was one of a few recipes Brett received for the dough that envelops meats and fish. Goody

Hephorn also gave Brett a recipe for pasty crust. Brett did not say which one she preferred; perhaps she experimented with both.

Was Brett operating under an egalitarian impulse when she included multiple recipes for the pasty crust?[16] Perhaps it was important for her not to exclude anyone because the community she lived in was small and its residents interdependent. Causing offense, even inadvertently, might have created tension among this network of women and men whose lives were profoundly intertwined. And there is another possible explanation. Many women accumulated more than one recipe for the same dish or medicine. In this way, they developed a repertoire that was varied and was more likely to ensure them at least one reliable and effective method. Whatever Brett's reasons for including multiple recipes for the same dish, the donors appear to have been of equal middlin' social rank (to one another), if not of equal culinary skill.

Should we assume that Brett was mistress of a manorial estate and met women of different social classes in that role? Or was she herself a good wife? From her book, I conjecture that she was a devout woman who, despite her wealth, traveled in modest social circles. The recipes she learned from Goody Fouler and Goody Weller were not elegant enough to serve at an elaborate dinner or feast.

Brett's recipes reflect a modest way of life. Her kind of cooking does not consist of fancy sugar works or clever conceits of marzipan, usually the dominion of the nobility. Absent from her culinary repertoire are "fancy biscuits, macaroons, meringues, gilded marchpanes, and striped sugar plate"[17] that would indicate an heirloom family manuscript with its overtones of aristocracy. Whereas some seventeenth-century manuscripts contain dozens of recipes for sweet dishes and preserved fruits, creams, and puddings, once called "banquetting stuffe,"[18] Brett had few recipes for the stillroom—a room set aside for making confections, cordial waters, and liqueurs, cosmetics, and healthful broths—that were the mainstay of many aristocratic receipt books.

Her recipes are straightforward and simple, the repertoire consistent with the good, hearty, middle-class English food of the seventeenth century: puddings and pies, potted and collared meats, sack possets (a drink made with milk and wine) and cheeses. A few medicinals are included, such as *"Doctor Eaton's medicine against the plague"* and *"Dr. Hasting's milk water for me."*

Rather than keep herbals and medicines in a separate section of her cookery book, which was common seventeenth-century practice, particularly in elegantly scrivened aristocratic texts, Brett interspersed medicines with her recipes for *"hog's pudding," "boiled bread pudding,"* and *"white mede."* This random order may be because she needed these items on a fairly regular basis or wrote them in her book as she received them. Her book appears far more useful than ornamental, suggesting that Brett directly supervised or labored over domestic duties with her own hands.

Unlike more opulent manuscript cookbooks compiled by a scrivener and consulted by the staff of an aristocratic household, even Brett's writing style for some of her recipes suggests that this was a book she used on a regular basis.[19] Like many women who kept these recipe books, Brett appeared to be eager to learn new and different ways of preparing foods.

> *This milk which bee hung in will bee cum brexe it will and stir it into youer milke for youer cheese and this is better then renit watter: scum off the cheese in the curd and sum in brin whitch is thus: take a galon of fayer water and a pottell of bay salt and boyle it keeping it skemed and when it is cold put in the Cheese keeping [——] turned once a daye less then to[o] dayse will salt hem if it bee a littell one: when the brin looeks [——] then [——] it a gain with a littell more water and salt: Clear it out into the celer: this is all you neede doe to youer Renit: Doe not cut nor breke the Renit Curd a ball for that doth cut make it wash the more: Goody Fouler waye put in the renit in the morning enuf in to the pint of milke*

Brett is intent upon capturing all the fine points of making cheese *"Goody Fouler way."* The precision with which she described the process suggests an emotional investment in her own culinary skills and pride in her craft. She also seemed to relish her own recipes (of which there were quite a few), an unusual detail for the period, simply because she titled them *"My Owne Way for making hogg's pudding"* or *"My littell tansy."* For her tansy she directed:

> *Take 6 eggs live out one whit abut half a pint of milk a littell above half a penny loaf bete a littell spunfull of flower in the eggs sugar salt and nuttmeg the jus of spinnage (tanse) wheat and sorril put in a littell butter first.*

She editorializes on making "*Caraway Comforts Wigs*" by adding "*I thinke the best way is to a bate sum of the yest and put in one egge all the white and half a custerd cup of new milke: colde.*" Brett scatters these editorial remarks throughout her manuscript, personalizing it, and presenting herself vividly, perhaps inadvertently so, to her readers. The personal tone of her descriptions of quantities and preparation techniques suggest that she prepared these foods herself, another characteristic defining her nonaristocratic status.

Moreover, noticeably absent from Brett's receipt book, with only one exception, are names of individuals of noble rank. Only one or two attributions to women or men with titles or honorifics graces her book. One of these is a recipe of Madam Westes's for a *Dyet Drincke*. Was Madam Weste an acquaintance, or did Brett learn or copy the recipe from another source, such as a published book or a manuscript circulating among her friends or family? If any of her sources was a social luminary, Brett gave no indication of that in her rendering of their names.

Although it does not appear that Hopestill Brett had patrician alliances, it was possible and, indeed, helpful to be associated with members of the powerful elite. In times of crisis, such relationships could be lifesaving or beneficial. When Sir Walter Raleigh's widow, Elizabeth Throckmorton, appealed her loss of property following her husband's imprisonment and execution, eighteen women from aristocratic families endorsed her supplicant's letter.[20] In early modern England, women formed alliances for different purposes,[21] and kinship and patronage systems offered protection to the interconnected nobility and gentry.[22] One expression of such alliance was in naming contributors to a household book. Yet recipe books did not merely display connections. They were a source of collective power enabling women to create and maintain vital links and mutual support among themselves and their households by fostering communication, social interaction, and the exchange of ideas.

Hopestill Brett's recipe book demonstrates her linkages; among them were her kin. As sources for four recipes she mentions her mother, Aunt Mills, "*my cousin Betty Pellat,*" and "*cos Phil Burritt.*"[23] With those attributions it is fairly clear that the contributors were relatives. However, she also called several women "*sister*" and mentions them throughout her book as donors of different kinds of recipes. With these names, there is some ambiguity about the relationship. Were they spiritual or biological sisters? The ambiguity is occasioned by Brett's use of the possessive pronoun *"my"* when referring to most of her *"sisters."* She refers to *"my sister Brewer," "my sister Knowles," "my sister White," "my sister Scutt,"* and *"my sister Higginbotham"* in several recipes. In doing so, Brett claimed these women either as blood connections or friends belonging to the same religious community. However, she is inconsistent. At different points, her text uses *"sister"* without the possessive pronoun to refer to the same women. The only woman she calls sister never using the possessive pronoun is *"sister Hills."* Is this mere oversight or a sister for whom she had less affection? Or is sister Hills a sister-in-law or a sister in faith?

If Hopestill Brett belonged to a religious community, she and her comrades may have been among those known in England in this period as dissenters: Quakers and other religious groups opposed to the opulent and autocratic Anglican church. Dissenters believed in an individual's direct relationship with God and an egalitarian association among church leaders and congregation. In keeping with these principles, members of these sects sought to live simply, concentrating on their spiritual rather than their material lives. However, Quakers, for example, were known for being acquisitive folks despite their conscientious and spiritual orientation.[24] Whatever her religious identity, from her cookbook we learn that piety nourished and sustained Hopestill Brett and her community as much as the food described in it.

Brett's recipe book, like other cookbooks, plays a role similar to the family Bible as a place for women to record important family events. At the back of her little recipe book Brett had written several scriptural verses. She also inscribed the deaths of members of her family and others in her network.[25] Perhaps recording the favorite scriptural text of each person she mentioned signaled their deaths, or perhaps she simply wanted to record the verses of her most beloved family and friends.

My mothers texx [text] *Ecclesiastes the thurde* [third] *Chapter and the 2 verse.*

A Time to be born and a time to die

My Uncle Goddard texx the 39 psalme and the 5 vers
verily every man at his best state is alltogether vanity

Mr. Sheppards texx Ecclesiastes the II Chapter and the 8 verses
But if a man live many years and rejoyce in them all: yet let him remember the
days of darkness for thay shall be many: all that Cometh is vanity.

Brett included her own favorite biblical verse as well:

My oune tex Jobe they 7 Chap and the 8 and 9 verce: the eyse of him that hath
seen mee shall see noe more: thine eyes are upon mee and I am not as the Cloude
is consumed: and vanished a way: soe hee that goeth doun to the grave shall com
ye no more.

Since Brett's recipe book largely abides in the world of women, it would not have been surprising if no mention were made of her father. However, Brett has included the verse that may have been her father's favorite:

Ecclesiastes the 12 chapter and the 7 verse; My Fathers texx: then shall the dust re-
turn to the earth as it wase: and the spirit shall return unto God who gave it.

Nearly all the selections concern the finality of death, the evanescence of life, and the capriciousness and futility of physical existence. I puzzled over the placement of admonitions against valuing an earthly life side by side with the sensual descriptions of the pleasures of food and drink. It may have been simply a matter of economy. At the time, paper was scarce and expensive. Moreover, in the course of Brett's daily tasks, her cookbook may have been a handy place for writing. Still, Brett shows us that her cookery book provided formulae for body and soul. For her, the illusory poles of life and death were entwined.

Thus, she felt the need to record for herself and for posterity the deaths of significant members of her social network. We are left to imagine how she felt when she dutifully recorded the death of "*my sister Knowles on April the 24th 1690.*" Her sister Knowles's favorite scriptural text was "*Proverbs the 31st Chapter and 30 and 31 verses.*" She memorialized Sister Knowles and others in her recipe book by chronicling their deaths. But Brett also honored others with the attributions in her cookbook. Among the people and the dishes that she commemorated was one that she learned from her mother. "*My own Mothers waye for hogs pudding*" may have been included as a tribute to her mother and a memory of a former life. She had "*my oune waye for hog's pudding*" among her recipes as well but wanted to preserve both versions. Thus, by including their recipes, she memorialized significant people from her past and her present in her cookbook.

Brett's manuscript leaves us with many unanswered questions about her rank, station, marital status, and religious affiliation. Nonetheless, the naming of "goodwives," men, sisters, and cousins, kinfolk in blood and spirit, who gave her recipes for vital medicines and commendable dishes are clues to her world. In the scriptural commentary that concludes the book, we glimpse the milieu in which Brett busied herself, a world circumscribed by daily tasks, spiritual comfort, and guidance on domestic matters from a considerable if not high-ranking social network. Like other women of the period, writes historian Belinda Peters, Brett sought "to connect herself and her household to the community through language, material goods, and piety."[26] The community commemorated in her cookbook was, like Brett's religious belief, predicated on shared understandings about what its members did and what mattered in their lives.

Mrs. Patterson's Receipt Book (Nineteenth-Century America)[27]

A clear contrast to Hopestill Brett's book is one that belonged to Mrs. Fred Patterson, a nineteenth-century American living in Pottsville, Pennsylvania.[28] Few personal cookery books are as explicit as Patterson's in recording the tales that everyone in the community knew, the stories that made that community cohere even amid turbulence and conflict. Such stories might be told in published community fund-raising cookbooks, as we shall see in the next chapter, for their compilers generally focused on a collective identity emphasizing a shared history and common purpose. For this reason, Mrs. Patterson's cookery book is unusual.[29] The large, black paper-covered text originally was a business account register of the Howard & Company's Express, which seemed to have specialized in the delivering of goods. Women commonly took books for their recipes that had been discarded from other uses.

Mrs. Patterson covered the ledger's pages lavishly with recipes, poetry, sermons, maxims, and journalistic accounts that she thought worthy of her commonplace cookery book. Everything from how *"to cook a turkey"* to remedies for the cholera, to creating custards like that in *"Charlotte de Russe"* found a place.

Handwritten recipes made up a portion of the book. Patterson had recipes for: *"Cinnamon Gingerbread," "Washington Cake," "White Cup Cake," "Annie's Peach Marmalade," "Maccaroons," "Annie's White Cake," "Soft Jumbles (Deborah),"* *"Soda Cake (Hannah's)," "Deborahs Ginger Pound Cake," "Mrs. Eiler's Sugar Biscuit,"* and *"Lizzie Downings Soda Cake." "Mrs. Frailys Plum Jam"* simply lists the ingredients and their proportions: *"1 qt. of stoned plums to 1 pound of sugar." "A Lemon Custard (Annie Pollards)"* required the *"rind and juice of 3 large lemons, 1 lb. of light brown sugar, yolk of 3 eggs, 2 tablespoonsful of cornstarch, 2 cups of water, and whites of 3 eggs."* It can be inferred that Patterson was familiar with the preparation method and needed no specific instructions on how to combine the ingredients. Many of the recipes in Patterson's book reflect the assumption that she and her contributors shared a basic cooking knowledge. A donor named Tillie Patterson, perhaps a relative, gave a recipe for pound cake about which she remarks, *"it is as good a [—] cake."*

Half Pound Cake
1 pound of Sugar
" " " Flour
½ " " Butter
1 Lemon 1 cup of Milk
2 of Royal B. P.
6 Eggs the whites and yolks
beaten Separated
the whites added last
Take two hours

As did many of her contemporaries, Patterson kept her valuable medicines and other household needs at the end of the book: *"Mrs. Lewis' Burn*

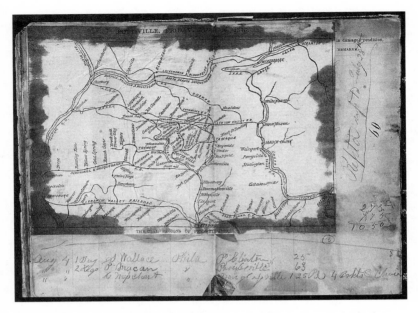

Figure 1.2   A map of the Lehigh Valley from Mrs. Patterson's manuscript receipt book.

Salve," "*Good healing salve,*" "*Miss Nimbleton Cholera Mixture,*" "*Mrs. Neals Sealingwax.*"

Patterson also pasted entire pages of recipes from the newspaper into her book. These were an assortment of foods in no particular order. Main dishes, desserts, preserves, and medicines all come together, included on a single page. Beneath Patterson's blanket of clippings, the ledger retains its original uses: "Memoranda of Freight Forwarded." Howard & Company's Express made deliveries to Danville, Reading, Pottsville, and Philadelphia among others. An accountant dutifully noted costs and payments. Overall the cookbook is a palimpsest (the original pages covered with new documents) with a layer of recipes covering—though not entirely—the names of nearby cities and towns. The juxtaposition of recipes with names of places to which Howard & Co. delivered is a fitting image for Patterson's curious cookbook.

Her recipe journal is a visual and textual montage of the community and the region, its economy, its divisions, and its unity. It is a home-produced book of history, current events, folk wisdom, recipes, and religious inspiration. Patterson's memorandum is, above all, about a place, Pottsville, Pennsylvania, in the Lehigh Valley, and the stories that comprised its identity. Pottsville was, in the late nineteenth century, part of the Pennsylvania coal-mining belt with an economy tied to mines and the mining industry. Lest we forget the region's geography, Patterson has pasted a map across two pages of her book. (See Figure 1.2) In 1875, a coal miners' strike in Wilkes-Barre and Hazleton provided the headline of a newspaper and captured Patterson's attention.

> AT WILKES-BARRE APRIL 9: An exciting rumor prevailed yesterday morning on the streets here that a large number of miners were assembling about nine miles below this city with the intention of making an attack upon the colliery of the Lehigh and Wilkes-Barre Coal Company at Hanover.

Patterson found the event consequential enough to enter into her cookbook. Over the following several days, she pasted successive articles about the strike into her recipe cum scrapbook. The newspaper drawings she added provide another dimension to the verbal accounts and a deeper understanding of the import of these events on family and community life. The drawings depict men gathering in a saloon deliberating a course of action during the strike. (See Figure 1.3) Some of the men look angry; some look disgruntled. From the illustration, one senses the frustration and anxiety caused by a lack of direction or action and the unknown outcome of their decisions.

Patterson's attention to this dispute between labor and management may have signaled her fear of potential violence, the result of Molly Maguireism. During the 1860s and 1870s in Schuylkill County, Pennsylvania, a rash of violence by Irish workers against management terrorized the community. The group, known as the Molly Maguires, has been portrayed by historians variously as immigrant working-class thugs randomly murdering or active unionists fighting injustice with sporadic assassinations. Some members of the Molly Maguires also joined trade unions such as the Workingmen's Benevolent Association, which was opposed to violence, and some joined a fraternal organization known as the Ancient Order of Hibernians. Both organizations were seen as structures within which the Molly Maguires could

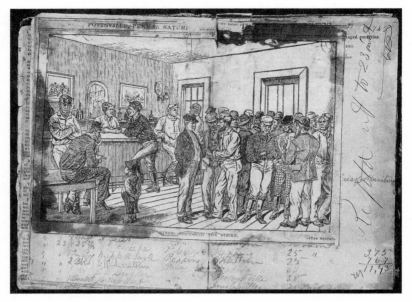

Figure 1.3   A drawing depicting the miners gathering in a saloon from Mrs. Patterson's manuscript receipt book

conspire against mine owners and municipal officials. More recently, historian Kevin Kenny has shown the ways in which the image of the Molly Maguires was manipulated by Nativists, Catholic clergy, newspaper accounts, and officials to stigmatize them and to undermine the trade union movement with which they were associated.[30]

If the Molly Maguires were an underlying fear or threat to Patterson, we do not read it in her cookbook. The faces and postures depicted in the drawing of the miners do not appear to be those of men on the verge of clashing. Rather the miners look like a disgruntled but orderly group trying to decide on the best course of action.

By itself, the miners' strike tells little about the social context of Patterson's recipes. However, in total, her cookbook—filled to the brim with printed newspaper stories of the miners' and railroad strikes, that year's devastating flood, and the social events, deaths, and professional accomplishments of the region's citizens—became a window into the community in which Mrs. Patterson lived. Did she choose these events as keepsakes because some of the incidents affected her directly? Or was she thrilled by the excitement conjured by these human and natural dramas?

This cookbook is unusual in providing the social context for the recipes that the women of Pottsville exchanged, developed, and wrote for one another. In her role as archivist, Patterson gathered not just recipes from her social network and the printed world with which she was familiar; she also collected the stories that affected the men, women, and children whose lives those recipes sustained. These were the current events that most likely riveted family conversations around the dinner table. No doubt while she and her friends were exchanging recipes, they discussed the miners' strike or worried about the men making a "voyage for supplies" and of women and men seeking safety from rising waters while waiting for rescue during the ice break up of April 1875. And while the newspaper stories report the *drama* of the events, the stuff of newspaper accounts and public attention, her recipes tell another portion of the story, one less easily discovered. It is the story of the women of the community and the heroic stories of their lives: the mutual aid and care they provided one another's families during these crises.

No doubt the miners' strike influenced what families ate during hard times. During periods of food scarcity or insecurity such as war or natural disaster, women have created innovative ways to cook even when lacking basic foodstuffs or fuel. Perhaps women devised special formulas during the crisis to enable them to prepare food without such costly items as butter and eggs. For example, during food shortages created by war, women have altered recipes in order to provide even sweets for their families. And as women traveled westward to Kansas, they found alternative sources of flour, using locally raised corn for grits, mush, pudding, or pancakes instead of the more precarious crop of wheat. As newcomers to the prairie, they used cow "chips" (dung), twigs, and dried grass for fuel because wood was scarce.[31]

After the Pottsville flood, when families were putting their homes back together, did women send food and other goods to help their neighbors through hard times? How did the victims manage to cook and feed their families? Were other women providing food for them? Most likely, the recipes

Patterson jotted carefully or hurriedly in her book came from neighbors, friends, and family, many of whom shared eastern Pennsylvania's bounty and cataclysms. Patterson portrays a community of divisions and difference as well as a group of people working together in times of crisis and disaster.

Patterson does not tell these stories explicitly, though, leaving unrecorded the acts of bravery and fortitude the community's women performed helping one another through this disaster. Rather the women's stories are embedded in the recipes. In their interaction around food, they secured emotional and material assistance for themselves and others. In times of crisis, they often shared costs and exchanged labor through these informal supports. They cared for one another through illness, childbirth, and dislocation.

In the recipes, rather than in the newspaper accounts, we find these un-written stories of relationships and support networks. For Patterson and per-haps for members of her family and friendship network, reading the recipes evoked memories of both heroic and quotidian events. What can we know about Patterson's friendships with Mrs. Eiler, Annie, and Deborah whose "*Soda Cake*," "*Peach Marmalade*," and "*Soft Jumbles*" respectively live on in this book? What relationship, if any, did these women have to the events Pat-terson recorded? We can only speculate.

It was in simple attributions that women acknowledged one another. They simply named the contributors both to their books and to their lives. They shared their culinary knowledge, exchanged recipes, and, in so doing, gave rise to communities—incidents the newspapers did not report.

Although local news was her specialty, Mrs. Patterson was also drawn to figures and events of national importance. Mostly she collected articles about men, since they were most often the subjects of newspaper accounts: the in-trepid acts of ordinary men during extraordinary times. A list of the men who fought and died in the Civil War and illustrations of those who rescued vic-tims during the flood in April 1875 were among the articles claimed for her book. A notable exception is the inclusion of a letter reputedly written by Mary Todd Lincoln following her husband's assassination. In her letter, Mrs. Lincoln speaks about her grief and sorrow "until God's love shall [—] me by his side again."[32] Patterson appears to have been an inveterate collector, gath-ering news and advice that buttressed and sustained her worldview.

On one page, Patterson gathered the Lord's Prayer and "A Beautiful Sentiment," which viewed sorrow and suffering as emotions that elevated the soul. Next to them she placed a sentimental poem extolling the virtues of married life, "Love in a Cottage":

Uncle Caleb and Ruth his wife,
Caring little for outside weather,
Fifty years of their wedded life
Spent in this tiny house together.
 .   .   .   .
Mossy the roof and gray the wall,
Narrow the window, low the door;
But love's own sunlight hallowed it all,
From raftered ceiling to sanded floor.

The poem describes the death of the couple and the solace they find together in their new and narrower earthen home. They had lived a loving, humble existence and, it is mused hopefully, were rewarded by an eternity similar to their tender earthly one. From these pieces we understand how Patterson wanted to represent her life and her values. A loving and lasting marriage sustained by Christian faith were more important than the inconsequential material rewards of position and wealth; the deaths of the couple reflected of the dutiful and harmonious life they lived together. Although the general Victorian preoccupation with death has been well documented,[33] one wonders if Patterson had more personal reasons for keeping these words of comfort.

Several other newspaper articles offered solace in the face of death. Not atypical of the period, Patterson focused on the good death, a peaceful finale surrounded by a loving family and respectful friends that was the apogee of a life well lived.[34] Patterson's collected meditations on dying are both poetic and journalistic. Among her newspaper clippings was a list of all "the prominent citizens" who died in "this borough" (of Pottsville) from 1860 to 1869. Sad to say, not one woman is mentioned in this nine-year period. Another clipping was the obituary of Mr. Edward Yardly, "one of the oldest and most respected citizens of Pottsville." The article on Yardly captures the sentiments about civic virtue, American aristocracy, and the commitment to place that pervade Patterson's book. Yardly had been a Quaker both in blood and in spirit, acting in a "just and honest manner his entire life." His family had been connected to "George Fox, the great Quaker" and also had married into the old Quaker family of George Lancaster, whose family had come to America before the Revolutionary War. Although he was born elsewhere, Yardly had lived in Pottsville almost his entire life, moving to Bethlehem only at the end of his illness to be cared for by his daughter. In one of the prevailing ideologies of the period, having led the life of an upstanding citizen, he was thus entitled to a "private, painless, peaceful death," the perfect resolution to old age.[35] Surrounded by loved ones and mourned by the entire community, Edward Yardly died the way he had lived: respected, admired, and loved.

Death is not the only subject of Patterson's recipe and household advice scrapbook. She also embraces notions of the good life in her clippings, ideals we conjecture were important to her and to her community. She valued guidance on conduct in a civil society. Etiquette books of the period were directed to the middle classes; they urged individuals to develop good habits and manners such as could be found among those of "high birth and good breeding."[36] According to the prescriptive literature, individuals needed to master the art of etiquette to ensure pleasant social interaction. One of the articles Patterson clipped from a newspaper, "Sound Rules," declared that respect and kindness toward others were desirable qualities.

> Never ridicule sacred things, or what others may esteem as such, however absurd they may appear to you. Never show levity when people are in worship. Never resent a supposed injury until you know the views and motives of the author. Always take the part of any other person who is censured in company, as far as truth and propriety will allow. Never think less of others on account of their differing with you on political or religious subjects. Not to dispute with a man who is more than seventy years of age; nor with a woman, nor an enthusiast.

The "sound rules" that demanded respectful and courteous individual conduct reverberated larger social and political themes affecting American society, particularly in cities.[37] These were pressures that Patterson and her community faced. As did many Americans, Patterson encountered changes in society following the Civil War: the evolution of "working, middle, and upper classes with diverging and at times antagonistic conditions, outlooks, and aspirations . . ." led to an increasing "distinction between manual and non manual laborers."[38] Market transactions and class interests may have deeply reduced face-to-face interactions that perhaps were characteristic of an earlier Pottsville. Whereas once workers and bosses had interacted directly, managers now may have intervened between the two. Just as Patterson's book pointed to the rupture between management and labor in the mine strike, the upheaval and divisiveness caused by that conflict were now taken up by newspaper accounts that described potential violence.

Where did Patterson fit in this social picture? We may conjecture that she was a middle-class woman frightened or preoccupied by the potential of violence on either side and who saw herself as nothing more than an observer, an archivist of her times. She may have simply decided to record the events and changes in her community and in the larger American society.

The proliferation of etiquette and conduct books after 1830, American historian John F. Kasson argues, was a response to the deep tensions in American society. Good manners were meant to teach individuals the rules of proper behavior in an egalitarian society that encouraged social mobility while attempting to preserve social order.[39] Patterson's collage of social disruption and codes of civility was an attempt to solve the dilemmas of class conflict in her locale, and it was, as well, a mirror of the larger society in which she lived. Her advice on propriety was surely not only an effort to remediate tensions in home spaces but also a tacit suggestion for structuring relationships in the more public domain of the workplace. What is most interesting perhaps is that Patterson engaged the prescriptive literature, reading and sifting and finally bringing portions of it close enough for her personal use. If we have wondered about the popular response to prescriptive literature such as etiquette and conduct books, from Patterson we learn the ways in which these edicts of behavior were actually read and used by people in their everyday lives.

The enthusiasm that Patterson showed for such counsel indicated her concern for appropriate conduct. Most of her selections instructed individuals how to behave toward one another. However, one item specified how *not* to behave. She brought into her personal repertoire of household advice an article called "Criticism in Rhyme," which pokes fun at pretentious pronunciation:

> Have you seen a dictionary, Of this new vocabulary,
> Which pronounces *Either* I-ther,
> And pronounces *Neither* ny-ther.

This poem and several others in her collection view conspicuous displays of rank and refinement as superficial marks of success and not authentic indicators of gentility. In speech as well as other social performances, it was difficult to balance simplicity and correctness. On one hand, etiquette writers suggested replacing polite language with dialectical speech and slang. On the other hand, as John Kasson notes, the writers also advised against "falsely refined speech."[40] In this instance, we may conjecture that Patterson upheld these principles of unassuming plain talk. We cannot know with certainty, but it is notable that her choices of material on the ideals of an egalitarian yet civil society reflected the tenor of the country.

The history of Pottsville and the Lehigh Valley compiled by Patterson is a public history, one portrayed in newspaper accounts and public documents. They describe centrifugal events that exposed the community's class, race, age, gender, ethnic, and political differences. These stories do not necessarily impose a sense of community on a group of people, yet common experiences can be starting points for the emergence of a sense of group identity. It was out of the strike, the flood, and other shared experiences that individuals and various groups maintained alliances and forged new ones.

Patterson's unusual cookbook provides a backdrop against which we might chart the ebb and flow of associations and ruptures that may have characterized her social life. Some of the alliances may have been temporary, others enduring. Above all, the interwoven woman-to-woman ties displayed in Patterson's cookbook and nearly all women's recipe books represent more than one social universe. Domestic and extradomestic relationships can be found in women's cookbooks, for the women often were part of several communities and fulfilled various roles in these different sectors. After all, they were often members of church or other religious groups; they socialized with neighbors and relatives; they held many roles in more than one family as mother, wife, child and aunt, cousin, and in-law. They interacted with doctors, pharmacists, servants, and laborers, among others. The difficulty lies in deciphering the conventions through which women designated the various relationships mentioned in their cookbooks.

Insiders and Outsiders

Cookery manuscripts, intimate documents of daily life, might lure us into believing that all the women who wrote or contributed to one another's books were social equals. We could believe that women's domestic spheres did not have hierarchies. Indeed, these personal recipe collections rarely reveal an explicit pecking order. However, looking carefully in these kitchen artifacts, we discover clues that women knew of the cultural and social differences among them. While many printed household advice books of the nineteenth century made a point of educating middle-class women about how to treat and teach their servants, personal recipe books were indirect in discussing class, race, and ethnicity yet provide subtle clues to these differences.

A small, beige and green marbled, paper-covered book, the nineteenth-century personal recipe book of Elizabeth (Lizzie) Emlen Randolph, a Philadelphia Quaker, handles the subject of servants and their tasks directly.[41] From Randolph's book we glimpse the domestic organization of a well-to-do, patrician household in nineteenth-century Philadelphia. Randolph's book reveals not only differences between mistress and servants but the differences among servants as well. There were clear distinctions in work assignments, and the book positions servants in a hierarchy according to the work they did. Households varied in the size of their retinue, and depending on the number of servants, more or less work might be allocated to each. Included at the back of Randolph's book, written out in her own hand, is a "to-do" list for servants in her household.

The section "*Servants Work*" begins:

Cook's Work
Everyday—Prepare men's breakfast—
parlour breakfast—wash kitchen
breakfast things—servants dinner
at 12 o'clock—parlor dinner at one
or two o'clock—wash kitchen dinner
things—parlor dinner dishes—
prepare men's tea parlour tea—
Mondays—Do the milking—wash
parlour breakfast cups, assist in
the washing, wash parlour dinner
and dessert dishes—do the milking
in the afternoon—
Tuesdays—Milking, washing parlour
dishes—ditto—make butter and
assist in the ironing—
Wednesdays—Bake bread—
Thursdays—Clean kitchen thoroughly—
scrub the pantry—scour the pans and
black the stove—
Fridays—Make the butter—
Saturdays—Bake Bread————

In previous eras, many households separated kitchen tasks from those of the dairy. But Randolph's cook carried out the responsibilities in both spheres. Besides preparing food daily for family and servants, the cook milked the cows (twice daily) and made butter. Randolph also asked her cook to scrub, scour, and clean the kitchen, pots, and pans, and to assist in washing and ironing. In larger households or in earlier times, this, too, might have been the work of a scullery maid or a laundress. The status of the household cook had changed. Instead of the pride of specialization, she was expected to be a generalist responsible for meals and whatever else needed doing. The diminishing, and often transient, supply of servants frequently lamented in nineteenth-century household advice books oddly did not elevate the position of servants. Instead, the tensions between the middle class and working class—particularly Irish women—were expressed in middle-class critiques of servants, sometime humorous and sometimes paternalistic.

Next came the work of the housemaid and chambermaid. In the years 1852–53, that included "*cleaning the baby's room, washing and mending baby clothes, and cleaning Mrs. W. dressing room. Sweep the back stairs every day— store room on Saturday—sew whenever possible and wait on the baby.*"[42] Live-in maids were at the beck and call of their mistresses. In this case, the maid was also responsible for Randolph's baby.

> *Waiter's Work—1852*
> *Monday—thorough cleaning of the dining room—*
> *Tuesday—Sweep and clean the large hall and scrub piazzas—*
> *Wednesday—clean smoking room—*
> *Thursday—do the chamber work and iron—*
> *Friday—clean dining room—clean the silks and dining room closets—*
> *Saturday—Sweep and clean the large hall—wash the oilcloth and scrub the piazzas—*
> *1853. Scrub the piazzas Monday, Wednesday and Saturday—do the third story rooms on wash day—& ironing day 1853.*
> *Cook to bake Monday, Wednesday, & Saturday—clean the kitchen Friday and Saturday, closets & tins—milk cellar every day possible & safe once a week.*

Clearly, the demands on servants in Randolph's household were heavy. Although chores were allocated to each servant somewhat differently, Randolph expected they would share certain tasks, ensuring some kind of cooperation among servants and also discouraging spare time. From the sheer number of tasks allocated to the cook and the waiter, their positions in the household must have been supervisory to some degree and superior to other household servants.

Lizzie Randolph's book parallels the structure of the household. She separates her own tasks from those of her servants. On the front page of the recipe section, she kept personal data, such as her name and the date at which she began her book, November 10, 1848, two years before she married Louis, son of John Wistar and Elizabeth Harvey, and records that she knitted an afghan for W. L. W. She placed the list of servants' duties at the back of the book, as women since the seventeenth century had separated cookery recipes from medicinals.[43]

Randolph's placement of servants' domestic tasks in her book distinguished the accomplishments of the mistress from the labor of her household retinue. As mistress and manager of the household, her duties were to see to the execution of all chores. Her vocation was to be wife, mother, gracious hostess, and guest. Her and her husband's position in society demanded that Lizzie Randolph develop the skills of a hostess and director of an efficient household.

A neatly written list on a page near the front of her book hints at the responsibilities of the young and novice hostess as Lizzie Randolph trained for her household roles. It is a list of foods and amounts suitable for a party of seventeen people:

First Tea Party—
For a party of twelve people—seventeen with the family—
—350 oysters
2 pans of chickens for salad—
50 cents of celery—
5 quarts of ice cream
2 quarts of jelly—
2 bottles of champagne
2 dozen croquettes—
1 dozen oranges
½ peck Lady apples—
3 lbs white grapes—
$1.39 cts worth of cakes—
An amply sufficient provision of everything—except perhaps cakes.

Planning the lavish tea for seventeen with oysters and champagne, ice cream, fruit, and cake was Randolph's responsibility. Imagine what combination of animation and anxiousness she brought to the task. Her criticism of the menu was that there were, perhaps, not enough cakes. Though this first occasion may or may not have earned her a reputation as a "notable housekeeper"—an accolade in this as in earlier periods—one has an image of a young woman striving to meet the expectations of society. While her servants attended to arduous and tedious housework, prepared meals, and cared for her children, Randolph could plan and give tea parties for friends and associates.

Lizzie Randolph's book explicitly demarcates mistress from servant, much as other women's books have more subtle and nebulous markers of social distinctions. As we have seen from earlier examples, women might have used kinship terms such as *"my mother's jumbles,"* or *"cousin Pellat's hog pudding."* Terms of address such as Mrs. Campbell and Mrs. Biddle and titles and honorifics such Madam West or My Lady Widderington designated the rank and status of the giver.

In other cases, it is impossible to determine the contributor's rank from name alone. Differences in status often were masked in unsuspecting ways: The use of a first name might indicate intimacy among equals but could easily denote a subordinate. So much depended on conventions of the time and the relationship between and statuses of writer and donor. It is difficult to determine with certainty just who was a close friend or who was a serving person. Elizabeth (Lizzie) Emlen Randolph mentioned a recipe for coleslaw done *"Ellen's way."* In this case, is Ellen her kinswoman Ellen Markoe Emlen and the recipe given by a social equal? Or is the Ellen who gave this recipe to Elizabeth Randolph an unknown cook or servant or friend?

In another instance, we read that Martha, Mrs. Jones's housekeeper, presented a recipe to Randolph for a much-enjoyed shortbread. Did Martha reluctantly give Randolph the recipe? Or was she flattered that Randolph wanted it? It is impossible to know how servants felt when their recipes were given to others. Even in the following case, we learn only that an unknown woman's cook gave her recipe for peach ice cream. Was she expected to part with her knowledge and skill as part of her employment? A letter in Ellen Markoe Emlen's recipe book is a case in point. It gives the following recipe for ice cream:

The cook says for this Ice Cream yesterday she used a pint of cream and a pint of rich milk. About a quarter of a peck of ripe peaches cut and sprinkled with sifted sugar, one and a half cups, letting them stand a little time for sugar to melt. After this she bruised the peaches with a wooden potato masher and [—] a coarse strainer leaving the fibered part out. Then pour in the cream and milk and turn all into the freezer which she turns about ¾ hour and leaves until ready to serve pouring off the water & refilling with ice and salt. Often she tries [—] lets turn [—] ¾ hour. [44]

The naming of a contributor does not reveal the specific nature of the relationship between donor and recipient. It only tells us that, however brief, an interaction occurred that resulted in the transmission of culinary information. The network of exchange may have been fluid, permeable, changing, and not always comprised of social equals. [45]

Only rarely can we learn those distinctions from the text alone. We need other documents to reveal the social network mentioned in some recipe books. Written contributions from servants, although they suggest collaboration and community, do not erase political, economic, and social inequalities. For example, Nelly Custis Lewis, the adopted daughter of George and Martha Washington, kept a housekeeping book based on Martha's recipe collection. Lewis, as the wife of a wealthy planter, frequently entertained visitors and guests. For many years, she and her husband moved in society's elite circles. Her receipt book recorded all of the sweetmeats and special dishes she served to the visitors and guests in her household but not everyday cookery. This was not unusual. First, everyday cookery was common knowledge, requiring no detailed instructions. Second, it is doubtful that Lewis did much of the actual cooking; she had servants and slaves to work in her kitchen. [46]

Lewis's kitchen help did more than prepare food. They often created the dishes for which her lavish table was known. Her cookbook had several recipes that were given to her by—or taken from—her laborers. There are recipes from *Dolcy* and *Old Letty* as well as *Hanson,* all of whom were the Lewis's slaves and servants. If indeed women shared recipes with one another and exchanged ideas about their work regardless of social rank or cultural group, it is still difficult to determine how, if at all, this collaboration affected their behavior toward one another.

Giving someone a recipe for cornbread does not require an equal exchange; it may be a token of affection, even of intimacy, but it is not necessarily evidence or indication of a symmetrical relationship. Thus, slaves and servants contributed to upper-class women's receipt books. They may have even been flattered and taken pride in the inclusion of their creations in their mistresses' books.[47] However, these contributions did not gain servants and slaves recognition, a raise in salary, or freedom. In other words, the exchange did not change behavior or transform status. Although the practice certainly acknowledged the talents and skills of servants and affectionate bonds that existed between women, it did not alter the status quo. Rather, it mirrored the economic and social relationships between mistress and servant or slave without encouraging those roles to expand and change. No roles or relationships were challenged. The conventions of the mistress/servant relationship permitted elite women to cross cultural and social boundaries by usurping recipes from women whose ideas may or may not have been given willingly.

Mementos of Friendship

While some women appropriated recipes from others, a rich tradition of recipe exchange existed among diverse friends and kin. In her pioneering work on recipes as gendered discourse, Susan Leonardi has pointed out that the exchange appears to be a way for women to cross boundaries of race, class, region, and generation.[48] Leonardi recognizes that recipes and food lore constitute a realm of activity that connects women despite differences. She traces the lexical origins of the word "recipe" to the Latin *recipere*, meaning "exchange." According to Leonardi, giving a recipe implies reciprocity, and women have seen recipes as tokens in a gift relationship. By the same means, withholding a recipe or an ingredient represents a lack of generosity, if not ill will. Sharing or withholding becomes a subtle, but still visible, act of largess or acrimony. As Leonardi insightfully interprets it, sharing a recipe is an act of trust.[49] Writing is a form of social action—not just social activity—and the exchange of recipes and the naming of contributors cements relationships fostered in daily life. It is one way to signal and affirm affiliations. Women's cookbooks, thus, could represent and have represented alliances and affinity, and often have been based on shared characteristics of race, class, and religion.

Women exchanged recipes with one another on remnants of paper, perhaps later to be written into the pages of a bound volume. In the process of transcribing the former into a text, transformations might occur. Sometimes deletions and additions were intentional, sometimes they were mistakes. For example, "Mrs. Downing," an early twentieth-century housewife, kept a cookbook that contained multiple recipes for many dishes.[50] Some she wrote on scraps of loose paper, inserting them between the pages of her composition book. Did Mrs. Downing hope that some day she would find a more permanent home for these recipes? Or was she hoping to incorporate the old recipes and the scraps into a new recipe book at some future time?[51] One recipe, *"Dandelion Wine,"* was written in two, slightly different versions, with one written on a fragment of paper and the other into Mrs. Downing's book. Moreover, the handwriting on the loose bit of paper differs from the one that inscribed the recipe in the book. The *"Dandelion Wine"* recipe written on a small piece of lined paper in Mrs. Downing's book reads:

Dandelion Wine

4 qts. flowers (gather A.M.)
3 qts. boiling water
4 lbs. sugar
3 lemons, 1 orange. 1 teaspoonful yeast (Flashmans)

On the reverse side the directions are provided.

put boiling water on flowers
let stand 6–8 hours. Strain
add sugar, lemons and orange
and yeast. Mix well. put in
2 qt jars to ferment.
when quiet bottle or
seal and put in cellar

Mrs. Downing may have tried the recipe for *"Dandelion Wine,"* then altered the text to reflect her own method and included that "improved" version in the bound volume. The recipe inscribed in her book differs by only one ingredient, adding gelatin, and she has added more explicit and detailed instructions for making the wine. In this way she has claimed the recipe as her own:

Dandelion Wine—1 gallon
Take four qt blossoms, scald with
3 qt boiling water take 1 orange 2
lemons cut fine and put in with the blossoms and scald together—
let stand 6 or 8 hours then press
out blossoms and put 3 lb. sugar
in and then put in jug and
let ferment for four or five wks [—]
and then carry in cellar and
let stand with cork on loosely and
after 6 months put in bottles and
at the same time put in a pinch of gelatin to make it clean
then it will be ready for
use

Why did Mrs. Downing keep the scrap after writing her own more elaborate recipe in her book? Frequently, such fragments of paper stored in recipe books were rewritten in the bound volume in the hand of the compiler. And just as often, even when rewritten, the scraps were preserved. Perhaps because the original might have been written in the donor's hand, it was kept as a memento, a visible token of the gift, a commemoration of the relationship.

Once the recipe had been included in the bound text, however, it belonged to the recipient as part of her own repertoire. Although there is no indication that Mrs. Downing has forgotten the donor, the original recipe exists only as a trace; there is no attribution of the contributor. The dandelion wine recipe, now permanently logged into Mrs. Downing's collection, is an elaboration of the loose-paper version. The recipe has taken on a new life as the combined efforts of the two women.

Another example may be found in Laura Bigelow's nineteenth-century cookbook from Waterville, New York, with dozens of recipes written into her book by other women or attributed to them. Many are dated, and for a few she records the names of the givers and their residences: *"Mrs. Morgan of Jersey City's Breakfast Bread"* logged in *"October, 1865"* and *"Mrs. P. G. Baker of Cold Spring's Apple Pudding"* was given to her in *"September, 1865."*

One recipe, in particular, depicts the social interaction around food that characterized many women's relationships.

> *Queen of Puddings*
> *1 pint of bread crumbs. 1 quart of milk. 1 cup of sugar. Yolks of four eggs, beaten. Grated rind of one lemon. Piece of butter size of a small egg. Bake until done but not watery. Whip the whites of the eggs stiff and beat in a small teacup of sugar in which has been stirred the juice of the lemon. Spread over the pudding jelly or any sweet [—]. Pour the whites of the eggs over this and bake until it is a light brown.*
> *April 27, 1865*
> *Maria Sherrill*
> *Maria Borton*
> *Witnesses to the merit of this pudding*[52]

Picture an afternoon tea party on a cool, crisp spring day. Laura Bigelow has served her latest culinary creation. She had gotten the recipe from her sister-in-law who said a woman in her fellowship group had served it the week before. Why not try it? Bigelow brings out the delicately browned pudding on a lovely porcelain plate. The women exchange news while drinking tea and nibbling on dainty cakes and the delectable *"Queen of Puddings."* It is a success!

Maria Sherrill, Maria Borton, and Laura Bigelow evaluated the dessert and found it an excellent one. They commemorated their afternoon tea and *"Queen of Puddings"* by recording it on the pages of Bigelow's cookbook. They were not alone in jotting down this recipe. I have found the identical recipe, or one with slight variations, in many nineteenth-century northeastern cookery manuscripts. Nearly all the recipes have the same ingredients and the same method of preparation. The *"Queen of Puddings"* was clearly a popular dish that circulated among middle-class women in, at least, the northeastern United States. Although the attributions in one woman's book do not illuminate the ways in which women's social circles overlapped, the widespread popularity of the dish indicates the breadth of women's networks. Whether the recipe first appeared in a cookbook or magazine is too complex a web to untangle. The search for a recipe's origins and authenticity is problematic since even minor alterations preclude certainty. From their recipe books, we learn that women's culinary knowledge issues from a variety of sources, print and friendship networks among them.

Some women, like Laura Bigelow, identified their recipes' sources in meticulous detail. Others did not but relied instead on memory. In some cases, the scrap of paper in the giver's handwriting was the talisman that mattered, a memento of a friend or an afternoon tea. The people and the social occasions they represented were inscribed as permanent reminders of the connections binding women to one another.

Epistolary Connections

Most cookery manuscripts contain correspondence bearing both recipes and the tracks of relationships near and far. For women who were literate, letters, like diaries and journals, were familiar forms of communication. Asking for a recipe may have been one reason for initiating a correspondence. It appears that renowned author Jane Austen took an interest in household matters. In a letter to her friend Althea Bigg, Jane requested the recipe for the drink she had enjoyed while visiting with the Bigg family at Manydown years before. Jane wrote to Althea:

> The real object of this letter is to ask you for a receipt. . . . We remember some excellent orange wine at Manydown, made from Seville oranges, entirely or chiefly, & should be very much obliged to you for the receipt. . . . [53]

One did not have to be literary to exchange news and sentiments with friends and family through letter writing. On Saturday, October 6, 1888, Clara Johnson of 64 Hammond Street, Boston, Massachusetts, sent a letter to an anonymous Philadelphian with a recipe for "*Sunday Morning Pudding.*" Written on an inexpensive sheet of white unlined paper, it remains, more than a century later, a tribute to the connection between two women.[54] Johnson tells her reader how to put the ingredients together:

Put one quart and 1 pint of milk to boil—dissolve a pint of milk in a full teacupfull of white Indian meal when the milk has boiled pour this into it and let it boil a few minutes—stirring it all the time until it thickens a little then let it cool—& break an egg in a bowl. Add to it one full cup of molasses and a dessert spoonful of salt beat these three together and stir into the milk—then put into your pan and place in the oven to bake until bedtime—bake it out—morning—thoroughly through.

Johnson's recipe for preparing "*Sunday Morning Pudding*" may be unclear to us, but the personal tone of the instructions—and their level of detail—suggest an informal and friendly conversation between friends or kin. It is as if Johnson were in the kitchen with her correspondent, telling and showing her just how to make this dish.

In letters like Mrs. Johnson's, women could sustain intimate ties by sharing the details of domesticity and cooking. Thus in 1871, "Pete"[55] sent a recipe for a rich wedding cake to Mrs. Jewett Cain who lived in Rutland, Vermont, or Elizabethtown, Kentucky.[56] Pete knew Cain well enough to know that she already had in her receipt book another recipe for a wedding cake attributed to Mrs. Dyer, yet the writer addressed her formally. The letter writer begins:

My dear Mrs. Cain—The recipe I send you makes the quantity of cake that I made for Hattie and for Belle Huntoon. If it is not enough I think if you take that recipe of Mrs. Dyers and add to it, it would be all you would want. I prepared the peel myself and will tell you how. I do not know as you can get oranges this time of year—I wish I could be there and help you—Pete

On the other side of the letter, which was folded in half, is the recipe for "*Preserved Orange Peel.*"

Take the rind of six or eight oranges let them soak in salt water overnight. Rinse them in clear water. Cut away a good share of the white part leaving only a thin yellow rind, boil till [—] in [ale] or water changing it once or twice, it will take it three of four hours to boil . . . in the last water put a pound and a half of sugar and boil the rind till it looks clear and the syrup is a little thick. Then can—it will keep a long time.

On the back of Pete's letter, in the same irregular hand is a list of ingredients for "*Wedding Cake.*" The recipe gives only a few instructions for combining the ingredients. Pete assumed that Cain was experienced in cake-making and did not need detailed instructions, just the list of ingredients.

Wedding Cake

19 Eggs: well beaten but not separately
½ lbs. of butter}stired to a cream
2½ lbs brown sugar}
2 Cakes of Baker's Chocolate }grated
2 quarts of flour
1 small teacup of Molasses. ⅔ cup of sour milk
1 teaspoon of soda
2 teaspoons of mace, 2 nutmegs, 1 tablespoon of ginger
2 tablespoons of cloves, 2 of cinnamon
1 tablespoon of allspice
½ pint of strong coffee
1½ pints of best brandy
10 lbs of raisins, one half of which chop very fine and the other half about half
    as fine
6 lbs of currants
3 lbs of citron
One lb of candied orange peel
2 lbs of almonds blanched and cut very fine

Although we will never know whether Cain used Pete's recipe (with or without Mrs. Dyers to extend it), whoever the letter writer was, the relationship between the two was familiar enough for the writer to express a wish to help Cain. Exchanging recipes in letters was one way family and friends separated by distance could continue to share the details of their day-to-day lives, the discovery of a new dish, or interest in and concern for one another.

Their recipes, scribbled on stray scraps of paper, in letters, and in each other's books, told the stories of women's connections within and beyond the household. As women worked side by side in kitchens in varied relationships and wrote to one another, they passed recipes from one family to another, their cooperative labor and exchange of culinary lore leaving as traces these imprints of social interactions. The recipes were delivered by mail, intermediaries, and messengers, clipped from newspapers and magazines, and copied from other manuscripts and printed books. As age mates and elders, women are the primary contributors to one another's recipe collections; yet children and men, travelers and guests, physicians and pharmacists also made their marks in women's recipe books.

Women's worlds are complex, bridging the household with the outside world in innumerable ways. Their cookbooks often have recorded these social and economic transactions as women began and augmented their own culinary repertoires with others', past and present. As we taste one woman's interpretation of a culinary creation, we remember that it is the result of many minds and many hands.

Two

Cookbooks as Collective Memory and Identity

How could an unskilled heart see past my bird-like mother's paisley dresses and cut-glass brooches to the passionate woman who kept a pair of elbow-length, white leather opera gloves wrapped in scented tissue in her drawer, and a postcard collection in a shoebox in her cupboard, who cooked to remember generations. . . .

—Anne Michaels, Fugitive Pieces[1]

And I grant, such mastery of the multiple gifts of cookery and language is rare indeed; yet I possess it. . . . And my chutneys and kausandies are, after all, connected to my nocturnal scribblings—by day amongst the pickle-vats, by night within these sheets, I spend my time at the great work of preserving. Memory, as well as fruit, is being saved from the corruption of the clocks.

—Salman Rushdie, Midnight's Children[2]

Women have conserved a whole world, past and present, in the idiom of food. In their personal manuscripts, in locally distributed community recipe compilations, and in commercially printed cookbooks, women have given history and memory a permanent lodging. The knowledge contained in cookbooks transcends generations. Grandmothers and mothers, sisters and aunts, friends and relatives of friends invest what tidbits and wisdom they can for the next generation. In addition, their culled selections from magazines, books, and other printed sources augment those recipes bestowed by their families and social networks.

Although many recipes remain nearly unchanged through the years, each new cook adapts some recipes to accommodate altered environments and the changes in fashion, and invents new dishes. Change is constant. The accidental or deliberate modification of centuries-old recipes takes place with the passing of each generation, with the movement of people from one locale or continent to another, with periods of crisis and scarcity such as war and natural disaster. Fashions ebb and flow, and a culture's culinary identity reflects its social and cultural place in an ever-changing society. Recipes that a century ago would have been the apogee of culinary chic may no longer be prepared because they are no longer in vogue; they may be considered unappealing, outdated, or unhealthful. Ingredients may be hard to find or expensive. Human ingenuity will create facsimiles of those old favorites and experiment with new recipes.

Yet some recipes are not forgiving. Cooks may closely follow the original for the purposes of remembrance. To alter even an ingredient would disrupt the evocative, symbolic qualities of a dish. For example, every Jewish family has its own recipe for haroseth, the apple and cinnamon dish[3] meant to represent the Jews' bondage in Egypt, or gefilte fish, which some claim should be sweet and others insist must be savory. Although there are many recipes for haroseth and gefilte fish from different regions of Eastern and Western Europe, each family tends to prefer its own and will change it little from one celebration of Passover to the next.

While some recipes signify an eternal (ongoing) connection to the past, other recipes (and sometimes the same ones) and dishes, associated with a culture of origin, may display changes in social life. This does not mean that the foods of our ancestors are discarded as simply as shedding clothing. Rather, as icons of cultural identity, a culture's cuisine may be used to mark the complex negotiations groups and individuals undertake in a new land. In many parts of the northeastern United States, Italian American families created a tomato-based sauce they called "gravy." They adapted their familiar regional foods to new settings, replacing foods they could no longer pro-cure with new items and incorporating their conception of an Anglo-American meal of meat, starch, and vegetable into their diet. For many Italian Americans in the northeastern United States, the American and Ital-ian meal systems existed side by side and signaled their cultural identities as Americans and Italians. For many Italian American women, their recipes and the recipes of their mothers and grandmothers were committed only to memory. Afraid that their knowledge might die with them, they recorded some of the ancient recipes, and their American variants, in local commu-nity cookbooks to be saved for posterity. Other recipes were collected from their mothers by a generation that did not want to lose the tastes and aro-mas of their family's table. Still others have been rediscovered and reinvented by reading commercial cookbooks popularizing the regional cuisines of Italy.

Whether the recipes are used as they are written or altered to suit con-temporary tastes and fashions, many recipes and memories preserved in these texts are savored as mementos of the past and a way of life that may no longer exist. Whether they are used or not, they are not forgotten. Their ex-istence in writing offers us a kind of permanence that, if and when we want it, is waiting for us to retrieve. Used or not, unchanged or transformed, these recipes and the rituals in which they are embedded continue to shape a group's current image of itself.

The past merges with the present as the cookbook and its user attract recipes from other women in the community and in the larger society, women connected to one another by virtue of religion, region, ethnicity, or common cause. Even the most sophisticated, knowledgeable, and talented cooks gather recipes from others. They may modify or transform a recipe— or never follow it precisely—but the recipe provides a blueprint for their imaginative interpretations. Thus, modifications may be personal and the selection of recipes themselves idiosyncratic, but culinary knowledge is col-lectively generated. Because it is knowledge accumulated over time, it ac-quires a patina of meanings that may be called upon to celebrate a culture, challenge prevailing stereotypes, and simply preserve a vanishing way of life.

I have selected three strikingly different cookbooks as examples of how women may use culinary writing as a way to define themselves and their cultural groups, to preserve the past, and to shape the future. Written by an African American woman, the first book challenges the stereotype of black Americans in the late 1940s. Freda De Knight's commercially published cookbook *A Date with A Dish* is a compilation of recipes from sources past and present. Her purpose is to depict a complex and heterogeneous African American culture that varied in class, region, professions, and educational backgrounds.

The second book, the 1972 *Rochester Hadassah Cookbook*,[4] clarifies for its women readers modern Jewish identity and its complex relationships to American and Israeli culture. Written by a group of Jewish women, it portrays its community, itself a composite group, negotiating the multiple identities of American, Jew, and Zionist in a multicultural society such as the United States. This cookbook, created by a local woman's organization for fund-raising purposes, provides a self-portrait of Jewish identity at a particular place and time.

The last compilation of recipes, *In Memory's Kitchen*,[5] although published in 1996, was written in the 1940s. A group of Jewish women who were inmates in the Theresienstadt concentration camp in Czechoslovakia dreamed of home and family and a way of life that was being extinguished. The women wrote their memories of food into a cookbook that took over fifty years to reach publication in 1996.

Each of the women and men who contributed to these cookbooks defined and memorialized a group of people and a way of life. Their goal was to celebrate their culture for themselves and others with the food and rituals through which they interpreted their past, represented their present, and gave shape to their future.

A Date with A Dish

Black culture and history are the subjects of Freda De Knight's 1948 cookbook, *A Date with A Dish*.[6] De Knight, as cooking editor of the widely circulated *Ebony Magazine*, was in a good position to act as a spokesperson. First published in 1945, the Chicago based magazine delivered a message of black achievement, experiences, and everyday heroism. Expanding her editorial role, De Knight cast her net widely, drawing on childhood contacts and a network of family, friends, colleagues, readers, and black cooks and caterers. With its culinary contributions attributed to individuals from across the nation, *A Date with A Dish* resembled a collaboratively written fund-raising community cookbook. However, De Knight's singly authored book (whose purpose was, most likely, as much consciousness as fund raising, only in the sense of private enterprise) made her sources and inspiration clear: the culture and creativity of black people. Beyond this, her mission was to take her readers beyond a stereotypical and homogeneous African American community. Although she does not state it directly, hers is a civil yet insistent plea to recognize the diversity within the black community with a recipe compilation from talented women and men: cooks, caterers, housewives, and other African Americans from all walks of life.

De Knight claimed that there was "an urgent need for a Cook Book of American Negro Recipes."[7] She must have seen her role as a writer/editor as critical: She was, after all, documenting African American culinary history as it was practiced, not as it had been depicted. Prior to *A Date with A Dish,* black cooking was, like black culture, considered nonexistent or stereotyped as Southern by many whites: African American innovations to American regional cooking other than Southern were generally unsung. In fact, the African influence on American cuisine, widely acknowledged today, had not yet been considered a defining characteristic of many regional cooking styles.[8] After World War I more than a few Southern cookbooks glorified black cooking but equated it with the South and with African slave cooks, thus perpetuating a stereotype of black culture.

In order to understand the misperception De Knight challenges, we will need to review the developments within Southern cookery literature from the antebellum period to Reconstruction and post–World War I. How were the contributions of black cooks depicted in Southern cookbooks prior to *A Date with A Dish?* Were these contributions to Southern cuisine neglected or masked as white elite women created an image of themselves and of plantation life in their cookery literature?

Southern cookery literature in its antebellum incarnation rarely depicted African cooks' ingenuity and creativity. Neither manuscripts nor published women's cookbooks did justice to the artistry of black cooks or the continuity of many African ingredients, dishes, and preparation techniques. The antebellum-period cookbook authors did not laud or single out black creativity when they recorded Southern recipes but focused instead on the generic Southern kitchen that was heavily influenced by talented and skilled African cooks. Instead, genteel white women of the Southern aristocracy, women of the planter class, compiled the manuscripts they used in their households and, later, published.

The Virginia Housewife by Mary Randolph (1824), *The Kentucky Housewife* by Mrs. Lettice Bryan (1839), and *The Carolina Housewife* by Sarah Rutledge (1847) are some of the antebellum South's most famous cookbooks.[9] Even *Mrs. Hill's Southern Practical Cookery and Receipt Book,* although published after the Civil War, in 1870, is exemplary of antebellum cooking and the lifestyle it represented.

Each of these books is an evocation of the South's emphasis on graciousness and hospitality, stressing the English cookery that is the basis of many dishes. The Southern identity that emerges from these descriptions is that of the planter class and the women who exemplified Southern genteel femininity. For this reason, these texts also enshrine the identity and collective memory of the Southern white elite. Even books that emerge during Reconstruction, such as *Mrs. Hill's Southern Practical Cookery,* describe the ideal of the antebellum mistress as well as the changing concept of femininity following the Civil War:

> A crisis is upon us which demands the development of the will and energy of Southern character. Its prestige in the past gives earnest of a successful future. As woman has been queen in the parlor, so, if need be, she will be queen in the kitchen; as she has performed so gracefully the duties of mistress of the establishment in the past, so she will, with a lovelier grace, perform whatever labor duty demands.[10]

With the exodus of slaves, white elite and middle-class women were required to assume the labor once assigned to others. In an introduction written by the Reverend E. W. Warren, a delineation of women's duties ironically continues: "They should not look forward as slaves to the task, or as idle pupils to the recitation."[11] Warren's figurative language admonishes his readers not to approach their duties and responsibilities with as much reluctance and despondence as their slaves reputedly had. Mrs. Hill reiterated Warren's description of the new role assumed by Southern women. However, hers is a decidedly gentler rendition.

> Thousands of young women are taking upon themselves the responsibilities of housekeepers, a position for which their inexperience and ignorance of household affairs renders them wholly unfitted. Formerly "mother" or "mother's cook" or one whom the considerate mother had trained to fill this important office in the daughter's menage, was, with many, the only authority considered necessary in the conduct of culinary operations. Now, however, things are changed. Mother, even if within accessible distance, is too much occupied with the accumulated cares of her own establishment to be able to devote much time and attention to a separate one; while "mother's cook" and "trained servants" are remembered as among the good spirits that ministered to the luxury and ease of by-gone days.[12]

Although Mrs. Hill notes that times have changed and that young women must now accomplish for themselves what others have done for them, there is still no acknowledgment of the culinary offerings African cooks had delivered to the tables of their wealthy owners or employers. However, behind the plantation mistress were the African cooks and white servants who made possible the image of the Southern white mistress. As historian Damon Fowler reminds us: "The contributions of Africans to Southern cookery are as numerous as they are undocumented; however, this influence is evidenced by a number of common elements—the use of okra, peanuts, sesame seeds, and eggplant, and such dishes as hoppin' John, calas (rice croquettes), tomatoes, and groundnut candy are just a few suggested elements."[13] The elaborate feasts for which many plantations were known "would not have been possible without slave labor," argues twentieth-century writer John Egerton in *Southern Food.* He continues: "In the most desolate and hopeless of circumstances, blacks caught in the grip of slavery often exhibited uncommon wisdom, beauty, strength, and creativity. The kitchen was one of the few places where their imagination and skill could have free rein and full expression, and there they often excelled."[14]

Not only did African slaves develop an entirely innovative cuisine in which the planter class took pride, according to anthropologist Sidney Mintz, they used the experiences of procuring and preparing food to acquire proficiencies and relationships useful in servitude and later in freedom.

Mintz has written that African slaves in the New World used their native food resources in producing, distributing, and processing foods for their masters' tables, as well as their own, as acts of submission and resistance. He says:

> Dealing in food was dealing in freedom at many levels. For example, working in the production of food legitimized certain claims that the slaves would level against their masters; working in the distribution of food legitimized freedom of movement, commercial maneuver, association, and accumulation; working in the processing of food legitimized the perfection of skills that would become important with freedom; and working in the emergence of cuisine (what they made for their masters) legitimized status distinctions within slavery both because the master class became dependent upon its cooks, and because the cooks actually invented a cuisine that the masters could vaunt, but could not themselves duplicate.[15]

Although cookery afforded African Americans some advantages under slavery, they were denied others such as reading and writing which were illegal. Thus, despite their talent and expertise, African Americans, for the most part, did not commit their recipes to writing. Instead, they entrusted their formulae to memory and most often passed them on orally from generation to generation. Because of the prohibitive costs of printing, particularly for wide dissemination, it was not until the twentieth century that cookbooks written by African Americans proliferated.[16]

There were two exceptions: In 1827 Robert Roberts, "a forceful Garrisonian anti-slavery worker, a strong opponent of African colonization schemes and an active member of the convention movement of free blacks," wrote an antebellum cookery and advice book for fellow servants entitled *The House Servant's Directory*.[17] Roberts' book taught servants not only their responsibilities in private homes but also the managerial skills necessary to the commercial venture of catering.[18] Catering parlayed the provision of food, drink, and service to private families into thriving establishments in Philadelphia, Boston, and New York. Further, the catering guild to which they belonged enabled the men who ran these businesses to assume leadership roles in the community to "a degree of affluence, culture and respect such as has probably never been surpassed in the history of the Negro in America."[19] Moreover, white socialites coveted the food prepared by the most famous of these caterers: Robert Bogle, Peter Augustin, and Thomas J. Dorsey, an ex-slave and abolitionist, among others. No social occasion was complete without them. Of Dorsey, W. E. B. DuBois wrote in *The Philadelphia Negro:*

> Dorsey was one of the triumvirate of colored caterers—the other two being Henry Jones and Henry Minton—who some years ago might have been said to rule the social world of Philadelphia through its stomach. Time was when lobster salad, chicken croquettes, deviled crabs and terrapin composed the edible display at every big Philadelphia gathering, and none of those dishes were thought to be perfectly prepared unless they came from the hands of one of the three men named.[20]

Adeptness in the kitchen placed black cooks in a critical position vis-à-vis white society. In the antebellum South, their authority in the culinary domain made them invaluable to their masters and, later, in the North as self-employed caterers to their clientele.

The catering profession appears to have figured prominently in African American history before and after the Civil War. In fact, it was a successful female San Francisco caterer named Abby Fisher who wrote the second commercially published household book by a black in 1881. Fisher, an ex-slave who could not read or write, became a successful professional cook using the recipes of the pre–Civil War South.[21] Fisher had accomplished in the West what Bogle, Minton, and Dorsey had achieved in the Northeast in the decades following the war.

Reconstruction heralded a new era in Southern cooking, of which *Mrs. Porter's New Southern Cookery Book* (1867) was the first published example. These books presented diluted versions of Southern food, including as they did recipes from other regions. During Reconstruction, cookery book writers, such as the popular Northern writer Mrs. Rorer and Southern writers such as Mary Stuart Smith, were redefining Southern cooking to include other regional cuisines. Women in the South were attempting to enter the national mainstream and also manage their scarce resources amid the post–Civil War economic crises. White and black women were still in kitchens together, but now they worked jointly as employer and servant rather than mistress and slave. Both had to make do under harsher economic circumstances.[22]

Following World War I, another spate of cookbooks finally recognized black cooks. However, they did so by nostalgically re-creating the Southern household, replete with images of "the Old Southern Mammy" on their covers. Such was Katharin Bell's *Mammy's Cook Book*. She begins mournfully:

> With the dying out of the black mammies of the South, much that was good and beautiful has gone out of life, and in this little volume I have sought to preserve the memory and the culinary lore of my Mammy, Sallie Miller, who in her day was a famous cook. She possessed, moreover, all those qualities of loyalty and devotion which have enshrined her and her kind, in the loving hearts of their "White Folks," to whom they were faithful, through every vicissitude and change of fortune."[23]

Bell's sentimental acknowledgment of her family's cook was an attempt to recapture memories of childhood, from her own point of view, not from Miller's experiences. In "an outspoken worship of the old ways and the days of black family retainers, with recipes named after 'aunt' or 'uncle' somebody [these cookbooks] presented an idealized view of the Southern household and black kitchen help."[24] Fiction, films, and textbooks portrayed the South and Southern blacks with the same nostalgia.[25] Stereotypical imagery and icons began to change in the late 1930s when the U. S. government attempted to redefine the contributions of Jews, immigrants, and blacks in an effort to create national unity.[26]

This undertaking intersected with those of black activists, intellectuals, and artists who were seeking to direct political and media attention to their "segregated fight for freedom."[27] To advance this enterprise and to bring attention to black contributions to the culinary arts, *Ebony* editor De Knight penned *A Date with A Dish*. In addition, she wanted to dispel the myth of a single black cooking style without forfeiting a recognition of black culinary talents. She says explicitly, "It is a fallacy, long disproved, that Negro cooks, chefs, caterers and housewives can adapt themselves only to the standard Southern dishes, such as fried chicken, greens, corn pone, hot breads, and so forth."[28] She asserts, "Like other Americans living in various sections of the country they have naturally shown a desire to branch out in all directions and become versatile in the preparation of any dish, whether it be Spanish in origin, Italian, French, Balinese, or East Indian."[29] Black Americans are a sophisticated and diverse group of individuals. The foods they have learned to prepare and enjoy are indications of the variations in their lifestyles, their environments, professions, talents, and training. In depicting African American culinary diversity, De Knight used food as a metaphor for the varieties of African American experience.

De Knight was also rescuing her heritage. Her book was part of the effort of many black intellectuals of the period to "provide the Negro people" (and ostensibly whites) "with a respectable past."[30] In 1949, sociologist Maurice R. Davie of Yale University described this as a movement: "Studies have been made of Negro history, of eminent Negroes, and of Negro cultural contributions—matters largely neglected by white historians. This movement is an expression of Negro protest, comparable to the role of the Negro newspaper in the contemporary field. Its purpose is to enhance self-respect and race pride among Negroes by substituting a belief in race achievements for the traditional belief in race inferiority."[31] *A Date with A Dish,* an extension and elaboration of her writings in *Ebony,* which "consistently presented working wives and mothers in a positive, and frequently positively heroic light,"[32] was De Knight's contribution to the protest movement.

De Knight's "urgent" call for a "non-regional cook book that would contain recipes, menus, and cooking hints from and by Negroes all over America"[33] was "the first of its kind: a cookbook written by a 'cultivated Negro woman' about the range of black American cuisines."[34] Gertrude Blair, who wrote the introduction to De Knight's cookbook, claims to mention this "purposely far from the beginning of my introduction to her work. *It is important that here is an authentic collection of very fine Negro recipes.*"[35] Why would she not assure the reader of the collection's authenticity immediately? In fact, she does tell the reader that De Knight "collected over a thousand wonderful recipes from Negro sources during the last twenty years."[36] In presenting De Knight as "a cultivated Negro woman," was she breaking a stereotype that would offend her audience? It is not clear why she wrote this or if, in fact, it has any meaning.

De Knight continues the emphasis on the authenticity of the recipes in this "collection [which is] as complete as can be found anywhere in the land."[37] Although she does not date individual recipes, she claims that she began her collection from such regions as Louisiana in 1906 and ended with the book's publication in 1948.[38] So comprehensive and voluminous were her sources that De Knight was "at wit's end" in New Orleans deciding which of the many recipes for the same dish was more authentic.[39] In keeping with modern conceptions of what is authentic,[40] De Knight, using gumbo as her example, concedes, "Each person feels his way is correct."[41] Authenticity is difficult to judge, she says, when you considered the alterations made for individual taste preferences. "To fully explore this land [New Orleans] of intrigue and unique recipes, we'd have to add hundreds of extra pages. So since we are trying to include everyone, we will just let 'The Little Brown Chef' momentarily stick his nose into a few pots and kitchens."[42]

The Little Brown Chef was the device De Knight used to judge a recipe's merit. If the Little Brown Chef was impressed with its taste, he would "date the dish" and thus include it in De Knight's collection. The metaphor of dating a "dish" (a slang term for an alluring woman) is a provocative one for it implies the possibility of a romance and sexual liaison. Although the Little Brown Chef was first to taste, he offered the recipe to the reader who might also choose to date the dish. De Knight's double entendres playfully allude to the relationship between food and sex. It seems the Little Brown Chef "has his eye set for a wife from either South Carolina or New Orleans."[43] It was more than kitchens and pots into which the Little Brown Chef was poking.

Nonetheless, using the benign persona of the Little Brown Chef, De Knight scoured the country for "authentic" recipes, from the acclaimed to the plebian, from "caterers to plain cooks, good chefs, fancy ones."[44] She gathered hundreds of extraordinary recipes, encoding the history of African Americans through the anecdotal accounts of extraordinary people like Mamie and Paul Scott and Zoah Hunt. It was they who remembered, adapted, and created the culinary delicacies in her collection. De Knight wrote as much to record their life stories as to collect their recipes. *A Date with A Dish* is a tribute to the black community and a celebration of its contributions, diversity, and creative people.

De Knight's goal is to "salute" black culinary artists, the "names and firms just too numerous to mention, along with any number of fine chefs in hotels and on the crack trains of every railroad. I must not forget the many fine teachers of the art, the experimental labs and kitchens, and industrial Negro schools to be given credit. Hundreds of names, unsung praises for other cook books and articles on food, as well as creations and dishes that have become renowned, origin unknown, and on and on."[45] De Knight wanted to tell the untold story of black contributions to American cuisine and of the cooks and caterers who achieved mastery in their field. Often without formal education, some illiterate, self-made men and women started successful businesses and worked against the odds in a racially divided America to achieve careers as teachers, chefs, and cooks in hotels, households, and railroad kitchens.

De Knight began her book with two tales. The first pays homage to "any number of little girls who, because of necessity, don't play, but can and do cook and take care of the younger kids."[46] Living in a "crowded tenement house of New York," the exemplar of such children, a girl of eleven, cooked breakfast, fixed lunches, and shuttled her younger brothers and sisters to their various schools. After school she cooked dinner to help her mother. Admiration for this child's creativity and natural talent as a cook warranted De Knight to add: "there are many children like this little girl, from whom women of the more fortunate class can learn a great lesson."[47] It is possible De Knight's commentary is either a criticism of middle-class women or a genuine show of concern.

The second tale related is that of a "kindly, plump, brown-skinned old lady in Tennessee . . . who told me a story of her version of cooks and of their ability during slavery days."[48] The mistress of a plantation returning from a trip to New York tells the cook about a delicious dish she had eaten. With very few clues about ingredients or how the dish was made, the plantation cook created a facsimile that became the talk of the plantation. Their culinary creativity was a result of their own imaginations, traditions, talents, and experimentation. "Those old cooks possessed vivid imaginations, keen sense of taste, and creative ability in the culinary art without the aid of book learning." These tales have two morals: The first is that talent and ingenuity can be found everywhere, even in the poorest of environments, from New York tenements to plantation kitchens; the second is that even without extravagant resources and the advantages of privilege, creativity and imagination will blossom.

An early memory and the desire to create a black culinary legacy not linked exclusively to Southern cooking kindled De Knight's mission. When her father died and because her "mother was a traveling nurse," Freda could not stay at home. She was sent to live with Mamie and Paul Scott in South Dakota, and young Freda found the Scotts "an inspiration for my early cooking aspirations." De Knight does not tell us if the Scotts were relatives or friends nor why they were chosen to shelter her. The Scotts were "famous as the middle-west's finest caterers."[49] Freda showed an interest in cooking at an early age. She tells us that "by the time I was five years of age, I was able to bake my first loaf of bread, make biscuits, and garnish plates. Instead of cutting out paper dolls and playing house, I was cutting out recipes and playing cook."[50] Perhaps her mother thought that Freda would benefit from the couple's culinary successes.

Freda viewed Mama Scott as a role model even though "Mama Scott's education was limited." In school, the rebellious young Freda found the Anglo-American recipes in home economics textbooks senseless and unpalatable. She recalled marking the pages with such remarks as "'Spinach tastes awful this way. Add tomatoes and onions.'" And "'Don't be silly; salt to taste! Mama Scott knows more than you.'" As with many American textbooks of the time, Anglo-American tastes were the standard. Just as primers in grade school portrayed history and literature from a white perspective, home economics texts were, with few exceptions, based on Anglo-American cooking.[51]

Books obviously mattered to De Knight, and it is tempting to conjecture that it was this experience that inspired her to document a black culinary legacy. Mamie Scott's recipes would no longer live only in memory or in the margins of home economics texts but in a book devoted to black culinary "genius." De Knight believed that "It is in our cookbooks that the experiments and genius of the naturally endowed have been collected and preserved for us."[52] And that is precisely what she accomplished. The recipes and the people who created and cooked them are memorialized in her book. In the years since her childhood experience, De Knight avers that "Mamie Scott died and Papa Scott retired." However, "their recipes live on"[53] in her collection. For example, she gives a recipe for "Mama Scott's Beet and Onion Salad," which asks for:

2 cups chopped pickled beets   1 cup onions, chopped or sliced thin
½ tsp. salt
3 tbsp. salad dressing

Combine salad dressing, onions, salt and beets. Save a few onion rings to decorate. Place salad in center of dish and arrange onion rings around salad. Serve. (We suggest you use Bermuda onions.)[54]

De Knight's cooking experiences early in life were also a source of culinary creativity. Her bookish sister Clare asked her, at the young age of six, to prepare her favorite meal of pork chops and creamed gravy.

I personally didn't care for pork, so to off-set my dislike I used to imagine them as anything but plain pork chops. After frying the chop to a delicious brown, I would place it on a plate as an island and surround it with snowy mountains of mashed potatoes. I then had a stream of cream gravy around the mountains with bits of parsley on the potatoes as trees. To me, it was a picture created in food, rather than a meal, a genuine "landscape" dish.

4 large, thick pork chops   ½ tsp. celery salt
1 cup milk or light cream   1½ tsp. season-all
salt and pepper (to taste)   ½ tsp. garlic salt
½ cup flour   1 pod garlic, chopped
1 tsp. paprika   ½ cup water
2 tbs. bacon fat

Mix flour and seasonings together. Marinate chops in flour well on both sides. Save remaining flour. Brown chops in fat on both sides, then cover and let steam thoroughly for about 30 minutes. Remove cover, add balance of flour and brown. Mix with fat. Pour milk or cream over chops. Add water. Let simmer another 15 minutes until gravy is thick. Serves 4. Serve with fluffy mashed potatoes.[55]

De Knight was a creative child who used food as a medium for art. From such personal experiences, she learned that education was not necessarily a prerequisite to inventiveness and ability. She provided more than a few examples of women who had no cooking training other than the world in which they worked but succeeded at developing reputations of excellence in their fields. Zoah Hunt of Cleveland, Ohio, worked in school lunchrooms and restaurant kitchens as a stock girl before opening her own catering business and restaurant. In addition, Hunt was a wife and mother who "was forced to advance against odds. Her story is one of perseverance."[56]

Here is another. West Indian-born Marianne Abramson Perez was still cooking professionally at the age of ninety-six. Her career began as the age of fourteen. Sent to England as a nursemaid, she learned cooking in the kitchens of aristocratic English homes. After returning to the islands a few years later, she discovered that her experience abroad was an asset in her quest for work. There she worked among English and Spanish families, learning to read and speak both languages fluently. Afterward her acquired name of "Nanana" served her well in U.S. households, where she continued to cook a blend of English, Spanish, and American cuisines. Without the benefit of formal schooling, domestic Marianne Perez educated herself in two languages and specialized in a cookery that demonstrated her understanding of several cultures. De Knight says of her: "she learned to combine her English and Spanish in an American way."[57] Perez's recipes include: "Cocoanut Mounds," "Rellenos," and "Bread Pudding That Slices."[58]

However, an education did not necessarily guarantee having a chance at a career. Texan Lucille B. Smith, a radio personality, writer, and teacher, struggled to succeed in her field of home economics. She spent more than fifteen years as a teacher in public service, "training maids and housewives, catering to dignitaries and demonstrating" food preparation throughout the state.[59] De Knight tells us about Smith only that "her climb to cooking fame has not been easy."[60] Ever the diplomat, she alludes to but does not detail Smith's struggles. Are we to read the inequality of educational and employment possibilities for blacks as a part of De Knight's message? By pointing to the differences, and often the limitations, of opportunities in both education and work for blacks, and, at the same time, by showing how individuals succeeded as professional cooks and caters, De Knight made her point without being blunt.

Freda De Knight's display of black Americans' cooking in all of its delectable variety may have been as much an effort to attract blacks to the cooking professions in an era of economic opportunities as it was to demonstrate black achievements in the field. According to contemporary sociologist Gunnar Myrdal, the post–World War II economic boom did not enhance job opportunities equally for all blacks. On the contrary, he pointed out that occupational and professional openings for blacks had worsened.[61] De Knight may have shared his perception, she does not say. However, her call to cooking was emphasized by stories about successful cooks and caterers. For example, she reminded her readers that in Baltimore there were several Negro[62] catering firms and "there has been ample room for all of them, and their success proves what Negroes can accomplish in this field."[63] One of her colleagues agreed. Chef Glenn Chase claimed that "A good cook is always in demand." Chase felt that "cooking is no longer classed as a common profession, and that it can lead to a great many fine positions, regardless of color or race."[64] Another of De Knight's contributors, Mrs. Cora Perrin, who had "extra-fine references as an 'extra-fine cateress,'" claimed that "the field of cooking offers vast opportunities."[65]

With few professional fields open to blacks, service occupations were avenues to entrepreneurship. De Knight may have believed that the catering business that had provided nineteenth-century blacks with well-respected positions in society was worth reconsidering in the twentieth century. Through the story of J. W. Holland, a Philadelphia caterer who managed one of the oldest catering businesses in the United States,[66] De Knight quietly intimated the difficulties black American entrepreneurs confronted. She noted that the commercialization of catering began in Philadelphia under Holland's direction.

And Holland's first head chef, William Newman, and Holland's daughter continued to build her father's prosperous business. De Knight believed it was extremely difficult for a black to succeed even in this northeastern city; she alludes to in this simple statement: "in order to cross the portals of Main Line Society, Holland's firm had to be just about the acme in its line."[67] "He is a credit to his race," she concluded, referring to Holland.

Although the service industry and cooking were acceptable occupations for blacks in this period, it was still difficult for black entrepreneurs to cross color lines in the United States.[68] Despite the persistent separation of the races, it was often black talent and industry that created, cooked, and served the food that pleased a nation. Writing in 1948, Myrdal found it "remarkable that it [racism] does not hinder the utilization of Negroes in even the most intimate household work and personal services."[69] After World War II, white households sought black domestic labor. However, black women were reluctant to return to these jobs. Efforts by organizations such the Women's Bureau and the National Council of Negro Women to recruit black women as domestics in white households show the aversion with which many did return to paid domestic labor after the war.[70] The black women described in De Knight's treatise spanned the gamut of cooking occupations: Some were cooks in others' households or professional cooks, others were housewives in their own homes, and still others were caterers.

To complete her portrait of diversity within the African American community, De Knight included recipes from people who were acknowledged for their contributions to American culture. Famous musicians gave their recipes; Lionel Hampton, whom she referred to as "King of the Xylophone," offered "Hamp's Stewed Chicken" as his contribution.[71] Next, "the modern Gabriel, Louis Armstrong, being from New Orleans, loves spicy foods." Although Armstrong enjoyed a range of foods, the "ham hocks and red beans" that he made himself was his favorite.[72] Armstrong's penchant for red beans prompted De Knight to encourage those who had never tried them to do so. Knowing that her audience might reject the dish as peasant food, she explained not only its tastiness but its nutritional value as well. In fact, when the beans were made with red wine, she advised her readers, "You can't go wrong serving them prepared this way at your most important dinner parties."[73] By adding wine, one of the more prevalent ingredients in French cuisine, she was attempting to elevate poor people's Southern food to "a dish definitely in the delicacy class."[74]

While she did not flinch from including the Southern version of beans à la Louis Armstrong, De Knight wanted to show the spectrum of regions and professions from which the African American repertoire was drawn. To that end she offered "Boston Baked Beans" as prepared by Nadine Wright Goodman, with as long-standing a lineage and history as any Boston Brahmin. "As long as there has been a Cambridge Mass., there has been a member of the Wright family who knows the traditional and exciting New England dishes. So it is no wonder Nadine Wright Goodman could look back through old papers and discover old recipes"[75] because it is not just descendants of the *Mayflower* who know how to cook the dish considered New England's emblem of Americanism.

Her own doctor, Jesse Miller, a great cook, found whipping up a meal relaxing. In order for Miller to achieve his goal of a career in medicine, he sought employment in traditionally black occupations. Apparently, while Miller was in school, "he worked as a waiter on a dining car and absorbed all the little tricks of the trade for his own pleasure."[76] In her travels, she met "lots of Dr. Millers, business and professional men who could be cooks, chefs or caterers."[77] De Knight plays with the stereotype of black people by inverting the image of a cook who wanted to be a doctor. Here she suggests that any of these successful professionals might have earned a living by being a cook. She is painting a portrait of the African American community that is one of diversity, artistry, hard work, persistence, and service.

De Knight assiduously avoided confronting the reader with the inequities between black and white opportunities. Instead, she let the stories of these individuals speak for themselves. She showed but did not tell the tales of struggle and racism, of lack of education and opportunity. She spoke instead of culinary achievements, of sumptuous cooking, and of doubly hard work in homes, hotels, and other institutions across the country. White historians had neglected culinary contributions such as these to the common fund of American cookery and culture.[78] The work of De Knight's people was backstage, behind the scenes, a creativity that was part of a largely unacknowledged American culinary legacy. Freda De Knight wanted to set the record straight.

Rochester Hadassah Cookbook

When, in 1972, the Rochester, New York chapter of Hadassah (a Jewish women's group) compiled a fund-raising cookbook, they memorialized their community[79] in 336 recipes, images, and household advice. Emblazoned across the cover in bright pink and orange stylized letters—in shape and angle reminiscent of the Hebrew alphabet—the words *Rochester Hadassah Cookbook* promised a modern yet still Jewish culinary repertoire. Among the diverse gastronomic offerings are such multicultural inventions as "Tuna Salad Luau," "Creole Pot Roast," "Israeli Liver and Eggs," "South of the Border Casserole," and "Easy Chop Suey." The cookbook brought together the fashionable food of the 1970s with traditional recipes for hamantaschen, a fruit-filled pastry prepared for the holiday of Purim; "Grandma's Great Chopped Liver"; "Passover Carrot Pudding"; "Sweet and Sour Brisket"; "Gefilte Fish" (chopped fish); and "Carrot Tsimmes." Polyglot recipes such as these, which still adhered to the Jewish dietary laws of kashrut,[80] indicated not only culinary inventiveness but also celebrated American pluralism while displaying the community's own ethnic, religious, and national identities.

Complementing the array of recipes, the illustrations accentuated the Rochester Jewish community's cultural and culinary uniqueness and adaptations. Seated around 1970s contemporary dining tables the men and boys wear yarmelkes (skullcaps). A young girl smiles broadly while wearing a cardboard headband boasting a large Star of David. In her hands are a knife and fork in a position of readiness to devour the large Thanksgiving turkey in front of her. Aside from the prominent Jewish religious symbols, the drawings depict middle-class American families, especially children, in various domestic scenes: eating meals, snacking on treats, enjoying holiday occasions. (See Figure 2.1) One drawing that catches the reader's attention is a stylized image of a Jewish housewife. She is perched atop a high stool in her short perky skirt, showing long lean legs, a representation of modern femininity, chic and youthful. It is a contemporary icon chosen perhaps to

Rochester
Hadassah
Cook Book

Figure 2.1   Jewish housewife reading her cookbook as depicted in the *Rochester Hadassah Cook Book*.

dispel the myth that conformity to tradition necessitates an old-fashioned image of womanhood.

According to the cookbook editors, women were the guardians of Jewish domestic life; it was their responsibility to surround their families with objects of symbolic significance, "the aromas and sizzlings of the Jewish kitchen,"[81] "to build up heart-warming experiences and fragrant memories for your family."[82] So important is the role of food and women in building Jewish identity that some researchers, such as folklorist Barbara Kirshen-blatt-Gimblet, have named it "kitchen Judaism."[83] Ostensibly these sensory cues bind children to their homes and to their faith with anticipatory joy in their early years, and, in later life, they harbor their memories. Sensory experiences lock memory into the body, and those same sensate keys may set them free. It was domestic life, the table with all of its artifacts, and its distinctive cuisine that betokened Jewish identity.

The *Rochester Hadassah Cookbook,* like other community cookbooks, is a guide to the identity and ethos of a community.[84] It is "a story they tell themselves about themselves."[85] In this record, the Rochester Hadassah gathered the culinary knowledge that was the heart of the occasions their families celebrated. Their cookbook was an archive of the food and of the ritual events that brought individuals together as a group to celebrate its history and identity. In the commemoration of holidays and daily meals, in the stories told around the dinner table, particularly at holiday reunions, they evoked, recounted, and reinvented the story of this community, Jewish history, culture, and religion.[86] Every occasion that unites individuals at a table is a moment for a culture to remember its past and celebrate "its unique identity vis-à-vis other groups."[87]

The women of the Rochester chapter of Hadassah saw themselves as "Jews, Americans, and Zionists"[88] who continued their long-standing tradition of service begun when the organization was founded in 1912. They saw their mission as one that took them beyond U.S. boundaries. They said: "In the decades since [its beginning] Hadassah has expanded its service to the people and the land which was Palestine and is now Israel."[89] The group of women who compiled this cookbook wanted to be recognized for their several allegiances: their religious and cultural heritage, their

American home, and Israel, the country that was their symbolic homeland. In their collaborative cookbook, the women of the Rochester Hadassah assembled the traditional and innovative dishes associated with the individuals and families of their community and of the wider society as a collective source of Jewish tradition.

They saw their cookbook as a reference for those who wanted to learn more about Jewish homemaking. Who was the intended audience: uninformed Americans or inexperienced Jewish housewives? Was the cookbook directed to both groups? Was the compilers' own seemingly inconsistent movement between American and Jewish identities reflected in their perception of their audience?[90] On one hand, the editors assumed that the cookbook reader would enter the Rochester Jewish community as a novice becoming familiar with some of the terms of food use, such as "pareve" (foods that may be eaten with either meat or milk meals). The editors also define and describe rituals such as "Shabbat" (the Sabbath) and holidays like Yom Kippur, the Day of Atonement observed with a day-long fast, and Sukkot, the celebration of the harvest.

At the same time, this was not most likely a guidebook for outsiders: The language was too esoteric to master, the references arcane. The reader was expected to have at least a basic comprehension of Jewish rituals, language, and tradition. The editors added only occasional definitions or explanations to the text. For example, the illustration that announced the Passover section required an insider's knowledge of the holiday. It depicted a boy, seated at the table, dreaming happily of the songs that end the seder's festive meal. The main characters—a farmer, a goat, an ox, and others—of the song called "Chad Gadya" dance in an arc around his head, enacting the chain folk tale of the farmer who smote the ox, put out the fire, killed the kid (goat), chased the cat, and so on. Without the knowledge of the song, an outsider could not decode the symbols on the page.

The cookbook was a catechism for those seeking knowledge in managing a Jewish kitchen and home. For example, one of the editors, Mrs. Abraham Karp, declares, "On Tu Bish'vat, our Jewish Arbor Day, we eat 'bokser' (or carob or St. John's bread) as Israeli fruit. Raisins and almonds also signify. We hope you know these 'roshinkes mit mandeln' (raisins and almonds) were the greatest treat for shtetl (Jewish village) children." She continues: "Purim afternoon is proper time for the Purim Seudah, one of the family holiday feasts. We all have already eaten hamentaschen, and have sent some of our baked goodies to friends for Shalach Manot (the custom of bringing sweets to friends and neighbors during the holiday)."[91] The editor musing on the origin of the triangular pastries that this community used to celebrate the holiday asks: "Is it possible that mon-taschen—poppyseed pockets—became hamentaschen?"[92]

References to European Jewish history and the name for its communities—shtetls—and the Hebrew Shalach Manot indicate that the authors had intended other Jewish women as its readers, women eager to know more about how to create and manage a Jewish home. A Jewish housewife needed to have knowledge of domestic rituals and the system of food purity. She also needed to know how to reaffirm social and religious bonds with family, friends, and neighbors. "In the words of Henrietta Szold, 'She is the center of all spiritual endeavors, the confidante and fosterer of every undertaking. To her the Talmudic sentence applies: It is woman alone through whom God's blessings are vouchsafed to a house.'"[93] Jewish identity is linked explicitly to maternal socialization and the domestic rituals that women orchestrate.

So the editors begin at the threshold of the house: A visitor entering a Jewish home may see the visible signs of a religious life through its material culture. The authors claim that Jewish homes are recognizable by a small artifact at the entrance: a rectangular container made of metal or wood, called a mezuzah, that contains a Jewish prayer. In a section entitled "The Jewish Home," the editors ask: "How do we recognize a Jewish home? We see the mezuzah on the door post as we go in or out."[94] Yet while they assert the presence of this basic symbol of a Jewish home, they do not describe it. Importantly, for the editors, Jewish homes must be marked as Jewish to signal the community's standards.

Once beyond the entrance of the house, sensory cues will envelop the visitor. A glance around the room will tell us it is a Jewish home. There will be a "silver wine goblet, a Hanukkah Menorah, paintings and objects of art from Israel. We will see Jewish books and hear music such as the song 'Jerusalem of Gold.'"[95] To be a Jewish home, it should be embellished by material objects that indicate that the home and its occupants have a "love for God and his commandments."[96] The Rochester Hadassah asserted a distinctive Jewish identity, now entwined with Israeli art, music, and literature, that was theirs to nourish.

Perhaps because the cookbook's table of contents appears, for all intents and purposes, to be like that in any other cookbook, it was doubly important to the editors to mark the distinctive nature of Jewish cuisine and its departure from Anglo-American cooking. At first glance, the chapter headings, from "Appetizers," "Beverages," "Breads," "Cakes," "Cookies," "Desserts," and "Extra Treats," to "Fish," "Meats," "Poultry and Stuffings," seem ordinary. However, there are some cues to the idiosyncratic nature of the cuisine, the cookbook, and the community. At the beginning of the book, prominently placed on its own page, a short paragraph offers a cautionary note from Mrs. Karp. She urges readers/housewives to "examine" the label of prepackaged foods to find the sign of the Union of Orthodox Jewish Congregations certifying ritual purity. For those who practice the dietary laws (kashrut), rabbinic supervision is required, from the slaughtering of animals to the preparation of packaged foods. According to British anthropologist Mary Douglas, the separation of meat and dairy and the prohibition against foods such as shellfish, pork, and game are a culinary code that delineate both a cuisine and a people as distinctive. In marking the borders of what they may eat, the Jewish people have circumscribed their borders as a distinct cultural group.[97] Ultimately, it was the housewife's responsibility to ensure that only pure foods were brought into the household. It was also her responsibility to ensure that her family remained within these cultural boundaries.[98]

There are other clues that the culinary code in this cookbook varies from typical American fare. Occasionally a subheading called "non-dairy" appeared, as with "Scalloped Potatoes," because Jewish dietary laws require the separation of meat from milk—in recipes and at a single meal.[99] The division between milk and meat is based on the biblical proscription "thou shalt not seeth a kid in its mother's milk" rather than for reasons of health. Some recipes were designated to alert the cook to their appropriate presentation at only certain meals, such as "Dairy Vegetable Soup" for dairy meals and "Tomato Soup with Meat" for meat meals.[100] To prepare meat dishes that also might call for milk products, nondairy substitutes were suggested: the recipe for "Chicken Kiev" called for margarine instead of butter.[101] A "Mocha Cake" recipe offered the cook two options: One version called for 1 cup of butter, the other, "½ cup margarine and ½ cup of vegetable shortening."[102]

However, in this atlas of culinary adaptations, the women of Hadassah also have expanded their borders by incorporating their neighbors' delicacies after altering them according to their rules of purity. At the outset, all meat must be made kosher, subjected to a special butchering process, before it can be incorporated into any dish. At the beginning of the section on meat, the editors have devoted a page to koshering meat.

> In the dietary laws of the Jewish people, the term "to kosher" is applied to the preparation of meat and poultry before preparing for the table. The animal must be slaughtered by a Shochet and purchased at a Kosher meat market.
>
> The meat must be put in a utensil specifically reserved for this purpose, with enough water to cover completely, and left to soak for half an hour. Then the meat must be put on a board placed in a slanting position, or on a board with grooves or perforations to allow the blood to flow freely. Then the meat must be sprinkled on all sides with coarse salt and allowed to remain for one hour. It is then removed and rinsed with cold water three times until all salt is removed.
>
> Liver cannot be koshered in this manner. It must be broiled in order to render it kosher, and it must be broiled before it can be sauted [sic] or used in any recipe. It should be washed, salted, then placed on a broiler. When it is finished, it must be washed in cold water to wash the blood away.
>
> Meat that is served broiled, such as steaks, hamburgers and chops does not have to be koshered.[103]

Since the meats used for "Shish Kabob," "Steak Nino," and "Steak au Poivre" are broiled, the dishes have already taken the first step to being made suitable for a Jewish table. Where the meat dishes of other groups might require animal fat such as butter, the recipe contributors substitute a pareve variety of margarine. As with the "Chicken Kiev" recipe, "Beef Stroganoff" is made with onions, mushrooms, chicken fat or margarine, flour, chicken soup, and white wine. In this way, the editors and contributors of the Hadassah cookbook acknowledged the multicultural society in which they lived even as they retained their distinctive identity.

As with the daily meals, celebratory meals required careful attention to culinary details, because both mundane and festive dining call attention to one's religious identity. For example, Passover, the holiday commemorating Jewish liberation from bondage in Egypt, demands discarding all foods made with or containing leavening. Only a separate set of dishes untouched by leavening should be in use during this celebration. To help plan these ritual occasions, the authors provide several "suggested festive menus." The content of the menus reflects esoteric knowledge: a shared pattern of food behavior identifying those who know (insiders) what to eat on particular occasions from those who do not (outsiders). In addition, menus are class markers, in this case for American Jews of the middle class. For example:

Sabbath Meal

Wine for Kiddush   Challah
Gefilte fish or Chopped Liver
Chicken soup and Noodles
Roast chicken with Tzimmes or Potato Kugel or Kishka
Or
Veal Breast with Potato Stuffing
Savory Green Bean Casserole Tossed Salad
Pumpkin Cake or Apple Cake Fresh
Fruit
Tea

Rosh Hashanah

Wine Apple Slices dipped in Honey Round Challah
Gefilte Fish or Chopped Liver
Chicken soup with Farfel or Kreplach
Roast Turkey or Chicken with Rice Pecan Stuffing
Carrot Tzimmes with Potato Kneidel
Rhubarb or Cranberry Gelatin Mold
Honey Cake Taiglach Fresh Fruit in Season
Tea

Passover Seder

Wine for Kiddush   Matzo

Hard Boiled Eggs in Salt Water
Gefilte Fish with Horseradish
Chicken Soup with Matzo Balls
Roast Turkey or Cornish Hens with Matzo Stuffing
Glazed Carrots Tomato and Cucumber Platter
Sponge Cake with Rhubarb-strawberry Sauce Tea

Although the *Rochester Hadassah Cookbook* described all of the holidays and provided menus for each, the celebration of Passover had a section of its own because of the special dietary requirements. Because flour and foods with leavening are prohibited during the week of observance, special ingredients such as matzo meal must be used. These extraordinary ingredients require specific formulations for their preparation. Passover, although universally important to Jews, garnered new significance in the American setting between the world wars.[104] Even families that no longer observed the dietary laws would have a Seder, the ritual meal beginning the Passover holiday in which no leavened bread is eaten. In the American context, Passover became the most elaborate and widely observed holiday in the Jewish ritual cycle.[105] It became a time to reconnect to a history of oppression.

Chanukah, the Feast of Lights, and Bar Mitzvah, the coming of age of young boys and, later, girls, were occasions reinvented and augmented in the New World as a means to captivate and enthrall young people and tie them to their faith, families, and communities.[106] In order to perpetuate Judaism, parents sought to develop rituals that would appeal to children to ensure the continuity of their religion and its customs and traditions. An emphasis on family and children in American life provided Jewish parents with an opportunity to create holidays and ceremonies that would be as appealing to Jewish children, for example, as Christmas was for other children. Ritual events such as Chanukah "stressed the primacy of the Jewish home as an agent of Jewish identity, cultural continuity, and 'beautification.'"[107] At the same time, the Jewish home was an agent of social change.[108] The culinary inventions and adaptations that coexisted with traditional recipes in the *Rochester Hadassah Cookbook* reveal a community that was continually shaping and reshaping social and cultural life and negotiating its own ethnic, religious, and national identities.

For example, at the turn of the twentieth century, Rochester's Jewish community was composed of Ashkenazic Jews from Western, Central, and Eastern Europe. When Sephardic Jews (Jews originally from Spain) moved to Rochester in 1906, a week before Passover, the residents had struggled to categorize them and their "strange" traditions as Jewish. Sephardim, according to editor Cohen, are Jews "who after their expulsion from Spain in 1492, found their way eastward to Italy and countries in the Eastern Mediterranean area or northward to towns such as Amsterdam and London and from there sometimes westward to North and South America."[109]

Mrs. Cohen recounted the story of their arrival: "They were strange because they did not speak Yiddish as all other Jews did. Although they adhered to the traditional in religious matters, their customs, language and national origin, marked them off as a distinct group."[110] They spoke a combination of Turkish and Judeo-Spanish called Ladino. "There was a great stir in the Jewish community in Rochester over these strange people who were so different from them."[111] Thus diversity, even within the Jewish community, was not always tolerated. The first arrivals were men. Although this immigration pattern was common, this too must have seemed unusual for this community of families. However, in time, the Sephardic Jews either married into their new community or brought over their wives and children. Eventually they established a synagogue of their own, which they dedicated in 1965, many years after their first settlement in Rochester.

The brief history of the Sephardic settlement in Rochester provided by the editors does not divulge the relationship between the two groups in the intervening years. In general, Sephardic communities build separate synagogues because their liturgy is somewhat different from the Western European service. Moreover, Haddassah groups are not affiliated with a particular congregation. Thus, the inclusion of Sephardic recipes, such as "Greek Lemon Soup," "Cheese Bourekas," "Passover Buenueloes (Matzo Fritters)," "Passover Pastele (Meat Pie)," and "Arroz con Letche (Rice Pudding)," among others, in the Hadassah cookbook is not surprising. The differences between the two traditions is observable, tellingly, by the Sephardic recipes' containment in a separate section. A few Sephardic dishes also were incorporated into the holiday menus for Passover and Shavuoth (festival commemorating the giving of the

Ten Commandments to Moses at Mt. Sinai) at the front of the book. Perhaps the editors thought that the food and history of the Sephardic Jews would add a touch of the exotic to the otherwise standard Jewish cookbook.[112]

In its entirety, the cookbook delivers a message of history, of modernity, of social change, and of culinary inventiveness. The Rochester Jewish community portrayed was not an assimilated community, nor did it exist in isolation from American culture. The community shared American middle-class values while displaying its distinctive Jewish identity and heritage. Food, a prominent symbol of Jewish identity, became a potent vehicle for the Rochester Hadassah's depiction of its own community past and present.

In Memory's Kitchen[113]

In contrast to the *Rochester Haddassah Cookbook,* which depicted an ongoing although changing tradition, the compilation of recipes published as *In Memory's Kitchen* echoes with the loss of a culture. This volume stands as one of the twentieth century's most moving and triumphant examples of cookbooks as artifacts of collective identity and memory, written by Mina Pachter and her Jewish women friends in Theresienstadt, Czechoslovakia, a ghetto/camp during the Holocaust.[114] The recipe manuscript compiled by Pachter and her friends contained the Central European recipes that represented their vanishing cultural world. "The lost world and its flavors"[115] enshrined in this book traveled a quarter of a century and a continent to reach its destination, Pachter's daughter, Anny Stern, who was then living in New York. The story of the book's origins and its journey testify to its creators' determination to preserve a way of life devastated by human atrocity.

The story began in 1941, in a Czech village named Terezin, forty miles north of Prague. The Germans renamed it Theresienstadt and brought Czechoslovakian, German, Moravian, Dutch, and Danish Jews to the village, purportedly a model ghetto meant to showcase their reputed good treatment of Jews. In reality, it was an overcrowded, pestilent village. From that ghetto, the Nazis transported the Jews to the "killing centers" of Auschwitz and Birkenau. Few survived.[116]

Subjected to the cruelest and harshest living conditions of everyone in the ghetto, the elderly and the young were least able to endure. Of the 15,000 children who passed through Theresienstadt, only 100 were alive at the end of the war. Few could eke out an existence on the scarce, barely edible rations. Bland soups and sauces occasionally made with tiny bits of meat, a loaf of bread, barley, and turnips were what inmates were given after hours of waiting. The food they were given was neither sufficient nor nourishing. Often meager meals had to sustain them for days at a time. Hunger was incessant. Some people, like the women who wrote their recipes on precious scraps of paper, escaped the hungers of the camp with flights of the imagination and memories of meals, homes, and people most would not see again. While an inmate, Mina Pachter transformed those scraps of paper on which she and her friends had written their recipes into a handwritten cookbook destined for the next generation.

The women who compiled this *kochbuch* (cookbook) participated in a "revolt of the spirit."[117] The camp boasted an inordinate number of musicians, artists, scientists, writers, and other intellectuals who tried to create a normal Jewish life for the children. There were operatic performances, lectures, and study groups to educate the young. It was with a similar and equally fierce determination that Pachter and the other women of Terezin, in their weakened physical condition, wrote their recipes and, with the recipes, their memories of the past. They talked about "food, to dwell on what they were missing—pots and pans, a kitchen, home, family, guests, meals, entertainment."[118] In the midst of misery almost beyond our comprehension, the women defied their captors by imagining another world, past and future, but not the present. They did this by "cooking platonically," cooking with their minds and mouths.[119]

"Talking about it [food] helped you," recalled Bianca Steiner Brown, a survivor of Terezin and the translator of the *kochbuch*. "Everyone did it. And people got very upset if they thought you made a dish the wrong way or had the wrong recipe for it," said another former inmate, Susan E. Cernyk-Spatz. The longing for food was unremitting, and the need to remember and describe it, to savor its flavors, aromas, and textures, was possible only with the mind. "Food, memories of it, missing it, craving it, dreaming of it, in short, the obsession with food colours all the Theresienstadt memoirs," wrote Ruth Schwertfeger in her book *Women of Theresienstadt, Voices from a Concentration Camp*.[120] It was a means of spiritual survival. Women and men engaged in the endless discussions about food that ignited debates about tastes, aromas, ingredients, and processes. Driven by hunger and aided by memory, inmates could sharpen their minds on the discussions and arguments that these sessions entailed.

Talking about the foods was a way to relive them, both to sustain the knowledge of domestic arts they had honed and to imagine the physical sensations of eating a well-loved dish. But these conversations were more than that as well. The women's talks assuaged not simply physical cravings for familiar food, but emotional longings for another time and place and a life they were denied.

At night, the women might remember a cake recipe to share with one another. "They would say, 'Do you know such and such a cake?' 'I did it in such and such a way.'"[121] One of the cakes in Pachter's book is for "*Ausgiebige Schokolade Torte*" (Rich Chocolate Cake). Perhaps it was one of the recipes the women discussed in their nocturnal debates. Pachter included two recipes for a Czech Cake:[122]

Czech Cake 1

25 dg hladke mouky, 8 dg tuku, 8 dg cukru, 1 vejce, 3 lzice mleka, ½ prasku, plnit podle chuti.

25 decagrams [smooth] flour [similar in texture to our all-purpose flour], 8 decagrams fat [margarine], 8 decagrams sugar, 1 egg, 3 spoons milk, ½ [packet] baking powder. Fill to taste.

Czech Cake 2

25 dg mouky, 15 dg varenych lisovanych brambor, 10 dg tuku, 10 dg cukru, 1 vejce, 2 lzice mleka, prasek, plnit.

25 decagrams flour, 15 decagrams boiled pressed potatoes [put through a potato ricer], 10 decagrams fat [margarine], 10 decagrams sugar, 1 egg, 2 spoons milk, baking powder, fill.

Perhaps Pachter was being tactful when she included variants of a recipe. The women must have known many recipes in common, for they shared a collective understanding of "the cuisines of the Austro-Hungarian empire," in particular that of "the Czechoslovak kitchen." Each of the writers may have had her own version of recipes they all knew. By including them all, Pachter's recipe book not only depicts the culture's culinary variations but embraces the life of the individual who provided the recipe.

More than one cookbook was produced in the horrors of Theresienstadt. Another inmate, Arnostka Klein, also wrote a cookbook during the long, hungry hours. Her book is now in safekeeping in Israel's Beit Theresienstadt.[123] She had recipes for a "sachertorte and a Londoner Schnitten made with marmalade, grated almonds, flour, butter, sugar, eggs, and lemon rind."[124] Although different in format from Mina Pachter's *kochbook,* Klein's cookbook served the same purpose: to keep alive their creators and a way of life.

That way of life included many hours spent with family and friends around a table laden with the specialties of the region. Cara De Silva, who edited Pachter's *kockbuch,* describes the food the women knew as

> robust with sophisticated overtones . . . it was well known for its soups; its roast birds and smoked meats; its savory sausages and wild mushrooms; its moderate use of spices (caraway and poppy seeds were popular); its goulash and wiener schnitzel; its large variety of dumplings (eaten from soup to dessert); and its cheese such as hoop cheese (similar to dry pot cheese); yeasted pastries (part of a great baking tradition); palachinky, sweet crepelike pancakes; and, of course, beer.[125]

The region from which these women came was extraordinarily rich in savory and sweet delicacies, and their food repertoire was inextricably bound to the languages (Czech and German) in which they wrote the recipes. Pachter's *kockbuch* written in the sensate language of cooking, must have encapsulated strong memories for its compiler and its contributors.

For remembering those who did not survive the camp, the languages and handwritings in Pachter's book are as important as the food. Composed sometimes in a faltering German (because German was most likely not the women's primary language) and sometimes with misspellings and grammatical errors, incomplete or faulty instructions, and unfinished lists of ingredients,[126] the recipes themselves "bear witness"[127] to the stress of living "in the face of death."[128] Although malnourished and weakened, these women reconstructed the recipes of the everyday meals and celebratory feasts that were once the hall-marks of capable Central European housewives.

According to Bianca Steiner Brown, the cookbook resembled the hand-written cookbooks that were common in this part of Europe, first written for their writers' use and later passed on to their daughters after their deaths. "Perhaps the writers of the Terezin cookbook were attempting to preserve this tradition."[129] It was with this urgency that Pachter gave her "fragile, hand-sewn" copybook to fellow inmate Arthur Buxbaum just before she died with the hope that it would reach her daughter, Anny Stern, who lived in Palestine.[130] Stern and others have reconstructed the book's history from what little is known. Many of the people involved in the transmission of the book have since died leaving many details undiscoverable. Before Stern left Czechoslovakia with her son David to join her husband in Palestine, she had begged her mother to come with her. Despite Stern's pleas, Pachter had de-cided to stay behind. She could not believe harm would come to her, an old person. Once she was transported to Terezin, she understood she might not survive. Buxbaum did not have Anny Stern's address in Israel, and the cook-book remained with him until he could fulfill his promise to deliver it. Not until 1960 did Buxbaum entrust the package containing the cookbook, let-ters, and photographs Pachter had given him to a cousin who was on her way to Israel. It was too late to reach Stern there; she and her family had moved to New York. Although no one knows exactly how the package got to Stern, she received a telephone call in which the caller said, "I have a package for you from your mother." And so it was that Mina Pachter's emo-tionally unsettling cookbook finally arrived at its destination, the daughter for whom it was written. When she saw her mother's handwriting on the package, she wept. "After all those years," she said, "it was like her hand was reaching out to me from long ago."

Recipe books allude to meals and events, people and places, successes and failures, joys and sorrows, lives and deaths of those loved and known. In sum, they represent the life worlds—past and present—of their creators. A culture's food as preserved in its recipes enfolds a group of people within its borders and, thus, comes to symbolize that culture and its homeland. Food and its preparation formulas represent the hungers and security that mark the history of its people. Recipes embed a culture's stories and myths, legends and lore in their cryptic texts. They embrace the past and locate a group in its present. Passed on to the next generation, cookbooks commemorate those who came before and create a bridge with those who will come after.

Food nurtures both the individual and the social body. Because it is shared, it may be used symbolically to demarcate a group's boundaries. It embodies a culture and those who eat together. Parents who provide food for their children create a bond through feeding. Exchanging food (as with the custom of Shalach Manot, sending packages of food during Purim) is a way a family both marks and sustains a wider network of social relationships.[131] Thus, a social group's cuisine may represent its collective history, identity, and memory.

In displaying their cuisine, the compilers and editors of these cookbooks also self-consciously portray and define an image of themselves, their cultural groups, and their own rendering of their group's history and identity. Sometimes the writers of these cookery books tell stories that differ from the mainstream versions of history. Freda De Knight's *A Date with A Dish* presented a "countermemory," an account of history that differed from the prevailing collective narrative.[132] It was an act of resistance. The women of Theresienstadt also wrote a cookbook as a form of resistance. Whereas De Knight corrected a stereotypical vision of African American cuisine and life, Pachter and her friends inscribed a world that was about to be lost. Both books commemorate a people and their histories.

But culture and heritage are not static. Social life is continually changing, and groups select aspects of their past to highlight and to suppress.[133] De Knight chose to celebrate the creativity, talent, and contributions of African American cooks. The *Rochester Haddassah Cookbook* gives us a view of the Jewish community of Rochester, New York, from the perspective of its women, as a social group negotiating multiple identities in a pluralistic society. The history of the Jews, their religious traditions and cultural memories, and their complex allegiances are all framed in the recipes that the

Hadassah presented to the reading public. Pachter's manuscript reified a cuisine and a way of life even as it was undergoing a cultural genocide. Those who received the manuscript would, of necessity, have to explicate it. Thus history is always reinterpreted in the context of the present moment. Yet present moments authenticate and validate themselves by looking back, by claiming ancient roots and history.

In these cookery texts presenting foods, recipes, and meals, ordinary and literary women have written a place into being, whether that place is a physical locale, a memorialized past, or a social location. As writers, these cookbook authors have contributed to shaping definitions of self, gender, community, and regional and national cultures and identities. The women who bring these texts into being create them as sentinels in their own lives and as guardians for the lives of those who follow.

THREE

Lineage and Legacies

Mothers pass down recipes not only for the haroseth for the Seder plate but for mezedhes, for cholent as well as ahladhi sto fourno—baked quince, for poppyseed cake and ladhera.

—*Anne Michaels,* Fugitive Pieces[1]

Some women leave diaries. My mother left recipes.

—*Linda Murray Berzok, "My Mother's Recipes"*[2]

An inscription on the inside front cover of the pocket-size book *New England Cookery,* (1808) by author Lucy Emerson reveals the history of Anna Dunsmore's copy. "*This book was given to Anna Powers Dunsmore by her father, at her marriage to Samuel Dunsmore, June 21st 1808 (3 mos after its publication). It was handed down to her eldest daughter Jane Dunsmore Jones, to her eldest daughter Clara Jones Staples, and last to her eldest daughter Minnie Staples Davis.*"[3] We may imagine a proud father giving this wedding gift to his daughter, who in turn began the transmission of this book, with its legacy of maternal wisdom, through four succeeding generations.

Trying to understand the history of a particular copy of any recipe book began each time I turned to the first page, the flyleaf. Sometimes I was disappointed to find nothing at all—no name, no date, no place. At other times, I discovered a woman's handwritten inscriptions stating her own name and sometimes a date, and occasionally a geographical location. The most revealing inscriptions name the book's owners and specify their relationships to the women from whom they received or to whom they gave the book. Certainly a statement of a book's ownership was proprietary, but I ventured that a proprietary inscription reflected more than an interest in the book's economic value.

In fact, women formally constructed their matrilineal genealogies and their relationships to one another in their cookbooks, binding together the different generations. Recipe books, although not always written only in the owner's hand, belonged to women and to the domestic sphere and culture they inhabited.[4] Because women's authority rested in the regulation of family relations, courtship rituals, leisure, and domestic space,[5] and a cookbook was so intimately connected with the functioning of a household and all of these activities, it was, de facto, an aspect of domestic space; it was a woman's property to give or bequeath.

In their recipe books, women formally acknowledged their blood ties and a hoped-for continuity of relationships that transcended time and space. Moreover, the offering of a recipe book was a sign of affection, a tie binding together women of different generations. Leaving a cookbook to the next of kin was a valued gift of vital practical knowledge, gathered by one woman from many others and, therefore, thick with personal, familial, and cultural memories.

Presumably custom dictated that a daughter would inherit her mother's cookbook, often at the time of the younger woman's marriage.[6] However, in the early modern period and into the nineteenth century, life was, even more than today, precarious and unpredictable. Too often a woman or her children did not survive to reach this milestone together. Many women died at a relatively young age in childbirth or from an illness. Children often died before reaching adulthood. Repeated widowhood led to multiple marriages, further obscuring patterns of inheritance. Because death and dislocation often interrupted the straightforward transmission of documents from one generation to the next, women bequeathed their recipe books and their descendants acquired them in ways that varied from one family to the next.

Getting or starting a cookbook may reflect a woman's entrance onto the stage of domesticity. The book, a symbol of a rite of passage, signals a child's taking leave of her mother and her birth family to start a life of her own. Taking her mother's book is symbolically taking that maternal presence with her. The knowledge in cookbooks is practical and necessary to sustain families from day to day, making it especially useful to young women who are less experienced in domestic matters when they begin their own households. Thus, a mother's recipe book and its contents are valuable in the present, not in an unforeseen and indefinite future. To be most useful, a mother's legacy might be given before her death.

Young women may have begun to acquire their mother's knowledge independently of the actual transfer of the elder's recipe book. Women of marriageable age or about to be married may have begun copying out favorites of their mother's recipes and techniques as they approached this rite of passage. This was the case with Margaret Savile. She had begun to copy out recipes—either from her mother's book, if such existed, or by writing out instructions as they were told to her—for "distilled waters and infusions" and thereafter for medicines. She died in 1683 of a fever at the age of fifteen before completing her task. Her husband to be, Jo. Brooke, the curate of Methley, completed her writing and gave the book to the Savile family, which has kept it for over four hundred years as a memorial to Margaret.[7] Margaret's death nearly interrupted the passage of a family legacy, but it is an example of one of the ways in which daughters gathered culinary and medicinal knowledge from their mothers.

In the seventeenth century, the young Elinor Fettiplace most probably began recording recipes for sweetmeets and preserves under her mother's supervision. At the time of her marriage and her move to Appleton Manor, her husband's parents' home, she brought with her some form of receipt book. Because of the out-of-order inclusion of cookery, preserves, banquetting stuff, medicines, and broths, it appears that she added to her original book over time and without concern for food categories. In 1604, a professional scribe recopied the book, this time attending to the proper placement of types of foodstuffs. Since no daughter survived her, Lady Fettiplace's book, in its 1604 version, passed to her niece, Lady Anne Horner.[8]

In some cases mother or daughter may have hired a professional scribe to write a recipe book as a gift for the younger woman's dowry and pending marriage. Dated July 4, 1737, Ms. Ann Lawrance's book is an example of what might have been such a ceremonial item. It is what is called a "fair copy," a carefully penned text, not one in rough or draft form. The book is written in a single hand; it may be Ann's or her mother's (or that of another family member), or even perhaps a professional scrivener. The recipes are written on one side of the page only, leaving the verso side blank, an unusual practice, given the high cost of paper. Each recipe is marked with an elaborate flourish, an embellishment not found in every recipe book. Although nothing conclusive points to its presentation as a gift to a young woman at the time of her marriage, its pristine condition suggests that it was never used. Was it a text meant to display Ann Lawrance's class and rank? Was it meant to be consulted rather than used directly in the kitchen? It is tempting to speculate that Ann Lawrance never married, that her book, like Margaret Savile's, became a memorial for a woman who died young or who never entered the socially expected next phase of the female life cycle.

Death and other unforeseen events made it difficult for women to specify the path of a manuscript. However, to the degree that it was possible, women controlled the distribution of this record of their life's work along with other household possessions. Despite this, oddly, by and large cookbooks were not mentioned separately in wills.[9] Although women's wills lovingly depicted the domestic goods—including books—they were distributing,[10] cookbooks are not among them. Perhaps the only documentation of the culinary legacy was the inscription within the object—the manuscript or book—itself. The cookbook became both testament and gift.

Why would wills contain no mention of the bequest of a receipt book? Was the assumption that daughters would inherit their mothers' books so pervasive that it did not warrant even a mention in a formal legal document? Personal recipe collections because they lacked monetary value were, perhaps, outside the bounds of the material possessions remaining for inventory by an appraiser. Were they so imbued with other meanings, more humble—or more sacred—than other household chattel such as linens, china, and silver that such a document was not a fitting place for a culinary legacy? After all, cookbooks contained the recipes for foods that sanctified the domestic rituals of families' feasting and fasting and brought comfort, if not healing, in times of illness and accident. Perhaps this odd combination of homeliness and reverence can account for the regard with which women who received these gifts might have viewed them.

Well-worn recipe books occupy a space between the sacred and profane. They contain learning that is critical and life sustaining. In recipe texts, women accumulated valuable, often arcane knowledge about the mysteries of birth and death—women's domains of responsibility[11] (and domains for which they were persecuted during turbulent times)—how to cook, comfort, and cure. Women's work has sometimes been described as magical for its abilities to transform raw materials into food and medicine.[12] The receiver of a manuscript containing such vital knowledge held a place as an intimate acquaintance of the giver. Mother and daughter, or other kinswomen, were united by vital knowledge and the bond they shared through a text handed down, literally and figuratively, through the generations. The evanescent worldly relationship between kin was given permanence in a cookbook. The living continue a relationship with the dead.

Cookbooks survived the women who used them, exposing the stresses of everyday handling with their residues of grease and flecks of batter, frayed pages, and singed edges. Because an individual used a book over time, it "acquired an aura"[13] that animated an inanimate object. Alive with the personal traces of its owner, a woman's cookbook became a talisman for those who followed. Perhaps, too, because they were "handheld"[14] and handmade, recipe books might be seen as "extensions of the body and of the maternal figure"[15] who created them. A daughter could now hold in her hands a visual representation of her mother in the script etched on the pages of the manuscript and hear her voice in the language of the book.

A silent narrator drives the descriptive instructions in cookery books. No longer present during the reenactment of a recipe, the absent narrator guides the reader in her task: "Take," "Chop," "Dice," "Peel," "Melt" are just a few of the imperatives that begin the discourse of the traditional recipe format. According to historian William Eamon, "a recipe implies a contract between the reader and the text. It is a prescription for taking action: recipe is the

Latin imperative 'take.' A recipe is a prescription for an experiment, a 'trying out.'"[16]

Despite the formulaic quality of the recipe format, in women's culinary manuscripts an individual voice may still be heard.[17] We see this in the way Grandmere Rappe meticulously numbered all of the recipes in her nineteenth-century recipe manuscript and gave ingredient amounts in whimsical terms. Number 168 is a *"Receipt to make an Indian Pudding Baked."* Moreover, her recipe is personalized by her expressions of quantity. She writes *"Scald two quarts skim milk; stir in one Pint Indian meal or enough to make very thin mush. Add a little salt, a tea cup full of molasses, a great spoonful of ginger or a little of any other spice you like."* I imagine Grandmere Rappe's grandchildren replaying their grandmother's instructions as they cook from her recipe book. How could anyone dismiss that voice? Its authority demands attention and deference. It also encourages creativity. A reproduction of her recipes brings her text to materiality and its creator to mind. Both the telling and the reproduction may be seen as vicarious representations of social interactions or encounters with the person whose recipes are recreated.

Because recipes do more than provide instructions for preparing food, and because they reenact social transactions, they also may signify social identity, particularly if some recipes become associated with a specific family and its members. Aristocratic culinary manuscripts functioned in this way. Their families' ancient histories and lineages were registered in these magisterial tomes and in the culinary and medicinal secrets they contained. We learn this when we read Lord Stanhope's inscriptions in his wife's receipt book. On the inside front cover of the seventeenth-century recipe book of Lady Anne Percy, daughter of Algernon, tenth Earl of Northumberland, he wrote: *"These receits are writ in my dear wifes the Lady Ann Percies own hand have been long kept secrets in the Northumberland family."*[18]

Why was it important for aristocratic families to conceal, or keep secret, their cookery and medicinal receipts? One reason many have been that the wealthy valued food as entertainment. Since the table was the site of conspicuous consumption and amusement, surprise was a key element in impressing one's guests. Delighting guests with a variety of dishes, some of which had never been served before to an array of guests, was a feat that earned one plaudits in elite social circles. Another reason was that concealing this knowledge was a way of closing ranks, protecting borders. A clan might know its members by their knowledge of its cuisine, and, conversely, a kinsman would know he had found safety in his clan by partaking of familiar food. A clan's history was represented in its long-standing family recipes; its borders protected by the secret knowledge available only to insiders.

Women were the guardians of the clan's food and medicinal secrets. Having her own book was a symbol of a lady's rank and privilege. It signaled wealth, lineage, and literacy. Beyond the status it displayed, possessing such a book also bore responsibilities. In a sense, a woman's pedigree was registered in the pages of her cookbook.

In Anno Domini 1669, Lady Frescheville announced herself on the first page of her receipt book. The large, opulent, red, Moroccan leather-bound manuscript bears the gilded initials "A*F" splintered by a golden crown.[19] From her title and the attributions in her book, there is little doubt that she came from a prominent family with noble connections. We do not know whether she wrote the book with her own hand as a self-proclamation or whether it was written out for her as a gift when she married. In either case, the inscription of Lady Frescheville's name tells us that she lived and when. Importantly, it also displayed the lineage from which she came. It spoke about the secret, guarded knowledge passed on in her family for generations.

Lady Frescheville's regal text opens with an index of cookery receipts. From the back, the book opens again with another index for sweetmeats that includes "*a thin summer cheese*" (see Figure 3.1), "*Quince Cakes,*" "*Orange Cakes,*" "*Gooseberry Creame,*" "*Spanish Creame,*" and "*cheesecakes.*" In addition, there are recipes for distilling and for making perfumes and cordial waters, preserves, potions, herbals, and cures. Both bodies of knowledge were important for a noblewoman. It was the mistress's task to manage the household, provision it, supervise the labor, and care for its members. She was also responsible for entertaining a variety of guests.

The mistress of the manor had to be prepared to feed the family and an entourage of others, from travelers seeking shelter to laborers. The manor house was also responsible for providing charity in the form of food and drink to the poor. At annual holidays such as Christmas, New Year's, and

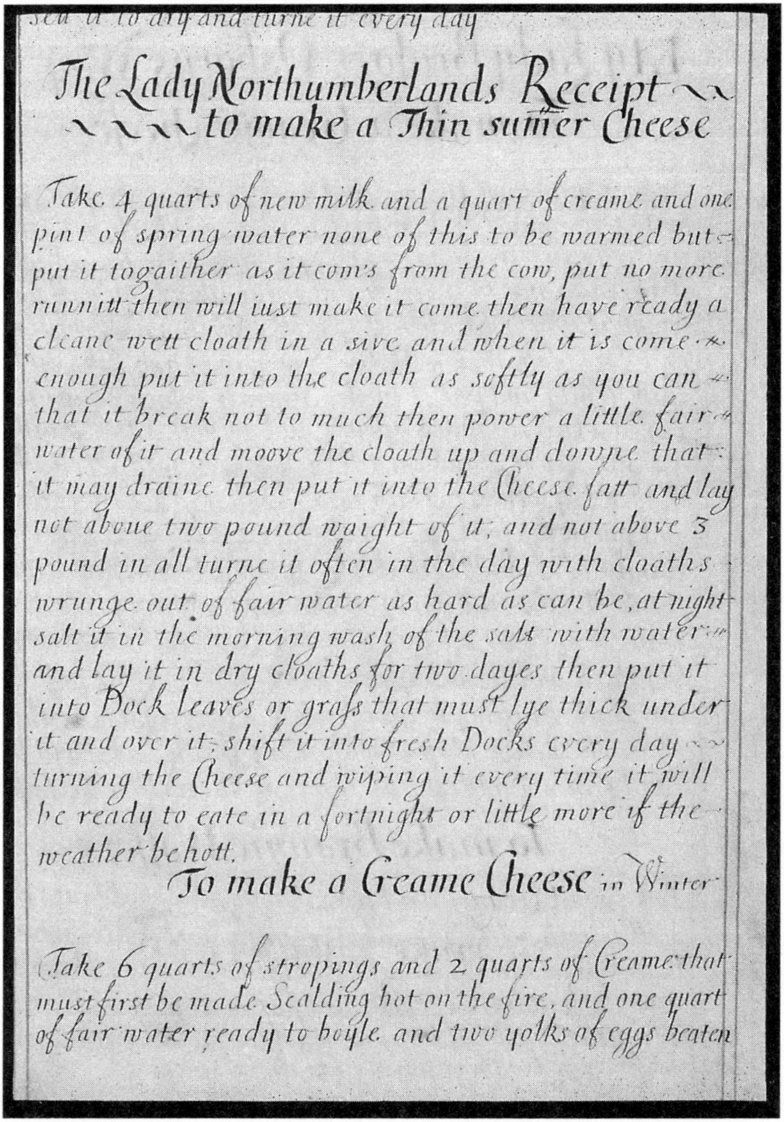

sed it to dry and turne it every day

The Lady Northumberlands Receipt
~~~to make a Thin sumer Cheese

Take 4 quarts of new milk and a quart of creame and one
pint of spring water none of this to be warmed but
put it togaither as it com's from the cow, put no more
runnitt then will iust make it come then have ready a
cleane wett cloath in a sive and when it is come
enough put it into the cloath as softly as you can
that it break not to much then power a little fair
water of it and moove the cloath up and downe that
it may draine then put it into the Cheese fatt and lay
not aboue two pound waight of it; and not aboue 3
pound in all turne it often in the day with cloaths
wrunge out of fair water as hard as can be, at night
salt it in the morning wash of the salt with water
and lay it in dry cloaths for two dayes then put it
into Dock leaves or grafs that must lye thick under
it and over it shift it into fresh Docks every day
turning the Cheese and wiping it every time it will
be ready to eate in a fortnight or little more if the
weather be hott.

To make a Creame Cheese in Winter

Take 6 quarts of stropings and 2 quarts of Creame that
must first be made Scalding hot on the fire, and one quart
of fair water ready to boyle and two yolks of eggs beaten

Figure 3.1   Contribution from an aristocrat to Lady Frescheville's opulent seventeenth-century receipt book.

Easter, food that had been grown and gathered on the manorial property was distributed to those who came to celebrate.[20]

Since servants, laborers, apprentices, neighbors, and the poor often turned to the local manor house and its matriarch for help in times of illness and accident, cookbooks also included time-tested, life-saving remedies for menstruation, difficult pregnancy, childbirth, or mothers who bore stillborn babies as well as for earaches, cancers, and constipation.

Not every woman was a gifted healer, yet women across the social spectrum engaged in healing activities. Some middle-ranking women earned their livelihoods as midwives and healers, while a virtuous Christian woman such as Lady Frescheville would aid her neighbors in distress. "All chatelaines of great houses were expected to be conversant with medicine, the arts of distilling cordials and healing waters and the cooking of restorative broths."[21]

Although it is not clear that Lady Frescheville experimented in chemistry—called "kitchen physick"[22]—many noblewomen engaged in scientific research and medical experimentation while occupied in domestic activities.[23] Medical cookery was related to other scientific and medical fields, such as botany and chemistry.[24] For example, many of the recipes of the seventeenth-century chemist Robert Boyle's sister, Lady Ranelagh, were medical, and most likely she shared them with her brother. In fact, he conducted chemistry experiments at her house.[25] Queen Henrietta Maria, wife of Charles I, was known to "descend to her closet and engage in these entertainments [experiments]."[26]

Another accomplished experimenter was the Countess of Kent, Elizabeth Grey, who was known for her herbals and powders. Her recipes were circulated among patrician families as recorded by, among others, Sir Kenelm Digby, published seventeenth-century cooking authority and courtly rogue, who reported that "my Lady Kent" cooked her nourishing broth "in a close flagon in bulliente Balneo."[27] Although her personal reputation was sometimes scandalous (she was known to have "promiscuous ways"),[28] her concern and care of the poor and the sick earned her a reputation as a charitable and generous woman, traits considered the natural duties of women of her station.[29] Lady Elizabeth was reported to have "'spent twenty thousand pound a year in physick, receipts and experiments, and in charity towards the poor.'"[30] Her charitable acts apparently redeemed her good name. Her reputation as a godly gentlewoman rested upon it.[31]

Other women of noble birth who had been socialized to assume these benevolent responsibilities but whose lives were dramatically altered by political and religious upheavals nonetheless maintained the tradition of keeping a manuscript for receipts. Wealthy and well-born Gulielma Penn, wife of William Penn and, like him, an ardent Quaker, found herself on the margins of her former social life due to her religious beliefs. Rejection and turmoil characterized her life as well as those of other Quakers in the mid to late seventeenth century. Beyond her Quaker activities, she was devoted equally to her husband, her children (only two of whom survived her), her household, and caring for the sick. She was noted for her healing skills and for her ability to apply the cures she had learned from her mother, Mary Penington, and her grandmother Springett. John Aubrey, a contemporary, described Guli Penn as "in person and qualities, virtuous, generous, wise, humble, plaine; generally beloved for those good qualities and one more— the great cures she does, having great skill in physic and surgery, which she freely bestows."[32] Among the first pages of Gulielma's receipt book are her grandmother Springett's ointments and herbs for curing eye ailments. Springett was renowned for her gifts in healing eyes, and Guli used her kinswomen's knowledge throughout her life.[33]

In 1703, a copy of Gulielma's recipe book crossed the Atlantic, although she never did. It was brought instead by her son, William, Jr. Although Guli died in 1694 at the age of fifty, her son had his mother's book transcribed "*in great hast*" for his transatlantic journey.[34] By then, his mother's original manuscript may have been in the hands of his sister, Laetitia. William Jr.'s copy is inscribed as follows: "*My Mother's Receipts for Cookerys Preserving and Chyrurgery—William Penn.*" On the last page the scribe has noted that "*Here ends the book of Coockary in great hast transcrided by Edward Blackfan the 25th of October 1702.*" William Jr.'s wish to have a copy of his mother's recipe book to take with him required that he or a scribe (in this case, Edward Blackfan) make a fair copy to take to his new home. While William Jr. must have believed that the contents of his mother's book would be of use to him in the New World, it is also tempting to conjecture that he had enjoyed an especially close relationship with his mother. William Jr. returned to England, but the manuscript remained in Pennsylvania for many years before it traveled to England and then finally came to rest in Pennsylvania once more.[35]

Many of America's patrician families continued the tradition of passing on women's culinary manuscripts. Martha Dandridge Custis Washington's cookery book is a complicated and puzzling example. George and Martha Washington's granddaughter Eleanor Parke Custis Lewis (1779–1852), who was called Nelly, inherited a manuscript that belonged to her grandmother Martha. The inscription in the book attributes Frances Parke Custis as its original author.

Not as straightforward as it appears, this inscription in Martha Washington's book has, according to culinary historian Karen Hess, perplexed historians, and there is some dispute about the book's originator and its succession.[36] The historical inaccuracies of the inscription suggest that inheritance was not linear; it also points to other readings and interpretations of these inscriptions. The flyleaf of Washington's manuscript reads:

Washington Cook Book
Written by Francis [sic] *Parke Custis the mother of Martha Washington's*
first husband. She gave it
to her daughter-in-law, and
Martha W, in turn—
bestowed it upon her adored
granddaughter, Nelly Custis
after her marriage to Lawrence
Lewis—

Hess argues convincingly that, despite the inscription, this manuscript, now in the possession of the Historical Society of Pennsylvania, was probably written in the mid-seventeenth century by Lady Berkeley, stepmother of Jane Ludwell Parke, who was Frances Parke Custis's mother. Hess contends that because Frances Parke Custis died in 1714/15 and Martha Dandridge Custis Washington was born in 1731, the book could not have been given to Martha directly. Further, she does not believe that Frances was the author of the book. Hess based her conclusions on the types of recipes and on the personalities, handwritings, and birth and death dates of the women involved. She asserts that the inscription was an afterword written in a nineteenth-century hand. This may likely be the case. However, the date when the inscription was written may not be as important as the sentiment it projects.

The Washington manuscript (as it is called) was copied out in one hand (whether by its compiler or a scrivener) and separated according to custom, with sweetmeats at one end and cookery at the other. In between were pages later written upon randomly by at least seven other hands.[37] The book was passed down to women of the family, notably the infamous Frances Parke Custis (Hess alleges that she was "not known for her generous disposition"[38]), whose husband kept it after her death. Custom dictated that Frances's daughter should have inherited the book; however, her only daughter died childless, so her son Daniel became heir to the recipe manuscript. When he married Martha Dandridge, the book passed to her.

If we assume that at least some of the inscription is accurate, then Nelly received her grandmother Martha Washington's recipe book after her marriage.[39] But Nelly also wrote her own household book, and it held two of her grandmother's recipes (perhaps copied out before her marriage?).[40] As did many Virginia plantation mistresses, Nelly kept a housekeeping book as a memory aid and to train her daughters in the arts of keeping house.[41] Thus, Martha Washington's cookery book may have been retired after it was given to Nelly. Nelly's own manuscript became the working document for her household, with Martha's perhaps kept as an heirloom, too fragile and cherished for daily use. Nelly's housekeeping book passed to her daughter Parke, who also kept it as a family heirloom.

The inscription in Martha Washington's manuscript may very well be historically inaccurate. Since it recounted the book's trail for three generations, the inscription had to have been written retrospectively.[42] However, the importance of an inscription may not be temporal precision but genealogical succession. In the case of the Washington text, the inscription may have reflected Nelly's—or someone else's—point of view of the intense bond between Martha Washington and her granddaughter and the Custis

line of descent. In their cookbooks, women's inscriptions may reflect idealized and real affectionate relationships between kinswomen rather than indicate accurate chronicles.

The custom of preparing a recipe book before marriage, perhaps as a
symbol of the coming rite of passage, continued into the nineteenth century.
Not unlike storing up a dowry of linens, it might have taken a young woman
months or years to gather the knowledge of cookery, medicines, and other
aids that comprised her household cookery book. It appears that Mary
Perkins, a resident of Virginia, began her book of recipes a year before she
planned to marry. Her engagement may have been the motivation for beginning her receipt book. She writes on the first page:

1872
I may be housekeeping
By 73.

Immediately following this inscription she writes:

Brought from home
When I went to house-
keeping
16 (fourteen)
bed covers 6 white
blankets 2 coverlets 4
counterpanes 2 quilts[43]

The first three pages of recipes in Mary Perkins's little book are carefully
written. What follows are pages of hastily scrawled recipes, sometimes only
lists of ingredients and abbreviated instructions for producing the dishes.
Did she write the first three pages while she was still at home, with ample
time to pen her household notes with care? Perhaps the rest of the book was
written after she had "set up housekeeping," in the stress and rush of everyday life. We can only conjecture that Mary Perkins began her household
book with hopeful promise and the resolve to be a tidy and efficient housekeeper. As her life's pace quickened with added responsibilities, her fastidi-
ous penmanship may have given way to the demands of daily life.

In the same fashion, Philadelphia Quaker Elizabeth (Lizzie) Randolph copied out at least a portion of her recipe book two years before her marriage to Louis Wistar in 1850: On the first page she signed and dated her book "*Lizzie Emlen Randolph November 10th 1848.*"[44]

One of the clearest examples I have found of the copying process is from a trio of books that were clearly related to one another because they arrived at the Winterthur archive in one batch. Two of them drew heavily from one another. After hours of browsing through both books, I became familiar enough with the handwriting in each to realize that some of the recipes in both were written in the same hand. Further, some of the recipes were identical, nearly word for word. Yet only one of the manuscripts was inscribed. It belonged to "*Mary Jane Hall of Muncy Farms, Lycoming, Pennsylvania.*"[45] The other, badly stained and torn, with missing pages, was anonymous.[46] If it once had an inscription, it no longer did. A significant portion of the recipes in Mary Jane Hall's book had the word "*copied*" carefully written above or across the recipe. The initial "*B*" was written beside it. Both cookbooks had attributions to the same women, "*Mrs. Morgan,*" "*Mrs. Shippen,*" and "*Fanny Arnold,*" indicating that their recipes had the same sources although not necessarily for the same dishes. Further, Anonymous's handwriting is also in Mary Jane Hall's book, indicating that before Anonymous copied recipes from Hall's book, she contributed to it.

As each recipe was copied from Mary Jane Hall's to Anonymous's book, the transcriber marked the recipe with the initial "*B*" in Hall's manuscript and neatly wrote the word "*copied*" across the recipe. Not clear is the relationship between "*B*" and Mary Jane Hall. At first I thought they were mother and daughter. However, it became apparent that this was not the case. In Anonymous's recipe book I found identical recipes for "*Eggplant*" (only one sentence distinguishes the recipes from one another), "*Good Coffee,*" and "*Dover Cake*" and recipes for "*Popovers*" and "*Jelly Cake*" attributed to Mary Jane Hall. A recipe for "*Cold Cream*" is also attributed to Hall. The recipe written in both books is in the same handwriting and its wording is identical. Since the recipes were not attributed to "Mother," we must assume that the two women were not mother and daughter but had some other relationship to one another.

Who they were and how they came to share many recipes remains a mystery since we cannot identify the woman who faithfully copied many of Mary Jane Hall's recipes. Surprisingly, only six of the recipes are found in Anonymous's book. What happened to all of the other recipes that were marked *"copied"*? Were Hall's recipes copied into another book? Even though the recipe books themselves remain, all we know is that a transcriber copied a good portion of the contents of Hall's book to other texts. We can only infer what may have occurred from the documents that have survived. Regrettably, only a few of the recipe books actually tell us the paths they have traveled to their descendants.

Because there are few explicit statements concerning the disposition of these artifacts, we can only wonder how some recipe collections passed from one generation to another. Individual cases suggest that the ideal pattern of mother-to-daughter transfer was contingent on a host of factors and circumstances. These included: Was there a female next of kin? Was there more than one daughter? Were any interested in learning their mother's skills or having a record of her work? What was the nature of the personal relationship between mother and daughter, and how did their class, ethnicity,[47] and economic circumstances affect how the book was transferred? And what happened when a book passed to the third generation?

Cookbooks in Search of Heirs

What puzzled me most about statements about kin relations and paths of transmission was that these often were stated retrospectively, not prospectively. Although the inscriptions were undoubtedly intentional renderings of kinship and affection, the books were not always specifically designated (in writing) in advance for the next of kin. Perhaps because of life's capriciousness, some women's cookbooks found their destinations by happenstance and the books' histories were inscribed only after they had found their heirs.

Instead of recognizing the mother-daughter bond, a recipe manuscript once belonging to Lady Frankland celebrates the links between alternating generations.[48] To the public, she was most likely known as Lady Frankland. To at least one of her grandchildren, she had another identity: *"Grandmama*

Lady Frankland." The recipe book that once belonged to her was begun around 1750. It contained housekeeping formulas and recipes for cooking, wines, and medicines. Among its contributors were women and men of rank and title: Lady Fagg, Lady Roche, Miss Colville, Baroness Philetsen, Dr. Bateman, Dr. Reynolds, and others. There is no title page, several other pages are missing, and no dates are entered into the earlier portions of the manuscript. Because the inscription is missing, we will never know if Lady Frankland signed her book or with what name. How did she refer to herself? The later additions have the notations *"1816," "1821," "1823"* to help date the manuscript. It was only after the book came into its inheritor's hands that the name of its original owner and a relationship between present and past was imprinted on the book.

A concluding remark written into the back inside cover reveals its new owner's sentiments: *"Dear Grandmama's Book. Several persons have written in it as well as myself. R. W."* The tenderness of the inscription suggests that, whatever else Frankland may have left as a legacy to her progeny, R. W. cherished the recipe book that once belonged to her grandmother. We cannot know if grandmother and granddaughter had a particularly affectionate relationship (or at what age she felt this)[49]—although *"Dear Grandmama's Book"* certainly suggests that—or whether R. W. idolized her ancestor because she had never had an opportunity to know her. In any case, Lady Frankland's recipe book became an emblem of her presence and her memory, and thus all the more valuable to her grandchild R. W.

It is noteworthy that R. W. felt she could tamper with the book by adding her own recipes to follow her grandmother's despite its value as an heirloom. And R. W. was not alone; others also wrote in her grandmother's book of cookery. Unlike Martha Washington and Nelly Custis's books, Lady Frankland's heirs did not treat her manuscript as a fragile document to be shelved. R. W. viewed her grandmother's book in a different spirit, as one to be prized but used.

We know nothing about how the book came into R. W.'s hands. It may have been passed directly to her from her grandmother or through her mother. Other grandchildren may have wanted the book, but Lady Frankland may have stipulated that the book should eventually go to R. W. As with so many culinary texts, we will simply never know just how and when R. W. took possession of the book.

Sometimes, either out of necessity or as a sign of self-conscious intimacy, the succession of ownership was innovative, and books moved laterally within a generation to sisters, sisters-in-law, cousins, and even second wives, who became guardians of this transitory legacy. Some women who married widowers inherited recipe books from their husbands' first wives. Such was the case for Anna McNeill Whistler, made famous by the painting of her by her son, James Whistler. Anna had a little recipe book her son called her "Bible,"[50] an indication of the esteem in which it was held by its owner. Yet the recipe book had belonged originally to Whistler's father's first wife, Mary Roberdox Swift, who began writing out the repertoire she had developed as a young bride. Mary's brother had given her the leather-bound notebook as a wedding present. She wrote her name once at the beginning of the book and then repeatedly, rehearsing her married name.[51]

After Mary's death, Anna married Whistler's father and inherited and faithfully added to the cookbook that her predecessor had begun. At Anna's death "she left her precious book of recipes with James."[52] Thus a cookbook begun by one wife continued as the valued possession of another, providing the recipes with which the husband and children were familiar. Was Anna's transition into an established family eased by the knowledge incidentally given her by her predecessor? Over time, Mary's personal legacy was enhanced by Anna's accretions; it became more of a family heirloom by taking on an identity greater than either of its contributors.

Some manuscripts indicate that an intermediary has acted as an emissary or has begun a new line of transmission: Husbands, uncles, aunts, grandmothers may serve in that role. If a woman had no daughters, a son, a daughter-in-law, sister-in-law, niece, or granddaughter might inherit the book. Jane Kane De Foulke's aunt preserved her mother's book until she found the right moment to give it to her niece. The history of the transaction is inscribed on the first page of the paper-bound volume.[53]

Recipe book belonging to
Jane D. L. Kane

*& sent to her Grand-daughter & only namesake by her Aunt E.D. Kane some
years after her marriage*
        Jean Kane Foulke

        *Jean Kane Foulke du Pont (Jane Kane's book preserved for her by her
aunt and passed to her niece).*

Why did E. D. Kane pass her mother's cookbook to her sister's daughter? Did
she have no daughters or children of her own? Or perhaps Aunt E. D. Kane had
searched for a token of affection to confer upon her niece and chose her own
mother's cookbook as a gift. If we take the inscription at face value, it is clear that
Kane felt that the book belonged to a grandchild with her grandmother's name.
Bestowing a name upon a child is another way of marking relationships: The
child stands in a particular position to her ancestor, perhaps, it is hoped, sharing
common personal features. The child's relationship to her grandparent is marked
twice, both as her namesake and with her keepsake. The travels of a book may
be irregular, but it was keeping it in motion that mattered, in general within a
family circle, keeping a woman, a family, and its memories alive.

Yet there may be other overarching reasons why women might want to
bestow these culinary guides on others. First, to give a gift is to exercise a
form of power. Throughout the early modern period and into the nineteenth century, not all women could legally bequeath "real property" (land
and buildings). According to English and American common law, husbands
subsumed their wives' holdings under the clause of "feme couvert" (a woman
was legally covered by her husband), which suspended a married woman's
legal rights as an individual.[54] Instead, women controlled and passed on
"chattel"—small and movable personal domestic possessions—and in those
acts, notes art historian Marcia Pointon, "established and maintained lineage."[55] It was through their bestowal of personal and domestic possessions
that women obligated subsequent generations of kinswomen to themselves
and to their memory.[56] In societies where descent is reckoned largely
through the male line, as heralded by naming, women found alternative
venues for creating their own female genealogy.

Less socially prominent women began culinary receipt books as a way
to mark both their newly created status and to record lineage and history

for their kin. Social changes swept in during the late seventeenth and eighteenth centuries: geographical mobility and a burgeoning market-place for art, literature, and all manner of foods. Women of the rising middle classes with wealth but without noble birth created maternal lega-cies by emulating the centuries-old tradition of keeping family receipt books. The collections of those women who began to compile or write a recipe book—without a long-standing family compilation—were en-hanced by the contributions of friends, neighbors, and others.[57] No mat-ter how briefly a recipe book stayed within a family, once the name of its compiler was registered on the front cover, the book acquired an emo-tional value for its recipient.

Women created cookbooks as gifts with the intention of affirming a par-ticularly affectionate relationship between a giver and receiver. In 1888, Bessie Howard received a Christmas present in the form of a small paper recipe book from her grandmother. The front cover, written diagonally in a flowing graceful script, read *"Bessie Howard, Merry Christmas, from Nannie, 1888."*[58] All of the receipts were for candy. The last page of the recipe book bore the metaphoric message of the entire book:

"Kisses for Bessie"

Beat the white of five Eggs with two pounds
Of Sugar, and a little citric acid.
Flavor with lemon and drop on buttered
Paper until cold
    From Nannie

Imagine these tender little meringue cookies melting on Bessie's tongue and, with every sweet mouthful, an image of her grandmother comes to mind. Nannie's gift to Bessie represented a bond between grandmother and grand-daughter, a relationship that did not need Bessie's mother as the vital link. The nature of Nannie's relationship to Bessie is invoked in the language of the little book and in its recipes for sweets, a symbol of good luck and love. It was the artifact of the book that would sustain a bond, one of their own, between the older woman and the child who was her kin.

Naming Lineage in Printed Books

In time, women began to use published cookbooks to construct their matrilineal genealogies. Just as women valued manuscript books as an inheritance, they could transform printed books into family heirlooms with an inscription. Printed books were, in any case, expensive items, commodities that had economic value and were inventoried as property at the time of an owner's death. Added to that, the book gained value, both as a personal and household possession, by its inscription.[59] In fact, some printed books contain more explicit histories of the book than the more elliptical manuscripts. In one engraved book produced by Edward Kidder for the pupils of his cooking school, the inscription reads:

> *This book belonged to my grandmother before she married. She then lived in Old Broad St. Her father Mr. Halloway was a Spanish Merchant with a house at Cadiz. Old Broad St was then considered a most respectable locality and the rich Merchants' Daughters went in their carriages twice a week to take lessons of professor Kidder.*
>
> *Miss Halloway took lessons about the year 1723—when she was 15. She married when she was 16 and had two children before she was 19. She had ten children who all grew up to be men and women.*[60]

In one volume of *The Art of Cookery or the Lady's, Housewife's, and Cookmaid's Assistant*,[61] an inscription describes the book's passage and its owners' genealogical relationships: "*Mrs. Fordyce, Having belonged to her Mother, Mrs. Macdougall, Inveresh, S. A. Dunghoff-Fordyce, Having belonged to her Grandmother.*" Because the inscription is in one hand, we may assume that the granddaughter provided the names of the two previous owners in her matrilineal record, a retrospective accounting of its history.

Another example of a book and its owner's family history is found on the inside front cover of an 1822 edition of Amelia Simmons's *American Cookery*, owned by the women of the Fiske family of Worcester, Massachusetts. The notation documents one of the Fiske (William and Frances E.) family's resources, their sheep and the wool that was spun into thread by Elizabeth [—]. On the flyleaf, another inscription repeats the name of the book's owner, "*Mrs. Frances Fiske, Worcester Massachusetts, July 26th 1826.*" Underneath another line reads

"*Given to Mrs. W. E. Fiske*" and again below that "*Gift to Frances Fiske by her Mother, May 1877. To be preserved with great care.*"[62] At least two generations of women owned, if not used, this volume written by the first American cookbook author, and they valued it perhaps as a symbol of patriotism[63] as well as for its potential for becoming a record of maternal history.

I found this dedication in an edition of *Bailey's Dictionarium,*[64] a popular household book of the eighteenth century in England and America (see Figures 3.2 and 3.3):

> *Abiah Darby, her book, 1746, given her by her husband, 7th month, 3:1746.* [subsequently owned by] *Mary Darby and Sarah Darby until 1827.*

The inscription catalogs the generational links forged between the women of one family for nearly one hundred years. Each of the two or three successive signatures adds to a carefully recorded genealogy. Although the book was a gift from her husband, Mrs. Darby passed the book down in the female line for nearly a century, it seems. Two separate inscriptions in the book suggest that it was passed from mother to daughter (and perhaps sisters), with each successor adding her name to the pages.

In most cases, only the owner's name and that of the giver are recorded. In another popular eighteenth-century cookery book, John Middleton's *Five Hundred New Receipts in Cookery, Confectionary, Pastry, Preserving, Conserving, Pickling*[65] is inscribed "*Mary Ann Hughes. This Book was given her by her grandmother, July Eighteenth 1804.*" Many books bear the name of their owner, if no other information. Some inscriptions describe where and from whom the book was received or, in this next case, purchased. An edition of Eliza Smith's *The Compleat Housewife*[66] bears the following inscription tracing the lines of acquisition. In 1775, the book was purchased from Elizabeth (Ella) Field, who had autographed her name on the front cover. "*Mary Wright at the Boarding School St. Lawrance bought of Ella Field in 1775.*" Perhaps the inscription signaled a personal bond between the two women, or perhaps Wright was merely recording a financial relationship.

Printed cookbooks, perhaps because they were already valued, became suitable sites for recording family histories and the history of the books. Published

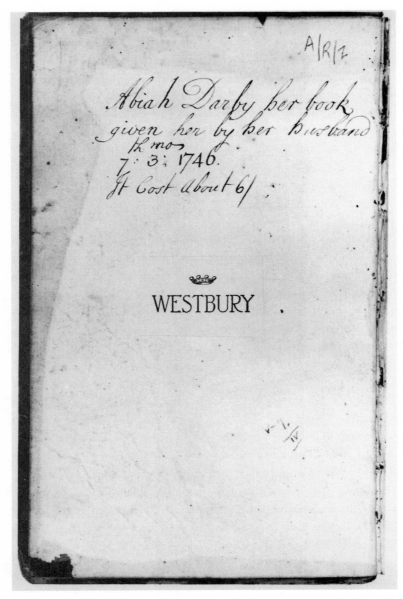

Figure 3.2 Inscription on the inside front cover of *Bailey's Dictionarium* belonging to the Darby family.

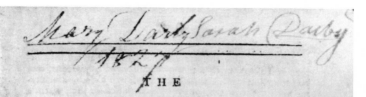

THE

FAMILY *Dictionary,* &c.

A B

ABSCESS, a difeafe to which poultry are incident. It is not an eafy matter to perceive when this diftemper feizes on hens, but by their being penfive and melancholic; upon which you are to examine their rumps, in which place the Abfcefs is commonly form'd, which when it has been for fome time, it will breed corrupt matter, and be painful to them.

This difeafe proceeds from their being over heated and coftivenefs, which corrupt the whole mafs of blood, obliging nature to difcharge it felf of what is burthenfome to it, to fome part or other, and chiefly upon this part.

The readieft method of cure, if not the only remedy, is to open or cut the Abfcefs with a pair of fciffars, and to prefs out the corruption with your fingers; which being done, give them to eat lettuce or blites chopp'd fmall, mix'd with bran, fteep'd in water, fweetened with a little honey. See *Poultry:*

ABSCESS [in *Human Bodies*] See *Impofthumation.*

An Old ACHE, mix two drams of oil of turpentine, with an ounce of *Lucatellus's* balfam, warm it and anoint the part affected, laying a piece of new flanel upon it.

For ACHES *and* Bruifes, *an Ointment.*

Put a quart of oil into a ftone jar, that will contain two quarts; then take camomile, fage, fouthernwood and wormwood, of each two handfuls, the quantity of half a quarter of a peck of red-rofe-buds; cut off the white and fhred all the herbs together grofsly, and put them into the oil; where let them remain for 9 or 10 days, ftirring them every day; and when the *Lavender Spike* is ripe, put in two handfuls of the tops,

A   corre

Figure 3.3   Inscription on the first page of *Bailey's Dictionarium* belonging to the Darby family.

cookbooks did not replace handwritten recipe books as family treasures but enlarged the category of gifts. By inscribing their published volumes with their names and affectionate sentiments, women transformed impersonal printed books into heirlooms. Women personalized the work of favorite or unknown authors with their own scripts and with the residue of daily kitchen use: grease, flecks of food, and marginal commentary! Women adopted and adapted printed cookbooks as handmade and handheld objects; they became personal legacies passed on from mother to daughter, who reckoned their ancestry through the female line and noted the line of descent in their cookbooks.

Lizzie's Legacy

Not only women related to one another by birth and name could pass on a cookbook to one another. Even strangers divided by age and class might create a bond with the gift of a recipe collection. In 1962, a friend of mine, Rosemary, married John Mitchell.[67] As a wedding present, John's family housekeeper, Lizzie Richards, gave Rosemary a three-ring binder "*designed to store recipes.*"[68] In the first portion of the book, Lizzie had written out recipes that she had created or adapted to feed the family of three boys and their father. The recipes were enclosed in a 5-by–7 pink plastic notebook, with "My Recipes" embossed in gold on the front cover.

By the time Rosemary met Lizzie, the housekeeper was in her seventies. They met for the first time the night John brought his fiancé to his father's apartment for dinner. Thereafter, Rosemary saw Lizzie perhaps only a half a dozen times, but she remembers the woman as a "bossy, fussy, old-fashioned" kind of housekeeper. "She was diminutive and not very pretty,"[69] in some ways a mysterious figure, or perhaps only an anonymous one. Her own history was overlooked in her role as housekeeper for a bustling family. Perhaps no one thought to ask about her early life, so caught up were they in their own. Therefore, little is known about Lizzie's childhood, only that she was English and had come to the United States as a young woman, with who knows what dreams. As did many young immigrant women in this era, Lizzie became a domestic.

According to Rosemary, Lizzie began working for John's grandmother in the 1940s. After she died, Lizzie began housekeeping for Mr. Mitchell and his three sons, who spent weekends with their father following his divorce from John's mother. Lizzie, who had no family of her own, might have thought herself a surrogate mother, or at least a mother figure in the boys' lives. She had, Rosemary told me, opinions about how they were being raised. Thinking their lives with their mother too sophisticated, Lizzie might have offered her straightforward, "good plain" food, such as hamburgers and mashed potatoes, on weekends as an antidote to their daily cosmopolitan lifestyle. John was the eldest and had, of all the boys, developed an affinity for Lizzie, since Rosemary remembers a fond teasing relationship existed between the two. This may account for the personal attention she lavished on her wedding present. Her concern for John, his bride, and their upcoming marriage resulted in what Rosemary calls a "kindly outpouring."[70]

Lizzie wrote a foreword to the book in the form of a letter to Rosemary, whom she called "Rosalie." Rosemary conjectures that Lizzie may have been hard of hearing and so misheard or misconstrued the sounds of her name. The mishearing and misspelling of Rosemary's name does not negate the sincerity of the gift, which is written with great care and some difficulty. Although Lizzie could obviously write and although her spelling followed standard orthography, her punctuation is flawed, indicating that she may have had little formal schooling or few opportunities to write. That did not seem to embarrass or deter her from her project of providing Johnny's bride-to-be with her advice and counsel.

Lizzie begins the book on a practical note, how useful the book might be, but soon reminisces about the family's growing years.

Dear Rosalie:

This book may help you some day the back of it is very useful, in a few recipes and weights and measures I am also adding a few recipes for you that are from my own head and what I have used in the family of Mr. Mitchell and boys, they were a very easy family to feed, they like everything I ever made, and I always knew what to give them, as long as it was plenty. Johnny was never hard to feed, he liked food but good plain food, so I hope you wont find him different. . . .

In this poignant way, Lizzie reveals that she had grown close to the boys, Johnny in this case, and that she knew them well. After so many years of feeding them, she had become familiar with their food preferences. She learned about the boys from the vantage point of a woman whose daily acts of nurturing included preparing their family's meals. In a moment of self-praise, she claimed that "they like everything I ever made, and I always knew what to give them."

We learn that Lizzie is not shy about taking credit for inventing a few of the recipes that she has included: *I am also adding a few recipes for you that are from my own head.* Making a gift of a recipe book that contained her own recipes was a way for "bossy" Lizzie to continue some symbolic control over the boys. It was, at the same time, a way for Lizzie to relinquish her charges and acknowledge her loss, the beginning of change for her substitute family and for her aging self. Among the cooking tips and recipes in her book was a list of "Johnny's favorites," meant to please the man who had once been the boy in Lizzie's care. Johnny's favorites included "lamb chops, veal cutlets, hamburgers and steak" and "baked and mashed potatoes, spinach, peas and brocali." There were many more foods on her list, the preparation of which had changed—as Lizzie noted in her letter—over the years because of the introduction of frozen foods and commercially baked breads.

Lizzie also alludes to the work involved in her cookery, which had changed with the introduction of these modern conveniences:

> *the frozen vegetables are now suberb* [sic]*, and will save you much time, needs little cooking, no cleaning, all kinds of frozen vegetables can now be had. Frozen orange juice is also good and frozen fruits, all year round. All kinds of lovely breads and muffins, which at one time I had to make and set overnight, no one has time today for such kind of cooking, I will give you the recipe for my brown cookies because they cant be bought, and they are easy to make. . . .* [71]

Lizzie acknowledged that it should be easier for Rosemary to cook Johnny's favorites since prepared foods had made kitchen work less arduous. Yet she expected Rosemary to continue preparing Johnny's favorite dishes, at least until the young woman had acquired her own kitchen prowess. She must have seen this as Rosemary's duty. After all, in Lizzie's world a woman's obligation was to please her husband. And feeding four men was also the work for which Lizzie was paid. It is this experience of her work that Lizzie wants to give to Rosemary: skills to ease the younger woman's work in the kitchen and advice on preparing meals for Rosemary's groom. After all, she continued to care about how Johnny would be fed.

The introductory note ends *"good luck to you,.* [sic] *Lizzie."* With her good wishes made clear, Lizzie announced gently that she was relinquishing her culinary knowledge and Johnny's care to Rosemary.

Still, throughout the manuscript, Lizzie added little tips and helpful hints: *"when you serve Consomme Hot add a little sherry, its so good"*; for *"Meatloaf," "this is so easy and good tasting, serve with Potato and green veg"*; *"Ham Cutlets with pineapple," "this is so good and easy to fix."* She advises Rosemary that *"Chicken Mousse makes a good buffet Dish because it is cold."* Lizzie suggested other dishes to serve when Rosemary entertains such as her *"good Pancakes"*:

> *2 cup of flour*
> *$\frac{1}{2}$ teaspoon Baking Powder*
> *1 " sugar*
> *1 cup milk*
> *1 tablespoon melted butter*
> <u>*1 egg, pinch salt*</u>

> *order*   *mix flour with Baking Powder and Salt, add sugar, egg well beaten,*
> *in*   *add milk gradually and melted Butter,*
>   *cook on griddle, serve with Lemon or Jam, or any sweet sauce*
>   <u>*or a brandy sauce below*</u>

> *Brandy Sauce*
> *12 tablespoon Brandy*
> *2 tablespoon butter*
> *$\frac{1}{2}$ cup Sugar, juice of 1 orange x rind*
> *to make*   *cream butter x sugar, add orange juice and rind, beat well and add*
>   *Brandy, (<u>no cooking to it.</u>*

> *{These are my special dessert*
> *Pancakes and are wonderful*
> *for a special affair}*

It is clear from Lizzie's marginal comments that she took pride in her cooking abilities. Her words of advice on how to fix a meal and for what occasions reveal a modest authority born of years of practice and experimentation. To affix her knowledge permanently in a book and give it to someone, although younger than herself, with quite a different social background alludes to Lizzie's self-esteem and also her generosity.

Indeed, Lizzie was a beneficent friend and ally. She closes her sweet gift with a page bearing only the following sentiment:

dear you go on from here
  Love Lizzie

Lizzie's recipe book is a personal token of affection that bridges the social distance between housekeeper and the young master's bride. It is a maternal act, and one that momentarily puts her in a more powerful position. She is older, more skilled, and more knowledgeable than Johnny's bride-to-be. Lizzie inverted her subservient role, asserting her authority on Johnny's life (as some mothers are sometimes apt to do). Yet in presenting her successor with a recipe book filled with personal knowledge, she offered a gesture of affection and acquiescence. It was an acceptance of things to come. The book marked the beginning of the end of her role in the boy's life and in the life of the family.[72]

Unlike a mother, she would have little further part to play. Lizzie's gift to Rosemary was more than a book of culinary knowledge. It was a memento of Johnny's childhood and a symbol of life's passage: Johnny's, Rosemary's, and her own.

With the transference of the recipe book marking that ending, Lizzie fully expected Rosemary to begin to develop her own repertoire. Only partially filled with Lizzie's recipes and hints, the rest of the pages of the book are blank. The idea that John and Rosemary's household would change was part of Lizzie's conception of the recipe book she gave. Wise and generous, Lizzie gave the fledgling cook enough to get her started, then prompted her to create her own culinary world.

Rosemary did just that. More out of gratitude to Lizzie than a desire to replicate stereotypical women's roles, she faithfully followed the recipes given to her. However, Rosemary and John had a broader culinary range than Lizzie's book allotted, and soon the old-fashioned book of recipes was shelved in favor of more eclectic tastes and exploration. Rosemary kept the book as a souvenir, a relic of the past, too outmoded to be useful, too precious to be thrown away.

A Little Cookbook for a Little Girl

Even a child's cookbook—a plaything—can become emblematic of the person to whom it belonged and carry a family legacy to descendants. In this poignant instance, a published cookbook for children called *A Little Cookbook for a Little Girl* (1905), which tells the story of Margaret who wanted and was given her own little kitchen, becomes the memento mori of Isabelle McCracken.

Isabelle died as a result of a riding accident that occurred at college.[73] The details of her death were written on the flyleaf of her cookbook after her accident on April 15, 1915: "*This book belonged to Isabelle McCracken who in her freshman year at the University of California was thrown from her horse and killed, April 15, 1915.*" We are introduced to Isabelle first, briefly. On the back of the front cover, written carefully in pencil but barely visible now, is the hand of Isabelle herself, "*isabelle.*" We learn nothing more about her or what the book meant to her. Nor do we learn who wrote the epitaph in her cookbook.

This particular copy of *A Little Cookbook for a Little Girl* and the story of Margaret, its heroine, whose idealized childhood surrounded by loving family, serve as a reminder to all of its subsequent readers of the life and the untimely death of its youthful owner, Isabelle. The lives of these two young people, one fictional, the other real, become entwined in this memorial. Isabelle's life and story are forever bound to that of Margaret's, a fictional character whose life is a fairy tale. The book begins: "Once upon a time there was a little girl named Margaret and she wanted to cook but she could not understand cookbooks."[74] So she went to her mother, her grandmother, her "Pretty Aunt," and her "Other Aunt," who decided to get her an apron, a set of tins, and a small table and "to make a cook-book all her own out of the old ones we wrote for ourselves long ago, just the plain easy things anyone can make, but, also, put in a few cooking school things besides."[75] The heroes of this tale are women; the seeker of knowledge is a little girl who must acquire their magical gifts in order to get wisdom and skill. The family surprised her on her birthday—in the kitchen—with a presentation: a little oilcloth-covered table made by her father, a set of tins and saucepans given her by her "aunties," three gingham aprons sewn by her grandmother, and "her mother's present, her own little cook-book with her own name on it, and that was best of all."[76]

Margaret's little cookbook is fashioned after—actually taken from—the cookbooks that her mother, aunts, and grandmother had owned. In her book are recipes for breakfast, luncheons, and dinners. Everything is included, from rice pudding and oat cereal to ice cream and cake. Contributions from her grandmother consist of "Grandmother's Cake" and "Grandmother's Sauce" and from her mother she received, among others, "Thousand Mile Shortcake," which is so named "because she sent so far for the recipe," a recipe she had enjoyed once on a trip abroad.[77] There are recipes from her "Aunties" and even one for "Margaret's Own Cake." "Pretty Aunt" put in a "cooking school rule" that "was the best sort of pudding for little girls to make."[78] Family stories are explicitly embedded in some of the recipes. In the instructions for easy-to-make muffins called "Barneys," author Caroline Benton describes how the family maid, Bridget, had to show Margaret "what was meant by 'cake batter'" since it was the necessary consistency for the muffin batter. The "Thousand Mile Shortcake" tells the reader that Margaret's mother had traveled and enjoyed this recipe in another country. This published, fictional family cookbook tells the stories many family members already know.

In manuscripts, family stories are rarely explicitly written into the recipe. The family member who inherits the book is likely to know at least some of the tales surrounding the dishes. However, those who come later must either discover or perhaps never know the anecdotes and legends behind the recipes.

In printed books, women often comment on or mark their favorite recipes, leaving a trail for their descendents. Moreover, they fill their printed books with recipes garnered from other sources in this way mimicking manuscript recipe books. Over time, many of the other recipes may gather new stories of their own. Modeled after the recipe books that adult women compiled, Margaret's little book socializes her—and her readers—into a gendered role and binds her to the women of previous generations. The fictional Margaret and her book are illustrative of the ways in which women recorded, exchanged, and passed on the culinary, familial, and community memories of previous and their own generations. As compelling as the communal histories these cookbooks perpetuate, it is the story of Margaret and Isabelle that envelops the reader. All we learn about Isabelle is her tragic death. Her brief life must be imagined through the lens of Margaret's story. The fictional Margaret and the real Isabelle whose lives and stories end with childhood are forever entangled in the history of this book.

Some of the recipe books women owned and left to their female next of kin may have met the same fate as Lizzie's and Isabelle's cookbook. More mementos than guides, they were stored away as sentimental legacies or delicate and fragile heirlooms. Others were handled again and again by subsequent generations of women who continued to use and add to the books of their forebears. Women who bequeath their handwritten or printed volumes—stained with grease, scrawled with comments, crammed with scraps of paper—to their next of kin bind the reader to a lineage and a network of women whose lives are symbolized by the recipes in their cookbooks. The storehouse of knowledge it contained, even the archaic wisdom, encoded the past and became an emblem of the woman who compiled it. It is that which gives the recipe manuscript or printed book both its immediacy and its timelessness.

The profound and unending relationship between past and present in their recipe books compelled women to use them to construct their own genealogies. Once imprinted in their recipe books, the names of family and friends were reminders of timelessness itself and of the repetitive cycle of women's work, all of which were memorialized in these culinary artifacts. The traces women left behind in cookbooks anchored their contemporary relationships to the pages of their books and also connected the living with the dead.

Frequently the manuscripts held prized recipes belonging to earlier generations; sometimes the manuscript itself was begun and handed down to the next of kin. In this way preceding generations and contemporary ones submitted their offerings to the same commonplace cookery book. A woman's cookbook became a meeting place of past and present, of individuals merging into a collectivity but safeguarded by an individual for posterity. An individual cookbook, then, is not only the creation of one person but a social context from which a singular voice emerges.

Taken as a whole, a woman's recipe book is the record of her life. The voice and script of the writer inscribed indelibly on the pages become synonymous with the text. The book may stand for its author as a part may represent a whole. The act of reading and cooking from her book makes possible a veritable communion with the writer.

FOUR

Cookbooks as Autobiography

The lemon chess pie is simple and remarkably delicious. When I make it, I make it for my mother, and she is tying my apron strings into a bow and flouring my counter to roll out the dough. She is modifying the recipe as I go along, her eyes catching the dearth of lemon zest and my hands rummaging the fruit bin for another lemon. The cursory directions are hers, her sensibility, her humor, and her thick love for Frances. So Frances materializes in my kitchen too, and the two of them start giggling about something shared as though they were young mothers again, cropped hair and bright red lipstick, remembering pregnancy and the hot fudge sundaes at Howard Johnson's after the doctor weighed them. . . .

Sometimes I know I am going to the kitchen to look for her [my mother], and sometimes I feel she is pulling me there to find her. Sometimes her presence comes alive in her recipes.

—*Nora Seton*, The Kitchen Congregation[1]

In her cookery book, Hannah Trimble[2] left a trail of clues revealing the contours of her farming life. Over the twenty-one years between 1859 and 1880, she painstakingly recorded recipes to nourish her family and kept an abundantly itemized account of the costs for maintaining a home first in Delaware and then in Pennsylvania. The fragmented stories in Hannah's cookbook connected me to the mid-Atlantic landscape I passed daily on my way to the museum where I did some of my research. As I drove past the little community of Fairville, Pennsylvania, I thought about Hannah's description of her move there in 1868 from McClelland, Delaware, just across the state line. Now gentlemen farmers own the large rolling-hill estates and the towns are punctuated with expensive designer homes, antique stores, and quiet inns. I tried to imagine Hannah Trimble's Fairville of more than one hundred years ago.

Hannah does not tell her story as it would appear in an autobiography or history book. To understand her life requires an imaginative leap into the past from the details Hannah has provided in her cookbook. Hannah's book, bound in leather, with a broken spine and badly stained paper, offers rich details of her life. Her manuscript opens conventionally with her name, but Hannah had embellished it with an insignia of an American eagle surrounding the printed block letters. She appears to have cut both name and insignia from a stenciled piece of paper and pasted them to the front page. Immediately after Hannah's name three poems follow, with the first announcing the themes of the other two:

> Father, take my hand, for I am prone
> To danger, and I fear to go alone.
> The way is dark before me; take my hand,
> For light can only come at thy command.

These are personal requests for God's guidance, help, comfort, and strength in the face of an unknown path: life. The verses reveal a woman who has put herself in God's hands. The book's opening prayers might safeguard Hannah's cookbook, symbol of home and family, and the enterprise of keeping it.

On the second page of her book, Hannah names three women: Hannah Way, Martha Mandenhal, and Lucretia Way. Their names, like Hannah's, are identically framed with the eagle insignia stamp, cut out, and pasted to the manuscript. Were they girlhood friends? Sisters? Sisters-in-law? Cousins? Although we do not know their exact relationship to Hannah, their placement beside her own name indicates a personal and uncommon bond. These women, I conjecture, played key roles in Hannah's life for they are mentioned throughout her cookery book in both the accounts and the recipes.

One family's name is still vital to the present community. For example, besides passing Fairville each day, I passed the community of Mendenhall.[3] Named after the family mentioned in Hannah's book, it is now an expensive retreat for tourists scouring the countryside for antiques.

The accounts Hannah kept, beginning on the third page of her book and continuing throughout, are the day-to-day log of a thrifty and industrious farmer's wife. At the back of the book she kept recipes—both cookery and medicinal—that she collected from friends, physicians, and kin. It is from these recipes and records—Hannah's clues—that I have pieced together an account of some of the events of her life.[4]

In February 1868, Hannah and James Trimble recorded the deed to their new Fairville property. They had waited eight long years to buy the farm. Although James was the official breadwinner, for years Hannah had supplemented the family income by selling milk, butter, and eggs. Sometimes she sold her farm-raised fowl as well. The additional revenue may have helped the family save enough money to buy their Pennsylvania farm. Hannah knew how to be frugal and economical. Her accounts were kept meticulously by day, month, and year, indicating she watched every penny she spent and carefully recorded her income.

Their old home in Delaware had been an asset, but it had also been costly to maintain the house and property. In October 1860, the Trimbles painted the east end of their house in McClelland. Three years later, Hannah must have decided to spruce up the house for she bought one piece of wallpaper border for 15 cents. Although they could not yet afford it, the couple dreamed of buying a new farm within a few years. The house and farm satisfied her for the moment but she longed for that particularly beautiful piece of property just across the state line.

Two months after they recorded the deed to their new home, on April 6, 1868, the Trimbles moved from McClelland to Fairville. They bought additional flour and meat to tide them over the first weeks in Pennsylvania. Although they brought their horse, Billy, and their cow, perhaps some of the livestock were sold or left to the new owners. They paid Prissy and George Pemberton $2.00 to drive the cow to the new home. Nearly a month passed before the Trimbles executed the deed and stamps to the new house. Their fee of $15.00 for executing the bill of sale and the conveyance of real estate was paid in Stamp Duties.[5] On the same day, they hired George Hutchins for the use of his carriage, most likely to move their possessions from Delaware to Pennsylvania. That day, too, they bought a key for the front door.

So it was that Hannah and James Trimble set up housekeeping on their farm just off Route 252. That summer they painted the house green and bought blinds for the front door and the third story of the house. They purchased 690 lights (panes) of glass for the greenhouse windows, 3 lights of glass for the cellar, and 2 for the kitchen. After plastering the parlor and the sitting room, they bought latches and locks, folding doors, and fixtures for the front door. To landscape her home, Hannah bought $1.50 worth of shrubbery and four peach trees at two cents each. Hannah was pleased as she surveyed their new surroundings; perhaps the farm was everything she had hoped it would be.

In November two years later, the Trimbles bought 1,000 bricks to pave the walk. Over the next few years Hannah bought an enameled tea kettle and a Britannia teapot, a parlor chair, and a cupboard. She was an affluent farmer's wife, most likely entertaining her neighbors and fellowship group often. Perhaps she used her teapot at afternoon parties at which she served Japan tea she bought at the Hamorton market and the cakes and puddings made from the recipes at the back of her book. These were, perhaps, social occasions for new and old friends and relations. Over the next few years, the Trimbles hired carpenters and laborers to maintain the house and grounds. Jacob Mendenhall painted, George Thomson added shutters and sashes, and William Cox did the carpentry and put up fences.

Hannah continued to cook, clean, shop, and manage her own dairy trade selling eggs and daily churned butter, the venture she had begun before she moved to Fairville. Members of her social network, women of the Mendenhall and Way families, shopped with her in the nearby market towns of Wilmington, Kennett Square, and Hamorton where she bought cloth and other goods from merchants with the same surnames. She shopped regularly, as she always needed staples and household goods that she did not produce herself. Knitting cotton, coffee, hard soap, stove blacking, and molasses were items she could not be without. In 1877, perhaps expecting a harsh winter, she bought husband James some sturdy brown cloth for a coat. She promised herself a new dress for church on Sundays and so bought fourteen yards of black silk. She thought some decorative buttons and a black silk bonnet would complement her new dress; they were too tempting to resist. She made rags out of worn-out sheets and pillowcases, and she bought unbleached muslin to sew new ones. Who wore the pair of green spectacles she bought earlier that year she does not say.

Despite the round of work inside and out of the house, Hannah still had time to exchange and compile recipes for cooking and medicines. Among her cookery recipes were "Floating Island," "An Egg Omelet with Oyster Sauce,"

"Cold Slaw Dressing," "Welsh Rarebit," "Beauregard Eggs," and "Soda Biscuit." Her medicinals were collected from several sources and included a recipe for "sore eyes," a "remedy for neuralgia," a recipe for "pneumonia" taken from *The Christian Monitor,* and a recipe "to prevent the hair from falling out." Cosmetics were also important to Hannah Trimble, as they had been to generations of women before her. She devoted a whole page to a recipe contributed by Lydia Brown of Nottingham for "the hair dye prepared by Bob Jones [that] colors beautifully." Her days continued as before until 1880, when abruptly her book concludes.

With the exception of her religious verse, Hannah's annotations leave no sense of her inner life. How she felt about her move to Fairville, the dairy products she sold, or the black silk bonnet she bought are missing from the account of her day-to-day activities. Yet it is in the writing of these details that Hannah Trimble leaves autobiographical traces. Without them we are likely to have lost even this fragmented, unfinished life story. It is through her cookbook writing that she survives for us at all. Possibly Trimble left correspondence or other documents to her progeny, but we only have access to the materials that have been luckily placed and maintained in archives. Although others may remember or keep alive memories of Hannah Trimble, others who may know her far more intimately than I can from her cookbook—it is through this account she wrote herself into being. She shaped her image as an industrious woman in the pages of her cookbook, an accounting not only of the material world surrounding her but of the good and virtuous life she lived.

Cookbooks tell personal stories. While many women left precious little behind—not even the faint trail Hannah Trimble gave us—often their cookbooks provide enough to catch a glimpse of the person. In evocative culinary memoirs composed of directions for cooking, accounts, textual fragments, marginalia, and paper ephemera stored between the pages of a book, women inscribe themselves in their recipe texts as testimonies to their existence.[6] After years of daily use, the cookbook becomes a memoir, a diary—a record of a life.

Self-conscious or not, recording everyday acts of cookery is an act of autobiographical writing and self-representation. When a woman writes even just her name on the first page of a book, she is committing an act of auto-biographical writing. A simple or elaborate signature is an act that defies anonymity.[7]

Cookbooks—printed or handmade—textually draw together vestiges of woman's work, intellect, and social interactions: the food she prepares or hopes to prepare daily and ceremonially for her family, the people who comprise her world, and the interests that distract her from or engage her in work. With the brief recipe texts and saved paper remnants, the writer constructs an image of herself, most often in keeping with society's values but here and there in defiance of them. Strictly speaking, of course, cookbooks are not autobiographies, yet they are opportunities for women to capture aspects of the work that they do, itself evanescent and often unnoticed. In these texts, women give permanence to this fleeting and repetitive cycle of tasks. And although their cookbooks do not tell stories in a chronological sequence or always tell us how women felt about their work and lives, they comprise what literary scholar Anne E. Goldman has termed "opportunistic autobiographies."[8]

In fact, cookbooks are one of a variety of written forms, such as diaries and journals, that women have adapted to recount and enrich their lives.[9] The cookbook is itself a hybrid that encompasses various kinds of women's writings: letters, memoirs, diaries, and scrapbooks blending raw ingredients into a new configuration, a form of daily writing centered on a woman's work.[10] Cookbooks are also convenient and safe places to save, to store, and to peruse—when one has the time—the countless tasks, bills, correspondence, and other documents that pass through a household and a woman's hands.

Although the cookbooks I have handled vary in size and shape, in content, and in labor, many of them are similar to scrapbooks.[11] In their "formal" scrapbooks, women self-consciously shape their identities by selecting significant memories and preserving them in images or textual fragments. In the same way, compiled recipe books are deliberate constructions of the women who kept them. They may have seen themselves as loving mothers, devoted wives, and good friends. These were the self-images they chose to project through their recipe books. In evoking or re-creating the sensate, culinary world of the book, the writer transports a reader in time and space into her own life world. The seasons of the writer's life emerge in the foods that she cooked or dreamed about cooking, the poetry and prose she placed alongside her recipes, the letters she received from friends and family that she tucked between the pages, and the particulars of her daily life she noted in her book. Unlike a work of fiction that may or may not resemble the world of the author, cookbooks, as memoirs, are saturated with the vivid details of the author's everyday reality.

Women announced in their books the achievements they had attained, the craft they had refined, and their cultural ideals. For example, Anne Hughes, an eighteenth-century farmer's wife, reveals the pride and satisfaction she derived from her daily tasks. After days of preparation, Hughes looked at her pantry shelves laden with cakes, preserves, and wines and reveled in her ability to provide such bounty. She sums it up in her "*booke*," a journal with recipes embedded: "*All the cookinge bee done and doe make a mitie brave showe, ande now I can rite in mye littel booke agen,*" she writes on July 10, 1797. Although cookbooks note much that is everyday, at the same time some recipes encode the highlights of a life. Women recorded favorite and successful recipes, those for which they were recognized or in which they took pride: the chocolate cake that may have garnered praise at a church picnic each summer; a daughter or son's first attempt at cooking; a best friend's most coveted, secret recipe for corn pudding. In Hughes's case, she basked in her domestic proficiency.

Cookbooks make evident the self-esteem some women developed as they matured in their domestic roles. Culinary interest may be a matter of temperament, but skills evolve over time and in many instances prowess might imbue women with cultural authority. With age-old limitations on the professional spheres women were permitted to enter, the domestic arena was one in which they could compete and excel. It may not have been many women's first choice of career, but, given societal constraints, it was one they made the best of and some strove to become best at.

A recipe book testifies to the development of a woman's craft, an archive of memory and knowledge. The text becomes an emblem of the self and may encode culturally appropriate images of the feminine, of the ideal family, and of the good life. Despite their overt guise as a symbol of ideal womanhood, some texts contain covert messages of resistance, signs of political activism, or, at the least, ambivalent and contradictory commentary about women's maternal and domestic roles. They also tell us that some women embraced both the domestic and the political without thinking of them as dual and segregated domains. These kitchen books unexpectedly reveal not only the domestic side of women but also other facets of a woman's life, interests, and personality.

Suffrage and Soufflés

Few of the women whose cookbooks I read are famous or well known. In most cases, all I could discover with certainty were their names. Attempts to track them down in census reports or birth, marriage, or death documents were futile. Their books left too few clues to flesh out lives with other historical evidence. Dates and places were often missing. Proper names were incomplete. Even so, the women who kept these cookery books called attention to themselves as individuals, not just as ideal wives and mothers.

Telling a life story is an act of interpretation possible only after one gathers the discoverable odds and ends that a life generated. There is no single correct story, not even if the person herself told it. Narratives about our own or others' lives are what we construct from the artifacts of history, themselves incomplete and often inconsistent. As I excavated history's mines—archives—in search of cookbooks, it was my hope that I would find just one instance in which a cookbook writer left behind another manuscript or cookbook in a collection with other documents, letters, or a journal. With one exception, though, they left nothing behind that I could find to supplement the meager evidence in their cookery writings. The cookery/receipt book belonging to Jane Campbell, a Philadelphian who lived in the late nineteenth and early twentieth centuries, was the anomaly. When I began to read this cookbook, the name of its author eluded me. I did not know then that the book I was poring over belonged to Sarah Jane Campbell, who lived from 1844 to 1928. I knew only that the large, marbled, paper-covered book, stamped with *"W. Campbell"* on the first page of the manuscript on "July 23rd 1864," had belonged to a man. As well as the stamped name I found a more complete inscription *"Wm. John Campbell"* under a clipping glued to the front cover.[12] Its masculine owner had been identified.

However, I suspected that this ledger, as had many others, had been taken into custody by a woman and transformed into a cookery scrapbook. The recipe book was a palimpsest and an encyclopedic array of domestic advice. From its scrapbook format, domestic contents, and stray scraps of paper with meager clues, I hypothesized that a woman had recycled this book into a personal recipe collection. Newspaper clippings of dozens and dozens of cookery recipes, herbal medicines, and gardening advice were pasted to the original pages of the book, covering them almost entirely. Of the few pages that remained uncovered, I was able to decipher a history of Pennsylvania's counties that I attributed to the book's original owner, W. Campbell. This was hardly an unambiguous clue as to the gender of the first author because many women's manuscripts were punctuated with snippets of historical information. However, because his name was on the inside front cover, I reasoned that William Campbell had written this portion of the manuscript. After all, I concluded, if the book's second owner had compiled this information, why would she have spent so much time covering it up? The final clue as to the feminine identity of its second owner came in the form of a fugitive scrap of paper with a recipe for a confection called "penucio" that bore the letterhead of the National American Woman Suffrage Association.

The book is divided into sections, beginning with household hints for laundry; caring for pots, pans, and other utensils; sickroom cookery; and soups and broths. Stews and stocks are next, followed by fish, fowl, beef, mutton, vegetables, and side dishes such as croquettes, potatoes, eggs, and omelets. Breads, muffins, and cakes comprise another section, and it is here that I encountered Jane Campbell's hand for the first time, although I did not know it. This carefully assembled scrapbook leaves one with a sense that the person who compiled this work was meticulous and thorough. I had assumed the second author was a woman. Her sections are remarkably homogenous, and only once in a while does a wayward recipe meander into another category. In the gardening section of the scrapbook, we find newspaper directives for getting rid of weeds and killing roaches. The book's creator had learned how to stabilize pea vines and eradicate poison ivy. Her interest in folk remedies is reflected in the newspaper articles claiming the virtues of yarrow, pokeweed, pennyroyal, and other herbs and describing their appearances.

How I discovered the identity of the cookbook's owner was as remarkable as if I had stumbled on an entire collection of documents written by the same woman. One evening in February 2000, quite serendipitously, the treasure I searched for found me. Mary Ann Leigh, a graduate student working on her master's thesis, was in a program that I directed. As it happened, I volunteered to teach a class one evening when a colleague went home sick. That night, as students discussed their respective research projects, Mary Ann told us that she was working on an Irish Catholic family named Campbell whose family papers were housed at St. Charles's Seminary. She was particularly interested in the correspondence of Jane Campbell, one of the women in the family. Mary Ann felt that scholars had stereotyped Irish Catholic women as servants and working-class immigrants. Her goal was to learn more about middle-class Irish women like Jane.

I mentioned that I owned a manuscript/scrapbook that had belonged to the most prominently displayed name on the cover, a W. Campbell, and that I was using it for my book project. We were both confident that our two Campbell families were related but not sure how. In my own research on the Campbell cookery manuscript, I had conjectured that the compiler of the cookbook was somehow connected to the suffrage movement. Mary Ann responded to my hypothesis: "That's interesting because Jane Campbell was the founder of the Woman Suffrage Society of Philadelphia in 1892 and active in the woman's suffrage movement in the United States."

"Perhaps these two women knew each other?" I asked.

Neither of us grasped the fact that we were studying the *same* woman and her family. When I mentioned that I had discovered a letter with the address 413 School House Lane, Mary Ann told me that Sarah Jane Campbell lived at that address.

A century later, two women, working independently with different documents, met by happenstance and learned they were studying the same family: Jane Campbell; her brother William; his wife, Bonnie; and their children. The names of others in this large Irish Catholic family appear in their letters to one another. Somehow as the family's other papers were donated to safe repositories such as St. Charles's Seminary and Temple University, the household book compiled by Jane and her brother William was separated from the lot. Years later it fell into my hands while I was browsing in a bookstore. Fortunately, a critical piece of evidence that had surfaced in my research had remained with the cookbook in the remnant of a letter from "G. P. Darrow."[13] It was the most salient among the fugitive scraps that helped to identify the family, if not the owner of the book.

Here was evidence that supported some of my speculations about this woman's life from the cryptic fragments in her culinary writings. Mary Ann was generous enough to share her research, providing me with letters and with pictures of Jane and their large rambling house.

I shared the cookery book with Mary Ann, and together we identified Jane's handwriting in it, the same that appeared in her letters. The book that had come into my possession was Jane's. It is one that both William and Jane literally had their hands in. It was he who wrote the histories of Pennsylvania's counties in this document, which served as the basis of his own published book on Pennsylvania history. Jane's contribution of printed recipes was layered on William's manuscript in scrapbook fashion.

Here and there, Jane's distinctive penmanship embellished the printed sources, but did William contribute to the scrapbook even after Jane had claimed it? Keeping a scrapbook was a popular pastime for both men and women in Victorian America. The ideology of the period required "separate spheres" for men and women; women were to remain sequestered in the home far from the defiling commercial world of business. Men expected to find a sanctuary in their homes, places where their wives created safe, harmonious retreats from the bustle and worrisome workaday world.[14] However, this was not always the case. Not only did women like Jane Campbell participate in public affairs, but men like William also blurred the boundaries by contributing to household knowledge. Just as evidence from earlier historical periods indicates that some men supported women's literacy, so, too, did some men participate in household affairs in cooperative ways. In one of Jane's letters to her nephew Will, a soldier during World War I, we learn that his father William (Jane's brother) was pasting clippings in a scrapbook. Jane writes: "*There was a letter in this week's Independent gazette from me of the embryo officers at Fort Oglethorpe. I cut it out and gave it to your father to paste in the book he is making.*"[15] It is possible that William also contributed to Jane's cookbook.

From her surviving letters, we learn that Jane Campbell had no trouble melding her intellectual interests and her domestic ardor. She may have enjoyed thinking about domestic life and contributing to the aesthetics of making a home, but it is unlikely that she was responsible for day-to-day household responsibilities. Other women, such as her sister-in-law, Bonnie, and a servant named Bridget, made it possible for Jane to engage in an intellectual and public life.[16] She was a traveler, writer, poet, historian, and music lover. She lectured widely and contributed to many periodicals including the *Rosary Magazine of New York* and the *Catholic Messenger of Ohio*. She published some of her historical articles in *The Philadelphia Record*.[17] Her appreciation for folk and popular music motivated her to translate two volumes of Danish songs and folk ballads.

Thus, her letters and other family documents reveal that Jane wrote and published essays, lectured, and worked for women's suffrage. Campbell's letters revealed another passion: gardening. I had noticed already the numerous newspaper clippings about plants in her cookery book before I read her lively correspondence. One of the clippings in her household book mentions the Germantown Horticultural Society, in particular, and its series of lectures on combating pests. Now that I had access to her letters, I learned that she often attended their meetings.

From her scrapbook, I had conjectured that at least one year produced a bounty of tomatoes from the Campbell garden; a blue penciled "x" marks several different recipes for tomato ketchup, tomato marmalade, tomato preserves, preserved tomatoes, and other ways of conserving the fruit. It may have been the year she wrote to her nephew Will about the "plentiful" crop of tomatoes. In her letter of Sunday, September 9, 1917, to Will, she describes the garden at 413 School House Lane: "*Your Mother's garden is a veritable riot of color. I give you no account of the vegetables for I know Elizabeth will do that. I only know results, as evidenced in corn, plentiful & fine tomatoes good and very beautiful to look at, beans, etc. etc. all right.*" To create a vivid picture of home for Will during his tour of duty, Jane portrays the details of home. She regales him with a description of the garden, a focus of attention for every member of the family.

In Jane's correspondence, she had a propensity to ask her family and friends to do small tasks for her during her many travels. Perhaps it was a way of sustaining the intimacy of face-to-face relationships in her absences. Among the correspondence at St. Charles's Seminary Mary Ann found a remnant of a letter in Jane's handwriting with one of "her commissions," as she called them.[18] In this instance, the addressee is unknown, but in it Jane requested a recipe: "*also please send in next letter—a copy of my receipt for stock orange cake—out of my own cook book—Bonnie has the book.*"[19] With the letter in my grasp, I hurried to her cookbook and found the recipe written in Jane's own hand and featured prominently at the top of her pages for cakes:

"Orange Cake"

1 ¾ cups sifted sugar
2 cups flour
1 teaspoon cream of tartar
½ teaspoon soda
Pinch of salt
6 eggs—yolks and whites beaten separately

1 orange grated
juice alone of one orange
1 small lemon—grate skin and use juice also
white of one egg beaten light
with about a pound of pulverized sugar

The cookbook gives no directions for combining but simply lists the ingredients. No doubt Jane knew how to produce the cake from this information. It is possible, even probable, that the other women in the household could also follow the recipe. They must have been familiar enough with how to make a cake that explicit directions were not necessary. Often recipes were memory aids for the cook, especially for baked goods, where precision in ingredients and measurements is critical. The women may have mastered the techniques of cake-baking by watching one another in the kitchen, learning by the age-old method of observation and practice. Who used the book? It is doubtful that Jane was the only one to prepare the recipes in it.

Amid the recipes there were two scraps of paper in her cookbook that led me to believe that this woman had varied interests. On the back of the first small paper for making *"French pickle"* is an excerpt of a speech written in her unmistakable hand.

> . . . *to these inconsistencies for the purpose merely of showing the confusion into which those are led who attempt to prove that you can benefit one man by legislation without taking something from somebody else—*
> *Here are two estranged products of one mental effort yearning for reconciliation.*[20]

This tantalizing scrap of a speech suggested several possibilities: The woman who compiled this book may have read and copied out speeches from manuals of rhetoric popular in the nineteenth century; she may have written or copied this speech for a discussion with a reading group or for a public debate; or she may have recorded a segment from a speech she heard. Had this been the only evidence of another side to Campbell's life, it would have remained an interesting but inconclusive piece of data. With the addition of another scrap of paper, equally suggestive of a woman whose interests ranged beyond her domestic sphere, I was tempted to guess that the compiler may have been involved in or, at least, connected to women who were engaged in political activism. This second revelatory piece of paper innocently bore a *"Receipt for penucio:" "The confection is made of three cups of light brown sugar, one cup of white sugar, three forth* [sic] *cup of milk, butter size of an egg, half pound of marshmellow* [sic], *one pound of English walnuts. Boil first four ingredients* [sic] *until when tried in cold water a soft ball may be fromed* [sic]. *Remove from front of fire and then add marshmellow when melted add nuts and turn on a buttered pan to cool."* This scrap of paper was imprinted with the letterhead "National American Woman Suffrage Association" from the "Office of the Vice-President, Philadelphia, Pennsylvania" and provided more clues about Jane's social network.

In 1892, the same year as she received the recipe for "penucio" from Anna Shaw's NAWSA office, Jane Campbell founded the Philadelphia Woman Suffrage Society. The Reverend Anna H. Shaw, a West Philadelphian from whose office this notepaper derives, was then vice president at large. Elizabeth Cady Stanton and Susan B. Anthony were honorary presidents of the national association. Anna Shaw had been named vice president of the association in this year and had since 1890 been designated by Anthony as national lecturer. Shaw had a gift for rhetoric and was known for her brilliant oratory.[21] But Jane Campbell was herself a gifted lecturer, and she, like Shaw, was deeply engaged in the mission of women's suffrage. If Shaw was helping Jane plan her local chapter, they also may have planned rallies and lectures together. If the women knew one another and worked together, it is tempting to imagine the two exchanging recipes such as penucio even as they worked.

Clearly even suffragists had to eat! Some may even have had to cook.[22] The image that we have of women who sought universal suffrage is one of political zealots, not housewives. Although Jane Campbell was among those middle-class women who had servants to ease their domestic responsibilities, some supporters of woman's suffrage were from other social classes.[23] While women like Jane could ask their cooks to think about what to serve for dinner that night, some suffragists had to prepare dinner themselves.[24] Jane's cookbook suggests the complexity of women's lives and identities. The coupling of recipes with suffrage politics is, at first glance, comparable to the maxim that politics make strange bedfellows. In other words, women from across the spectrum of class and race, ethnicity, age, and occupation may have been united in seeking the vote. However, their agreement and joint action for this common cause did not necessarily unite them on all social issues. Class and race did, in fact, create factions within organizations and groups with different issues and interests. While many were able to devote themselves entirely to social reform and the cause of universal suffrage, many others had to attend to family matters and fit reform into their other domestic responsibilities.

To be a wife and mother, to be a domestic woman is not to eschew political action, or the reverse. To be engaged in the political issues of the times does not preclude nurturing others. Importantly, women could have multiple roles and identities. They could even hold superficially paradoxical opinions. Their worlds sometimes collided and often overlapped. Suffrage and soufflé could coexist on paper and in the minds of the women who would prepare them for dinner that night.

A Cookbook, a Note Book, and Shakespeare:
Recipes and Reading Clubs
A Downingtown Housewife—1914

As I mentioned earlier, one of the challenges of doing this kind of research is that we are often missing biographical information about the women who compiled the manuscripts. However, the cookbooks may still bear an impression of their owner(s) from which we may discern the compilers' hobbies, preoccupations, and, even, a glimpse of their personalities.

In my collection of old cookbooks, I discovered a locally published cookbook enclosed by a notebook filled with recipes dating to the early twentieth century. From my repeated readings of its tattered pages I imagined the following scene and the women who used these documents.

It is 1914, in southeastern Pennsylvania, somewhere in or around the towns of Coatesville or Downingtown. Gas is being touted as the most liberating and convenient of fuels, offering many advantages: immediate availability, no storage, cleanliness, low cost, and "no kindling is required but a match." Ice is still the surest way to preserve fresh foods, and spices are purchased at the grocer or the druggist's shop.

A woman, Mrs. Downing, is sitting at her kitchen table, cutting sections from the newspaper.[25] She is dressed in a blue-flowered cotton housedress that is covered with an apron reaching from neckline to knee. Her hair is tucked away from her face, gathered in the back with a chignon. On the table in front of her is a blue composition book to which she turns her attention from time to time, writing occasionally and reading. It is in this book that she pastes the newspaper clippings in between trips to the stove where she is preparing dinner.

She is interrupted twice while she works. A knock on the door signals the delivery of ice for her icebox. She pays the man 90 cents for the month's bill. A girl, her daughter, enters the kitchen. She asks some questions about the food on the stove. They talk briefly. After taking her mother's pen, the daughter begins to jot down a recipe in the book. She is pleased to do this for the recipe is one she has learned and cooked in her home economics class at school. The recipe book is filled with penciled notations, handwritten recipes, and newspaper clippings. A printed recipe book, *Housekeepers' Favorites,* lies open beside the manuscript. Both mother and daughter refer to the printed book and discuss some of the recipes for chocolate cake. Both books are worn, the pages spotted with grease and flecks of food.

Together they begin baking. While doing so they make notations in the printed cookbook; they have decided to alter the proportion of sugar in the recipe for chocolate cake they are preparing. At the same time, the woman and the girl peruse other recipes, deciding which ones would be suitable for other occasions. While they pore over the volumes, they unsystematically return to their storage space the many scraps of paper that spill out of the books. As the daughter begins to set the table for the next meal, the mother places the two volumes side by side on the shelf next to the cupboard from which they had been taken.

Years after Mrs. Downing put her kitchen books to use, they were given to me as if they were one text, an assemblage of several kinds of documents: a blue-lined paper book with the words "Composition Book" embossed in gold on the blue front cover, an amalgam of manuscript and newspaper clippings pasted to the pages, a printed local cookbook, and many loose scraps of paper inserted into the blue text. I assumed that the two texts belonged to the same woman. An address in the composition book reveals Downingtown as the area in which this woman shopped for goods, and the handwriting in the manuscript matches the penciled marginalia in the printed text. And I also assumed that when Mrs. Downing used them in her kitchen, the two volumes were discrete. Over time, and with use, bindings broke, pages were no longer confined, and a new configuration emerged. What I held in my hands eighty years later was a federation of texts, related to one another but neither entirely separate nor united. Inserted into the composition book are the pages of a printed recipe book called *Housekeepers' Favorites* within which dozens of local merchants from the Downingtown/Coatesville area advertise their shops and goods. The pages of *Housekeepers' Favorites* had migrated into the composition book, giving the illusion of a single work. The tome, with its component parts, is worn, its covers separated from the torn, yellowed, and frayed leaves lying loose and unbound.

Housekeepers' Favorites was a locally produced cookbook, replete with local merchants' advertisements, with recipes contributed by a network of women perhaps connected to one another through church or another organization. Each of the recipes in the printed book is attributed to its donor, and the compiler of this receipt collection may have been one of them. But the composition book bears no trace of the author's name. Perhaps her name did appear in *Housekeeper's Favorites* or in the notebook at one time but, over the years, it has disappeared.

On the pages of her composition book, the manuscript portion of her collection, the housewife from Downingtown recorded recipes given to her by friends, acquaintances, and family members. One recipe is titled "*Our Improved White Cake*," which suggests that this recipe was a communal affair, worked on together by several women. Several names are repeated throughout the book—Mrs. H. E. Spessard is one—indicating a long-term relationship. The handwriting is identical whenever Mrs. Spessard's recipes appear in the manuscript, and it is different from the two predominant in the text. Most likely Mrs. Spessard wrote her recipe into the Downingtown housekeeper's book herself. Another recipe squeezed between "*Chocolate Kisses*," contributed by Miss Marion Fox, "*Icing for White Cake*," and "*For Mixing White Cake*" is a small, boxed-in recipe for "*Walnut Cakes*"; it, like others, is signed "*Mother*" in one of the two prevalent hands in the book.

It is difficult to sort out the intergenerational relationships in Mrs. Downing's text, but clearly one was between a mother and daughter. On several occasions, the book alludes to a relationship between mother and daughter, but without a chronology or proper names, it is impossible to determine if the parent is Mrs. Downing herself—and the book now in her daughter's possession—or if the parent was Mrs. Downing's mother. From the handwriting and the attributions, I suspect that the book belonged to a senior female for a period of time and was passed along to a daughter, by then a full-grown woman. Yet a few of the recipes suggest that even after the book had been given to its new owner, its previous compiler—Mother— added to the book; a few of the receipts are signed "Mother" at the bottom of the recipes, as if they were signatures on letters. This is different from the titles that precede recipes, such as "*mother's way*" or "*Mother's version*" or "*my mother's cookies*." This latter style of attribution signals recipes that have been written into a recipe book by a daughter, now steering her own household and acknowledging her mother's versions of recipes.

Some of the hands in the book are childish, written by a younger person, and so it is possible that a school-age daughter lived in Mrs. Downing's household.[26] Girls were introduced to home economics in school curricula; thus, women of all ages were familiar with the domestic science movement and its principles. Perhaps a school-age daughter contributed recipes she learned in home economics classes to the cookery book while she was still living at home. However, most of the handwriting in the book is an adult's script. This manuscript follows the pattern of many other compiled cookery books. It was a multigenerational affair.

Imagine the woman, Mrs. Downing, whose cookbook bore such scrupulous notations about the food she was served, the food she ate, and the food she planned and prepared. Her notes, though spare, describe table decorations and social encounters with members of her social network and her sales of food to strangers. Between the pages of her book are loose bits of lined notepaper, with recipes from many sources written in different hands indicating friends and family acknowledged in her cookery book. Numerous newspaper clippings of recipes are pasted to the pages of the composition book, for everything from "peach compote with ice cream" to "potato balls" and "oyster pie." Often both sides of the page are used, one side pasted with printed and clipped recipes, the other side handwritten, showing her eclectic sources if not tastes. Recipes taken from *The Ledger, Youth Companion,* and *McCall's* tell us something about what Mrs. Downing might have read. While many, but not all, of the recipes in the handwritten text are for sweets, the printed *Housekeepers' Favorites* spans the gamut of savory soups and main dishes, pickles and relishes, puddings, pies, and cakes. Menus are provided for luncheons and dinners and a "private entertainment for fifty people." From these menus we learn that entertaining was, most likely, part of Mrs. Downing's social life and occupied some of her thoughts. Throughout the book, we learn about the recipes Mrs. Downing tried and liked, those upon which she improved, and those that she hoped to try one day. Comments above or below the recipes indicate her responses to them: "*very good,*" "*nice,*" "*a little bland,*" "*want to try,*" "*have tried.*"

It is clear that Mrs. Downing is not a novice cook and can recognize an omission when she sees one. She noticed something amiss in the listing of ingredients for this recipe for "*Jenny Lind Cake*" and commented upon it.

(?) cups sugar
1 cup butter
4 " flour
4 eggs
2 teaspoonsfull of baking powder

In parentheses beside the list she wrote, "*It gives no milk. It must have been forgotten.*" Such attention to detail implies that Mrs. Downing was a knowledgeable cook who took pride in her collection of recipes. Apparently she was perfecting her culinary repertoire, just as an author might amend her prose in search of a more perfect word or an artist blend tones and hues on a palette. Mrs. Downing was not likely simply to have added a recipe to her collection without first evaluating it.

There is no doubt that Mrs. Downing enjoyed thinking about food, trying out new recipes, and planning meals. Her cookbook revels in the details of her craft, revealing both recipes for specific dishes and accumulated menu ideas for meal preparation. Some scraps of them, written in her own hand, are apparently descriptions of meals she had been served at others' homes or perhaps meals she actually had or hoped to prepare and serve in her own home.[27] Fairly typically, this menu came from a number of sources, including newspapers:[28]

Menu for Dinner
Sliced Roast Beef
  Mashed Potato Cakes
Buttered Beets
Bread   Plum Jelly
Head Lettuce and French Dressing
Sliced Peaches   Date Filled Cookies
  Iced Coffee

Menus like these could be found in such books as Fannie Merritt Farmer's *The Boston Cooking School Cook Book* (1903) and on the pages of local newspapers. Lighter than the Victorian dinners of the previous century, they reflected the domestic science movement's new emphasis on nutrition, along with variety, cleanliness, and efficiency.[29] Mrs. Downing's menus may have been meals she was longing to test, meals that pleased her imagination and taste or that she thought her family would enjoy. In writing at least, she was a woman who sought variety in foods and preparation styles.

While she actually may have prepared the dishes she read about,[30] it is equally likely that she only daydreamed about preparing them. In these flights of fancy, women can both transcend and escape their quotidian world and still remain firmly rooted in it. These were momentary excursions through which Mrs. Downing's imagination could roam, offering a moment's distraction in the midst of her work. The menus she recorded and clipped from newspapers were fashionable repasts for proper middle-class social gatherings. Perhaps she fantasized about whom she might invite to one of these dinners. Or perhaps she dreamed about the meal she would prepare. In either case, Mrs. Downing gave a lot of thought to the delectable and proper meals she would serve her guests.

Her book was a mixture of the imagined—the future—the lived—the past. The culinary details of occasions with friends and family were promptly recorded in her book:

Supper at Wm Garretts on the eve of May 31st 1906
Everything was placed on the table—
    Roast beef with gravy
    potatoes, boiled whole parsley and
    dressed with cream
corn—potato salad—and rhubarb sauce
with oranges sliced—pickles were on the table—
Last course was ice cream with coffee cake and pretzels and crackers—
    cheese—

Why was Mrs. Downing recording these details of a meal? Was she a woman who enjoyed the sensuous details of her physical world? Her brief description of decorations reveals her delight in the aesthetics of the table:

Dinner at Pres. Funkhousers
Table center of yellow tulips
four lighted candles with yellow shades

These were important details to Mrs. Downing. Perhaps she noted them as much to emulate a standard to which she aspired as to remember the loveliness of an evening's meal. At this time, theme dinners were popular. The table and everything on it was inspired by a single color.[31]

On the same loose sheet of paper that describes the table setting at President Funkhousers' dinner, Mrs. Downing records the food that was served:

1st course salad of pineapple and oranges
2nd course Veal chops garnished with parsley
    sweet potatoes
    asparagus on toast
    bread and butter
    olives—nuts
3rd course tomatoes on lettuce
    served with wafers
4th course Ice cream cake and coffee

This meal in the same sequence of courses turns up on another piece of paper, this time labeled "*My own dinner.*" She did add corn, celery, and cranberries to the menu as well as mints but she eliminated the fourth course. Did Mrs. Downing imitate the Funkhousers' dinner or did they reproduce hers? On the reverse side of the page titled "*My own dinner,*" Mrs. Downing offered another conception of a meal called "*My Own course.*" The writing of this menu suggests that this meal had not yet happened: in the third course, she has written only "*some kind of salad,*" too vague a description for someone like Mrs. Downing, who identifies and names every item.

My Own course:
1st, fruit salad
2nd croquette, peas in patties
celery or olives and sandwhiches [sic]
3 Some kind of salad
4 Vanilla ice cream with walnuts

and chocolate sauce
Small cakes coffee

We learn from her household book that she loved enumerating courses and describing foods. Although we may not know the event that occasioned the meal or who the guests were, nonetheless we can see, smell, and taste the meals she described, visualize the table setting, and let *our* imaginations fill in the gaps. For Mrs. Downing, food represented her social world. To entertain her social peers, she had to learn appropriate decorum from table settings and the etiquette of service to the foods that were au courant in her group.

We learn also that writing and reading played an important role in Mrs. Downing's life beyond the kitchen. As did many women from all segments of society, Mrs. Downing may have belonged to a reading group. Social historian Anne Ruggles Gere has described the role of women's clubs in late nineteenth- and early twentieth-century America and their struggle to defend or even deny their hidden agenda in fostering literacy practices for club members while, at the same time, offering them a chance to engage in important cultural work for their society.[32] Subjected to male scrutiny and criticism, the women in these clubs emphasized their social contributions, charity, and reform work. Their commitment to self-improvement through reading and writing for one another and other educational leisure activities, such as attending lectures, may have been covert. But they engaged in these activities anyway. They met, they talked, and, most likely, they ate.

Mrs. Downing includes a menu of a meal served at a reading club meeting.

Refreshments served at Mrs. Gossard and Mrs. Gringinch Reading Club,
February 4, 1927
Patties filled with creamed chicken peas, lettuce with a lovely mould of lemon
gelatine and filled with lemon, Buttered rolls,
2nd course. Very rich ice cream with cherries. Very good cake with cocoanut
icing
Angel food—coffee nuts & candies.

A fragment dated thirteen years earlier than the reading club menu also may have been a club meeting. Mrs. Downing jotted down the menu:

Refreshments at Mrs. Gossards, February 21, 1914.
First course pineapple with whipped cream and cherry————
Second course—patties filled with chicken potato chips butter sandwiches olives
Third course Asparagus tips on celery
leaves ball of cheese. Asparagus was cold
with a dressing on it, banquet wafers
were served with this course—
fourth course—nut ice cream
some kind of Marguerites with peanut
dressing—nuts—chocolates mints
last course coffee————

Mrs. Gossard appears to be the leader of the reading group in 1927, but that, by itself, is not definitive evidence that the club existed in 1914 or that, if it existed, Mrs. Gossard and Mrs. Downing were among its members. The refreshments that were served on both occasions—unbelievably similar menus separated by fourteen years—suggest that both events were reading club meetings. Meal formats such as this are often linked to specific occasions.[33] Birthdays might be celebrated in one family with a dinner, in another with a party. Dinners and parties are two different meal formats. The first requires sitting down together at a table; the second, helping oneself from a buffet and sitting or standing as one chooses. The choice of meal format often signals that the occasions have similar social value. Still, another interpretation is possible: The meal of chicken in patties served with either lettuce and gelatine or asparagus tips on celery leaves was perhaps a serviceable menu for several different kinds of events, from social dinners, to birthdays, to reading groups.

Even so, through this rendering of genteel meals Mrs. Downing constructs an image of herself of respectability, class, and, importantly, erudition. The women of this reading club epitomized a middle-class lifestyle, in their tastes for food and its service. The menu and its presentation reflect late-Victorian eating patterns comprised of elaborate meals served in several courses, the earlier menu more closely resembling this turn-of-the-century pattern. If the two meals are any example, however, what Mrs. Gossard lacks in ingenuity she makes up for in redundancy. Or perhaps even slight varia-

tions constituted novelty. Or were they simply the casual and normal variations in an expected dietary pattern? From the food served on these occasions, we may only speculate that the world in which Mrs. Downing moved
was remarkably small and may signal the stability and cohesiveness of the
community to which she belonged. The women of the reading group also
may have been her neighbors, friends, and family—her community.

One of the ways in which Mrs. Downing and the women who compiled
the printed cookbook brought literary activity into daily life was through
their cookbook. Literary quotations and poetry were placed side by side with
recipes. It is noteworthy that each chapter of *Housekeepers' Favorites,* the
community cookbook that Mrs. Downing used until it was in tatters, begins
with short readings from literature. Is it possible that the reading club itself
compiled the cookbook as one of its cooperative efforts? If the reading club
produced the local cookbook then the cookbook also served another aim: to
provide its readers with brief quotes from literature so that they might read
the masterpieces as they went about their daily tasks. In one instance Swift
introduces a section. The heading "Chapter XVIII—Menus" is followed by:

> Give no more to every guest
> than he's able to digest;
> Give him always of the prime,
> And but a little at a time.
>   —Swift

The opening lines of "Chapter II: Fish, Oysters, Etc." are from Shakespeare:

> "No, they are both as whole as fish"—*The Taming of the Shrew*
> "Drenched in the sea, hold, notwithstanding, their freshness"—*The Tempest*

Shakespearean quotes were a common addition to many household advice
books and magazines in this period.[34] Placing elite literature beside the
recipes served several functions. First, it demonstrated these women's familiarity with high culture, and, second it brought literature into their most
mundane activities, validating and elevating their vernacular writing projects
by bringing elite art into the service of their kitchen work, enlivening their
tasks, and affirming their vision of themselves as literate, educated women.

The women who compiled their prized recipes for *Housekeepers' Favorites* incorporated literary quotations to demonstrate that though they were at home and busy with domestic responsibilities, they were not entirely preoccupied by them. Primarily conscientious and busy housekeepers attending to the needs of their families, they displayed their education and their knowledge of elite culture even in cookery books.

Whether the cookbook *Housekeepers' Favorites* was produced by Mrs. Downing's reading club, it nevertheless acknowledges the role of reading in the lives of middle-class women like the Downingtown housekeeper. Educated middle-class women were expected to know literary figures. The modest "I" of our anonymous author becomes more prominent and forceful when embedded in a "we," a community of local readers, whose interests were in nurturing and helping others as well as themselves.

Mrs. Downing also delved into poetry. Perhaps a contest asked women to employ kitchen terms in creating a poem. She, or the sponsors, provided a list of kitchen utensils as the verbal elements of the poems: "mixing bowls, casserole, custard cups, colander, saucepan, double boiler." As she used each term, she crossed it from her list. Only a portion of the poem was completed:

A colander you'll find and its
The regulation hue
A double boiler if you want
To boil your beans in two.

The unused words on her list and unfinished verses show that her poetry was still a work-in-progress. The frequent appearance of poetry in her cookery book, either the printed work of famous poets or her own homespun verse, the notations of daily meals, and the commentary that punctuates the published *Housekeepers' Favorites* leads us to believe that Mrs. Downing was a woman who took pleasure in words.

Mrs. Downing seems also to have been somewhat entrepreneurial. The woman who compiled this print-and-manuscript recipe book seems to have ventured into the candy-making business, prompted by more than the mere pleasure of making candy. A portion of several pages is devoted to an accounting of the cost of ingredients for making candy. At the end, the author subtracts the cost of materials from her earnings and shows a small profit. What occasioned this financial junket? The following yellowed advertisement was among the loose papers in her book and may have spawned her interest:

Dr. Miles' Candy Book

Almost without exception both young and old have a "sweet tooth" which is always ready to sink into a confection, especially if it is a homemade one. To the young candymaking is almost a necessity, and while learned doctors may deplore the tendency to eat too many sweets, it may well be doubted whether any great number of children or young people really get "too much."

Again, candymaking is a pleasant pastime that serves to occupy the attention of the young at times when other pursuits, far more dangerous, might be indulged in. Who, indeed, will be fool enough to decry the old fashioned "candy pull" or to assert that the eating of even a goodly portion of "taffy" is injurious to humanity?

Anyone with a little bit of practice and care, may learn to make a delicious plate of candy as toothsome as the product of the professional "candy butcher." Candymaking, moreover, is a popular occupation and it is safe to say there is scarcely a household that does not have a number who knows how to turn out a dish of fudge or some equally pleasing confection.

The receipts given in this booklet are as a rule not of the complicated kind and may be followed without misunderstanding by anyone at all familiar with a kitchen. It is believed those interested in the making of sweetmeats will find in them a reliable guide as well as something new.

What dangers Dr. Miles refers to we can only guess. Did Mrs. Downing (and perhaps her daughter) want a wholesome and "old-fashioned" way to earn money? Perhaps with the incentive of Dr. Miles's brochure, the Downingtown housekeeper or her daughter began making candy for fun and profit. She was careful to keep an accounting of the costs and profits of her candy-making business, which were penciled on two pages of her notebook:

Account for making home made candy—cost for making candy Sept. 13   =38cts

   "   20 67

   "   21 32

   _____

   $1.37

Cleared $1.73 Have sold $3.00 worth Sept. 21, 1912.

On September 13, Mrs. Downing (I assume) made *"fudge, maple fudge and orange balls."* It cost her a total of 38 cents. *"Elizabeth"* furnished butter, which *"paid half of the expenses."* On September 20, 1912, she made *"orange and lemon balls"* and *"chocolate fudge"* at a cost of 18 cents. Later, the orange balls cost 19 cents to make and the lemon balls, 12 cents. She made a second batch of chocolate fudge out of which she got 28 bags of candy and sold each for 5 cents, earning $1.40. On September 21 she made two batches of fudge, yielding 12 bags of candy. Again on October 2, 1912, she made lemon balls and orange balls and *"sold"* them to *"college girls."* West Chester University is about eight miles from Downingtown. Is this the college the college girls attended? If so, how did Mrs. Downing encounter them?

The comments about her meeting the young women, like so many fragments of information in her book, are intriguingly, frustratingly spare. One is left to imagine the exchange between the housekeeper from Downingtown and the young women as a longing for what the other had and knew. Mrs. Downing may have envied the freedom and unrestricted future of the young women while the college girls looked forward to achieving Mrs. Downing's role and status as a married woman. We will never know what transpired in that conversation or interaction—if anything happened at all.

We shall never know whether the profits met Mrs. Downing's expectations or goals for her financial enterprise, but her foray into the world of confectionery seems to have been short-lived. If Mrs. Downing again hazarded the candy-making business, we hear nothing more about it.

A few cryptic notes indicate that someone in the family was getting or giving music lessons. The name Anna Krieder appears twice in the cookery book, once as the contributor of *"canned corn in glass jars"* and then as a person connected to music lessons. Whoever Krieder was, teacher or student, Mrs. Downing wanted to keep an accounting of the costs incurred by or owed to this woman.

> *In account with Anna Krieder—*
> *Owe two music lessons*
> *1 sheet music*
> *Saturday—14 Sept. 1912 / lesson .35*
> *Sat. 21 Sept. 1912 / lesson .35*

Once again, we are left with tantalizing clues: Was Mrs. Downing a student? If so, of what instrument was she a pupil? Was she a teacher? There are endless possibilities to ponder, but any of them would be speculation. All we can say is that among her other interests, music may have been one.

The accounts Mrs. Downing kept of her candy-making venture and music lessons also reveal her concerns with managing money, an aspect of women's household responsibilities. Mrs. Downing's work-worn book is simultaneously both a conscious construction of an image of femininity and an unselfconscious account of this woman's life. What we learn is that this ordinary housewife was resourceful, curious, innovative, and literate. She surrounded herself with a network of women who shared her interests and provided her with a community of support, and with whom she had extended and apparently long-lasting relationships. A mother-daughter bond figured prominently in her life, and the child was most likely the inheritor of the book. (What we do not know is if Mrs. Downing was mother to the child or child to the mother.) Mrs. Downing's cookbook shows her to be a domestic woman, a mother, a friend, and a musical, literate, and educated woman. This autobiography does not disclose the nuances, sorrows, and longings of her life. However, in this textual self-portrait, Mrs. Downing has fashioned a representation of femininity and womanhood she valued for herself. The mere presence of her recipe book was a sign to others of her dedication to the ideals of domesticity and her commitment to the responsibilities of caring for her family.

A Metaphor for Life:
Carol's Cooking Stinks Cookbook[35]

Clearly some women kept cookbooks as symbols of maternal devotion, as sources of inspiration for the relentless task of providing meals for a family, or as a way of recording their knowledge. The very act of writing—especially for women who had few opportunities to write in the course of a day—may have provided them with a sense of pleasure and pride in what they had accomplished. No matter that the book was a record of recipes; it was an accounting of what they did with their time, quite often suffused with a love of the art and craft of cooking. Writing a cookery text certainly was not all that women accomplished in the course of their lifetimes, but, in many instances, it occupied a significant chunk of time. However, the use of recipe books does not necessarily mean that all women loved kitchen work.

The kitchen is not a place where all women want to be, even if some women enjoy cooking and find it a satisfying and creative task. It is still a burdensome job for most women at least some of the time. In her turn-of-the-twentieth-century diary, Magnolia Le Guin communicates her frustration about the endless meals she prepared for her family and the incessant stream of guests and visitors to their home. On September 1, 1905, she writes:

> How sick I've been since April! Oh, how hard it has been to keep up! To cook! To make beds! To sweep floors! To care for babies!—Ralph and Mary. How I've dragged around doing absolutely necessary things! How I've prayed when strength failed for help to get the meals done. Summer is ending. I am glad. All summers are trying to me—weakening—making strength easily overtaxed, and cooking and entertaining the crowd who visit us—it is always overtaxing to my strength. . . . [36]

She found little joy in cooking under these circumstances. The laborious, tedious, repetitive nature of preparing meals for a household can make daily cooking a tiring chore. Still, women might have taken pleasure in the act of recording their knowledge and recipes. Does writing make this act of labor less of a drudgery? Does record keeping transform the tedium into an important resource for the practical information it conveys, for even the unpleasant memories it encodes, and for the release it provides? Does the act of writing give women's onerous chores dignity? In the act of inscribing their knowledge, women exalt the ordinary work that they do in the routines of everyday life. The text renders the invisible and transient—often thankless and taken-for-granted—work indelible, noticed, and worthy. Women used recipe books, these artifacts of everyday life, as forums for self-expression. In a written record of their work, they expressed everything from pride and pleasure in their accomplishments to resentment, anger, and frustration with all that they were expected to do.

Several years ago, an auction-loving colleague brought me a loose-leaf binder he had found in a box of books bought for a song at a nearby market. The contents were disarming. On the first page of this slender handful of papers the author had scrawled a tirade of resentment in a bold, angry script with the title: *"CAROL'S COOKING STINKS COOK BOOK, ALSO A DIARY AS WE GO ON."* On her title page she asserts rancorously: *"Dedicated to all my fellow 'ladies of the house' who would rather be reading, sleeping, drinking, and smoking, playing with the dog, the baby or her own belly button—anything—rather than face that what to have for dinner crisis everyday. But do it we must or feel so guilty! Out for dinner is a cop out—at least this way you don't have to wear a girdle."* This, she decides, is much worse than cooking at home. At least at home she has the freedom to wear comfortable clothes.

Carol kept her notebook most probably during the 1960s or 1970s, when both girdles and bland food were conventional. Although she kept an account of what she ate in the form of nightly menus over a several-month period, Carol does not indicate the year during which she kept the book. She begins her book's first section with a question: *"What Am I Going to Have?"* Another page in the same section is devoted to the announcement that the book is beginning: *"Here it Comes—from the kid who couldn't make Jello."* At the bottom of this page she has a key to reading the recipe book. An asterisk denotes that the dish mentioned in the menu has a recipe included in the book, and two lines under the first letter indicates *"the letter under which you can find it."* In comparison to recipe books of earlier eras, Carol's book shatters conventions. Her opening is not the self-confident table of contents or index found in seventeenth- through twentieth-century recipe manuscripts. Instead, Carol reveals her chagrin and indecision. While her own recipes are included and indexed, Carol's recipe book consists mostly of menus made with many commercially prepared foods.

Reminiscent of the fashionable food of the 1970s, its trendy tastes were an amalgam of commercially prepared foodstuffs with some natural edibles. Women yearned for foods that promised ease of preparation but were natural and nutritious as well. It was the era of Betty Friedan's *The Feminine Mystique,* and women were becoming aware of society's gender inequities.[37]

Friedan's book described the malaise of domesticity that had long afflicted women, a longing for more than the household routines.

Carol kept a log of her domestic customs with day-by-day menus of the dinners she prepared. Perhaps she needed to demonstrate that even she, who hated cooking, gave thought to feeding herself and her husband. On Monday, October 3, she prepared Weaver frozen chicken with buttered noodles, lemon Jell-O, and pear salad. Her husband had canned chili. She served cheeseburgers with canned potato sticks and sliced tomatoes on Tuesday. Both show the pattern common in Carol's household menus.

The next night, Wednesday, Carol writes: "*Wed. 5: goof-off nite—Beef stew from freezer (made it 8/13) split toasted rolls butter and bleu cheese powder on top, salad—takes about 1 hour to reheat—sip slowly.*" (Is she talking about a drink she may have made while waiting for her dinner, to stave off hunger?) She continues "*Yeah, well—we lugged 7 bags of animal food yesterday & 5 people food today. We do feel secure with plenty food in the house—like money in the bank. Avoids 5:30 panic. Plenty available=pick what you feel like.*" This then was her strategy: Keep an assortment handy so that meals can be created with little thinking ahead. Last-minute shopping is kept to a minimum, and there will always be the makings of a meal in the house.

Carol distinguishes between *"store-kind"* food and homemade; she obviously recognizes the value of the latter. Yet her dislike for cooking overwhelms her guilt about not eating healthful food. Her cookbook is less about how to prepare food than it is about how she manages to put food on the table when her feelings about her housewife role are, at best, ambivalent. Most often her rage and frustration at her multiple roles as breadwinner, shopper, cook, and house cleaner are evident in this book. She punctuates her menus with comments that describe the pace of her days and the expectations made of women to do it all.

In the fourth week of October, Carol's coworker Sally went on vacation, obviously leaving her with additional responsibilities at work plus the household tasks with which she alone is fettered. Like a banner headline across the top of the page, Carol announces: "*Sally out all week—Carol will do her job as well as her own—menu's will be interesting studies in 'fatigue cuisine.'*"

She begins on: "*Monday, 24th: chili/chicken, noodles, lettuce salad catalina dressing for me, Italian for Bob.*" "*Tuesday 25th: ham slice, brussell sprouts, salad, corn toaster pop-ups.*" "*Wednesday 26: Easy cheese fondue, lettuce, tomato, catalina dressing—long day today, little pooped, folks.*" The menu for Thursday, 27 includes: "*turkey croquettes, corn, celery sticks, biscuits—long day today—big pooped—the dingbats haven't changed in thirty years.*"

We learn more about Carol's age and her determination in the next entry. On Friday, the twenty-eighth of October she served "*Hot roast beef sandwiches with gravy, string beans—throw up tired today—maybe 50 can't hold up like 25, but we'll TRY or croak in the attempt.*" Her week is made more difficult on Saturday by an incident that upset her. "*Basket case today—food shopped anyway. Also today the day of the big mouse trauma & Andy in Willow Grove Avenue day. Ok to bleed a little? (trapped a mouse—it chewed its tail off to escape trap—oh god!)*" She closes the week's entries with an envious and sarcastic comment on her colleague's expected return and the vacation tales she will tell. At the bottom of the page Carol writes: "*CAN HARDLY WAIT TO HEAR HOW SALLY GOT AWAY FROM IT ALL and was elegant too! hoo boy!*" Clearly Carol's envy of her colleague's vacation and what she perceives as her pretensions are evident in her sarcastic commentary about Sally's trip. She expects Sally to regale her with the details of her "elegant" vacation and feels as if she will have her nose rubbed in it. Not only was Carol unable to go on vacation, but she had to fill in for her coworker to boot.

There is every reason for Carol to be disgruntled about her circumstances. As is the case with many working women, she finds herself earning a livelihood for the household and carrying on all of the labor to maintain the home in which she and her husband live.[38] Sociologist Arlie Hochschild calls this "the second shift," the inequitable arrangement by which women work full-time jobs during the day and at night and weekends take on the additional job of housekeeping, childcare, and cooking.[39] Not only was Carol expected to be the household caretaker, but she paid a penalty at work as well.

In the first week of November, while "*Glamourina (Sally) is still out for 2 more days because 'she has a problem,'*" Carol worked "*42 ¾ hours this week— whatta way to treat a senior citizen (me—only when it suits me). The tiredies are the giveaway tho—. If only I were paid by the hour—still on 23 hour week*" *pay—I'd be rich.*" Finally, she is rewarded the following week. Carol's colleague, Mike, insists on compensating her for the additional hours she worked the week before. She's tired but happy about the additional income, "*$225.00, about $160.00 net—am rich.*"

As is often the case with working women, Carol may have been underpaid (at least she feels she is) and just as often overworked. The folk wisdom that has been plastered in offices around the country seems to hold true in Carol's case: "Women have to do twice as much as men do for half the pay." For Carol, as for many working women, entering the workforce did not mean equal opportunities for career or job advancement. According to Hochschild, it is not because women limit themselves or have no role models. It is not that institutions discriminate against women. Hochschild explains the inequity in career mobility by holding men accountable: "Men do not share the raising of their children and the caring of their homes. Men think and feel within structures of work which presume they don't do these things. Women who enter these traditional structures and do the work of the home, too, can't compete on male terms."[40] According to Carol, her husband Bob did not help with the care of the household. While there is no evidence that children were present and needed care, nonetheless, Carol felt overburdened by her sole caretaker's role.

It is not clear what Carol's occupation was, although she may have been a nurse. In her cookery book she says that she took a "*nutrition course at nursing school.*" She is proud of her efficiency and her competence, if not exhausted and somewhat piqued at the number of tasks she crammed into her off day (Sunday) while cooking dinner, presumably for her husband and herself. She lists the chores she completed with the same relish as she registers the food: "*baked glazed corned beef, sour cream/chive potato casserole, baked carrots and parsley (tonite I shoved it all in the oven); boiled the corn beef this AM while doing the wash, kitty pans, balancing bank statement joint (Bob made his usual error in math) & pushing vacuum & waxing kitchen floor—3 ½ hours—just about right.*"

At times such as that Sunday, she is pleased with her self-reliance and her ability to manage. At other times she is barely able to cope. The second week of November, she is on the edge. She writes bitterly in her book:

"*Oh Mommy, I'm so tired—am either crying or flaked out or screaming. Let your son-in-law know last nite* [sic] *that while I'm shopping for food, doing his shitty pants laundry, cooking his meals, taking total care of the animals & trying to earn money, which he doesn't—the LEAST HE CAN DO IS DO THE FREAKING CLEANING esp when 17 years of paint is chipping off the walls. I DON'T HAVE ANY MOTIVATION—Damn near walked out, to leave him to pursue the further exploits of William Richards*[41] *alone and without me. GODDAMN there is the present and future bearing down—screw the past! end of subject. He cleaned beautifully but does sulk a bit & hollered a lot. Well he had good rest first, stayed out all week because he had a cold—Ahhh-hhhh (next page—Ok?)*" We are left to wonder what past Carol refers to. A past may be all that keeps her bound to her husband. What she wants from him is a helpmate, someone with whom to share the workload.

Constantly tired, Carol struggles to balance her own needs for rest with her sense of obligation to be a good wife and caregiver. "*Sort of spun out this evening either from fatigue or hormones—redeemed my conscience for easy dinner by sectioning 2 grapefruits (sort of small—7 for a dollar—tho red).*" Once again she shows pride in her ability to manage under the circumstances. Serving sectioned grapefruits, she mentioned, as "*one of the few things I learned of value*" from her nursing school "*dingbat*" nutrition course. Her easily prepared meal was enhanced by something of nutritional value. Yet she is never satisfied with her performance. Here she both applauds her economy—"*7 for a dollar*" at the same that she denigrates the quality of the produce "*sort of small.*" Is it the result of her own lack of self-esteem, or is it because of the economic and work-related inequities that permeate her life?

Although she feels overworked while Sally is away, her coworker's return is unwelcome. Another woman, Judy, has been called in "*to cover the front desk*" in Sally's absence. Apparently this feels "*like heaven*" to Carol. "*Judy doing superfine on front desk—official word is Sally has mini nervous breakdown—out all next week Hot Dog—hope forever. Nerve break my ass—she's being cute have been around that stuff enough to smell a phoney.*" So happy is Carol about Sally's absence that she writes in the third week of November: "*If Sally comes back, I'm gonna commit suicide.*" But Sally comes back. On Thursday Carol writes "*Sally comes back—doesn't let out a peep—is like a stunned robot. Is either drugged out or maybe a MD told her to not tell her stuff to others as shrinks often do—don't know if she is seeing one—now—she's a bit pitiful—anyway dinner is"* (leftovers from Sunday night's meal). Perhaps Carol sees something of herself in Sally—a tired, frazzled woman. Carol ends her discussion of Sally with some feeling of empathy, *"she's a bit pitiful."* Perhaps she recognizes the stress of the double shift?

Yet when the work schedule relaxes a bit, so does Carol. On the days when she arrives home early from work, she prepares meals that satisfy her sense of duty. And she actually takes pride in her culinary prowess for the Thanksgiving meal she writes about. Having worked only eight hours on the Wednesday before Thanksgiving, Carol prepared their nightly meal while making advance preparations for the next day's festive one. Thrilled that she was home from work before six o'clock, she prepared a simple meal of hot dogs, mustard and relish, celery, and potato sticks while making a pumpkin pie, chilling the cranberry sauce, and defrosting the turkey. On Thursday she writes:

> *a lovely Thanksgiving dinner! Damn!! that girl can cook—tho there <u>were strings on the celery</u>—so maybe not—anyway, we had:*
> *Turkey, homemade stuffing, gravy (not from a can) string beans, creamed onions au gratin, baked yams, cranberry sauce, cole slaw, ripe olives, celery, Aunt Reba Spancake's green tomato relish and pumpkin pie & water with ice cubes and ATE AT THE TABLE on my precious Staffordshire. Charley <u>made</u> the meal by zooming downstairs with a sanitary napkin in his mouth—<u>USED</u>! Animals were confused—cook was too pooped to enjoy. In bed at 7:45—forgot to tell—washed & ironed curtains this AM.*

At Thanksgiving, she almost admitted without reservation that she was a good cook. However, she could not let this self-congratulatory claim go unchallenged. She had to mention the *"strings on the celery"* as the fatal flaw of the meal and her own inadequacy. Overall, Carol is critical of just about everything and everyone in her life with the exception of her beloved animals.

Carol had a Scottish terrier named Charley whom she adored. She loved animals, and they seemed to be her preferred source of companionship. From her account of Thanksgiving, one of the highlights of the evening for Carol—if for no one else—was her dog zooming down the stairs with a used sanitary napkin in his mouth. She tells us at the outset of her cookery book that "*anything—playing with the dog or the baby*" would be better than facing the decision about what to have for dinner. Dog shows and other activities that involve her animals are her preferred way of spending time. The day after Thanksgiving, she celebrated Charley's second birthday with a specially prepared "*birthday cake*" made of ground round to be shared with the cats. On Saturday she is content: "*lovely day today—washed & hung 3 pairs of drip dry curtains and THAT'S ALL. Spent the whole day reading with Daisy* [one of her cats] *on my chest & doggie beside me—a beautiful day!*" All Carol seems to want and need are a few hours to herself—to rest and to read. The rage of her cookbook writing is about the lack of time and help in keeping her household maintained.

Even Carol's weekends consist mainly of household chores, although a little extra sleep and some time for play seem to make her feel happier. "*On weekends, if I get up at 7:00 (well, that's 45 minutes later than weekdays) can start chores at 7:30 and be finished by lunch time. Today, we changed beds, did litter, 4 loads of wash and 6 bags at the Acme. Had wash folded and put away, same for 6 bags by 10–12—and could goof-off all afternoon—a little goofing makes the hip*[42] *feel better—then we don't get the wake-ups during the nite— real BLISS YOU KNOW.*" At first her use of the pronoun "we" gave me the impression that on this day she and her husband had done the shopping, bed changing, and other tasks together. However, in the next sentence she used the pronoun "we," again to talk about herself and her nighttime wakefulness. Now I realized that she had only distanced herself from her own feelings. By referring to herself as "we," she used a belittling and demeaning tone to ridicule herself.

Carol continues her culinary tale in her cookbook along with her backbreaking days. The constant pressure to do two jobs every day each day leaves her angry and dissatisfied. She complains of pain, fatigue, and poor sleep.

Still, as Christmas approaches, the tone of the book changes. On December 4 Carol writes, like a child anticipating Santa Claus, "*did the Christmas cards today—it's coming, IT'S COMING!!*" She ends her narrative just a week before Christmas on a hopeful and joyous note. Carol's anticipation of the holidays, of excitement and the respite from the quotidian as she moves into sacred time, gives her hope. Almost childlike, Carol looks forward to the rewards of the season, gifts and food, time to withdraw from the world and to dream about the future.

Carol's cookbook reveals a woman with, at best, ambivalent feelings about cooking. Most often, it is drudgery and tedium to perform, a housewifely act her conscience dictates. Carol avoids the skillful cooking required for making home-prepared food because between work and other chores, there is little time for her other interests. Yet when she has the time to cook, she seems to take pride in her accomplishments. For the rest of it, trying to fit a second shift into each day, every day, leaves her tired and angry. Food and cooking have become a target of her rage, a symbol of her husband's lack of support, her long, tiring hours at a job, and her sense of alienation and abandonment. Just as it was for other women in the era of Betty Friedan's liberating sexual politics, for Carol cooking is just another assignment, one she would rather do without.

The women who compiled and annotated their cookery books became synonymous with them. Women created their own singular, idiosyncratic texts by accumulating, appropriating, and transforming the material they collected into their own visions of the world. Each shaped communal memory to her own tastes: preserving, omitting, and altering the material she had collected. Each left a literal and figurative fingerprint of her daily work on the pages of her recipe book. In doing so these women rewrote a cultural legacy into a personal vision of and testament to their individual lives.

How important the activity of recording the details of their lives was we can only infer from the recipe/scrapbooks themselves. Their very existence alludes to the important role they played in the lives of the women who created and used them. Reading and writing offered women opportunities for reflection and developing self-awareness. Keeping a recipe book, ostensibly a record of mundane tasks and accomplishments, was simultaneously a way of inscribing one's life, writing oneself into being. The books are an accounting of days and tasks, the accumulated wisdom and knowledge that a woman garnered over the years of her life as wife, mother, daughter, kin, friend, healer, reader, writer, and as an individual. On the pages of these texts she celebrated her successes, documented her own and her children's development, and dreamed about and longed for new and different experiences.

FIVE

Cookbooks, Literacy, and Domesticity

January 5, 1903: . . . Children around me almost every stroke of the pen. . . .
January 23, 1903: But my deepest regret is that I can't read more. Want
to read my new Bible more, my magazine and now what I'm especially in-
terested in is a borrowed book, a large thick, good one "The Ideal Life."
There are some sweet pieces of poetry especially to my liking in it and I
want to copy some of that and some paragraphs and sentences particularly
good that I wish to copy so that I might read again. I'm going to get me a
new ledger if I can find time and copy it full of such things. . . . Now this
is a poor apology for a Diary. An old acct. book of Ghu's. Yet I feel so anx-
ious for a diary that I use this and maybe by and by I'll have a nicer book.
May 5, 1903: I sometimes hunger to read—sometimes to write in my
diary. Ere I get the chance, the things I so much want to write have been
forgotten. . . . Well must stop and cook supper. . . . Askew has [written] a
letter on the other side of this leaf. He is 7 years old. He likes to write.

—From the diary of Magnolia Le Guin, 1901–1913[1]

To write down their lives, women had to be literate. However, in centuries past, not all women learned how to write.[2] Determining just
how many women in any historical period were able to write is fraught
with difficulty.[3] Estimates vary by region and time period. In seventeenth-
century England, estimates are that 52 percent of urban women and 80 percent

of provincial women were illiterate.[4] In colonial Windsor, Connecticut women's literacy rates "climbed from 27 percent for those born in the 1660s and 1670s to 90 percent for those born in the 1740s."[5] Their formal education was, in general, subordinate to men's.[6] There were not as many educational opportunities for them as for men, and the prevailing social norms did not encourage women to write.[7] Even when education and literacy were open to women, it was expected that they would use their skills to improve domestic life and educate children.[8]

In spite of this limitation, women, by their own ingenuity, may have achieved what they were denied formally and publicly. Some women found alternative avenues for self-improvement, self-expression, and education through the church or in their homes. For example, in colonial America, an upper-class woman might have had access to her husband's library,[9] and some girls benefited from the presence of a brother who was tutored at home.[10] Around domestic life and its responsibilities women thus were able to construct a socially sanctioned world that was theirs to value, dissect, and embellish.

It is not surprising, then, that culinary activities provided women with a context for reading, writing, and communicating with one another without neglecting their domestic responsibilities. From their cookery books, we learn that the kitchen was a place where mothers, servants, children, and others read and wrote. Just as the social interactions around cooking provided women with a shared purpose, cookbooks gave them a common place to raise their level of literacy. Cookbooks and recipe collections were a "place" where they could engage in compiling, editing, categorizing, composing, and responding to written texts. Women wrote letters to request recipes, compiled cookbooks for publication, and submitted their own creations to newspapers and magazines. Likewise, they read and wrote in the margins of the published works that they used for cooking.[11] In this way, they practiced literacy, even when they were denied it by formal institutions of learning.

Also, while working in the kitchen with children underfoot, mothers may have used recipes to teach their children—primarily daughters—how to read and write. They allowed, even encouraged their children to practice their letters in these books. Cookbooks from as early as the seventeenth century provide ample evidence of children's doodling, practicing letters, and copying recipes. Moreover, some literate housewives acted as mentors to servants through face-to-face teaching, sharing their books, or publishing cookery books that stressed the importance of reading and writing.[12]

A Mother and Daughter Practice Writing

One of the first recipe books to capture my attention was the large and elaborate seventeenth-century English manuscript belonging to the Maddison family. [13] The grandeur of this work in both its size and its historical scope promised to reveal a culinary adventure. Its opening pages, with "*receipts to cure gout*" and "*Certaine Necessary Observations for health,*" had most likely been written even earlier, in the fifteenth and sixteenth centuries. Yet an ordinary scrap of paper bearing a recipe for "*hooping cough*" carried on its reverse side an act presented to Parliament to "*inclose the fields of St. Ives parish, Huntingdon*" in 1801.[14] As this scrap of paper shows, the Maddison manuscript had already been used for three hundred years.

This text opened a world to me, a world I wanted to explore and understand. I was curious about the women and men who recorded their lives in the volume. I recall how it felt to touch the smooth, silken surface of the book: a large, worn, leather-bound volume with gilded fleur-de-lis ornamentation on the cover. Opening it for the first time, I was thrilled by the various scripts and the seemingly indecipherable inscription on the inside front cover. I had opened a historic document with receipts for cooking and healing; I would soon discover that I had also encountered a human one.

I returned to the manuscript day after day, compelled to discover what I could about its writers. It took weeks just to decipher the scripts, and some remain inaccessible. Yet over the months that I would work with the text, familiarizing myself with its contents, I came to recognize the handwritings of many of the various contributors, especially the few who appeared repeatedly on the pages. The more familiar I became with a few of the names and hands, the more inspired I was to ask general questions about women's writing and reading in cookbooks.

In the Maddison manuscript, two writers stand out against the backdrop of recipes: Mary, the child, and Mrs. Maddison, the mother.

"I am . . . Mary Madcap"

I encountered the scribbles and signature of Mary Madcap the first day I examined the cookery manuscript. It was her handwriting that touched me most, some three hundred years after its penning. It was the hand of a child, a girl who called herself "Mary Madcap."[15] Based on a list of her clothing someone (most likely her mother) had written on an earlier page of the manuscript—*"August Mary Maddison, a bill of hur cluse the 12 1673"*—she was between the ages of five and fifteen. Among the articles of clothing mentioned were *"6 bebes."* During the seventeenth century, children wore bibs from infancy through adolescence.[16]

Although her handwriting was clear and carefully executed, it was nonetheless the script of a child. I had to turn the book upside down to read her signature because she had written her name on the bottom of the page opposite the recipes. The year she inscribed herself in her family's book was 1679. On several other pages and on the back cover she practiced her initials *M M M M* repeatedly, trying different-shape letters as if trying on different personalities.[17] Each new letter she executed altered her initials slightly. With a shift in the upswing or a change in the downstroke of her pen, the curl that began the letter "M" grew or diminished. On one page she repeats the letter "M" until it embroiders the page like a lace coverlet. Peeking out from beneath the sampler of shapes are the words *"I am."* (See Figure 5.1) Even the young Mary Madcap had a sense of herself as a presence in the world.

Did she give herself the nickname, Mary Madcap, or did others give it to her? I picture an exuberant child, joyful, zany, nonconforming. In writing at least, to my twentieth-century eyes, she had a demeanor to be explained. On the one hand, her initials were graceful representations of her name, suggesting an awareness of status and rank. On the other hand, her nickname suggests a fun-loving child. There may be, however, another reason for her name. In the seventeenth century, "madcap" was the name given to an insane person or a deviant.

In any case, the child saw herself as a distinct entity and etched her name

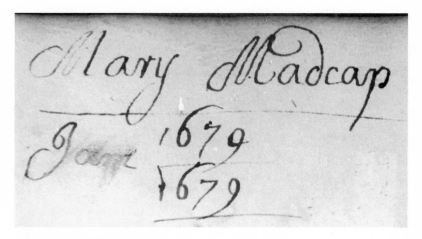

Figure 5.1   Mary Madcap's signature and announcement "*I am.*"

forever in her family's book of cookery. Perhaps this is all we will ever see or know about Mary Madcap. Yet with her nickname and her initials, she inscribes herself in history. "To sign your name, your mark," as poet and critic Susan Stewart says, "is to leave a track like any other track of the body; handwriting is to space what the voice is to time."[18]

Mary Madcap's enthusiasm for writing her initials has other precedents in the seventeenth century. Women's needlework traditions in the early modern period are another medium through which they advanced their literacy. Women were expected to become skilled in making samplers and accomplished at fancy embroidered linen work. In these crafts, women literally "wrought" (wrote) their initials in the fabric. According to literary scholar Susan Frye, "initials express a sense of identity, but they also reach out to connect women with the names of powerful figures into whose company they might literally work themselves."[19] This act of sewing, a performance of bonding individual threads into a pattern, is analogous to linking oneself with a family. Although Mary Madcap inscribes her initials on paper instead of fabric, the effect is the same. The Maddison family cookbook became a place for Mary, the child, to identify herself both as an individual and as a member of the family. A site to practice her manual dexterity, the cookbook was also a place to announce her existence. Women may have encouraged

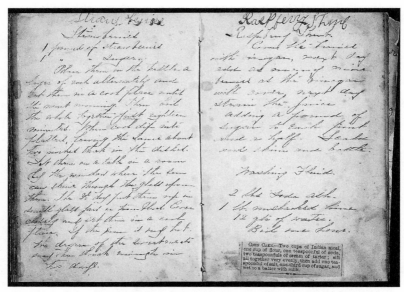

Figure 5.2   The words "*raspberries*" and "*strawberries*" copied in a nineteenth-century manuscript receipt book indicating someone practicing writing.

these concrete acts of writing for their children; they may have merely tolerated them. Either way, in the achievement of writing, children forged links with previous generations and with their successors.

Although some manuscripts, such as the Maddison text, offer clear examples of children's writing, some hands are more difficult to decipher. More than a few manuscript cookbooks provide evidence of *someone* practicing her letters, but it is difficult to determine if the copier was a child or an adult. In Laura Bigelow's nineteenth-century Waterville, New York, manuscript, for example, a child—or perhaps a servant—has practiced her penmanship on several pages of the text that was in use from 1845 to 1881.[20] On two successive pages, the copier penned the words "*raspberries*" and "*strawberries*" above the recipe titles themselves. (See Figure 5.2) "*Sarah's Cake*," a recipe found in Bigelow's manuscript, was written with great difficulty. The letters were almost geometric in shape rather than softly rounded, the pen haltingly held, for each letter seemed to tremble beneath the writer's nervous or aging hand. Numbers were also practiced in Bigelow's book as amounts of ingredients were laboriously etched onto the pages.

"I cannot write it right"
—Mrs. Maddison's concern

The Maddison text shows a second woman struggling to master the pen in the act of writing a recipe. In her attempt, she reflects explicitly on her writing. I believe this woman is Mrs. Maddison and that she is Mary Madcap's mother because through her hand she traces connections to her daughters. It is this hand that wrote *"My dater Margret"* (see Figure 5.3) and *"My dater that is at home Mary"* on other pages of the manuscript. It is she who writes Mary's *"Bill of hur cluse."* And it is the same handwriting that keeps accounts in 1688 stating that *"money is due to me and to my husband."* Given the large sums of money she is owed—upward of fifty pounds in some cases—I assume that this woman who also wrote a significant number of recipes in the book was not a servant but rather the lady of the house. She was, most likely, the wife of Christian Maddison, who inscribed the front cover of the cookery manuscript on June 24, 1675, with the following: *"I cam to Thos. house to dwell in."* His hand is found only once more at the back of the book computing sums.

Given Mary Madcap's costly list of clothing, the wealth signaled by her household accounts for 1688, and the opulent leather-bound receipt book, I would have expected the mistress of this household to have been of aristocratic lineage and therefore well educated. I thought her handwriting and her prose would correspond with her social status. In other words, I expected Mrs. Maddison to be able to write with ease.

Yet surprisingly, in comparison to other scripts in the book, Mrs. Maddison's hand is awkward, her letters uneven, her penmanship unpracticed. In addition, unlike many of her aristocratic contemporaries, Mrs. Maddison has not inscribed her name in the front of her book. Herein lies the difference between it and many other receipt books belonging to seventeenth-century women from affluent families.[21] It is this fact, among others, that

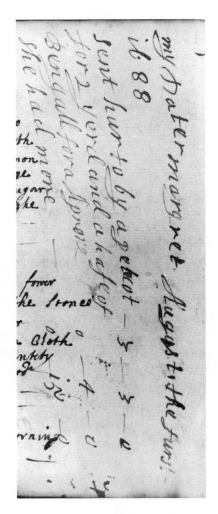

Figure 5.3   Maternal commentary on the pages of the seventeenth-century Maddison manuscript receipt book.

heightens the mystery surrounding the Maddison book and the identity of one of its primary writers, the woman I believe was Mrs. Maddison.[22]

In the midst of writing a recipe "*for a dropsy,*" the writer, Mrs. Maddison, stops in midsentence to make a comment that is one of the most fascinating and revealing in all the documents I have examined. Instead of directions for the cure she writes: "*I cannot write it right.*" (See Figure 5.4) What prompted her to enter this personal admission—perhaps an expression of frustration—in her book?

The recipe, with its title, "*for a dropsy,*" begins in a script called the Secretary hand, a popular but formal handwriting of the seventeenth century, most often associated with the execution of public documents such as wills and deeds. The writer continues in the same formal script, "*Take a pecke of sliced.*" With only this much of the recipe written, the half-finished sentence ends abruptly. Suddenly the writer changes her script to one known as italic, a popular one preferred by gentlewomen of the period, and finishes her recipe with her confession.[23] We will never know why Mrs. Maddison interjected this comment in the middle of her recipe writing. However, its presence alerts us to her concern with writing. Was she a woman who wanted to improve her penmanship? Was she concerned about appearances? Did she wish to identify with an elite group? She may have been someone who had learned to write in her youth and who had few opportunities to use her skill. Or was she simply ill that day?

If my suppositions about her are correct, then this manuscript may be an example of a gentlewoman who could read but was not confident about her writing. Women who could read did not necessarily learn how to write. Although aristocratic women were more likely to be literate than women of other social groups, some may have been more comfortable with writing than others. Another explanation might be that she was not a member of the aristocracy at all. Perhaps she was the wife of a wealthy farmer or merchant, who had learned to write for commerce but not for polite society.[24] She may have married up. In this case, her literacy skills may have been rudimentary, and she may have been practicing the fashionable script of the day. Her statement, however, points to the importance that *she* placed on writing and her desire to master it.

Not all recipe manuscripts are so explicit in declaring the importance of writing in women's lives. This work is the best example of many books from the seventeenth to the twentieth century that contain instances of women, children, and others practicing their penmanship.

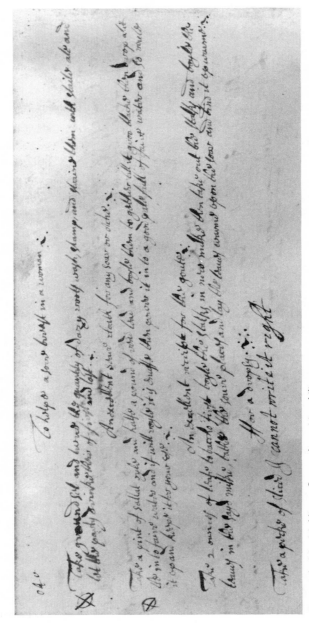

Figure 5.4 Mrs. Maddison reflects on her writing ability.

The Kitchen as a Place to Read and Write

Literacy is a key to empowerment and transformation, to economic gain and social mobility.[25] The extent of women's literacy is thus a rough measure of the degree to which women in different eras were able to participate, or not, in arenas other than the domestic one. But how many women were literate in each historical period is difficult to determine. This difficulty in assessing the rates of women's literacy stems, in part, from the nature of the evidence, which has rested largely on public documents such as wills and deeds.[26] Other sources, such as diaries and journals, most often belonged to women of the middle and upper classes.[27]

Moreover, definitions of literacy are complex. Is it the mechanical skills of reading or of writing, or both? Or does literacy include all the ways different cultures, and various groups within a society, value their forms of speech: oral and written, script and print?[28] And what are the consequences of these concepts for different people within the same society? Who might have access to these communicative tools? Soon after the American Revolution, the prevailing ideology valued women for their role as nurturers of the country's future citizens. To teach their children to read, women had to be literate themselves, but such opportunities were available only to those living in comfortable economic circumstances.[29] In this case, women were taught to read, but they did not necessarily learn to write.[30] Similarly in England in the same time period, women were expected to teach children and servants to read.

Attitudes toward and opportunities for women's education and literacy were affected by factors such as race, class, ethnicity, region, and religion.[31] In the early modern period, from the fifteenth through seventeenth centuries, for example, a merchant's wife living in London and participating in commercial life beside her husband was more likely to be literate than a poor farmer's wife in the north of England. A patrician woman was more likely than her servants to be educated and to be knowledgeable about books and letters. This fact is what makes Mrs. Maddison's book ambiguous. From the richness of its cover and the amount of expensive paper it encloses to the attributions linking its owners to noble and titled individuals, its compiler's rudimentary script is puzzling. However, Mrs. Maddison was not unusual. With the exception of some aristocrats, women seldom acquired the tools for written communication.

Instruction within the context of religion was one way that some women learned how to read. While in early modern Europe, Catholic convents may have educated young women of upper-class families, Protestantism, in the Old and New worlds, encouraged women as well as men to read and write.[32] Yet while Protestantism promoted reading and writing so that both sexes might directly engage in biblical study and spiritual introspection, it also may have narrowed women's roles to domestic ones as it shifted fealty from God to husband.[33]

Colonial New England women had better access to schooling and were taught to read more readily than those in the Southern colonies. However, even within particular regions, race and social class influenced literacy. For example, in the South until the Civil War, law and practice both generally denied slaves the right to learn to read and write. At the same time, some Southern free blacks were literate.[34]

From the seventeenth through the late nineteenth centuries in England and America, the acquisition of literacy was crucial for women to participate in an increasingly print-oriented society. Economic and social changes altered existing communication structures. The transformations included the increased dissemination of print in vernacular English to a wider reading public in the form of weeklies, broadsides, newspapers, periodicals, and magazines.[35] Once again, these changes were tempered by national and regional differences that varied people's experiences with literacy. Movements of people to urban centers, for instance, involved the development of occupational opportunities for men and women.[36] The ability to read and write was implicated in many of these social and economic changes.[37]

Moreover, there are other potential consequences to literacy, including gaining the ability to join in challenges to existing political and economic power structures.[38] Becoming literate does not guarantee equality for an individual or for a group, but it is a vehicle that may engender social change. While literacy may spawn social change for groups, it also may enable personal growth and development.[39] During the American Civil War, for example, Southern women's only communication with absent husbands was through correspondence. In their letters, they engaged in self-reflection, expressed love, and shared the mundane details of their daily lives. "Writing is inescapably an act of discovery," writes historian Drew Gilpin Faust.[40] Although Faust's book centers on Southern women's writing during the Civil War, the process of writing may have held equal importance for women writing in domestic contexts.

In the domestic context, women could engage in literate activities without censure. Despite the constraints imposed on them by male prerogatives, women were actively constructing social and utilitarian worlds of their own in the context of the kitchen. For women and their social networks, the exchange of recipes for their books was also a form of communication. It provided women with opportunities for reading, writing, and socializing across class lines. Such was the case for Anne Hughes and her servant, Sarah.

"I bee goinge toe teche Sarah nexte winter": A Farmer's Wife Teaches Her Servant How to Read and Write

Anne Hughes, the eighteenth-century wife of a well-to-do English farmer, is one of only a few women below middle class who kept a diary that survives to this day. Although her entries lasted for only one year, between 1796 and 1797,[41] her diary leaves an account of her yeoman's life in some detail.

As the wife of a farmer, Anne's daily tasks were considerable. Rising early each day, she fed the livestock before attending to her housekeeping chores. She cooked, baked, cleaned, and sewed. She worried about the health and illness of family, friends, and neighbors as well as strangers. On several occasions, she helped the itinerant poor who came into her life either by begging at her door or by requesting work.

Significantly, she worried most about the hungry, dirty, and homeless women and children connected to these laboring men. Her entry on March 11, 1796, mentions the first of several of her acts of kindness: "*In cums Mistress Prue att midd daye toe tell me Joe Shorts wifee does hav a childe and e shee wyth little clothes for itt bein verrie pore. Mistress Prue doe say can I helpe her, wyche I will moste willen bein sorrie to anny who doe suffer frome wante, so I wyth her later toe see thee pore wretche, ande didde finde her lying moste wearie, and comfurtless."*[42] The next day she revisits Emma Short in her cottage *"toe washe her. I didde . . . also wype the babes fase and mayke itt tydie and cumfurtabel no boddie else doin itt."*[43]

Anne is quite aware of her gender. As she fusses over the wives and children of workers, she sees her husband, John, as one who needs coddling and handling, *"hee bein a mere man."*[44] On February 6, 1796, their third wedding anniversary, she writes in her diary that she *"didde doe mye butter maken"* while she left Sarah *"To cooke moste off thee dinner."* The results were predictable, according to Anne: *"Sarah didde burne the dinner, like she always doe, ande John was verrie crosse therebye, he mislyking Sarahs cooken, so I doe sometime have to lett him think itt is mee. Men be verrye tiyresome sometimes."*[45] The theme of men's insufficiencies is replayed in her diary on many occasions. Because she feels she cannot count on John to be as generous as she, she deploys other tactics.

To carry out her intentions of helping others, Anne often finds a subtle way to enlist John's backing, or sometimes she decides to deceive him. On March 11, 1796, she writes, *"I backe home toe gette sum clene sheetes and a blankit toe make thee pore sowle better, ande sum mylk for her toe drynk wyche didde warme her, wee then home wyth her blessinge us, I didde nott tell John of mee givinge her thee shtes ande blankit, hee bein a mere man, soe itt nott wyse toe doe soe."*[46]

Nonetheless, Anne feels lucky to have married her well-to-do farmer husband. She has the necessities of life and some luxuries. One of them is a full-time servant named Sarah. Another is her ability to read and write. Sentiments such as the following appear frequently in her journal: *"I doe feel that Gode bee verrie goode toe mee ande favvourede mee muche, wyth a goode home ande plentie to ett ande toe kepe mee warme ande abel too rede ande rite."*[47] Anne wrote a great deal about cooking and included recipes in many of her daily reports.

Even more remarkable are her comments on the importance of reading and writing in her life. For example, on March 6, 1796, Anne Hughes called on her childhood friend, Lady Susan. As she was going to tea at Susan's house, she took with her, as a gift, a

*pott of mye pickelled strawberries wyche didd plese her grately she nott hering talk
of suche, ande didde saye woulde I tell her howe toe doe itt whych I shall rite oute
and sende her. Shee didde give mee thee recept off sum ginger bredde cake wee
didde ett ande wiche was verrie tastie, ande shee didde tell me was made thys
waye, you doe take off wite flower 2 punds, 1 pund of sugger wyche wee doe putt
in our tea, 1 pund off buttyr, ande 2 teespunfulls off ginger, thys muste bee mixed
thee daye before, nexte daye you doe putte itt in a hotte oven ande bake verrie
quicke wythe a piece of sweet peele on thee toppe.*

In her brief description of the visit to Lady Susan, Anne Hughes points
out the ways in which her interaction with her friend fosters literacy. First,
she tells us that she will write out her recipe for *"pickelled strawberries"* and
send it to her friend. Should we have expected Lady Susan, the gentlewoman, to be the writer of the recipe and Anne, the farmer's wife, to communicate her recipe orally? If so, Anne quickly undermines our expectations.
Her desire to emulate *"people of qualitie"* may be the motivation for writing
and sending her recipe. "Telling" instead of writing, on the other hand, may
be Susan's way of crossing class boundaries, at least in this interaction.

Indeed, we know very little about Anne's social background. We do know
that she married a wealthy farmer and that she had friends and acquaintances from varied social strata. How she came to know *"Lady Susan"* she
never tells us. We only know that they have been friends since childhood.
From her descriptions of social life, we may infer that she was eager to be associated with, in her own words, people of *"qualitie."* Her own literacy was
fortuitous. Mistress Prue, *"a fine lady,"* had taught Anne to read and write.
On July 24, 1796, she admits, *"I shall aluss bee gladd thay my owne dere
mother didd lett Mistress Prue show mee howe toe rite ande figger."*

Because Anne valued the skills she had acquired, she wanted to teach her
maid, Sarah, how to read and write as a sign of affection, as a reward for
good service and compliance with domestic standards, and a gesture of noblesse oblige. On July 12, 1796, Anne vowed, *"I bee goinge toe teche Sarah
nexte winter, shee sayeing shee wyshe see could. Shee bee a goode cooke nowe,
ande dont nowe spoil the vittals, ande verrie clene ande tidie."*[48]

The generosity of women such as Mistress Prue may have inspired
Anne to assume a similar role in Sarah's life. It was a benevolent gesture

and also a tender one. Over the year of her journal, we learn that Anne has developed a relationship with Sarah. When faced with Sarah's upcoming marriage, Anne admits that she is reluctant to let her go. Sarah has become Anne's confidante as much as her servant. Much of Anne's diary comments in the second year of writing focus on the tension she feels between a wish to help Sarah reach her potential and unhappiness at losing a servant. Nonetheless Anne's desire to do good wins out. She provides Sarah with clothing and linens, and she herself prepares a fine wedding feast.

Anne's desire to be benevolent stems not only from her personal history—losing her mother when she was still a young girl—and her generosity (which she demonstrates repeatedly in her journal) but also from contemporary ideals of femininity that she emulated. Acts of charity were especially associated with aristocratic women and thus were doubly valued in terms of class and gender. Her desire to be compassionate was supported in some of the conduct books of the period, such as Dorothy Leigh's *The Mother's Blessing,* which advised women to teach their children and servants how to read and write.[49] It appears that Anne made good on her promise because, as the journal closes, she tells the reader that Sarah has written a thank-you note to a wedding guest, who had been unable to witness the marriage but who nonetheless sent gifts for the couple.

Literacy was thus a means to denote rank and power. For all of these women, writing—in this case, about food and cooking—was a way to signal standing and class, regard and authority. Literacy, like other currencies, may act as a bridge or a barrier depending on the circumstances. In her relationship with Lady Susan, Anne Hughes "sent" her recipes, as much out of courtesy and respect as out of the desire to demonstrate her status as a literate woman. In imparting literacy skills to her maid, Sarah, Anne was doubly motivated. For Anne and her social network, reading and writing served to bind and reward, to mark differences and similarities.

If cooking was their craft, literacy was their tool. By putting one in the service of the other, women could weave together their lives, shape representations of themselves, and create meanings around the written as well as the spoken rituals and traditions of cookery.

Cookbooks: Common Ground for Women and Men

Not only women interacted with one another through their written recipes; sometimes men and women also found common ground in culinary documents. Men and women's spheres of activity have never been as exclusive of one another as popular ideology suggests.[50] Manuscript cookbooks further challenge the idea that men and women inhabit entirely separate worlds. Although women created, utilized, and enjoyed culinary productions, men frequently participated in the endeavor. In fact, men authored the earliest cookery books, even though they were written for women and household use.[51] Until 1640 men predominated in the field of household writing. Gervase Markham, Richard Allestree, and Richard Braithwaite were among those writing domestic advice literature for women in the early modern period.

However, it was not just through published texts that men contributed to women's cookery and medicinal lore. The stereotype of men's exclusion from the world of the kitchen falls apart under close examination of these cookbooks. Instead, some men "sponsored" women's reading and writing, whether inadvertently or directly.[52] Yielding the material goods necessary for writing and reading was one way that men indirectly contributed to women's literacy. In the seventeenth century especially, books and paper were scarce and expensive commodities, and it appears that many women were not entitled to these luxury goods.[53] Women's reuse of men's books is a fairly obvious sign that women's literacy was subordinate to men's. One of the earliest examples I found of a recycled text was that of an anonymous seventeenth-century woman who either took or received a book used first for mathematical exercises and accounts. The first twenty-seven pages are devoted to the manipulation and calculation of sums through addition, multiplication, subtraction, and division. Thereafter the book becomes a book of what its writer called "*cookrey.*"[54]

The Maddison manuscript, which had been inscribed "*Chr.* [Christian] *Maddison*" was intended for use as a man's commonplace book (a notebook in which one copies out useful information) and had been in use for at least a hundred years before it was used for domestic cookery. There are innumerable examples from the seventeenth through the twentieth centuries of women scavenging ledgers, diaries, and address and telephone books as raw materials for their own use. Such borrowings may reflect other indirect acts of sponsorship, such as sharing and giving books, discussion, and correspondence.[55]

The Delightes for Ladies:
A Cook Book as Love Token

Men also gave, perhaps in courtship or as a gift of friendship, books of culinary and medicinal matters. In 1602 one proficient author, Sir Hugh Plat, an English inventor, agriculturist, and epicure, penned *The Delightes for Ladies,* one of the most popular cookery books of the time.[56]

So valued were cookbooks, Plat's among them, in the seventeenth century, and so popular with ladies, that in 1655 one rejected suitor gave his beloved a recipe manuscript "scrivened"—written by a professional scribe—to resemble Plat's printed favorite.[57] Joseph Lovett bestowed on his lady, Mabella Powers, a volume of receipts for making conserves, candies, potions, and creams as well as valuable, life-sustaining, medicinal remedies. The title page of Lovett's text was artfully copied to resemble Plat's original, but the recipes came from other sources. Perhaps some of them were Lovett's own creations.

Since many seventeenth-century men and women were not literate, it was customary for professional scribes to write for those who could not. These scriveners were paid to write a letter or copy an entire text. Interestingly, the writer of Mabella's text was inadvertently or deliberately not faithful to the printed version. But given the cost of paper and binding, this text was not inexpensive. A pocket-size book bound in leather, it has no adornment on the cover. It is a dainty book, one meant for a lady's hand and use.

Written in the literary and social conventions of the period, the poem inscribed on the front page tells Lovett's story of unrequited love. Who the lovers are, other than their names, we do not know. Joseph inscribes his gift with avowed eternal devotion, still in hope of winning his lady's affection:

a presumption to disstorb yr
attractive Eloquence to admit it a

loging in yr studdy, but since my
indevors cannot lite such delights
as my deserve your essteeme, be plesd
but to forgive my fall, & I shall
acknoligg the happinis two great to
him that prayes for your Eternall
filycities and remanes Mrs.
The hum(bl)ist of all yr
exskommunicated
Servants
For Ever Jose: Lovett

From Joseph's inscription, we might infer that Mabella had rejected a number of her admirers. Or he may have been simply forsaken by his patron or lady. Joseph ironically designates himself "*the humblist*" of *all* her "*exskommunicated servants.*" He may not have been humble at all. He had the wherewithal to have a book made for his lady, so we must assume he was not poor. But about his pedigree we know nothing. Lovett may have been an inappropriate match for a patrician woman. Or was he her parents' choice of husband whom she rejected? We know that Mabella had social standing. We learn from the poem at the beginning of the book that Joseph asks Mabella "*to admit it* [the book] *a loging in yr studdy,*" which reveals that Mabella was wealthy enough to have a room to herself, a "loging" Joseph wanted to share.

If not Joseph, then his culinary missive would remain in his beloved Mabella's study, a private space from which he was excluded. The gift Joseph gave would be a stand-in for him in Mabella's inner sanctum. Each time she referred to her book, she would be reminded of his devotion. The receipt book was one way in which Joseph and Mabella could be united, just as cookbooks offered some other men and women at least textual common ground. Although Joseph's gift was an indirect contribution to women's literacy, others were more pointed.

There are, in fact, indications that men actively brokered literacy for some women in their families and social networks. Some men contributed either medicinal or cookery recipes to women's books. Other men were themselves collectors and culinary aficionados who kept kitchen books of their own or shared the texts with women in their families.[58] More often contributors and scribes, men were sometimes compilers of texts, a role usually reserved for women.[59] Although some men certainly refrained from displaying knowledge of culinary tasks, others took pride in understanding and remembering the sensory properties of a dish and the manner of its making. Among the latter was Samuel Pepys, the seventeenth-century essayist and gastronome, who devoted volumes to his daily culinary explorations and regimen. In the same period, John Evelyn, a noted writer, recorded hundreds of medicinal receipts and authored a classic study of salads called *Acetaria.*[60]

"The recipes were copied out for me by my brother"

Men might act as amanuenses and actually write out a text—from a sermon to a recipe—for women who could not write themselves.[61] At first glance this practice might not seem to further women's literacy, for it could be a way of creating women's even greater dependence on others for their ability to communicate. However, women could, if so inclined, put this practice to good use: They could use these scrivened texts to read and as models to practice their own writing.

One mid-eighteenth-century woman, Lydia Grofton Jarvis, may have done just that. Lydia kept a manuscript recipe book apparently not written in her own hand.[62] However, her signature appears, in pencil, on the first page of her text. Her slender and modest book opens with the explanation that *"the recipes were copied out for me by my brother."* (See Figure 5.5) His elegant hand begins the book with a section on *"Puddings."* My immediate conjecture was that Lydia Grofton Jarvis was illiterate. Yet more puzzling was the discovery of a list of *"discheveled books—in barn, for self-education"* written in the last pages of her recipe book. (See Figure 5.6) She included among the volumes for her self-improvement *"Mothers bible, Salmon's Gazeteer, School Journal, Locke's Notes on St. Paul, Walker's Dictionary, Osgood's Milestones, Frederic III and 4 volumes Rollins American History."* This list was written in pencil in the same hand that signed *"Lydia Grofton Jarvis"* on the first page of the book. From the books she has chosen, it is obvious that Lydia

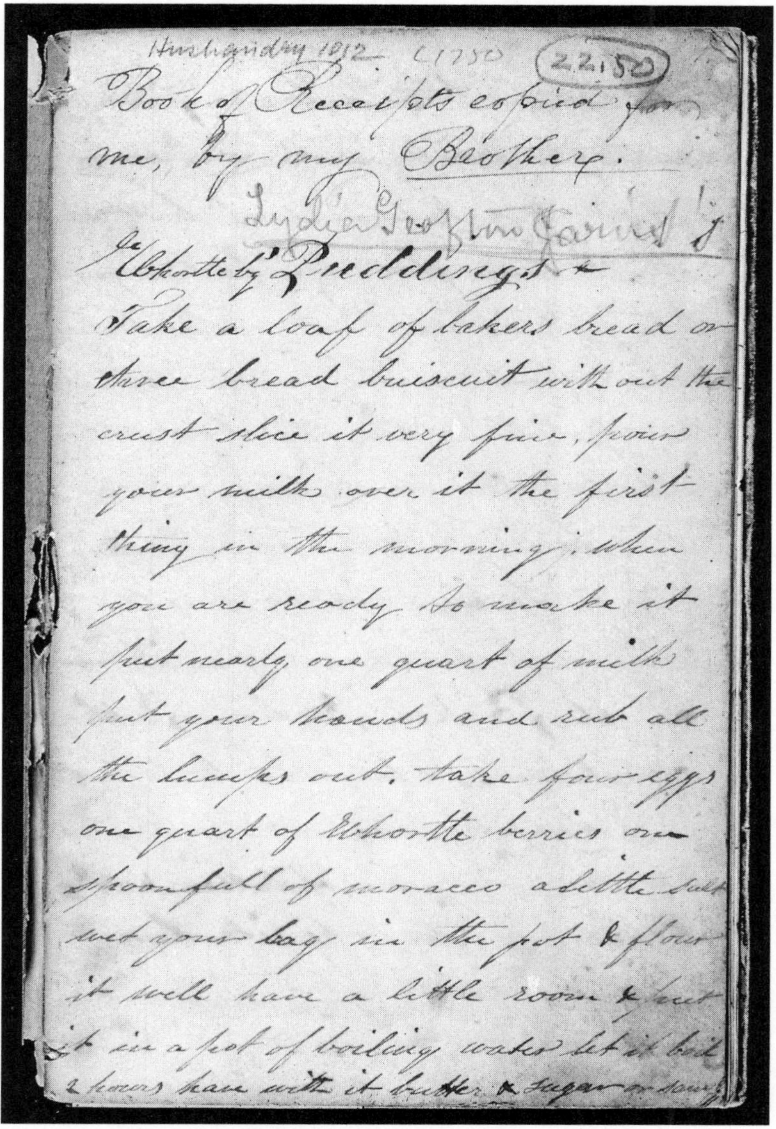

Huckleberry 1812 · (1750) · 2.2.15

Book of Receipts copied for me, by my Brother.

Lydia Grofton Jarvis's

Whortleberry Puddings

Take a loaf of bakers bread or three bread biscuit with out the crust slice it very fine, pour your milk over it the first thing in the morning, when you are ready to make it put nearly one quart of milk put your hands and rub all the lumps out, take four eggs one quart of Whortle berries one spoonfull of morases a little salt wet your bag in the pot & flour it well have a little room & put it in a pot of boiling water let it boil 2 hours have with it butter & sugar or

Figure 5.5   Lydia Grofton Jarvis's manuscript receipt book *copied out for me by my brother.*

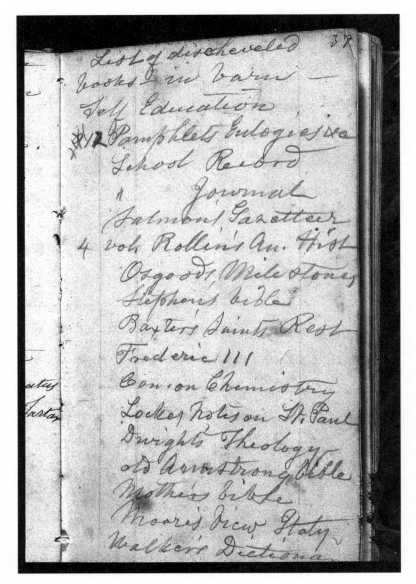

Figure 5.6   List of "*discheveled books—in barn, for self education*" on the last page of Grofton Jarvis's receipt book.

fashioned an education for herself comparable to a man's. It is also likely that the books on her list once belonged to others, perhaps her brother.

Even more perplexing than the presence of Lydia's signature in a book written by her brother is that, in several of the recipes, a pencil script is overlaid with the same elegant penmanship found throughout the book. Was it Lydia who first penciled in a few of the recipes but asked her brother to cover in ink what she may have perceived as her own flawed hand? In the eighteenth century, penmanship was viewed as a reflection of the character of the writer. Control over the pen was metaphorically also control of the body. The handwritten text was a "sincere human expression" that reflected the worth and disposition of its maker.[63] Did Lydia think that her own handwriting was not beautiful enough to inscribe her recipes for posterity? For women, writing was seen as much as a visual art as a sign of literacy.[64] "'Graceful lines and curves,'" as "'pure and chaste and beautiful'" as the writers themselves, were what women sought to emulate in their scripts. Their hands might then characterize them as refined and elegant ladies.[65] Was Lydia an aspiring socialite who was afraid her script would designate her otherwise?

There may be yet another explanation for her brother's role in writing Lydia's recipe book. Perhaps Lydia asked her brother to write her book as a means of acknowledging her affection for him or vice versa. Because recipes were exchanged, then and now, between women as symbols of bonding and affection, scribing her recipe book may have been a gift from brother to sister, a token of affection between them. A final alternative is that perhaps Lydia's motives were more pragmatic. She may have extracted as much knowledge and assistance from her brother as she could. It was not uncommon for girls to share their brothers' books, teachers, and lessons, so perhaps Lydia read her brother's cast-off books and used his script to practice her own penmanship. We will never know exactly how she used his literacy—if, in fact, she did—to foster her own. Yet from the list that mentioned "Stephen's bible," "Stephen's cologne," and other references to books used for male education, we learn that men were important in providing models for Lydia as she constructed a curriculum for herself.

There is little more to know about Lydia from her cookery book—where she lived, her social class, her education, her familial and friendship network are beguilingly unfathomable from the evidence she left behind.[66] Still, Lydia Grofton Jarvis has told us, in her receipt book, that such issues as reading, writing, and self-improvement mattered to her.

A Commonplace Book for Women

Just as cookery and receipt books are among those genres, such as letters, that offered women an opportunity for self-improvement in the arena of domesticity, one especially ubiquitous form adopted by women for their culinary writings was that of the commonplace book. In a departure from the teaching methods of antiquity, students (more frequently men) starting during the Renaissance were schooled in a system of information storage and retrieval called the commonplace method.[67] This method required taking "notable fragments" of authoritative texts and placing them—literally—in a book for easy recovery. The purpose for doing so was to compile a storehouse of common though memorable knowledge from which all could borrow, including the individual compiler.[68] During the Renaissance, authorship and knowledge were collective enterprises. From the writings of well-known and respected philosophers, historians, naturalists, and literati, individuals selected and arranged their bits of wisdom to create arguments and speeches bolstered by the authoritative knowledge of the ancients. For some compilers, other sources were valued as well. Local wisdom, learned orally, might be placed side by side with biblical verse and an Aristotelian adage. Direct personal experience also played a role in commonplace books.[69] These books thus display a fluid relationship between oral and print cultures of the periods as compilers gave equal weight to word of mouth and print sources, placing them side by side in their copybooks as vital knowledge from respected sources.

Although some women, usually from the upper echelons of society, may have learned to compile commonplace books much as their brothers and fathers did, most women were not exposed to a humanist education.[70] In fact, customarily many women were denied such entitlement. Consequently, it is not clear how and why women discovered or learned how to compile commonplace books. It is tempting to conjecture that some women whose brothers, fathers, or other male relatives played a supporting role in their education learned the method because they modeled their own education after the men's, but we cannot know for sure.

In women's hands, however, the commonplace book changed its focus, as women adapted the features of these books—if not the pedagogical philosophy underlying the genre—for their domestic writings. They compiled their recipe cum commonplace books with the same spirit: Knowledge was shared; ideally it belonged to everyone.[71] Authorship was collaborative. However, they altered the content to reflect their own needs and interests. Cookery and medicinal recipes predominated in their texts, but these were interspersed with aphorisms, poetry, and other forms of folk wisdom. Like many women's journals in our time, these culinary commonplace books were women's compositions: a site to compile knowledge, practice writing, and address domestic as well as personal concerns.

One example, an unidentified poem found in the seventeenth-century Maddison commonplace receipt book is a poignant lament on aging and the loss of beauty. Written in Mrs. Maddison's hand, the title, "*Like Swallowes*," has been recopied beneath the verse in Mary Madcap's own unmistakable script. (See Figure 5.7)

Like Swallowes

Like swallowes when the summers done
they fly and seeke some warmer sun
then wisely chuse one to your friend
whose love may: when your beauties end
Remaine still firme by you

This very personal, poignant expression of fear of aging and loss of beauty speaks to many women's concerns. And not only was the child, Mary, practicing her penmanship, she was introduced to her mother's feminine world through this commonplace recipe book.

Besides including poems, women also updated their own handwritten recipe collections by copying out recipes from printed books. In Mary

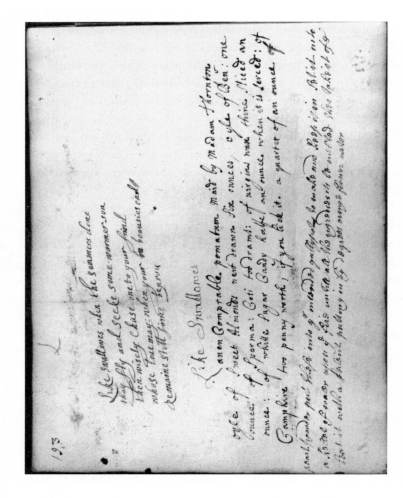

Figure 5.7 The poem "*Like Swallowes*" penned by Mrs. Maddison, the title copied by Mary Madcap.

Maddison's manuscript, a recipe for a powder attributed to Elizabeth Grey, the Countess of Kent, suggested that the receipt had been copied, nearly verbatim, from a contemporary and very popular printed book, the Countess of Kent's *Choice Manuall, or, Rare and select secrets in physick and chyrurgery, collected and practised by the right honorourable the Countess of Kent, late deceased; whereto are added several experiments of the virtues of Gascon pouder and lapis contra yarvam by a professor of physick.*[72]

In the Maddison manuscript, even the funnel-shape title of the receipt is written so as to resemble the printed version.[73]

> *The true [—] Receipt of the Countess of Kents powder*
> *Which is most mos soveraine against all malignant and*
> *Pestilent diseases, french Pox, measles, Plague, malignant*
> *or Scarlet Fevers, against Melancholy. 20 or 30*
> *for a man, 10 for a child to be given*
> *In Sack or harts horn jelly*[74]

The curative ingredients of the powder and the technique for combining them are reproduced as faithfully as the title:

> *Take of the magistery of pearls, of Crabs eyes prepared, of white Amber prepared, Harts-horn, Magistery of white Corrall, of* Lapis contra Yarvum, *of each alike quantity, to these pouders infused put of the black tips of the great clawes of Crabs, to thefull weight of the rest, beat thesee all into very fine pouder, and fearce them through a fine Lawn Searce, to every ounce of this pouder add a drachm of true Oriental bezer, make all these up into a lump or masse, with the jelly of Hartshorn, and colour it with Saffron, putting thereto a scruple of Ambergrice, and a little Musk also finely poudered and dry them (made up into small Trochiss) neither by fire nor Sun, but by a dry aire: you may give to a man twenty grains of it, and to a Child twelve graines.*[75]

The Countess of Kent's powder also was copied by many published authors of the period, including Robert May, a well-known seventeenth-century chef.[76] It is clear that Elizabeth Grey, Countess of Kent, had become an authority in the domain of medical cookery. Housewives and others thus justifiably appropriated her receipts for their own. In this way women began the process of developing their own authoritative texts to be used in their homes and communities.[77]

Women compiled examples of their knowledge and their own authority in several steps. First, they appropriated texts from well-known published sources. But they also copied recipes learned by word of mouth and observation and from other written sources such as letters. These borrowings usually were taken from an authoritative source, sometimes attributed to "a notable woman," often a relative or a neighbor noted for her own experience in domestic and culinary matters.[78] In other words, the receipt was proven through a respected woman's firsthand experience. When learned from oral tradition, the writer had to transform the spoken word of a recipe into a written text, committing to paper a formula that may never have been written out before.

For women who had learned only a rudimentary script or fundamental compositional skills, this must have been a difficult undertaking. But they clearly persisted. Not only did domestic commonplace books provide women with opportunities for developing and enhancing their reading and writing skills, but proficient deployment of their contents may have earned them prestige and influence in their households and communities. The form of culinary commonplace books endures not only through this period but also in recipe books dating to the beginning of the twentieth century.[79]

Women Take the Printed Word

Into the nineteenth and twentieth centuries, women continued to hand-copy recipes, poetry, and biblical texts from neighbors and friends as well as from printed books. However, by the mid-nineteenth and into the twentieth century, the accessibility of inexpensive print media such as newspapers, magazines, and pamphlets gave women additional ways to augment their own culinary repertoires and compile their cookery books. Biblical verses and other spiritual expressions, items of local historical interest and national importance, biographies and obituaries, poetry, and philosophy were penned, pasted, or pinned to pages of recipes for making quince marmalade or potting a pig.

Commonly, these home-produced books resembled a collage or a scrapbook in which print and script were placed side by side. With the inception of this technique for compiling cookbooks, women who could not write well or could not write at all—"who could but read"[80]—were able to create texts of their own design and of "mine own inventions."[81] The affordability of print sources made it possible for women to create texts, whether they had acquired fluency in writing or not.

The East Falls, Pennsylvania, housekeeper and suffragist Jane Campbell, mentioned in chapter 4, chose a scrapbooklike arrangement for her book and used print and script on the same pages.[82] Many nineteenth- and twentieth-century recipe books look like this.

A second format might include a text comprised of two sections: one handwritten and the other produced of printed excerpts or an entire published text, but kept together as one assemblage instead of two. Recall Mrs. Downing, from Coatesville, Pennsylvania, the early-twentieth-century housewife who belonged to a book club. She kept two volumes as one, a manuscript and a published cookbook. In another example, the anonymous, nineteenth-century reader of Edward Lear whose poem of a daughter's death lingers in her manuscript chose an address book in which to paste all of her printed sources, reserving her copybook for only script. This pattern suggests that this cookery compilation may have belonged to women of different generations: One wrote her recipes by hand while the other decided to leave the manuscript intact and produce another text entirely from print.[83]

But the most dramatic example of this form is presented by nineteenth-century Philadelphian Mrs. Hannah Keen, wife and widow of J. Seymour Keen, a lumber merchant, who kept a manuscript cookery book from 1854 until at least 1882. On the first page of her book someone is practicing penmanship and the names "*Mrs. Hannah M. Keen,*" "*Mrs. Hannah Keen,*" which several times cover the page from top to bottom. Perhaps it is she? Perhaps it is a child? The book is inscribed several times with more than one address, including 3312 Race Street, West Philadelphia. Hannah Keen's text is entirely handwritten. Although she appropriates recipes from printed cookery books of the period, she prefers to hand-write the recipes into her book rather than clip and paste them.

Filled with handwritten recipes attributed to several women and one man named "Jack," along with loose scraps of paper, Mrs. Keen's cookery book reveals that she was obviously fond of the recipes found in a popular contemporary cookbook, *Widdifield's new cookbook, or Practical receipts for the housewife* by Mrs. Widdifield (1856).[84] Eight recipes are attributed to Mrs. Widdifield's published work, although each is handwritten into Keen's book in her own beautiful script.[85] In the published cookery book, the recipe for "Balloons, (or Baked flour pudding)" consists of:

One pint of milk;
Three eggs;
One pint of flour.

Separate the eggs, beat the yolks until light, and mix with the milk, and stir into the flour gradually. Beat it well with one salt-spoonful of salt; then whisk the whites until stiff and dry, and stir through lightly, half at a time. Butter small cups, fill them half full of the mixture, and bake in a quick oven. When done, turn them out of the cups, place them on a heated dish, and send them to table hot. Eat with wine sauce, or nun's butter.[86]

Hannah Keen's version is nearly verbatim, although she rearranges the list of ingredients, placing the flour after the milk followed by the eggs. She also omits the wine sauce and suggests only nun's butter. The recipe for nun's butter is found on the preceding page of Keen's manuscript; it is identical to Widdifield's and may also have come from the printed book.

Besides creating their own collections in various combinations of print and script, women used published cookbooks as foundations for their own books. In these they felt free to strike out, alter, comment upon, and respond to the recipes and the authors whose texts they owned. Further, they altered and updated the printed books with additional clipped print sources as well as handwritten ones just as women added to their manuscripts. Multiple clipped newspaper recipes are affixed to a page in a copy of Marion Harland's *Common Sense in the Household* (1871). (See Figure 5.8) The compiler had done the same with other dishes and sweets. The anonymous owner of Mrs. Raffald's popular eighteenth-century book, *The Experienced English*

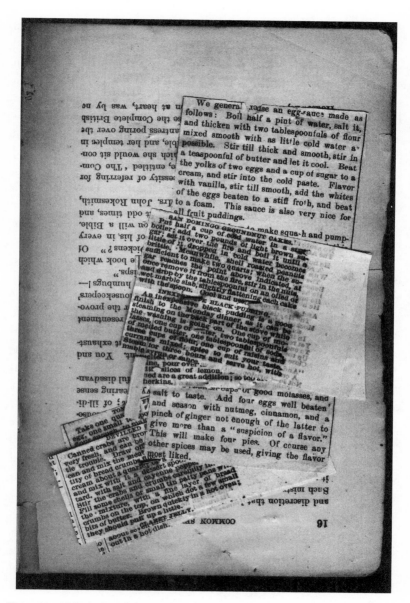

Figure 5.8   Multiple clipped newspaper recipes affixed with a straight pin in Marion Harland's *Common-Sense in the Household.*

Housekeeper (1787), felt free to strike out "cumin" and other spices in bold black ink from every recipe that called for them.

Many readers also editorialized their editions with marginalia, from mundane comments, such as "*want to try,*" "*good,*" and "*terrible,*" to scathing social commentary.[87] The anonymous owner of a copy of *Mrs. Putnam's Receipt Book & Young Housekeeper's Assistant* (1854), for example, was an articulate critic of Mrs. Putnam's authoritative stance toward the reader. Since it is not unusual to find notes, questions, opinions, and comments written in the margins of these texts, the fact of this reader's commentary is not unusual. What is surprising is the vehemence with which the reader critiques the book. In this popular nineteenth-century cookbook, the author boasts about her "twenty years' experience . . . in housekeeping." The reader retorts in her handwritten commentary: "*Query with the rest of the household.*"[88] In other words, "Whom do you think you're kidding?" On the next page their dialogue continues. The author writes: "One of the greatest conveniences to a young housekeeper is a Cook Book, on the excellence of whose directions she may rely; while few things embarrass her more than one which is filled, not with a selection, but with an indiscriminate collection, of receipts, good, bad, and indifferent, brought together haphazard, without any reference to their real value." The reader has bracketed this long sentence with the sardonic comment: "*True as per sample.*"

A recipe for "a Mountain Goose" is written as follows: "Cleanse it the same as a turkey. Make a dressing of bread crums, one onion chopped very fine, two spoonfuls of sage, pepper, salt, and a little pork chopped fine, and one egg. To roast a large goose requires two hours' cooking. The gravy is made the same as for common goose." To this our reader/ commentator adds: "*which must be the goose of the valley.*"[89]

The very next recipe is for "A Mongrel Goose": "Is dressed the same as the common goose, but <u>as the mongrel has so much flavor, the dressing is unnecessary.</u>" (See Figure 5.9) The reader replies with a bold underline of the sentence, and retorts, "*You good woman! How did you find this out?*"[90]

What is interesting here is the intense dialogue that the reader has with the author/text and the apparent status display alluded to in the commentary.

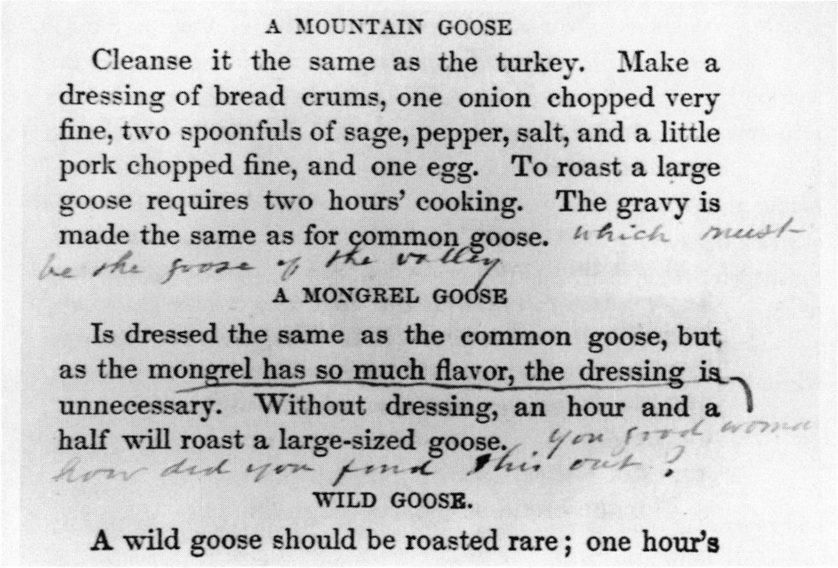

A MOUNTAIN GOOSE

Cleanse it the same as the turkey. Make a dressing of bread crums, one onion chopped very fine, two spoonfuls of sage, pepper, salt, and a little pork chopped fine, and one egg. To roast a large goose requires two hours' cooking. The gravy is made the same as for common goose. *which must be the goose of the valley*

A MONGREL GOOSE

Is dressed the same as the common goose, but, as the mongrel has so much flavor, the dressing is unnecessary. Without dressing, an hour and a half will roast a large-sized goose. *You good woman how did you find this out?*

WILD GOOSE.

A wild goose should be roasted rare; one hour's

Figure 5.9   Marginalia from Mrs. Putnam's receipt book (1854) critiquing the author.

Through her marginalia laden with sarcasm and irony, the reader has alerted us to positional differences that, in this instance, separate writer and reader. The characteristics of mountain and mongrel, which distinguish geese, also distinguish humans. The reader views such distinctions as pretentious and absurd. She has suggested earlier that the author had no claim to expertise, despite Mrs. Putnam's claim. Declarations of long experience in the kitchen were often claims for authority in domestic matters. It is difficult to say whether the reader is mistress or maid, although from the beautifully penned commentary, I would infer she is mistress. It is clear, however, that there is a battle being waged on these pages between high and low, between theory and practice, and between those who work and those who supervise.

Cookbooks, as they are used in daily life, are works-in-progress. They are added to, altered, and transformed to suit the idiosyncratic needs of each household. As texts poised between generations, genders, occupations, and statuses, cookbooks are welcoming sites for pen, pencil, and print.

Thus, cookbooks invite editorializing. Printed books often have blank pages for the reader to add recipes of her own. Well-known authors like Marion Harland asked readers to test the recipes and submit changes and recommendations to her. Improvements on the author's work were claimed to be welcome. This invitation to the reader is not altogether different from manuscripts that offered three or four versions of the same recipe, using the expression "another way." Other manuscripts simply added several recipes for the same bread, pie, or pudding learned from different sources and, most likely, at different times.

All of these documents show how kitchens and cookbooks were places where women could and did practice reading and writing and where they also taught others to do so. Manuscript recipe books and printed cookbooks provided women the opportunity to read, write, and reflect and to engage in reverie and fantasy while working in the kitchen. In the process of learning and practicing their literacy skills on the pages of their cookbooks, pasting in recipes from other printed sources, and editorializing, women were not only readers and writers, they became authors.

Women did not merely receive texts but participated in their creation. Thus, as each woman created a book of her own, she engaged in book production. A few women took the next step and used cooking knowledge and writing as a sanctioned path to cultural authority, economic independence, and public visibility.

Six

Becoming an Author:
Cookbooks and Conduct

*Feminist critics and even general readers have embraced books by women
as one of the few places in which women could speak for themselves, could
represent women's experiences, could express their needs, their nightmares,
and their utopian hopes, and escape the masculine myth of the female.*

—*Paula R. Backscheider and John J. Richetti,*[1]
Popular Fiction by Women

Since we know comparatively little about early women cookbook
writers,[2] we must start to find our clues from their published
works.[3] By looking at title pages, portraits, and prefaces as well as
the recipes themselves, it is possible to piece together information about
these authors: how they presented themselves to readers, why and how they
wrote, and for whom.

Print publication made it possible for women to reach beyond their immediate family and friendship circles. By becoming authors through print
publication, women could extend the boundaries of their influence and, if
successful, profit economically from the venture. In their self-presentations,
they emphasized their own day-to-day experiences, identifying with those of
their readers. They rendered their instructions with self-conscious simplicity,

enabling comprehension, in the words of Hannah Glasse, one of the eighteenth century's cherished writers, "for every servant who can but read."[4] They chose language as prosaic and nontechnical as they could muster to reach the widest possible audience. These cookbooks, addressed primarily to British audiences and exported to the colonies, were not simply a reflection of the social and occupational hierarchy of eighteenth-century England and the gentry's dependence on a servant class, but attempts to reach entire "communities of readers."[5] What better way to accomplish this than by embracing the gamut of household workers, paid and unpaid, and by addressing an audience that ranged from ladies to cook-maids?

Although social class was certainly explicit in these writers' presuppositions about their readers, they emphasized the ways in which women of different statuses apportioned the work of maintaining a household. They achieved inclusivity without neglecting status and role by focusing on a larger social unit, the household. They directed their texts to a social space inhabited by women and often, but not always, to the culinary activity that presumably occupied them. However, by aiming their writing at the range of workers in a household, they embraced a diverse community of readers.

If class and literacy were implicated in their choice of unadorned language, then resistance to French influence was an impulse in their unadorned cuisine. The cookery they championed was suited for an English family; their goal was to provide elegance without extravagance. Many of the eighteenth-century cookbook authors disparaged expensive French cuisine, opting instead for good, simple English cooking. Women were not entirely alone in this mission, although they stressed the suitability of their receipts for English tastes.

They were writing side by side with their male counterparts, many of whom were writing for professional chefs, while others were also writing for a domestic audience.[6] Until the mid-seventeenth century, as we saw in chapter 5, although women wrote and circulated their own documents in other ways, it was primarily men who published domestic advice and cookery books.[7] In their books, male writers, who occasionally acknowledged their original female sources, offered women guidance on everything from female decorum and comportment to recipes for cooking and healing.[8] Once women found their way into print, they did not differ dramatically, in this respect, from the male authors beside whom they published.[9] Women, too, shaped their books with an author's individual stylistic imprint, creating texts that varied in scope and content.

As a result, some cookbooks were more than cookbooks. Besides providing recipes, authors used cookery books as a venue for the exploration of domestic life, women's roles, education, and demeanor. Printed cookery literature was a place for women to shape the images of femininity that were being debated in other forms of literature.[10] This was not an unusual strategy. Novels often were fictionalized conduct books, and other types of literature also encompassed other genres. The point of creating such hybrids was to provide a comprehensive household manual in a single text. Depending on the author's purpose, these manuals took different forms, ranging from culinary specialization to the regulation of domestic social relationships; each book was idiosyncratic in content and its author's signature style.

Cookbooks differed as widely from one another as did the women who wrote them. This fact also had implications for a book's commercial success. Each author tried to outdo the other by promising original, never-before-published recipes or including other didactic literature. Some books were encyclopedic in scope, covering topics from bee-keeping and brewing to the home production of cosmetics, conserves, and medicinals. Other books contained dictionaries and model letters or aphorisms and maxims. As we look at each of the books in this chapter, we can see how similarly and differently each author, bookseller, and printer conceived of their projects, purposes, and audiences. The differences among the books sometimes outweigh their similarities. Variations of the common cookery book template were due to an author's style, the intended audience—still unknown to booksellers—and burgeoning culinary tastes.

Approaches to Publication: Manuscript versus Print

We can only guess at why and how some books became classic culinary models and their authors achieved immortality while others were relegated to the margins of history. It seems that some writers never sought publication at all. It is important to remember that print was not the only vehicle by which women and men shared their culinary and medicinal secrets. Besides print publication, there were two main ways to distribute (or publish) one's written work in the early modern period.[11] The first was by circulating one's manuscript discretely to a selected group of readers. The second was by selling copies of a handwritten text.

Into the eighteenth and nineteenth centuries, many women who wrote for audiences other than their immediate family and friendship networks circulated their writings prudently,[12] controlling who had access to their manuscripts. Many of the women and men who composed literature confined their writings to their own social groups.[13] In this way, as authors they controlled their readership, a choice, according to literary historian Margaret Ezell, that "permitted and encouraged participation in literary life of groups of people whom print technology effectively isolated and alienated."[14] Printers, publishers, and authors negotiated their dominions and often manuscripts were sold outright, leaving the author without jurisdiction over her work.

However, manuscripts could be and were sold. Buyers could purchase manuscript copies of texts handwritten by the author or scrivened by a professional scribe.[15] This form of distribution was called scribal publication. Mary Eales, confectioner to England's Queen Anne, sold a few manuscript copies of her *Compleat Confectioner* in 1713 or so, before her books were printed and sold in the marketplace in 1718. The cost of the manuscript, five guineas, a considerable sum of money in those days, limited the sale to individuals of what she called "Prime Quality." It is not clear whether Mary Eales wrote out her own manuscripts in order to confine her audience to elite families or whether they were professionally hand-copied and sold to anyone who could afford her recipe collections.[16] However, it appears that manuscript copies of *The Compleat Confectioner* predated the book's printed publication.[17] When contrasted with the cost of printing an edition, hand-copying was a more economical way of producing a small number of texts for sale.

Mary Statham, Her Book, September 22 d A.D. 1724

Another example of a circulated manuscript in England is Mary Statham's 1724 text. In appearance it is an unassuming volume made up of, in her words, "*2 Hundred thirty-six ~ ~ ~ Receipts or above never before this made publick."* Slender, bound only in paper, its seventy-five pages stitched together carefully, the manuscript holds only a few clues about its author's intentions. Each recipe is carefully written in the same clear hand throughout. The manuscript's pages show no signs of daily use: no hurried scrawls, no unfinished notes, no doodles, no personal musings or accounts. Statham's manuscript is a polished piece, each recipe a perfect copy. But this is not the only indication of its author's intention to share her work—for pleasure or profit—with a reading public beyond her family's use. Her title page and preface also lead me to believe she had other readers in mind because such prefaces are not found in private, housebound manuscripts.

Most manuscript receipt books intended for private use bear only the name of their owners, and often the date they were given or begun.[18] Her first page reads: *"The great and Rare art of candying, cooking, distilling, Preserving, Pickling, and Physick containing 2 Hundred thirty-six ~ ~ ~ Receipts or above never before this made publick now made publick thro the intercession of some friends for the use good and Benefit of the Country. with Severall others for making Severall sorts of wine."*

In this formulaic preface, Statham claims that she is publishing her recipes at the behest of her friends, perhaps enabled by their advance purchase of her book. In keeping with the literary conventions of the eighteenth century and the obligations of modesty, Statham tells her readers that she is making her manuscript "publick" (publishing) only for the good of her country (which has not been identified) and because her friends have urged her to do so.

It was immodest for an author to admit writing for economic gain or personal glory. Did Mary Statham pen or have someone scriven her book of receipts for private but extended circulation or for sale? Since there is no extant printed version (or record of one), her book could have been one of those manuscripts that reached its public through scribal publication.

Eliza Smith's Preface
to *The Compleat Housewife*

Prefaces such as Statham's were fairly standard in printed books of the period.[19] Seventeenth- and eighteenth-century literary conventions were similar across genres: From poetic to prose forms, most authors did not admit they were writing for money or vanity. Women and men, for example, pleaded innocence about contracting with a printer, asserting that their work was taken without their knowledge and consent. Some authors claimed that friends obliged them to publish their knowledge for the public good.

Other writers, especially women, claimed that they were compelled to write by revelation and God's divine intervention. Some women wrote to defend or gain their rightful property while still others needed to clear their names from scandal.[20] Cookbook authors thus deployed the same conventional and sanctioned motivations for writing found in other genres. Sometimes the books they authored were published anonymously. Sometimes, after several successful editions, their names appeared in print.[21]

In 1727, Eliza Smith, the English author of *The Compleat Housewife*, published the first edition of her cookbook. *The Compleat Housewife* would ultimately appear in sixteen editions, becoming one of the most popular cookbooks of the eighteenth century in both England and America. Smith wrote her cookery book out of her own experience as a housekeeper and told her readers, "what I here present the World with, is the Product of my own Experience, and that for the Space of Thirty Years and upwards; during which Time, I have been constantly employed in fashionable and noble Families."[22] Very little else is known about Smith. Yet in her preface there were echoes of the writings of other women of this time. They, like Smith, were amateur authors who wrote books from their everyday knowledge and not from formal education or training.

Since most prefaces were formulaic in the eighteenth century, it is hard to sift fact from mere convention. Printers and publishers took liberties with texts, adding and changing the writer's work to make the book more appealing and increase sales. Eliza Smith's preface is no exception. Smith uses her introduction—if, indeed, she wrote it—to ridicule the required prefatory remarks. Smith tells her readers candidly that "it being grown as unfashionable for a Book now to appear in Public without a Preface, as for a Lady to appear at a Ball without a Hoop-Petticoat; I shall conform to Custom for Fashion sake and not through any Necessity."[23] While apparently surrendering to fashion, Smith ridicules its tyranny. With her petticoat metaphor, she graciously but ironically bows to style and the ways in which a book must be window-dressed for acceptance by a wide reading public.[24] Its clever use of a sartorial emblem—the hoop-petticoat—stamped her cookbook for female readers.

The petticoat was a well-chosen image, familiar to many eighteenth-century readers; it carried with it the suggestion of contemporary social tensions between the growing wealth and values of the middle classes and those of the waning aristocracy. If it signaled the difference between opulence and economy in the class structure, for women the cumbersome hoop-petticoat was a symbol of both power and restriction. On one hand, it was a potent representation of female seductiveness. On the other, the petticoat's sheer physical size and shape were constraining. In either case, for Smith the tensions symbolized by this garment highlighted the pretensions of class, gender, and the marketplace.[25] Smith could not have chosen a more resonant icon to signal the difference between her cookbook and others, particularly men's.

Books, like women's clothing, must be attractive and fashionable. They must artfully disguise, emphasize, or display the texts (bodies) concealed by the ornamentation of paper, type, and binding (the layers of cloth and wire that adorn the body). The hoop-petticoat is also an appropriate symbol to designate a book written by a woman for women's use. However, Smith also views the petticoat as a symbol for artifice and guile when she describes male cookbook writers. Smith chides the great professional (male) culinary writers, "which bear great Names, as Cooks to Kings, Princes, and Noblemen." She felt "deceived in [her] Expectations," for they "conceal their best Receipts from the Public" (under the cloth and wire of hoop-petticoats or the paper and binding of books) without the substance of the straightforward cookery, "wholesome, toothsome, all practicable and easy to be performed," that she wishes to teach to her female audience.[26]

Smith identifies herself with her readers by first noting her own disappointment with the books produced by famous professionals. She complains about their recipes:

> many of them to *us* are impracticable, others whimsical, others unpalatable, unless to depraved Palates; some unwholesome; many Things copied from old

Authors, and recommended, without (as I am persuaded) the Copiers ever having had any Experience of the Palatableness, or had any Regard to the Wholesomeness of them; which two things ought to be the standing Rules, that no Pretenders in Cookery ought to deviate from.[27]

In this sentence Smith has allied herself with her readers, an intimate gesture of identification and inclusion. Unlike her male competitors, who, she claims, did not concern themselves with everyday cookery, she is offering her knowledge and experience to women like herself, women who must offer wholesome, practical, and palatable food to families. The "Pretenders to Cookery," as she calls them, are guilty of chicanery as authorities as well as being inept and pretentious communicators. Smith won her audience because she spoke as a woman with years of experience in the kitchen to other women. This, above all else, established her authority.

Smith tries further to undermine her male competitors by raising the question of whose domain cookery is. Unnecessary as she claims the preface is, Smith nonetheless uses it to regale her readers with a history of cooking. Her lengthy preface outdoes those by her contemporaries in its scope: "having three or four pages to be filled up previous to the Subject itself, I shall employ them on a subject I think new, and not yet handled by any of the Pretenders to the Art of Cookery; and that is, the Antiquity of it." Beginning with the Bible, Smith explores the question of whether Esau was the first cook:

That Esau was the first Cook, I shall not presume to assert; for Abraham gave Orders to dress a fatted Calf; but Esau is the first Person mentioned that made any Advances beyond plain Dressing, as Boiling, Roasting, &c. For tho' we find, indeed, that Rebecca, his Mother, was accomplished with the Skill of making savoury Meat as well as he, yet whether he learned it from her, or she from him, is a Question too knotty for me to determine.[28]

She agrees that a man first transformed the simplest cooking techniques into more elaborate ones, but she will not concede that men had culinary knowledge before women. Rebecca, Esau's mother, had equal skill in the practical art of cookery. Smith does not know whether Esau learned from Rebecca or vice versa, and she would prefer not to decide.

The First Professional Cookbook Writer:
Hannah Wolley

Women's experiences were different from men's. In order to perpetuate their own perspectives of knowledge, women entered the world of print.[29] The first woman professional culinary writer to enter the arena of print publication in seventeenth-century England was Hannah Wolley.[30] Known not only for her cookery and medicinal receipts, Wolley has been remembered as a defender of women's education. However, some claim that her most trenchant statement about education has been erroneously attributed to her.[31] In a book she may actually *not* have written, *The Gentlewoman's Companion*,[32] the unidentified author makes a mockery of contemporary women's schooling:

> The right Education of the Female Sex as it is in a manner everywhere neglected, so it ought to be generally lamented. Most of this deprav'd late Age think a Woman learned and wise enough, if she can distinguish her Husband's bed from another's. I cannot but complain of, and must condemn the great negligence of Parents, in letting the fertile ground of their daughters lie fallow, yet send the barren Noodles of their sons to the University.[33]

We may never know whether Wolley would have agreed with this witty and provocative statement. That this book and this statement were attributed to her suggests that her celebrated literary persona made her a medium through which others could speak. As far as we can determine, Wolley did not have the benefit of a formal education. Her entrance into the world of print initiated a practice that recurred repeatedly: women without formal education who earned their living by writing for publication and teaching others to cook.[34] In Wolley's case, as later in others, the publication of her cookery book also advertised her cooking classes. Moreover, as she transformed herself into a professional writer, she commented on social relations, literacy, and female comportment.

Apparently her knowledge about managing households came from years of experience as a housekeeper. There are conflicting accounts of Wolley's life, but it is fairly certain that she had developed domestic competence as a housekeeper in various settings, including a noble household, while also developing a reputation as a healer. Orphaned at the age of fourteen, she later married and ran a school in Hackney with her husband. After her husband's death, she wanted to succeed him as head of the school but was denied that position. Some have speculated that she then turned to writing as a way to earn a livelihood. Although she married again briefly, she was soon widowed once again. Her writing career began in 1661, after her first husband's death, with the publication of a cookbook called *The Ladies Directory*. The title page of this book says it was "'printed for the authoress,'" indicating that Wolley bore the expense, in some form, of this first publishing venture. During this time, it was not unusual for an author to pay for the cost of printing. Sometimes printed editions also were paid for by subscription preceding publication, meaning that the author solicited a group of people to pay in advance for copies of the book, in that way mitigating the financial risk.

Another way for an author to safeguard the venture, to seek public approval for her work, and perhaps to increase sales was to dedicate a book to a famous patron. By the time of her second enterprise, *The Cook's Guide* (1664), Wolley had learned how to promote herself and her books in the marketplace.[35] *The Cook's Guide* "published and set forth particularly for Ladies and Gentlewomen" was dedicated to Lady Anne Wroth and her daughter Mary. Wolley's selection of these two famous and noble patrons could have been useful in persuading an elite audience to buy her book. Further, Wolley justifies her published writings as a way to "preserve her reputation" and to be "usefully employed."[36] She writes: "I would not willingly dye while I live, nor be quite forgotten when I am dead; therefore have I sent forth This book, to testifie to the scandalous World that I do not altogether spend my Time idley."[37] Her ostensible need to defend herself may have been nothing more than a rhetorical device to justify publication. However, Wolley was well known in her time, and it is possible that her life was the subject of some contemporaries' critical speculation. As a result, she may have felt the need to protect her reputation by claiming virtue and industriousness. In fact, several controversies have come down to us concerning Wolley's life including her outrage at the poaching of her texts and the publication of a false biography by hack writers later in her life.[38]

Whereas *The Cook's Guide* "was published and set forth particularly for Ladies and Gentlewomen," in *The Queen-like Closet* (1670) Wolley speaks to a wider audience: "Very Pleasant and Beneficial to all Ingenious Persons of the Female Sex." In this introduction she addresses her readers: "To all Ladies, gentlewomen, and to all other of the female sex who do delight in, or be desirous of good accomplishments."[39] Not only does she approach women of several stations and ranks, but she does so in unpretentious language. She eschews the pompous and more scientific language of her competitor Robert May, who wrote explicitly for a male professional audience. Instead Wolley writes her text in a straightforward, accessible way:[40] "Here is to be noted, that in divers of these receipts there are directions for two or three several things in one, not confounding the brains with multitudes of words to little or no purpose, or vain expressions of things which are altogether unknown to the learned as well as the ignorant; this is really imparted for the good of all the female sex."[41]

Her interests in reaching a wide audience may reflect her own sensitivity to the issue of who her readers were or her publisher's more mercenary goals. Whatever the motivation, the consequences were that her book provided understandable instruction for women of different classes.

In this period, the nascent publishing trade did not always know who its readers were, and printer-publishers as well as authors were appealing to a wide readership.[42] By offering her authoritative guidance in language as clear as possible, Wolley addressed her readers with mastery but not with condescension. As she matured as a writer, she used her authority to advise her readers on more than cookery, and her topics began to embrace other aspects of women's work and concerns. For patrician women she urged productivity in domestic duties, as in the following poem that compares her own diligence with the leisured life of the rich:

I sit here sad while you are merry,
Eating dainties, drinking perry;
But I'm content you should so feed,
So I may have to serve my need.[43]

In an ironic twist, Wolley points out that the indulgences of the rich provide her with a livelihood.

Beyond her satiric poem, Wolley described women's comportment appropriate to their socially stratified roles. In keeping with her text's focus on household tasks and the women (a potential community of readers) who do them, she legislates social relations both within and outside of the household. In this way, Wolley introduced advice about proper behavior to mistresses and servants.

Since a mistress's job was to create a well-run household in which each member knew how to behave, Wolley offered guidance on how mistresses should treat servants. She also admonished servants to serve guests by "watch[ing] the eyes of visitors to deduce whether they might want something, to save them the embarrassment of having to make demands in front of their host."[44] In addition, Wolley asked women to be generous to the needy and to remember that under different circumstances, they too could be hungry and poor. It is to virtue and charity that she turns her reader's attention: "If any poor body comes to ask an alms, do not shut the door against them rudely, but be modest and civil to them, and see if you can procure somewhat for them, and think with yourselves, that though you are now full fed, and well clothed, and free from care, yet you know not what may be your condition another day."[45]

Wolley's book was not unusual in giving such advice; male cookery book authors of the period, and later, embedded conduct literature within culinary texts. What was different about Wolley's book was that she, a woman, wrote it. There is debate about whether publishing in this period was a bold move for a woman.[46] Many argue that women faced vilification if they published their work. Others claim that women could publish without difficulty but that their work was judged against a male standard. Literary historian Elaine Hobby argues that as men encroached on previously female domains of knowledge and responsibility, women's writing in the arenas of cookery and midwifery may be seen as "an upgrading of traditional feminine activities." Women writers "struggled to prevent their complete exclusion from all remunerative fields of endeavour."[47]

In conformity with convention, Wolley's prefaces continue to maintain an image of a modest writer who was cajoled by friends into publishing. She justified the publication of her third book, *The Queen-like Closet,* with the conventional report that her friends urged her to do so: "Methinks, I hear some of you say, 'I wish Mrs. Wolley would put forth some new experiments'; and to say the truth, I have been importuned by divers of my friends and acquaintance to do so."[48]

Assuming she was vulnerable to criticism, Wolley was always careful to appease those who might condemn her continuing appearance in the marketplace. She felt the same need to protect herself in her final effort, *A Supplement to A Queen-like Closet* (1674). This time, more than persuasive friends and readers motivated her text. Although her readers "had not heard from her in awhile," she was also roused by civic duty and God-given talent to complete her final work.[49] Her progression from "a cook who writes to a professional writer"[50] may account for her poetic introduction. With the success of her first books, Wolley felt confident in writing other types of literature for her readers. In the following she once again addresses her readers in verse:

Tis twelve years past since first in print I came
More for my country's good, than to get fame.
My study was to impart to others free,
What God and Nature hath informed me.
I must not hide that talent God me gave,
Content I am others a share should have
To practice what I teach; if pains they'll take,
Amends for all my care they will me make.
Servant to ingenuity I'll be,
Such ladies shall command all arts from me.
Nothing from them I'll hide, that's in my heart,
To wait on them I think it is my part.
And to confirm to them what I have writ,
Fearing no censures, 'mongst they that have wit.[51]

It is not surprising to find poetry like this in printed cookery texts. Poetry and recipes were common in familial compilations as well as printed cookery texts. In her poetic flourish, Wolley's text is reminiscent of her well-known predecessor, Sir Hugh Plat, who also deferred to his readers with flattering lines. This seductive poem by Plat introduces his *The Delightes for Ladies*:

. . . now my pen and paper are
perfum'd,
Rosewater is the inke I write withall:
Of sweetes the sweetest I will now command,
To sweetest creatures that the earth
Doth heare;
These are the Saints to whome I sacrifice
Preserves and conserves both of plum
And peare.[52]

There is little doubt that Plat's audience was an elite one. The contents of his beautifully ornamented book focus on the traditional lady's accomplishments of the stillroom, a room where "delights" such as cosmetics, medicinals, and sweetmeats were prepared. Although Wolley also has sections devoted to such "delights" and "entertainments," as they were called, she differs from Plat by including servants among her readers and enlarging the scope of her advice.

Hannah Wolley was among the first in a succession of women cookbook writers who "turned her hard-won housewifely competence into a source of income for herself, both by advertising her willingness to teach, and by being paid as a writer."[53] Whether she did so defiantly or simply out of her own economic need, Hannah Wolley dared to compete with male cookbook authors such as Robert May and Hugh Plat and commented on more than cookery, broaching issues of conduct, literacy, and education. She wrote and taught women the culinary arts from 1661 until her death.

Of those writers who followed in her footsteps, some would and some would not venture beyond the domain of cookery. But by the eighteenth century, it was middle-class women like Wolley who became the arbiters of taste and the guardians of domestic life.

"Wrote out of my own experience": Mrs. Elizabeth Raffald's *Experienced English Housekeeper*

In the eighteenth century, with no more than their own experience as guides, women "seized the pen"[54] and began to publish a plethora of household advice and cookery books.[55] Like her seventeenth-century predecessor Hannah Wolley, Elizabeth Raffald, a paragon of notable housekeepers, was the Martha Stewart of her time. Noted for being an extraordinary housekeeper, she also became an entrepreneurial phenomenon in Manchester, England. Once a servant, later a pastry shop owner and caterer, director of a servants' registry, tavern keeper, compiler of the *Manchester Commercial Directory*, wife, mother, and best-selling cookbook author, Mrs. Raffald rose to a position of prominence in her city and her era. Her book of cookery, *The Experienced English Housekeeper*, was one of the most popular of the eighteenth century.

Raffald's ascendancy is all the more remarkable because of her unassuming origins. Years of day-to-day experience as a housekeeper in a noble household supervising the preparation of daily meals and lavish feasts formed the basis of her publication. Although she could read and write, she was not formally educated. As she tells us in the preface to her book, the receipts in her book "are wrote from my own experience."[56] Learned while she was a servant in her mistress's house, Elizabeth Whitaker Raffald's culinary expertise was the foundation for her career as an author, a career that offered the possibility of income and influence.

A portrait of the author gracing the frontispiece of her book is the opening device. Portraits such as these were commonly used by printers as advertising strategies linking a book with its author. However, Raffald's image suggests that perhaps her reputation as a housekeeper preceded her rise as an author. Here, encircled by a brick frame, Raffald's demure bodice and scarf and a bonnet perched gingerly on her upswept hair depict a robust middle-age woman with a composed demeanor. Her outstretched hand presents a book to the reader in a beckoning gesture. (See Figure 6.1)

At first glance, the image of Elizabeth Raffald is that of a properly decorous English housekeeper, belying her extraordinary life as a popular cookbook author and prominent citizen of Manchester, England. Yet a closer examination of the frontispiece reveals more than a staid, pleasant woman dressed modestly in an apron and headdress partly made by her daughter.[57]

First, Mrs. Raffald does not avert her eyes from the reader's gaze. On the contrary, she looks her reader squarely in the eye. Modesty and submissiveness were two of the virtues of femininity in the eighteenth century.[58] The

Figure 6.1   Mrs. Elizabeth Raffald's frontispiece portrait in *The Experienced English Housekeeper.*

prescriptive literature of the period dictated that women were expected to look shyly to the floor or away from their male conversational partners. Even between women, displays of boastfulness and pride were considered impolite. Yet Raffald's stance is not insubordinate. Her steady gaze is balanced by another slightly exceptional feature: Raffald's extended hand breaks through the constraining frame of sturdy brick that encircles her likeness. It is a personal and intimate gesture, one that draws the reader to the author, connecting them through the presentation of the book. These two unusual features, the gaze and the break in the frame, drew my attention to Raffald's text and life as an exemplar of what some unlettered working- and middle-class women attained by authoring cookery books.

Although details of her life are difficult to reconstruct, her career as an author is traceable. The four daughters born to Joshua (a teacher) and Elizabeth Whitaker, Elizabeth Raffald's parents, "certainly could read and write when they left home to go to work."[59] One of her sisters, Mary, became a confectioner. Elizabeth went into service, a term that meant working as a servant for a family either as an apprentice or for salary. In either case, this period in young people's lives was meant to prepare them for an occupation. Elizabeth probably worked for a number of prominent and noble families, which benefited her when she authored her book. In 1760, she took a post as housekeeper at Arley Hall in England's North Country, where she worked in the home of the Warburton family. She and Lady Warburton, familiarly known as Lady Betty,[60] seemed to enjoy a warm relationship. Elizabeth managed the female servants, kept the accounts of all but the meat bills, and saw to the day-to-day running of the kitchen. She had already learned the techniques of conserving, preserving, and the fancy sugar work that were the hallmark of dinners, balls, and teas on wealthy dining tables. While at Arley Hall she met the gardener, John Raffald, an event that began the next phase of her life.

John and Elizabeth married in 1763 and soon left the Warburton family's employment. For many servants, especially women, marriage often signaled the end of service and frequently a ruined relationship with the employer. Yet this was the beginning of a rapid rise for Elizabeth Raffald. She and John moved to Manchester, where his family owned market gardens. She established a shop where she sold a variety of meats, portable soups (ingredients dried in the sun), sweetmeats, and preserves. Already a regular advertiser in the city's weekly *Manchester Mercury,* Elizabeth realized that she might enhance her business by combining it with a register office, an employment agency for servants. She also developed or contributed to the *Manchester Directory,* which listed workers available to the cottage industry—labor that was done at home and paid for by the piece.

To add to her list of accomplishments, Elizabeth was also a mother. Some say she had sixteen daughters; others claim nine. It is now believed that although Elizabeth had six daughters who were baptized, "only three survived their mother."[61] Her daughters benefited from their mother's success as an author, which placed them all in "comfortable circumstances." "Moreover," social historian J. Jean Hecht points out, "because of the way in which it was achieved, her prosperity lifted her above the usual social status of an innkeeper's wife; she was highly regarded by the most respectable people of Manchester."[62]

Elizabeth Raffald's growing businesses served not only an aristocratic clientele but a growing middle class. Many newly wealthy merchant and commercial families had moved to the country in order to own land, which was the way to achieve political power and social status. Elizabeth's integrated businesses offered it all—the fashionable foods and the servants to provide newly rich bourgeois families with the accoutrements of aristocratic life. Apparently while she was engaged in this entrepreneurial activity, Elizabeth was also writing her cookbook. It is probable that she kept a receipt book of her own while working as servant, cook-maid, and housekeeper to some of England's prominent families.[63] Even if the recipes she published were perfected—even learned—as a servant in another's household, Raffald became author of these culinary creations. Her receipt book from those years of service may have been the basis of her published work.[64]

Raffald minimized her economic liability both by selling copies in advance of publication and by seeking patronage. With over 800 subscriptions sold in advance, the book dedicated to her former employer, Lady Elizabeth Warburton, was a careful investment. Knowing her place, Raffald sought protection by enlisting her former employer as her patron. In her dedication she writes:

To the Honorourable Lady Elizabeth Warburton

Permit me, honoured Madam, to lay before you a work for which I am ambitious of obtaining your Ladyship's approbation, as much as to oblige a great number of my friends, who are well acquainted with the practice I have had in the art of Cookery, ever since I left your Ladyship's family, and have often solicited me to publish for the instruction of their housekeepers.

As I flatter myself I had the happiness of giving satisfaction during my service, Madam, in your family, it would be a still greater encouragement should my endeavours for your service of my sex be honoured with the favourable opinion of so good a judge of propriety and elegance as your Ladyship.

I am not vain enough to propose adding anything to the experienced housekeeper, but hope these receipts (written purely from practice) may be of use to young persons who are willing to improve themselves.

I rely on you Ladyship's candour, and whatever ladies favour this book with reading it, to excuse the plainness of the style; as, in compliance with the desire of my friends, I have studied to express myself so as to be understood by the meanest capacity, and think myself happy in being allowed the honour of subscribing, Madam,[65]

Your Ladyship's most dutiful, most obedient, and

most humble servant,

ELIZABETH RAFFALD[66]

The patronage system, which for centuries had been the means by which artists and writers were supported, was beginning to erode in the seventeenth century, yet there were remnants of the practice in Raffald's time. Authors sought patronage in several forms: One was an outright gift of money to support the author; a second form of patronage might come from the dedicatee's advance purchase of the book through subscription. One reason for seeking such sponsorship is that it might well entice the patron's friends and acquaintances to buy the book in advance. Finally, if nothing else, it was hoped that the patron's name in the book would increase sales. Certainly such a recommendation could assure that the reading public would receive the book without censuring the author. Raffald preempted criticism by asking readers to withhold judgment until they have tried out her book: "When I reflect upon the number of books already in print upon this subject, and with what contempt they are read, I cannot but be apprehensive that this may meet the same fate from some who will censure before they see it or try its value."[67]

Moreover, in another move for self-protection and in keeping with custom, Raffald attempted to exempt herself from any desire for personal gain in her preface. After all, she tells us, "a great number of my friends . . . have solicited me to publish for the instruction of their housekeepers."[68] Yet her deferential tone was modulated by a frank appraisal of her experience and ability to offer her composition to the public:

> The whole work being now completed to my wishes, I think it my duty to render my most sincere and grateful thanks to my most noble and worthy friends who have already shown their good opinion of my endeavors to serve my sex by raising me so large a subscription which far exceeds my expectations. [As] I can faithfully assure my friends that they are wrote from my own experience and not borrowed from any other author, nor glossed over with hard names or words of high style, but wrote in my own plain language. . . . [69]

In the net she cast for readers, Raffald reached up and down the social scale, drawing in even those who could barely read.

The Use of Plain Language in Print

To appease the more literate and high-born among her audience, Mrs. Raffald apologizes for her simple prose, "whatever ladies favour this book with reading it, to excuse the plainness of the style." She has carefully chosen her language: "I have studied to express myself so as to be understood by the weakest capacity."[70] In the prefaces of their cookbooks, seventeenth-, eighteenth-, and later nineteenth-century authors discuss their use of language. Just as Mrs. Wolley eschewed "words to little or no purpose," her successors also used the most direct language to reach the widest possible reading public. Since cookbooks were directed to the range of readers within stratified households, the title pages were addressed to multiple audiences: ladies, mistresses, housekeepers, maids, nurses, and mothers. In order to serve such a broad audience, authors used language they believed would be accessible to all readers, from aristocratic to plebian.

Women were known to be a growing group of consumers of print publications in the eighteenth century. The highly popular novels and romances of the period may have reflected the interests of only a segment of the reading public, cookery books may have had a broader appeal.[71] Servants increasingly joined the ranks of women readers. However, the cost of books was sometimes beyond the meager incomes of working-class women. Yet there were a number of ways that texts might find their way to servants: They could sometimes purchase them in less expensive serial form; receive them as gifts; "borrow them"; or be read to from them.[72] Servants who could read might benefit by developing culinary skills and have better opportunities for employment. Glasse suggests that the ability to read and follow her directions "will be capable of making a tolerable good cook, and those who have the least notion of Cookery cannot miss of being very good ones."[73]

Another reason for women's emphasis on the use of "plain language" or avoiding "the high polite style" of fashionable society, as Hannah Glasse said in her preface, was to retrieve cookery from the professional male chefs with whom some women were competing in the marketplace.

Many seventeenth-century male chefs who were writing for publication, such as Robert May and William Rabisha—although they promised to disclose the art and mystery of cookery in clear terms—wrote in a manner that women, mistresses, and cook-maids alike could not follow. Particularly as some of the male authors were continuing to direct their writings to male professionals, the complexity of the techniques and the lack of familiarity with the technical jargon made deciphering the recipes an overwhelming task for an uninitiated audience.

When this is coupled with the perception—and the reality—of the lower rates of women's literacy, it may be understood why women cookbook authors were perpetually trying to reassure their readers that what followed would be replicable and, above all, comprehensible. By choosing to write in straightforward and unadorned prose, these authors were writing for a wide audience from mistresses and middle-class housewives to servants. While some wrote simply in direct English for barely literate women, others explicitly addressed the importance of reading, writing, and education. This was an important, if inadvertently, political attempt to reach women readers of all ranks and stations. If cookbooks did nothing more than instruct women in cookery, then by itself developing cookery skills would have enabled some young untrained women to find more lucrative employment.[74] While female cooks were never paid as well as male ones, housekeepers and cooks were not as far down on the pay scale as some other servants. As time went on, more women could read. Consequently, when authors did embark on discussions of women's roles, their opinions could reach women across the social spectrum.

Madam Johnson's Present: The Knowledge of Letters

Despite its conservative appearance in a dignified brown leather cover and a frontispiece image of its properly feminine author, *Madam Johnson's Present* (1754) takes a stance on educational reform liberal for its time by advocating that some form of education should be available to everyone.[75] It is a bumpy, roller-coaster book covering subjects from law to literacy, through marketing and cooking, to the proclaimed eternal rewards of service meant to embrace a wide readership up and down the social scale, from mistresses of households to servants.

If read from front to back, Johnson's book is a textual finishing school for young ladies who wish to learn proper middle-class behavior. Reversed, it is a manual for servants.[76] In between are sections useful to women from all ranks and stations. When conceiving the book, the author thought it a useful text for entire households. In this regard her work, like Wolley's, addresses the gamut of women's household responsibilities including general cooking instructions (how to boil a ham and a tongue, how to make a pease pottage and a fine syllabub) and, further, the correct spelling of words used in marketing, cooking, pickling, and preserving. Unlike Wolley and Raffald, however, Johnson's skills ostensibly arise from the management of her own household, not the households of others. The lofty place from which Johnson writes is quite different from the hands-on experience of her author-cook predecessors. In fact, a portrait of Madam Johnson on the frontispiece shows no hands at all.

Her frontispiece portrait rests delicately on a pedestal inscribed "Madam Johnson, the accomplish'd Lady." Johnson thus has announced herself as a woman of status who has mastered the domestic arts from cookery to confectionary, from sewing to supervising. On this mastery she rests her authority. It is a confident authorial voice that she presents to the reader.

Her image is of a modestly seductive, demure woman. Mary Johnson averts her eyes from the reader by turning her head in the direction in which her curls lie delicately on her bosom. Her hands rest out of sight. They are, perhaps, hands that do not labor. Interestingly, Johnson makes no apology for the publication of her book; perhaps this omission is an indication of her class. We do not learn what prompted her to write this treatise for young women or what reputation she enjoyed either as a historical figure or an authorial one.

Since her book was popular on both sides of the Atlantic,[77] we can infer that the author of this 1754 household manual was "no improper pocket companion for the most able and experienced housewife" and "young women" presumably of the middle class. For its young middle-class readers, Madam Johnson's text shapes an image of genteel femininity and lauds marriage as a pinnacle of a woman's life. Madam Johnson says:

> Marriage being one of the most important Events of Life, and the End to which the Attractions of Beauty, the Arts of Dress, and the internal Accomplishments which heighten and stamp a Value on these Charms, principally lead, every law relating to this great Transaction must be considered, not only as a matter of Curiousity, but as an Affair of such Moment as to deserve to be particularly and carefully attended to. And indeed, since the marriage State, when wisely entered upon, is the source of the truest and most solid Happiness, every unmarried Lady must look upon the Forms of Admission into it as something in which she is peculiarly concerned.[78]

Hers is a primer on how a woman can achieve the goal of marriage. She tells the reader that marriage is a woman's ultimate aim and that everything the reader strives to become should be directed to that end. Beauty should be embellished with clothing and feminine accomplishments: domestic competence, grace, and education befitting a woman's rank. From the first page to the last, the text describes the talents, skills, and discipline a woman requires to cultivate her "Charms" to become more marriageable, to enter into that blissful state, and to manage a household with utmost grace and feminine capability.

The text opens with the author's interpretation of the recently passed 1754 Marriage Act, an act of Parliament that attempted to prevent unapproved or clandestine marriages. The Marriage Act passed in the same year as the book was published required the "Banns of Matrimony [to be] published in the Parish-Church, or some Publick Chapel . . . three Sundays before the marriage."[79] Johnson cautions that "the notice must be done in writing at least seven days before the announcement." Parental consent was required for both parties. Without it the marriage was considered void. The law did not include inhabitants of Scotland, the colonies, or Quakers or Jews.

Johnson wants to inform her readers about the right way to go about getting married. In order to comply with the Marriage Act with refinement and gentility, Johnson offers her readers a few model letters for couples announcing their intentions to marry. Although Johnson's intention may have been to impart proper decorum to her readers, her emphasis on the importance of literacy presages her sections on the instruction of reading and writing. But before she embarks on these lessons in literacy, she feels the need to advocate for proper education for women first.

Overall, more women were literate during the eighteenth century than in the seventeenth century and literacy was greater among women in urban areas than in rural areas. Women of gentility were expected to read, to teach others to do so, and to write "in a neat legible hand." Johnson, however, takes her guidance one step further than many cookery and household advice books by reprinting a lecture by the "celebrated Dr. Watts" on the value of education and reading and writing, in particular. Dr. Watts was an eighteenth-century advocate of education even for the poor. It has been said of him "that he was in advance of his time in his views on education."[80] Watts enjoyed immense popularity in America, where his hymns, devotions, and essays enjoyed a wide reading public. By reproducing Watts's views on education, which were progressive and liberal for the period, Madam Johnson has tacitly given her support and approval to his stance.

"'The Knowledge of Letters (Says that ingenious Author) is one of the greatest Blessings that ever God bestow'd on the Children of Men,'" Johnson quotes Watts. Without the ability to read and write, she cautions, we would lose the "'the rich Treasure of Knowledge'" of the past "'for those that shall come after us.'"[81] Johnson continues to quote Dr. Watts:

> Thus Letters give us a Sort of Immortality in this World, and they support our immortal Hopes in the next.
> Those who wilfully neglect this sort of Knowledge will live and die in Ignorance both of the Things of God and Man.[82]

Through literacy, Watts says, "we may acquaint ourselves with what is done in all the distant Parts of the World" and "revive all the past Ages of Men but the greatest Blessing of all, is the Knowledge of the Holy Scriptures, wherein God has appointed his Servants, in ancient Times to write down the Discoveries which he has made of his Power."[83]

For Johnson, Watts, and others, to read and reflect on God's word directly was the impetus for learning how to read during the early modern period. The ability to read the Bible and become conversant with scripture had long been an argument in support of literacy for both women and men. Using Watts as her authority, Johnson makes a case for the wider uses of reading and writing: as a link to the past, to the future, and to other parts of the world.

Interestingly, Johnson attributes the dispositions of passion, appetite, and lust to the male gender. On the other hand, knowledge, learning, and the soul are feminine and potent. It was the feminine capacity for knowledge and learning that could awaken man's "reasoning faculty" and unfold the soul's "intellectual powers."[84] Animal instincts may be quelled by knowledge, science, and reason. Like a butterfly emerging from its cocoon, the soul is freed with knowledge. Johnson continues: "When Learning has spread her Influence on the soul, by which I always mean Science and real Knowledge, she wakes, as from a Dream, and begins to be acquainted with herself, her Powers, her Connections, and Relations to Things without her, and learns that first and greatest Branch of human Science, a Knowledge of herself."[85] Here is Madam Johnson at her most eloquent and poetic about the power of knowledge. But knowledge for Johnson is scientific and rational. Is she arguing that with education comes freedom and possibility? Does education unlock an individual's potential to reach beyond her circumstances? For Madam Johnson education can liberate an individual only within certain limits.

Johnson soon leaves aside the general discussion of education and singles out her "fair" reader with specific assertions about learning.

> Having premis'd thus much, we shall devote the remaining Part of this preliminary Discourse to the peculiar service of the Fair Sex, and shall therein take the Liberty of pointing out to them, not only those Accomplishments which are within their Reach, but such as must necessarily be put in Practice, if they ever expect to shine, and live with any tolerable Degree of Credit and Reputation in the World.[86]

Women may become accomplished by first achieving competence in housewifely skills. They may embellish their talents with a passing familiarity of "polite Literature," such as sermons, histories, and epics. Next Johnson elaborates on what she means by a "well-directed education in a woman's life": "The Acquisitions of the following knowledge [in the book] are therefore requisite to make her 'the ornament of her sex.'"[87] And further:

> In the first place she should be able to read with Propriety and a good Grace; to write a neat legible hand; to have a tolerable Insight into the first Rudiments of Accounts, and the methods of keeping a proper Diary; and in the next, to know to lay her money out with judgement abroad; to be conversant, in short, with all the various Branches of Cookery, confectionary &c at home; and to be dextrous in the Art of Carving at Table, in private or publick, when Ever Occasion should require it.[88]

In this respect Johnson does not differ from many of her contemporaries who felt that a woman should be educated in the domestic arts. Beyond that, reading and writing enhanced a woman's charms as long as her skills were employed in domestic concerns. Johnson values learning for women that is focused solely on the welfare of the household.

For the rest of humanity, she imposes the limitations of fate. Education should not exceed one's birthright. Neither men nor women should be "so thirsty after knowledge" that they move beyond their social roles. Knowledge should "render them most useful in that particular Station of Life in which Providence has cast them."[89] While education is critical to conducting one's life, the education Johnson champions does not engender upward mobility. It is an education that will enable women to perform better in the position to which they have been born.

But Johnson is not content to leave the reader with the exhortation to read and write and to gain an education appropriate to her rank and station. She proceeds to deliver specific instructions on how to master the alphabet in reading and writing, presumably for her middle-class readers:[90] "The Alphabet is divided into Vowels and Consonants, the former signifying a Simple Sound; and the latter sounding with, or in Conjunction with another."[91] Directions on how to hold a pen and form the letters are written in a chapter entitled "A New and Easy Introduction to the Art of Writing." Johnson provides a rationale for developing the skill: to make the "blushing scribbler" more desirable for marriage.

All should be fair, that beauteous Woman frames;
Strive to excel, with Ease the Pen will move,
And pretty lines add Charms to infant LOVE.[92]

For her middle-class readers, Johnson argues that writing increases the likelihood of attracting a suitable husband. And education encompassing reading, writing, and figures is essential to managing a household. Literacy skills enhance a genteel woman's appeal and desirability on the marriage market when coupled with "modesty," "sense," and "good nature." Johnson makes her statement about women's proper comportment as boldly as she cautions women against boldness: "The second Qualification is Modesty—modest demeanor and bashfulness which is the peculiar ornament of her sex. In men boldness designates courage, in a woman boldness suggests haughtiness and assurance. Even if she has feminine softness, no one will notice it if masculine characteristics are evident."[93]

Despite this emphasis on writing as a means of attracting a suitable husband, Johnson's instructions on the art of reading and writing are not explicitly exclusive. She addresses her advice to "every Young Woman" : "There can be no edifice erected without a Foundation. Every YOUNG WOMAN, therefore, who is desirous of attaining to a compleat Knowledge of her native Language, must, in the first Place, make herself a Mistress of the Letters, whereof all the various Words made use of in that Language are compos'd."[94]

Shall we take Johnson at her word? Does she mean *every* woman? Were her lessons directed only at middle-class readers? Compounding the confusion is an advertisement, perhaps written by the publisher and not with Johnson's consent, for her book that appeared in 1770 that stated that the book would be "A very proper Christmas Box, or New Years Gift, for Servant-Maids. This day is published, The Fifth Edition, to which are added, some plain and very necessary Directions to Maid-Servants."[95] Who might the reader be who ponders Johnson's instructions on how to read and write? May we assume that this book is meant as much for servants as for mistresses? Johnson does not explicitly address one social group but rather embraces the range of women who would be found in a middle-class household. Though class is never diminished in importance in the book's advice for readers, the book as a whole is directed to a common cultural space, the entire household.

Having finished schooling readers of all classes in middle-class feminine arts, Johnson moves on to the specific duties of other members of the household, the servants. In fact, she concludes her book with a section devoted to the comportment of servants. It is no surprise that a section devoted to servants appears at the back of the book. The placement of the components of a text reveals as much as the words themselves. Books, like bodies and other physical structures, may be used to symbolize such things as the social order. Eliza Smith noted this in the preface of her book, *The Compleat Housewife,* discussed earlier in this chapter. Servants lived below or behind the main living quarters; they ate separately often in the company of their peers. In Johnson's book, being last was being least, although it is likely that this placement was an invitation for servants to read their mistress's book from the beginning. Here is what Johnson told servants: "The first Duty incumbent on you, in that humble Station allotted you by Providence, is to pay a just Regard to all the lawful Commands of those in Authority over you; and this Obedience is expressly required of you by the Apostle Paul, in his Epistle."[96]

Johnson uses divine authority in her "serious Exhortation too Maid-Servants, in regard to the Regulation of their conduct." For Johnson, rank and

station are inextricably bound to a divine moral code based on religious prescription. Obedience, submission, and integrity in conduct despite even
harsh conditions of employment were required by biblical precept.

Furthermore, servants should strive to serve their masters and mistresses
with "chearfulness and a willing Mind." They should at all costs avoid becoming "eye servants." By that Johnson meant that even without supervision—the mistress's observation—servants should conduct themselves as if
such authority were present. In other words, servants should have integrity,
performing always as if they were being watched. To serve well and dili-
gently, without succumbing to the temptations of dishonesty or slothfulness,
were a servant's first commandments. Reward would come eventually from
God for having accepted "the humble Station allotted you by Providence."[97]

Despite her own biases, Madam Johnson nonetheless made the tools of
literacy readily available to women of all stations and ranks. It is easy to
imagine servants—as well as mistresses—poring over her sections on the
value of education and instructions on how to read and write. Was *Madam
Johnson's Present* inadvertently a conduct book for young women who might
cross class boundaries? Was she offering models of middle-class decorum and
domesticity that inspired passage not only from single to married life but
from working-class servant to middle-class mistress? We cannot know how
the book was read any more than we can know with certainty why Johnson
wrote it. Her message, however, advanced standards of education that by the
end of that century would be widespread.

Eliza Haywood (1693–1756):
A Present for a Servant-Maid

If Madam Johnson's text prepared readers for a world in which women
reached for one goal, marriage, the works of Eliza Haywood suggested that
men could destroy women's autonomy. One of the most prolific and popular writers of English amatory fiction of the early eighteenth century, Eliza
Haywood considered herself an educator of young women. Yet her notion
of education included more than learning letters. In her writings she warns
young women about the dangers of "male tyranny."[98] Her romances turn on

the themes of love, loss, and sometimes the redemption of heroines who suc-
cumbed to men's seductions. Haywood's novels warned young women about
the perils of love and taught them how to resist men's control. In her slender conduct/cookery pamphlet, *A Present for the Servant-Maid or, The Sure
Means of gaining Love and Esteem, The Whole Calculated for making both the
Mistress and Maid happy,* Haywood tackles the same issues:[99] concern for
women's virtue and mindfulness against seductive men.

Haywood's own life was unconventional. Little is known about her early
life. Born Eliza Fowler (c. 1693), the daughter of a shopkeeper, she educated
herself in literature and languages, "more liberal than is ordinarily allowed to
Persons of my Sex,"[100] she says. She married a man much older than herself,
a clergyman, the Reverend Valentine Haywood. After a few years of marriage, Haywood left her husband. Having already published her successful
first novel, *Love in Excess* (1719), Haywood first became an actress and later
succeeded in supporting herself and her children as an author. Whether her
scandalous reputation resulted from her brief career as an actress or the topics she took up in her novels is disputable.

As a novelist, Haywood's early career was marked by criticism. Because
her romances were "known for their passionate intrigue and amorous, often
titillating, adventure,"[101] and her heroines often behaved rebelliously,[102] her
male literary contemporaries considered her disreputable; her novels were
judged to be corrupting to young women.[103] Others contend that her de-
tractors, among them Alexander Pope, simply reviled all women scribblers;
Haywood was only one of many hack writers for whom Pope had little respect. But despite her contemporaries' critical reviews, Haywood was a popular success. However, as a result of Pope's attack in *The Dunciad,* Haywood
stopped writing under her name for a period of time, although she continued to write and publish anonymously.[104] Her literary career languished for
years before she returned to public life as editor of *The Female Spectator,* a
magazine for women.[105]

After Haywood had resumed writing, more than a few of her contempo-
raries claimed she had redeemed herself by becoming a "virtuous" woman.[106]
Clara Reeve, author of *The Progress of Romance through Times, Countries and
Manners* (1785), declares that Haywood "repented her faults, and employed

the latter part of her life in expiating the offences of the former . . . she certainly wrote some amorous novels in her youth."[107] Reeve continues: "Mrs. Heywood had the singular good fortune to recover a lost reputation, and the yet greater honour to atone for her errors.—She devoted the remainder of her life and labours to the service of virtue."[108]

Perhaps her early and later careers as a writer should not be seen as worlds apart. Some have argued that *all* her work was directed to the instruction of women.[109] Haywood's early work is characterized by what critic Mary Anne Schofield has called eighteenth-century women writers' "quiet rebellion," a "double writing" in which women authors describe in fiction what cannot take place in reality.[110] Renewed interest in Haywood credits her with revealing to eighteenth-century women readers their "imprisoned and exploited state."[111] Moreover, she contributed to the period's changing images of women as "seekers after personal freedom and identity."[112]

In her writing, Haywood depicts independent and authoritative single mothers, women in supportive relationships with other women who move confidently and unencumbered in a female world. This self-sufficient world collapses in the presence of men; women's strength and autonomy is possible only in isolation.[113]

The stories of women's treacherous relations with men that characterize Haywood's prose fiction are also woven into her nonfiction writing, including her cookery and conduct book. They too reiterate her moral instructions for women related to, among others, "Chastity," "Temptations from Men," and "Lying."

Haywood was not the only eighteenth-century author to depict the troubling situations in which young women might find themselves.[114] However, she may have authored her cookery/conduct book to address the same practical issues in another literary form because different readers may have chosen different kinds of reading. Class, region, levels of literacy, available leisure time, occupation, taste, and position may have been factors in women's reading choices. Thus, delivering the same message in different genres would more likely reach a wider audience.

Thus, in 1743, between her career as a novelist and her guardianship of *The Female Spectator,* Haywood wrote her advice manual and cookbook for servants. Although her advice book is written from the perspectives of both employer and servant, the first section of the book addresses maidservants directly and solely. In contrast to Johnson's volume, which is directed to mistresses first and servants last, Haywood's volume singles out the servant-maid.[115] Haywood begins familiarly:

> Dear Girls,
>   I Think there cannot be a greater Service done to the Commonwealth, (of which you are a numerous Body) than to lay down some general rules for your Behaviour which, if observed, will make your Condition as happy to your-selves as it is necessary to others.

She advises her readers not to accept a position unless they intend to "*stay in it.*" In this admonition she writes from the position of employer. (Apparently a problem in eighteenth-century England was the incessant movement of servants from one position to another.)[116] Yet after this admonition her perspective changes back again to that of a servant looking for a job. She warns readers that they must be careful in finding a post. Here Haywood points out how young girls may be misled by appearances:

> There are some Houses which appear well by Day, that it would be little safe for a modest Maid to sleep in at Night: I do not mean those Coffee-houses, Bagnio's &c . . . for in those the very Aspect of the Persons who keep them are sufficient to show what manner of Trade they follow; but Houses who have no public Shew of Business, are richly furnished, and where the Mistress has an Air of the strictest Modesty. . . . Yet under such roofs, and under the Sanction of such Women as I have described as would startle even the Owners of some common Brothels.[117]

Haywood urges her unsuspecting readers to be wary of people who might deceive them. Luxurious but respectable-looking houses also could be sexual playgrounds. A not-infrequent scenario in this period was the luring of attractive young girls, fresh from the country, into prostitution. Unsophisticated, they could not imagine the situations into which they might be brought, so the worldly Haywood was determined to educate and warn them about the dangers.

Haywood also admonishes young women to have realistic expectations about their positions and to develop good working habits. Maidservants are to avoid "sloth," "excessive eating" and "drinking," "idleness," "snuff," and "alcohol." Among the many vices of which serving maids are guilty, "liquorishness" is unacceptable. Haywood advises,

> As small errors frequently lead on to greater, there are two things I wou'd advise you not to give way to: The first is a Desire or a Craving after Dainties, by which I mean Such things as either are not in the House, or are not allowed to come to your Table; It looks silly and childish in a Servant to be laying out her money in baubling Cakes, Nuts, and things which she has not real occasion for, and can do her no good; and no less impudent to presume to touch any thing her Mistress has order'd to be set by; who, tho' she may not be of so cruel a Disposition as a certain Lady, who not long since sent her Maid to Brideswell for taking a Slice of Pudding, has Reason to be angry at having any thing diminish'd she reserv'd for her own eating, or those on whom she intended to bestow it.[118]

Prison is quite a harsh punishment for a dish some would call unappetizing.[119] Clearly sweets were a category of food declared out of bounds for servants. Their employers discouraged them from spending money on sugar treats by labeling them "silly" and "childish." At this time, there was a general cry of alarm that even working-class families were drinking tea with sugar, clearly an indication that luxury foods were filtering down the social scale.[120] Servants might actually contract with their employers to permit this luxury.[121] Food, like clothing, was one of the markers of class.[122] It was one way to discern who was a peer and who was not.

If food and clothing were class-bound, so too were relationships that could lead to marriage. The pitfalls Haywood's fictional heroines face in her romances and novels are also explored in her conduct and cookery book. She devotes five sections of this book to servants' temptations from men: "Temptations from the Master"; "Behaviour to him if a Single Man"; "Behaviour if a married Man"; "Temptations from the Master's Son"; "Temptations from Gentlemen Lodgers."[123] Servant girls were to avoid delicate and dangerous situations with men, masters, their sons, and gentlemen lodgers: "Suffer not, therefore, your Hearts, much less your Innocence, to be tempted with a

Prospect wherein the *best* that can arrive is bad enough."[124] Haywood's predictions are harsh. Young women could too easily be snared by flattery and the hope of finding love and marriage with a man of higher social status. Haywood believes that such marriages are never happy, let alone likely.

However, there is some cunning in her prescriptive advice.[125] A maid's response to the temptations of her master should depend on his marital status. If he is single, Haywood suggests:

> Let no wanton Smile, or light coquet Air give him room to suspect you are not so much displeased with the Inclination he has for you as you would seem; for if he once imagine you deny but for the sake of Form, it will the more enflame him, and render him more pressing than ever. Let your Answers, therefore, be delivered with the greatest Sedateness; shew that you are truly sorry, and more ashamed than vain, that he finds anything in you to like . . . but if you fail in this laudable Ambition, if he persists in his Importunities, and you have Reason to fear he will make Use of other Means than Persuasions to satisfy his brutal Appetite . . . you have nothing to do, but, on the first symptom that appears of such a Design, to go directly out of his House.[126]

It is difficult to say whether Haywood is effectively teaching her female readers how to succeed in snaring a husband by enflaming his passion but refusing to yield.

Despite her advocacy for women, her stance reified the class structure; rank and station determined customary behavior. Haywood oscillates between educating servants for their own protection and advocating for employers. Departures from the norm were inexcusable. The category of servants known as "eye-servants"—servants who were responsible only if they were supervised—was particularly loathsome.[127] Haywood points out that "People who keep Servants, keep them for their Ease, not to increase their Care; and nothing can be more cruel as well as more unjust than to disappoint them in a View they have so much right to expect."[128] Integrity, faithfulness, and obedience were characteristics for servants to develop. The reward for such service was a good relationship with employers and perhaps a future entitlement of protection and assistance.

Haywood concludes her book of advice with "Directions for going to Market," and the most basic recipes for "dressing meat, fowl, fish," "for making puddings, pyes &c.," and "for washing." Her primary concern in this book is not the performance of cookery, but the realization of character.

Haywood's cookery and advice book was published one year before she became the editor of *The Female Spectator.* What was her motivation for writing this book? Did she write it only to earn money? Or did she want to reach an even broader audience of young women through this venue? Was she attempting to rescue her reputation? So allied was domesticity and feminine virtue that authoring *A Present for the Servant-maid* may have been an act of redemption, one of several in Haywood's later career "in the service of virtue." Another edition followed in 1771. This one, with its slightly altered title, *A New Present for the Servant-Maid,* may not have been written by Eliza Haywood at all. If it was, it was published posthumously because she died in 1756.

A New Present for the Servant-Maid was somewhat different from Haywood's first effort in the genre. Whereas the earlier book was primarily an advice book and a cookery book second, the latter was most definitely a cookbook with some advice to servants. The remarkable frontispiece depicts a young woman in a kitchen bent over a cookbook. (Looking closely, one discovers it is the very book being sold.) Intently reading the recipes, she is poised, spoon in hand, ready to return to her work using Mrs. Haywood's book as her reference and guide.

This illustration is not the first image of a woman reading. However, it is among the first portrayals of a woman *reading while cooking.* Earlier illustrations in cookbooks depict women working in kitchens or portray women reading while at rest or planning the day's work. They were not toiling over a stove but instead were sitting in reverie or in discussion with their maids.[129] (See Figure 6.2) The illustration from Haywood's cookbook suggests the role that cookery and conduct books and their authors played in the eighteenth century. Although it is not a straightforward cause-and-effect relationship, this literature of the everyday helped to shape the attitudes and behaviors of women from all classes. By the close of the century, literacy had become widespread and books were directed noticeably to female servants.

Engrav'd for Haywoods New Present for a Servant Maid.

Figure 6.2   Frontispiece to Eliza Haywood's *New Present for a Servant-Maid* depicting a woman reading instructions from the cook book while cooking.

Women authors such as Raffald, Glasse, Johnson, and Haywood had become cultural authorities in the domain of cooking and conduct, and the next generation of young women embraced their publications.

Whether Haywood authored this *New Present for a Servant-Maid* or not is insignificant. Even fifteen years after her death, her name and reputation as an educator were thought to be prominent enough to sell this book. Like Haywood, all of the women authors examined in this chapter used their knowledge of culinary and domestic arts to reach further goals—both for themselves and for the women who read their books. They parlayed the culinary skills they developed in day-to-day living into areas of expertise and became published authorities. In turn, they offered this knowledge to other women, who used it to enhance their skills in their own households or to earn a livelihood. In the arena of cookery and domestic advice, women had become strong and influential voices. Those public voices, and all that they epitomized, were carried across the Atlantic to the colonies to guide readers in the New World.

SEVEN

Recipe and Household Literature as Social and Political Commentary

> *More than that, it is wrong—morally wrong, so as the individual is concerned; and injurious beyond calculation to the interest of our country. To what are the increasing beggary, and discouraged exertions of the present period owing? A multitude of causes have no doubt tended to increase the evil; but the root of the whole matter is the extravagance of all classes of people!*
>
> —*Lydia Maria Child*, The Frugal Housewife[1]

As much recipes for living as formulae for cooking, cookbooks are forums for discussing the conduct of life. Even the most pragmatic of cookbooks alludes to both a moral world and an aesthetic to be tended. Although the most salient function of cookbooks is to provide instruction in the domestic arts, women have used them and household manuals in subtle and ingenious ways. Living within the constraints of their respective eras, they have used these texts to examine and shape their own and others' lives.

For women of varied cultural and religious backgrounds, the genre of cookery literature—and the terms of kitchen practice—have provided a vehicle for constructing, defending, and transgressing social and cultural borders. Rather than conform to the images and ideals that cookbook authors constructed, women found them useful points of departure for reflection. Prescriptive literature does not necessarily represent the "reality" of the period in which it was written nor does it reflect the ways in which women (people) actually behaved. None of the cookbooks I discuss is meant to suggest typicality. What *is* remarkable is that women of diverse experiences and backgrounds have chosen the genre as a suitable place to probe issues of social and cultural identity.

In dedications, prefaces, and introductions, as well as with recipes and titles and other explanatory material, the writers told stories. Some books were elaborate, if not coded, explorations of identity—of self; of other women; and of home, community, and country—which supported or challenged (sometimes both) the status quo. *The New Housekeeper's Manual,*[2] coauthored by Catharine Beecher and Harriet Beecher Stowe, is one such text. Other texts, such as Amelia Simmons' *American Cookery,*[3] offered modest prefaces in keeping with prevailing norms about women's public demeanor, social disruptions disguised by unassuming rhetorical strategies. These introductions, large or small, encoded images of the "feminine," some of which were sanctioned by an authoritative culture and some of which were in opposition to normative standards. What the cookbook authors put forward as "feminine" was entangled with other social features, among them race, class, ethnicity, and religion.

Because gender embraced other features of social life, the discussion of women's roles, obligations, and responsibilities in these texts was also a site for what literary critic Anne E. Goldman calls an "autobiographical presence, self-reflection, and political commentary."[4] In these texts and through them women debated the merits and flaws of customary kitchen and culinary practices that highlighted and demarcated social and cultural boundaries. The texts—neither univocal nor without ambivalence and contradictions—encoded messages of vigilance and transgression.

Even while cookbook writers valorized women's work and embraced an expanding consciousness and community of women through an increasingly literate readership, often other women were excluded from the community defined by the authors. It was not just published, prominent author-cooks, such as Amelia Simmons, the Beechers, and Lydia Maria

Child, whose work informed and shaped the changing images of American women and cultural standards from the late eighteenth through early twentieth centuries; the vernacular writing of women whose works remained unpublished or printed in limited quantities for charitable and fund-raising purposes also had an effect.

"How to make a right Presbyterian in two days": Catharine Cotton, Her Booke, 1698

Although this chapter focuses on American cookbooks, antecedents of social commentary in women's culinary writings may be found in English manuscripts and published books, such as those of Hopestill Brett and Hannah Wolley, dating to the seventeenth century. Secreted in the middle of an otherwise ordinary seventeenth-century recipe book, a poem discloses the attitudes and values of its compiler. In keeping with other manuscript texts belonging to affluent women, Catharine Cotton's text is luxurious. Her name appears prominently in several places: embossed in gold on both the back and the front leather-bound covers and on each of the first three pages, with the word "piety" in tiny script beneath the inscription on the first page. The word "piety" at the beginning of her book suggests that Cotton sought or wanted to convey an image of godliness and devotion to duty. The first half of the book contains recipes for cooking; the second half, turned upside down and opened from back to front, discloses medicinals. The inscription on the first page reads: "*Catharine Cotton, Her Booke, given her May the 21th, 1698.*"

Cotton lived during a tumultuous period in English history. The seventeenth century had been marked by civil war and religious foment sparked by Protestant sects known as dissenters. During this civil and religious strife, and because society was in upheaval, opportunities arose for women to hone their skills as writers and speakers. Although still limited by societal norms of appropriate female conduct, women found fissures in the foundations of society, and they used them. On behalf of God and country, of husband and children, they preached the word of God, wrote petitions to save their lands and homes, and defended their reputations against slander.[5]

By the time Catharine Cotton wrote her book, at the close of the seventeenth century, the monarchy, although undeniably changed, had been restored to power. With the Restoration, women once again were installed in traditional feminine roles, which were perhaps more intensely conventional than before the war. Moreover, reactions against the secular and religious reform movements that had toppled the monarchy were equally fervent.[6] It is perhaps with this reactionary spirit that Cotton includes among her medicinal and cookery recipes a verse that bitingly describes a dissenting religious group, the Presbyterians.[7] We do not know whether Cotton was its author or if she copied it from print or oral tradition. However, she writes in her own hand: "*A receipt how to make a right presbyterian in two days.*" (See Figure 7.1)

Take the herbes of hypocrasie and ambition of each two handfuls of ye flowers of formality two scruples of ye spirit of pride and malice two drams each of the seeds of contention & stubbornness of each four ounces, of the cordial of reflection and lyes of each fifty ounces, of the root of moderation as small a quantity as you please.

Drink the cordial, chop the herbs, powder the seeds, slice the roots, bruse them alltogether in a morter of vainglory with pestles of contradiciton & deceit, put them in a pan of [—] water to be infus'd over a brimstone fire of fained seal which is hypocrasie adding thereto a hundred ounces of ye syrup of self-conceit, covetousness & self-ends, when luke-warm let ye person that is to be made a presbyterian take ten spoonfulls night and morning, and when his mouth is full of this hellish compound let him make wry mouths and squeese out some tears of dissmulation.

This will do wonders and make the schismaticks maintain of [—], run down the church, delude the people, justife dissention, forment contention, & rebellion & call it all liberty of conscience.

Although women's cookery books often incorporate religious texts and beliefs, the rituals of life and death inscribed for remembrance, Cotton's religious verse was not meant to comfort. It was meant to rankle and mock; it is stinging and critical. The dissenting religious group may have been threatening or odious to Catharine Cotton's social world. It is tempting to guess that her rank and station were aristocratic and that Cotton and her family were royalists, faithful to the crown; they may have been adherents of the Church of England. The verse's placement in a book of recipes indicates the salience of religious conflict in Cotton's times.

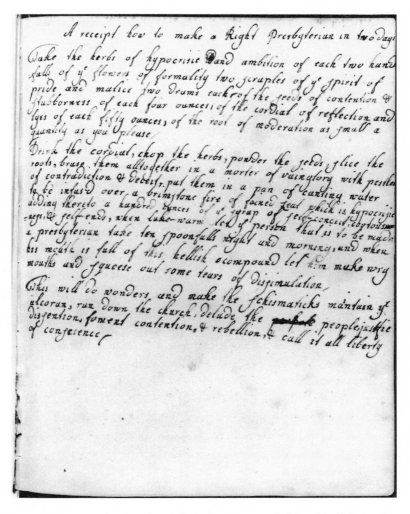

Figure 7.1   *"A receipt how to make a Right Presbyterian in two days"* found in Catharine Cotton's seventeenth-century cookery manuscript.

This late-seventeenth-century mistress hid her opinions in the recesses of her cookbook. Once found, the recipe poem calls attention to itself. Versified recipes had been in existence for centuries.[8] And although this poem is not rhymed, in the rhythmic and repetitive structure of the lines and its formulaic quality, it is similar to recipes of ancient books.[9] What is different is that Cotton's recipe is not about making food but about making human beings. Human vices correspond to ingredients for cooking: "*Take the herbes of hypocrasie and ambition of each two handfuls of the flowers of formality two scruples of the spirit of pride and malice two drams.* . . ." The human vessel in which the malevolent traits of "*self conceit*" and "*contention*" are compounded is likened to a "*morter of vainglory.*" In proportions equal to their negative effects the list of vices is enumerated; the outcome is a malevolent being. It concludes with the recipient taking "*ten spoonfuls night and morning.*"

This allusion to the creation of evil, through the mysteries of alchemy and experimentation, suggests the devil's own handiwork and witchcraft. Not only are the "*schismaticks*" themselves evil incarnate, but the outcome of their malevolence is divisiveness, a rupture in the social fabric. The poem calls attention to the personal characteristics a pious and devout woman would find repugnant and unsuitable in human behavior, among them self-conceit, stubbornness, pride, and malice. Above all, the disruption of the social order with "*contentiousness,*" "*dissention*" and "*rebellion*" compounds the sins of pride. In a society predicated on rigid hierarchy, stratification, and the maintenance of the status quo then in the midst of social and geographic mobility and change, a disputation was seen as a breakdown in the social order.

Accusations of witchcraft play a role in societies in which individuals and groups threaten to disrupt the social order.[10] Whenever social and cultural borders are transgressed and endangered, those who seek change become vulnerable. Attacks may be redirected at those who violate the boundaries. As the tables are turned, the violators become culpable for crimes—witchcraft—they did not commit.

Yet Cotton also may have enjoyed the poem as much for its style as for its sentiments. It is cleverly written and displays the kind of wit and wordplay then in vogue. Although it is not unusual to find poetry on the pages of cookery books, its placement in the center of her book, surrounded only by blank pages, indicates that this particular poem was perhaps not quite suitable for everyone to see. Cotton may have tried to conceal it from servants. A more mundane explanation is that she simply needed a piece of paper on which to write the poem but did not want the verse to interrupt the cookery and medicinal sections of her book. Whatever the reason for its positioning, the bitterness of the poem's sentiments may have reflected Cotton's sentiments and others of her class and station.

American Cookery:
"For the rising class of females"

It is, then, in the Anglophone tradition for cookbook writers to speak about other than culinary matters. It is not surprising to find America's first cookbook is both a political and gastronomic treatise. Until that time, English cookbooks, such as those penned by Richard Bradley, Susannah Carter, and Eliza Smith, were imported or published in America for American readers. Although "America came late to cookbook publishing," *American Cookery* has been acclaimed "a culinary declaration of independence."[11] A rising middle class, a burgeoning publishing industry, and a country that had "recently acquired nationhood" required a cookbook of its own.[12] The author, Amelia Simmons, who declared herself "an American Orphan" on the title page, set the stage for a compilation of recipes for conduct and cooking.

In the years following the War of Independence, an emerging focus on women as invaluable nurturers of the republic's future citizenry,[13] and "the selling of patriotism"[14] so-called by social historian Ann Fairfax Witherington, engendered this "original work in this country."[15] Twenty years after the Revolution, signs of patriotism for private and public consumption were produced. Visual icons and designs for newspapers, plaques and other objects celebrated America's victory over the British, instilling, according to Witherington, a national consciousness.[16] Simmons's cookbook, which asserted a national identity, was as much symbolic as practical. This first printed American culinary voice provided recipes in a vernacular idiom for food preparation in the New World.

American Cookery offers not only guidance in cooking; its brief preface also advises women on the importance of a virtuous character and how to achieve it. Simmons promotes the egalitarian ideals of the new republic to all while she entices her readers with an intimate glimpse of the good life by revealing upper-class culinary secrets. In her prefatory statements, Simmons

departs only slightly from her English counterparts, who were still influenc-
ing American cuisine and providing guidance to women. Yet in these seemingly trivial departures, she alludes to prevailing conceptions of women in
postwar America.

Moreover, Simmons's introduction focuses on the social and political tensions that existed in the new republic.[17] In her modest introduction she
sought to strike a balance between tradition and innovation, age and youth,
and resistance and flexibility, among other issues. However, her admonitions
and instructions were directed primarily to women. Simmons's depiction of
the fickleness of fashion in the domestic sphere may be seen as an opportunity to highlight the debate about the fledgling nation's competing values for
women. Once active patriots in the war effort, with its close, women were
again relegated to domestic life, albeit with a slightly altered mission: the
moral education of the young.[18] With this goal, existing educational structures were the locus of debate by women (and men) as they struggled to balance tradition and innovation and women's roles in a new political and social
context. For the moment, women remained at the margins of society.[19]

Why was the first American cookbook ostensibly written by an illiterate
orphan, with recipes requiring indigenous resources, and in a vernacular
idiom that championed sentiments of self-improvement and self-sufficiency?
Written by a working woman, *American Cookery,* designed to be used by "a
rising generation of females in America,"[20] presupposed both the literacy of
her readers and the need for a distinctly American text using indigenous
foodstuffs. The book evokes the New World and republic as deftly as any
cookbook as it rewards its readers with a sensate portrayal of cuisine and culture and a social lens through which to view them.

The importance of *American Cookery* resides not only in its inclusion of
novelty; it is the first to present both adaptations of English recipes *and* innovative recipes using New World ingredients.[21] It is the first to suggest serving
turkey with cranberries, the use of a crookneck "squash," a Native American
term, for a pudding, "a pompkin pudding" (melding British puddings with
native ingredients that had not been used in this form before), and cornmeal
products: "Slapjacks," "Jonny Cakes," and "a Tasty Indian Pudding," all requiring indigenous products. The Jerusalem artichoke, long ignored in Euro-

pean cookery books, was mentioned in Simmons's text, another departure from English preferences. Adaptations of Old World cuisine were renamed for the new social context as "Election Cake," "Independence Cake," and "Federal Pan Cake," and a recipe for soft gingerbread, a New World adaptation of the crispier European variety, are all found here for the first time.[22] Simmons's use of the vernacular to title her recipes and describe her dishes blended Old and New World flavors, language, and ideas, simultaneously merging and distinguishing the two cultures, English and American.

Beyond defining a new culinary repertoire, this American orphan spoke for women whose familial circumstances, or lack thereof, limited their opportunities. In spite of her own marginal social position, she claims cultural knowledge and authority through her expertise in cookery. We know little about her and her life as a historical person except what we have garnered from her books. We learn from an errata sheet at the back of the first edition that she relied on a scribe to write the book. She apologizes for its flaws, which she attributes to this individual's negligence: "The author of the *American Cookery,* not having an education sufficient to prepare the work for the press, the person that was employed by her, and entrusted with the receipts, to prepare them for publication, did omit several articles very essential in some of the receipts."[23] In this postscript, Simmons also points to the class differences between herself and the scribe and alludes to both her dependency and the role of knowledge in defining cultural authority. From the postscript and the title page announcing the author as an orphan, we learn that Simmons was an uneducated woman. This persona of orphan she—or her editors—has constructed is revealing.[24]

Let us assume for a moment that Simmons's preface is fictional and not autobiographical, that Simmons is a literary device created by the publishers. Was she a trope for the new society and culture? Orphaned much like the new republican country, she was without parents, lineage, genealogy. She was also unprotected. Simmons had broken from her parents, as did colonial America. Reputedly with the split came independence from the pedigrees of the past.

Despite the losses of parentage, there were gains. Without the constraints of lineage, one could move more freely in society. The orphan—country or daughter—could, without the heavy weight of the past, invent new ways of cooking, coping, and being. Amelia Simmons used her cookbook to emphasize her humble origins as she argued for a woman's right to determination and will. Simmons wrote from the vantage point of an upwardly mobile orphan trying to break social barriers; she spoke for the "rising generation of females"[25] in her young country. Not unlike her country, the borders she negotiated were those of class, generation, lineage, and authority.

Despite her claims for universality—the book is intended "for all grades of life"[26]—in her preface she identifies her projected audience. The book itself, she argues, is useful in all households, but the audience she emphasizes is women who seek self-improvement, ideally *all* women, but particularly those in "unfortunate circumstances"[27] and thus dependent on "virtuous guardians"[28] and, most important, their own resourcefulness. Judith Sargent Murray, a contemporary of Simmons, wrote in 1798, "The Sex should be taught to depend on their own efforts, for the procurement of an establishment in life."[29] Simmons's rhetoric departs from that of her British counterparts only slightly. They also wrote ostensibly for the improvement of their sex and addressed a similarly wide-ranging audience, from gentlewomen and ladies, to housewives and servants. However, whereas they exhorted women to achieve a position suited to their "rank and station," Simmons wrote for women who might rise beyond the constraints of birth and circumstance. Historian Linda K. Kerber explains that "in the early Republic, female learning was thus explicitly put to the service of upward social mobility."[30] Albeit brief and subtle, the difference in Simmons's expectations for women's upward mobility is significant.

Simmons was, however, also politically astute. She did not want to arouse the enmity of another segment of the reading public. Although she stressed the usefulness of her book for women in unfortunate circumstances, she was careful not to alienate her audience—she was, after all, revealing secrets belonging to wealthier households—and asked that:

> . . . the Lady of fashion and fortune be not displeased if many hints are suggested for a more universal knowledge of those females in this country, who by the loss of their parents, or other unfortunate circumstances, are reduced

to the necessity of going into families in the line of domesticks, or taking refuge with their friends or relations, and doing those things which are really essential to the perfecting them as good wives, and useful members to society. The orphan, though left to the care of virtuous guardians will find it essentially necessary to have an opinion and determination of her own.[31]

By advocating the dissemination of knowledge from one class to another and from one generation to another, Simmons underscores the differences between the "ladies of fashion" and the "women who are in unfortunate circumstances." In her emphasis on differences between those more and less fortunate, she is attempting to bridge the gap between both classes with advice on cookery and decorum. Simultaneously self-effacing and confident, her implied autobiographical presence nonetheless asserts that even women in humble circumstances should develop strength and persistence. "By having an opinion and determination I would not be understood to mean an obstinate perseverance in trifles, which borders on obstinacy—by no means, but only an adherence to those rules and maxims which have stood the test of ages, and will forever establish the *female character,* a virtuous character— although they conform to the ruling taste of the age in cookery, dress, language, manners, &c."[32]

For Simmons, the dictates of the decade should not deter women from achieving the universal and transcendent qualities of the feminine ideal that could be learned from the long-standing traditions of the past. Had she learned from her own experience the difficulties of working in another woman's home? Was she eager to advise young women in similar circumstances against the "obstinacy" they showed toward their mistresses?

In eighteenth-century America young women who may have been in positions similar to Simmons—hired or indentured helps—were not noted for their compliant attitudes. The letters and diaries of several colonial mistresses comment upon the difficult relationships with their helpers. A girl could be accused of being "under no regulations" or "as bad as she can be."[33] Martha Moore Ballard dismissed Elizabeth Taylor in December 1795, commenting, "'I am determined not to pay girls any more for ill manners.' The self assertion of these 'helps' hardly suggests an obeisant temperament among young women who earned their keep."[34] Simmons was preoccupied by the issues of generational difference, and she points to the ways in which old and young respond to a changing world.

> The world, and the fashion thereof, is so variable, that old people cannot accommodate themselves to the various changes and fashions which daily occur: *they* will adhere to the fashion of *their* day, and will not surrender their attachments to the *good old way*—while the young and the gay bend and conform readily to the taste of the times, and fancy of the hour.[35]

A thinly veiled disdain for the fickleness of fashion and the rigidity of age suggests that only with strength of character will a young woman in "unfortunate circumstances" cope with a changing world. "Opinion and determination"—those male traits—are softened into timeless feminine qualities in keeping with women's morality and virtue. Resilience and suppleness, assertiveness and conformity are juxtaposed and then intertwined in Simmons's view of womanhood, at least for the "rising generation of *Females*" who concern her in this text.[36] Her apparent ambivalence and final integration of these opposing personal characteristics urges women to temper their strength with virtue and to master both strategies in order to succeed. In keeping with republican norms, Simmons's apparent conservative posture does not depart from the contemporary philosophy on education for women. Schooling should prepare them for life and for their roles as wives and mothers.

Even those women writers who espoused conservative views (women should be concerned with home and family) about the position of women in society were—by the very act of writing—behaving contrary to the norms of their era. After all, women were not encouraged to engage in public life, although publishing cookbooks may have been an exception. Although women were exhorted not to publish, some did. In fact, they published their ideas in many genres. In England, the range of literature written by women spanned the same breadth as literature by men: novels, spiritual and religious essays, autobiographies, and poetry, among the genres.[37] As we saw in chapter 6, many women resolved the contradiction of their own assertiveness by claiming that their motivation for writing was the encouragement of friends and the desire to help their countrywomen.[38] Above all, they wanted to be

viewed as "useful members to society."[39] If the prefaces were not autobiographical statements or motivations for writing that were meant to disguise
the authors' brashness, then they were fairly formulaic introductions quali-
fying the author and exempting her from audacity. Prefaces such as Simmons's were the standard formulaic prefaces found in cookery and other
books from the fifteenth century.[40]

Simmons uses a strategy of feigned reticence not unlike that of her contemporaries in Britain, yet she departs slightly from this rhetorical device. She
never tells us how her book came into being. She never claims to have been
encouraged by others to seek publication, although she offers her "treatise" for
the benefit of her young women compatriots. She makes no apologies for writing her cookery book. And, at the end of her preface, which is itself both bold
and conservative, she makes her appeal: "The candor of the American Ladies
is solicitously intreated by the Authoress, as she is circumscribed in her knowledge, this being an original work in this country. Should any future editions
appear, she hopes to render it more valuable."[41] Simmons's subtle advocacy of
women's social mobility is concealed by rhetoric that would be acceptable to
the reading public. While she extols the virtues of the old—"only adherence
to those rules and maxims which have stood the test of ages"—she argues that
women should develop a resolute character and other personal attributes that
women—particularly those making their own way in the world—should have.
It was important to pass on these virtues to subsequent generations.

By expressing her desire to follow the maxims of the past, Simmons's prescriptions are compatible with the educational ideology of the period. According to William Gilmore in his study of literacy in rural New England
during the period in which Simmons published, the prevailing educational
philosophy was the inculcation of the young in the traditions and customs
of the past. [42] "The whole point of reading was the 'practical investigations
of wisdom.' . . . The purpose of reading as it was then conceptualized was to
maintain the status quo. However, it had unintended consequences."[43]

In the 1780s there was concern about how women could carry out their
roles as nurturers of the young and future citizens of the new republic if
they were themselves illiterate. For these reasons women's literacy became
more common and more acceptable. Many works of the time were directed
to women who were upwardly mobile or middle-class mothers; the postwar

educational ideology was aimed especially at them. They were the republican mothers for whom this literature was intended because it was they who would rear the next generation of citizens.

What is different about Simmons's text is that it addresses, in particular, women in unfortunate circumstances as well as those of the middle classes. Simmons muted her ardor, and perhaps her defiance of the limitations for mobility placed on her by her class and gender position, by ultimately appealing to feminine modesty and goodness. She advises women with a background such as hers to develop determination and opinion, qualities once reserved for men. Historian Linda K. Kerber describes "The model Republican woman [as] competent and confident. She could resist the vagaries of fashion; she was rational, benevolent, independent, self-reliant."[44] Although there were differences between expectations for women before and after the war, authors such as Benjamin Rush and Judith Sargent Murray,[45] who espoused the new ideals, spoke and wrote for the middle classes. According to Kerber, "Few spoke to the nascent class of unskilled women."[46] Furthermore, even those who advocated for a liberal education for women were careful to temper their endorsements by agreeing that women should not neglect their proper domain—the household.

Reprinted into the nineteenth century, Simmons's book remained a popular favorite of American women. It is not clear what role *American Cookery* played in the dissemination of a rhetoric that politicized the domestic economy and brought women slowly into the political arena. However, after about 1825, according to Gilmore, the tensions between "tradition and innovation" heightened. It became increasingly difficult to reconcile the changing mores with the old order. As pious mothers charged with the responsibility of raising future citizens—male and female—women needed to be able to read in order to educate their children. However, as historian Joan Gunderson has said so concisely, "What society intends an institution to do, and what participants absorb from that experience can vary. No matter how much reformers thought they were creating an education for mothers in the new republic, some students . . . had their own motives for learning. Whatever its intent, the academy did not domesticate all of its first charges."[47]

Ironically, the old framework and the emphasis on women's traditional roles engendered social change, and Simmons's text is an example. Although her explicit message conforms to the pedagogical stance of the period—"adherence to the rules and maxims of the past"—Simmons persists in her critique of society. The tensions between "tradition and innovation" that William Gilmore describes as irreconcilable by 1825 are already evident (presaged) in Simmons's book and her description of young and old.

Although she employs a slightly scornful tone in her deference to the "Lady of fashion and fortune" as one who "conforms to the fancy of the hour," Simmons nonetheless is appealing to the vanity of the Ladies of Fashion by suggesting that being in step with the times is an indication of those who are willing to accept the new social order of egalitarianism. Using double-edged flattery, Simmons praises those who embrace the ideals of the new republic. In this artful disguise, she transgresses class and generational boundaries. While appeasing the ladies, she offers the "hints" belonging to fashionable families to servants and housekeepers. Offering secrets was a breach of the upper classes' privacy at the same time that it was an enticement to her working-class readers. What more intimate view of the life of the upper classes than through the kitchen and the dining room!

In her text, Simmons was developing a site at which mistress and servant could negotiate the boundaries of authority.[48] An inversion of the more customary relationship between servant and mistress could occur in the cookery text, a site in which Simmons, a working woman, could assume an authoritative voice. Although she was writing dutifully for the benefit of her sex, Simmons struck a strong chord for women in less than privileged circumstances. In the publication of *American Cookery*, Amelia Simmons was scripting herself and others of her sex and station into the fledgling republic's social structure.

The New Housekeeper's Manual: "Good servants do not often come to us. They must be made . . ."

In the fewer than one hundred years after the publication of Simmons's book, a proliferation of household advice flooded nineteenth-century America's literary marketplace. In contrast to Amelia Simmons's humble origins, two influential women of a prominent American family, Harriet Beecher Stowe, noted abolitionist and author of *Uncle Tom's Cabin*, and her sister, Catharine Beecher, advocate for women's education, together co-authored *The New Housekeeper's Manual.*[49] The 1873 primer in household management was encyclopedic in scope, covering, among other topics, architecture, interior design, and cookery. Essentially *The New Housekeeper's Manual* was a revised edition of their *American Woman's Home*, published in 1869. Stowe's contributions to the manual were primarily in the sections on architecture and home decorating. Both books were an attempt to capitalize on the national reputation of the author of *Uncle Tom's Cabin*, and the collaboration was for the two women an emblem of their sisterly closeness.[50]

The Beechers were part of a cadre of well-known women writing books for household use. While Harriet Beecher Stowe was most known for her novels and stories, Catharine Beecher employed household advice literature as the podium from which to speak about women's education and women's sphere of influence. The Beechers urged women to recognize the importance of their role as shapers of culture and of family life. Both Stowe and Beecher argued that women could—from the kitchen and the parlor—engender social change. They agreed that women should be educated in both the liberal and the household arts, be economically independent, and be recognized for their contributions to society through the care of home and family. This, they felt, would create a better society, albeit one divided by gender into separate spheres of influence.

However, the sisters differed in the degree to which they felt women should be permitted to participate in the wider public sphere. Stowe advocated for universal suffrage while Beecher was uneasy about women's place and abilities in public life. She distrusted the public sphere, where "a mingling of all grades and the absence of distinct classes presaged chaos in the Republic." Her suggestion was to "domesticate it [chaos] within the walls of the middle-class home."[51]

Indeed, by the mid-nineteenth century, influential reformers like Beecher and Stowe had helped to create a platform of power for urban middle-class women anchored to the realm of home, domesticity, and the matrix of morality domestic life embodied. From this vantage point, indeed, because of its association with religion, the nineteenth-century housewife managed to exert substantial influence on political and other ideological issues, including the education and socialization of new immigrant groups. With domestic prowess as a foil, women like the Beechers lobbied for and engaged in social reform as they had earlier on behalf of abolition. Their efforts were two-pronged.

One audience for their propositions was the immigrants they could reach directly. Middle-class matrons taught immigrants how to arrange their domestic space, what foods to buy, and how to prepare and serve them.[52] The Beechers believed that by teaching acceptable, sanitary, and sound principles of nutrition and domestic practice, the hardships of immigration could be minimized. Under pressure from social reformers to adapt, to incorporate novel resources, to adjust to the absence of familiar foods and methods of cookery, and from their desire to become American, the immigrants did transform their traditional cuisines, creating some of the culinary hybrids with which we are familiar.[53]

The second audience for the reformers' ideas was the middle-class housewife whose job it was to educate those within her household: family and servants alike. As they did with immigrants, reformers worked assiduously to improve health, nutrition, and sanitation, all in the name of morality and home.

Cooking was more than a metaphor for cultural difference. It was a custom to be changed. Beecher had transformed her zeal for a spiritual heaven on earth into a secular domestic agenda.[54] The homogenization of American life would occur through the standardization of domestic principles, from architecture to cookery. The nation's internal conflicts would dissolve when differences among its inhabitants were eradicated. It was thus vital to the Beechers that untrained immigrants learn the techniques and practices of American housekeepers. By patrolling and amending the kitchen and domestic practices of racial, ethnic, and religious newcomers to America, they could protect home—and nation.

The Beecher sisters believed that equality could be achieved through common household practice.[55] By eradicating or transforming the traditional cultural practices of immigrants, particularly the Irish servants about whom they wrote, Beecher sought to eliminate class differences and kitchen conflict, the conflict between middle-class matrons and their working-class servants. It is at this juncture that the paradoxes of their mission are visible.

In their book of household management, *The New Housekeeper's Manual,* the Beecher sisters presented their audiences with an elevated image of womanhood even if the women it depicted were white, middle-class, and Protestant.[56]

Implied in their ideal model of womanhood was a matron whose domestic skills, patience, kindness, and authority had been learned on a Yankee farm. In *The New Housekeeper's Manual,* the Beecher sisters were evoking a place—New England—and narrating an idealized history of an idyllic agrarian past, an Arcadia in which all were equal. Nonetheless, despite their claims for social equality, their descriptions of the relationship between servant and mistress reveal both the negative racial rhetoric of the era[57] and the contradictions and ambivalence of their agenda.

The Beechers were living in an era of prolific immigration to the United States. Among those who came between 1870 and 1900 were more than 1.5 million Irish immigrants.[58] Associated with urban ghetto blight and crime, the Irish Catholic immigrant was often the target of prejudice.[59] Stereotypical images of the Irish female servant swelled in the popular press, fiction, and letters.

The Beechers, among others, authored books for the middle-class, white housewife whose duties included the supervision of servants: a "Bridget" or a "Biddy." Clearly the responsibility born out of the relationship between mistress and servants is one of noblesse oblige and the asymmetrical ties that bind women of different classes. Embedded in the description of the mistress's obligations towards her household help is an infantilization of the servant and a patronizing stance toward educating and training.

The Beechers' sentiments about Irish servants are voiced in *The Housekeeper's Manual.* More than that, in this text they transform the rhetoric of race, class, and religion into one of gender.

The Beechers' manual was dedicated "To The Women of America, In Whose Hands Rest the Real Destinies of the Republic, as Moulded by the Early Training and Preserved Amid the Maturer Influences of Home, This Volume is Affectionately Inscribed." The dedications signal a woman-to-woman lineage—as they did in manuscripts and cookery books from at least the seventeenth century. In this inscription, the Beechers acknowledge and attribute the development of American society to women's labor, a modest but potent recognition of women's work and contribution to cultural life. They argued that:

> the honor and duties of the family state are not duly appreciated, that women are not trained for these duties as men are trained for their trades and professions, and that as the consequence, family labor is poorly done, poorly paid, and regarded as menial and disgraceful. To be the nurse of young children, a cook, or a housemaid is regarded as the lowest and last resort of poverty, and one which no woman of culture and position can assume without loss of caste and respectability.[60]

They felt that an education would give women equal footing with men for whom training was a prerequisite for an honorable profession; however, they viewed paid housekeeping in another's home as the most demeaning work of all—work unbecoming a lady. There is a tone of disapproval that this should be so. With education and training, they might argue, the domestic arts would be regarded with as much respect as other professions and a career that women might enter with dignity and self-esteem.

In keeping with their views of the importance of domesticity, they noted and chastised others in the women's movement for belittling women who chose to stay at home.

> So much has been said of the higher sphere of woman and so much has been done to find some better work for her that, insensibly, almost every body begins to feel that it is rather degrading for a woman in good society to be much tied down to family affairs; especially since in these Woman's Rights Conventions there is so much dissatisfaction expressed at those who confine her ideas to the kitchen and the nursery. . . .
>
> Many of the women connected with these movements are as superior in every thing properly womanly as they are in exceptional talent and culture. There is no manner of doubt that the sphere of woman is properly to be enlarged. Every woman has rights as a human being which belong to no sex, and ought to be as freely conceded to her as if she were a man,—first and foremost, the great right of doing any thing which God and nature evidently have fitted her to excel in.[61]

Clearly, the Beechers argued that all women had the right to choose a profession for which their natural talents suited them. Women who chose to remain at home to care for families were not to be belittled; their contributions to society were as vital and significant as those of women activists.

Even as champions of all women and of women's work, the Beechers did not see their own contradictions in their position on women's status and women's rights. Catharine's position was built on a hierarchical vision of society, one ordained by God: women subordinate to men as children to parents and as servants to masters.[62] Whereas other activists, such as the Grimke sisters, believed that women had the right to engage in political activity, Catharine did not. Instead Catharine proposed to eliminate racial, ethnic, and class differences by dividing the nation in two: male and female.[63]

Within this bipartite structure, the hierarchical relationship that, according to Catharine, ordered all human society also existed between women. Thus, the Beechers advanced the image of the New England woman as the one against which all others women should be measured. And it was the middle-class mistress who bore responsibility for teaching her servants proper domestic skills. It is through the relationship of mistress and servant and the intersection of religion, race (ethnicity), class, and gender that their ethnocentrism is revealed.[64] This ethnocentrism muddies the Beechers' well-intentioned appeal for tolerance and respect to be shown to the "uncultured" immigrant Irish in the chapter in *The Housekeeper's Manual* entitled "The Care of Servants."

The chapter expresses a longing for a not-so-distant and perhaps imaginary past—a nostalgia for the time when families sent one another "helpers," not servants:

> to be employed in all respects as equals and companions, and so the work of the community is equalized. . . . Then were to be seen families of daughters, handsome, strong women, rising each day to their in-door work with cheerful alertness—one to sweep the room, another to make the fire, while a third prepared the breakfast for the father and brothers who were going out to manly labor. . . . In those former days most women were in good health, debility and disease being the exception. . . . Long years of practice made them familiar with the shortest, neatest, most expeditious method of doing every

household office, so that really for the greater part of the time in the house there seemed, to a looker-on, to be nothing to do."[65]

Help came not in the form of servants but neighboring farm girls who sat equally with their mistresses at the family table. Yet both help and domestics, as the immigrants were now called, were servants. Both were paid. The difference between them is that help was not an occupation, it was a form of intermittent and flexible work. The shift in terms reflects the changes taking place in American urban industrial workplaces and in homes and families as well.[66]

Women, both servants and mistresses alike, experienced social change in the nineteenth century. The Beechers' articulation of the changes within the middle-class household was framed in the domestic contrasts between past and present and American and foreigner. Compare the Beechers' vision of New England's native daughters cited above with that of the immigrant domestic in this moralistic tale: "a raw Irish maid-of-all-work, a creature of immense bone and muscle, but of heavy, unawakened brain. In one short night she established such a reign of Chaos and old Night in the kitchen and through the house that her mistress, a delicate woman, encumbered with the care of young children, began seriously to think that she made more work each day than she performed and dismissed her."[67] The Beechers conjure up not only the unskilled methods of their Irish servants but their physical attributes as well. The rough and clumsy Irish maid, "a creature of immense bone and muscle," had no knowledge of domestic arts. Her unbridled manner wreaked havoc instead of order and required the services of another to repair the mess.

The exemplar continues with a portrait of the newcomer, once again stressing her physical appearance as well as her work habits:

Forthwith came into the family-circle a tall, well-dressed young person, grave, unobtrusive, self-respecting, yet not in the least presuming, who sat at the family table and observed all its decorums with the modest self-possession of a lady. The newcomer took a survey of the labors of a family of ten members, including four or five young children, and, looking, seemed at once to throw them into system; matured her plans, arranged her hours of washing, ironing,

baking, and cleaning; rose early, moved deftly; and in a single day the slat-
ternly and littered kitchen assumed that neat, orderly appearance that so often
strikes one in New-England farm-houses. . . . That tall, fine looking girl, for
aught we know, may yet be mistress of a fine house on Fifth Avenue; and if
she is, she will, we fear, prove rather an exacting mistress to Irish Bridget."[68]

The New England goddess knew just by "intuition" the proper and most nutritious foods to prepare for her family and how to prepare them and even
from her bedchamber could direct a child to carry out her instructions with
"mathematical certainty."[69] Alas, if only the mothers of New England had
written down their kitchen codes, the United States would be a better place.

According to the Beechers, democracy has given hope to the servants who
have come to this country believing that "this is somehow a land of liberty,
and with very dim and confused notions of what liberty is. They are very extensively raw, untrained Irish peasantry, and the wonder is, that, with all the
unreasoning heats and prejudices of the Celtic blood, all the necessary igno-
rance and rawness, there should be the measure of comfort and success there
is in our domestic arrangements."[70] Precisely what the Beechers consider
"dim and confused notions of liberty" is unclear. One may conjecture from
nineteenth-century accounts of the middle-class matron's struggle to hold
onto Irish servants that the Beechers are irked by a notion of liberty that
benefits Irish servants' mobility from household to household. Ironically,
this may, in fact, have been one reason why the American mistress and newly
immigrated servant were successful in their negotiations. Those of the immigrant population who assumed such roles came "more or less infected
with the spirit of democracy."[71] They expected to be treated as equals. As a
result, according to the Beechers, "life became a sort of domestic wrangle
and struggle between the employers . . . and the employed, who knew their
power and insisted on their privileges."[72] Because Irish servants were much
in demand despite the alleged dissatisfaction with their work, they could
move in and out of positions, much to the chagrin of their employers who
complained bitterly about the situation.[73] Second, employment in middle-
class homes was useful for the Irish newcomers to learn about middle-class
life firsthand. They self-consciously exploited their employment situations

to become familiar with middle-class domesticity and in time Americanized themselves and their families in the process.[74]

Diarists such as Caroline Barrett White depict a faceted portrait of the relationship between servant and mistress, one fraught with anxiety about work standards, privacy, and loyalty on both parts. White referred to her servants whom she hired and fired regularly as "the cook, my girl, my second girl." Yet when one of them left to find more suitable employment, she declared them unfaithful: "My cook left today and the one I had engaged to take her place has failed to keep her engagement. *Irish fidelity!* Mary Whalen, chambergirl, informed me she should leave this eve—she has accordingly gone—this is a specimen of Irish kindness and willingness to oblige—She has left me with the four children and no one to assist but the cook."[75]

Yet the ethnocentric description of the Irish working class does not leave the middle-class housewife blameless or without responsibility. She has a role to play. Her job is to teach: "The first business of a housekeeper in America is that of a teacher. It requires only a little tact, some patience, some clearness in giving directions, and all comes right. . . . Good servants do not often come to us; they must be made by patience and training. . . . The most difficult situations are not teaching 'girls' who know nothing but those who work 'contrary to the genius of one's housekeeping.'"[76]

On one hand, the Beechers extol the importance of housekeeping and the skill and intelligence required of women as housekeepers, but the genius belongs clearly to the middle-class mistress of the house.[77]

In the end, the Beechers urge tolerance and kindness as they conclude their thoughts on the care of servants. After all, the daughters of Erin were far from home, stripped of motherly guidance, shipped abroad and into service. In the end, despite the differences between Irish servants and American mistresses, the Beechers acknowledged that American mothers would, under similar circumstances, consider such sacrifice and contributions heroic.[78] The authors conclude that respect and tolerance are missing from the interactions of mistress and servant and that such mistreatment leads to dissatisfaction: "It

is because the young women who become servants are not treated respect-
fully . . . they are not willing to place themselves in a situation where their
self-respect is hourly wounded by the implication of a degree of inferiority,
which does not follow any kind of labor or service in this country but that of
the family."[79]

The Beechers' final note is one of tolerance, yet the relationship they depict between employer and employed remained unequal. It required from
the mistress a willingness to suspend harshness but never to relinquish her
role as educator and authority. In carrying out her responsibilities as teacher,
the mistress could transform the untrained Irish servant into her own image
of middle-class matron. They were not at odds in that regard: Both mistress
and domestic shared that same goal albeit for different reasons. Both sides
benefited. For the servant, achieving upward mobility was the reason for em-
igration in the first place. For the matron, successfully training servants
would create a better home. Thus, in the very writings made possible by
their servants' labor, women like the Beechers could affirm the rightness of
their own customary practices—symbolized by cooking and domestic practice—and guard the boundaries of their own class position.

Mrs. Patterson and Elnora Blanchard: Irish Humor in Manuscript Books

The Beechers were not alone in their descriptions of the Irish maid-of-all-
work. The popular press swarmed with derisive and benevolent images of the
Irish servant maid. (See Figure 7.2) *Godey's Lady's Book and Magazine* depicted
the Irish servant /mistress relationship in detail. In an article entitled "Mrs.
Deming's Troubles," author Mary W. Janvrin describes the utter frustration of
Mrs. Deming in her efforts to teach her domestic, Kate, how to prepare a pudding. After showing her how to make the dish on Tuesday, Kate has forgotten.
"'Well, Kate, I'll show you today, but you must remember in the future so as
not to call upon me again; for you know I directed you how to make this very
pudding last Tuesday.'" The lesson continues and as Mrs. Deming finishes
demonstrating the making of the pudding, she says, "'There! Do you think
you can remember now, Kate?' she asked, as a few minutes later, all the ingre-

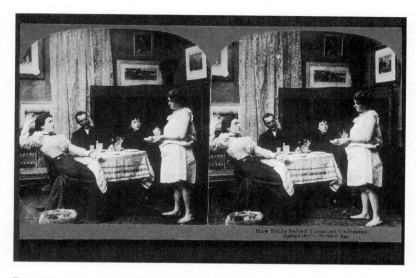

Figure 7.2   A stereopticon slide debasing an Irish servant.

dients added, she poured the mixture into the baking pan. 'Or will you be call-ing me again every time you have this pudding to make.'"[80]

Kate responds: "'Ah, but I see through it now, jist intirely! Sure, it wasn't *the mixin* ov it all, but the quantities that bothered me, for it had gone clean out ov me memory, whether it was the sax eggs or the dozen I wud be afther usin.'" The scene continues with one final query from Kate to her mistress about preparing the roast beef for dinner. "'Just hould on a bit, ma'am, if ye plaze! There was something the masther said about the cooking ov the bafe, an' I don't jist seem to recollect, ma'am.'"[81]

"'Why you heard him say it was to be cooked rare, I suppose, and that was my order, too, you know; beef always to be rare done, I charged you. How stupid you are, Kate!'"[82] Kate's ineptitude was the result of being "raw, as the latest specimens of that genus 'just over' are apt to be."[83]

Ordinary women made use of their recipe and cookery books in similar al-beit vernacular ways. They chose articles to include in their manuscript cook-books that resonated with their day-to-day experiences. Although Patterson's Pottsville, Pennsylvania, cookbook (discussed in chapter 1) emphasizes the tensions that affected her community, from the men's perspective, in particular, the differences among and between women may be found in more subtle allusions. Patterson pasted a newspaper clipping with a joke about an Irish maid into her culinary scrapbook. This column was entitled "Humor":

> It was in Dublin that a good humored maid-of-all-work, Molly, once related to her young mistress a most marvelous dream she had had the night before. "Pooh, Pooh!!" cries the latter, at its conclusion; "You must have been asleep, Molly, when you dreamed such nonsense." "Indeed I was not, then," replies the indignant Molly; "I was just as wide awake as I am this minute."

Both mistress and maid look foolish in this joke, but it is the maid whose sense (and work ability) is questioned. Humor and other narrative accounts (such as that found in *Godey's Lady's Book*) provided a framework for women like Patterson to interpret these encounters.

Elnora Blanchard kept a recipe book, into which she pasted a column of newspaper jokes called "From the funny Columns." One of the jokes refers to the violence that reputedly characterized Irish family life in the cities: "Kitchen Scene.—'These potatoes are better than the last ones, Bridget?' Bridget—'they are, mum. The boy said they was Irish potatoes, and sure and I think they must be, for whin I opened the oven door to see if they was done, one of them flew out and hit me in the eye.'"[84] The pervasiveness of this stereotype in the format of a joke veiled the ethnocentrism that affected middle-class women's interactions with their domestics. It is difficult to know how readers would interpret these jokes and stories. Humor functions in several ways: It may act as a release from tension and it provides pleasure because of its clever word play. It serves other functions as well.

Framed as "not to be taken seriously," jokes still may sanction fear and antagonism toward outsiders. Justifying the mistresses' beliefs, the stories enabled these women to abrogate any share of responsibility for tense interactions and misunderstandings between mistress and maid. In this way, humorous stories maintain the status quo. In some cases, however, humor may have another effect: It may bring into high relief the contentious relationships between Anglo mistresses and Irish maids and motivate some women to reflect on what they had assumed to be acceptable practices.

The Presbyterian Cookbook:
Poetry and Beans

Beginning with the Civil War in the United States, women used recipes to raise money for charitable causes. Through the compilation and sale of church and community cookbooks, women funneled the proceeds into hospitals, poorhouses, missions, churches, synagogues, and orphanages.[85] As women continued their humanitarian efforts and their household labors, they engaged in what Anne Goldman calls "sotto voce" (in a subdued voice) debates about their own and others' proper place in society.[86]

In 1873 the Ladies Society of the First Presbyterian Church of Dayton, Ohio, "hastily compiled and published a 'Cook Book,' *The Presbyterian Cookbook,* a small collection of recipes for plain household cooking."[87] As ordinary housewives, they "begged indulgence for the manner of their writing"[88]—they had, after all, never written for publication before. In this slender volume, published locally, we find a recipe that gives directions for "Cooking Beans" reprinted from *Moore's Rural New Yorker.*

Innocently enough, the recipe is in verse:

Cooking Beans

If, my dear Rural, you should ever wish
For Breakfast or dinner a tempting dish
Of the beans so famous in Boston town,
You must read the rules I here lay down.

.   .   .   .

Then if, in the pantry, there still should be
That bean-pot, so famous in history,
With all deference bring it out,
And if there's a skimmer lying about,
Skim half of the beans from the boiling pan
Into the bean pot as fast as you can;
Then turn to Biddy and calmly tell her
To take a huge knife and go to the cellar;
For you must have, like Shylock of old,
"A pound of flesh," ere your beans grow cold;
But, very unlike that ancient Jew,
Nothing but pork will do for you.

. . . .

Like an island of pork in an ocean of beans;
Pour on boiling hot water enough to cover
The tops of the beans completely over,
Shove into the oven and bake till done,
And the triumph of Yankee cookery's won![89]

In denoting the proper code for making beans—itself a symbol of the New England elite—the poem alludes to improper conduct, that of Shylock, the ancient Jew, whose pound of flesh was taken in the form of usury, the stereotypical behavior of the Jew. Pork, the forbidden food of Jews, is in this instance the delectable and necessary—the centerpiece—ingredient in cooking beans, the Bostonian equivalent of the all-American dish. What more compelling way to show the dangers of the foreign than to contrast a preferred food in one culture with the tabooed food of another? At the same time, the poem's mention of "the bean-pot, so famous in history" mythologizes an artifact that is a symbol of the New England agrarian roots of American culture.

The poem's placement in the text signals another feature of the women's cultural life. Not only did the reference to Shylock highlight the differences between Christians and Jews and between Americans and foreigners, but it also displayed the Presbyterian women's erudition. Quotations from venerated literature, such as Shakespeare's plays, often graced the pages of nineteenth-century cookery books. White, Anglo-Saxon, Protestant women were expected to be familiar with elite literature as a reflection of their respectability and refinement. In this cookbook they found a forum for their own cultural commentary about contemporary issues, in particular, the perceived threat of foreign incursions through immigration. Although the poem itself may not have been written by a woman, its inclusion in the local cookbook acknowledges the concerns of many women in this community about racial matters.[90]

It is no surprise that home-grown, grass-roots cookbooks that serve humanitarian goals are reflections of very particular and parochial concerns. The charitable effort is meant to serve a local community or, in some cases, a proselytizing mission far from home. In service to their own cause, the fund raisers celebrate their own culture and community while, at best, ignoring other communities and, at worst, denigrating them.

This is not to demean the many successful charitable efforts by women on behalf of other groups as well as their own. Still, it is ironic that in engaging in charitable activity to benefit their own group, the compilers of the *Presbyterian Cookbook* [1886] invoked negative images of Jewish cultural otherness and difference.

Ordinary women attended to and commented on the political and social issues of their times. Attitudes toward cultural difference, in this case anti-Semitic expressions, could be promulgated in their quotidian writings and disseminated in local circles. Women who were barely literate could use such artifacts of daily life as the cookbook to express their fears about ethnic, cultural, and religious differences, and the negative impact that things foreign could have on American life.

Cooking as an Act of Translation: How to Cook and Eat in Chinese

If native-born and mainstream women were using the venue of the cookbook to express their views on social and cultural life and to protect cultural and class boundaries through the codification of kitchen practice, a few non-native-born women found the cookbook a handy genre for crossing the very cultural, linguistic, and social boundaries established in household advice literature by women such as the sisters Beecher.

One immigrant woman who used the cookbook to cross cultural boundaries was Buwei Yang Chao, who in 1945 published *How to Cook and Eat in Chinese*.[91] On the surface, the book is an effort to educate American women about Chinese civilization by introducing them to Chinese food and cooking. Culinary writer Betty Fussell has said eloquently that "eating is the primary act of translation. One ingests the world of things and articulates a world of ideas."[92] Chao's book is such an act of translation. It interprets Chinese home cooking for an American kitchen and alludes to the thorny processes of acculturation and assimilation—another act of translation—for newly immigrated families.[93]

Chao, in her brief introduction, states: "I am ashamed to have written this book. First, because I am a doctor and ought to be practicing instead of cooking. Secondly, because I didn't write the book."[94] In these opening sentences, she sets the stage with the problematics of her cookbook enterprise— an enterprise that implicates the process of immigration. The difficulties that she and her family experienced in writing the cookbook are similar to the difficulties that she and her family encountered in their new country. Both required learning how to adapt familial patterns and relationships learned in one cultural setting to another.

We are enlightened by her statements that she "ought to be practicing [medicine] instead of cooking" when Chao tells us that she "grew up with the idea that nice ladies should not be in a kitchen."[95] With this disclaimer, she underscores her socioeconomic class as a physician, a mark of rank. She also tells us that she is a wife and mother. All of these personal characteristics will be deployed in her efforts to gain the American reader's attention and trust. Although she is Chinese, she draws attention to the personal characteristics of middle-class marriage and motherhood that she shares with her reading public: She has the expertise of a native, the long experience of cooking for a family, and social standing. In making these claims for cultural knowledge and authority, she distinguishes herself from the ordinary immigrant.

As World War II was drawing to its close, Chao would also have us understand that there is a distinction between Chinese and Japanese cultures. With broad anti-Asian sentiment in the United States following the war, it was imperative for her to differentiate and distance herself from the Japanese. When she tells us why she learned to cook despite her class prerogative not to do so, we discover her own anti-Japanese attitude. She claims, "I never stirred an egg until I went to college—the Tokyo Women's Medical College. I found Japanese food so uneatable that I had to cook my own meals."[96] This statement signals the painful relationship between the Chinese and the Japanese during World War II as clearly as a declaration of hostilities. In this and later in the title of a recipe—"Bomb Tokyo"—Chao alludes to Chinese sentiments toward Japan and the enduring effects of war on a culture and country.[97]

Besides learning how to cook while in Japan, Chao undertook a study of regional Chinese cuisine. While her husband, a philologist, surveyed regional dialects in China, she learned how to cook its specialties. "I like to talk to strangers and I wanted to learn more about my country. I learned about many of the local customs and recipes in this way."[98] Her interest in cooking and in learning about her own culture were united in this journey, a culinary pilgrimage in her homeland, a country that was to change dramatically.

Armed with the cultural authority she had accrued on this expedition, Chao used her expert knowledge to enter American homes via the dinner table. She intelligently views the intimate knowledge of food and language, and the activities of eating and speaking, as deeply initiating one into a culture and, conversely, preventing outsiders from crossing borders. To be an insider is to know how to speak and how to eat. By bringing an "authentic" version of Chinese food and Chinese ways of eating into American homes, Chao is likewise crossing a cultural boundary. She has chosen the alimentary canal as the road to understanding.

In addition to her own attempts to create alliances with an American audience, she is aided by a notable American and winner of the Nobel Prize for Literature, Pearl Buck, whose devotion to issues of Sino-American relations won her a place in history. In her preface, Buck argues that Chao's book is a contribution to world peace and suggests that the author should be nominated for a Nobel Peace Prize. Buck sees Chao as a cultural mediator: "For what better road to universal peace is there than to gather around the table where new and delicious dishes are set forth, dishes which, though yet untasted by us, we are destined to enjoy and love? I consider this cookbook a contribution to international understanding."[99]

Buck is careful as she addresses her intended Anglo audience. She states her loyalty and identity first and foremost as that of an American housewife. "I am trying to write this preface as an American housewife who is daily responsible for the meals of a large family and for occasional guests as well. . . . I have steadily remembered that I now live in the United States and that I am limited to American meats and vegetables, fats and fruits. It is as an American woman therefore that I should like to say that it seems to me this is a perfect cook book."[100]

By allying herself primarily with American women, Buck's testimonial to the usefulness of the book for an American kitchen becomes credible. More than that, as a renowned expert on Chinese culture, Buck both attests to the cuisine's authenticity and speaks on behalf of the American readers who regard her as a fellow national. Her dual role enables Buck to act as a cultural broker for Chao, her text, her cuisine, and her culture.

Reviewers such as Clementine Paddleford agree with Buck's assessment of the authenticity of Chao's cuisine. With Chao as a guide, you may "walk right though China's kitchen door . . . while she is cooking and you sit there with your mouth watering."[101] Furthermore, according to the Literary Guild review on the book's dust jacket, "with nothing more exotic than a bottle of soy sauce and a copy of *How to Cook and Eat in Chinese* you can turn out dishes that are easy on the ration points, amusing to cook and satisfying to eat."[102] Americans can cook foreign foods and remain patriotic.

This style of cookery was in keeping with the reduction of the use of meat and milk products touted by governmental agencies. At this time, in service of the war effort, American anthropologists such as Margaret Mead and Ruth Benedict, sociologists such as John Bennett, and nutritionists were encouraging Americans to model their eating habits after the cuisines of other cultures. Some of these peasant diets required little meat, fat, or vegetables and sustained hardworking and vigorous populations.

We are told that

> the recipes she [Chao] concocts, and there are hundreds in this book, haven't a spoonful of anything in them that you cannot get right here in the United States; but they are true Chinese dishes. Some of them call for ingredients found only in Chinatowns, but usually the author marks these "optional." For a very few recipes, Chinatown ingredients are indispensable. (Incidentally such ingredients can be bought by mail.) In short, the great majority of the recipes require only items obtainable in any American food store.[103]

Thus, according to the dust jacket, readers can venture as far from home as they are able or dare. They can buy exotic products and never step foot into the Chinese community. The cuisine presented by Chao allows Americans to travel without ever leaving home. It is up to the reader to decide how far she will go on her voyage to cultural understanding. In this process the only person to cross cultural boundaries is Chao.

At the same time as Chao is infiltrating the cultural borders of her new country, she is reserving for Chinese their rightful place as insiders to their culture, a place that few Americans may inhabit. It is through a knowledge of cooking and eating practices that Chao guards her *own culture's* borders. To be Chinese her readers must know how to eat. She cautions Americans:

> . . . the greatest difficulty is that you do not feel natural when you eat Chinese food in American. You feel you are missing something essential. You do not feel that you are eating a meal. It is not ch'ih-fan. Now when I say "you" I mean "we" of course. So far as *you* are concerned, I would recommend first concentrating on preparing one dish or so in your usual scheme of meals and then try occasionally community eating as a lark. When you know how to shovel rice or congee gracefully over the edge of your bowl and leave a clean bowl at the end of your meal, then you are doing better than even some American old-timers in China, and we will feel that you belong.[104]

Chao is explicit about who constitutes "we" and "you." Americans who are not familiar with the rules of Chinese table etiquette are beyond the pale. To understand the people and its culture, one has to grasp their civilities. In the intricacies of eating politely may be found the door to their culture. In order to be "insiders," her readers must know how to eat rice from a bowl, sip tea from a cup, and be hospitable.

Chao is clear that the Chinese dishes Americans have learned to eat in restaurants are as foreign to the Chinese as American food. In a step-by-step fashion Americans may slowly adapt to Chinese patterns of eating. Chao encourages the reader: "The next step you may take in eating in Chinese may be to have all food Chinese but served and eaten with the framework of an American meal. In China, especially when there are foreign guests not used to Chinese ways of eating, this is sometimes practiced and is called 'Chinese meal foreign eaten.' Each guest is served individually and there is no common dish or dishes you eat directly out of." According to Chao, if nonnatives are willing to learn both the methods of cooking and eating, they, like Pearl Buck, may be considered "fellow provincials."[105] Americans may have no difficulty enjoying Chinese cuisine, but they may stumble when invited to partake from a common bowl. To eat from the same dish as others is to symbolically share a bond or an identity.

Throughout the book, Chao takes us on a journey—in time and in space—and repeatedly lets us know that we are the outsiders to this culture. In her descriptions of meal systems, we learn the difference between a meal—"fan, a period of rice"—and a snack—"tien-hsin, something to dot the heart."[106] We also learn about customary behavior at the end of a banquet when heavy foods are served. "This is the time to serve rice or congee if you can still eat anything. But most experienced eaters can, because they know the program beforehand and know the motto of 'Ten, jen, hen!' It means something like: Await, avoid, attack! That is you wait and avoid eating too much of everything, but when something really good comes, attack!"[107]

Chao describes the etiquette specific to these occasions in a spirit of frivolity and playfulness. Dignitaries and outsiders often are accommodated at these large and formal occasions. Hospitality is paramount. Formality is high; expectations of intimacy are low. Only those familiar with the meal systems are knowledgeable and socially competent enough to override the decreed presentation. They may do so without censure. By the same token, those who do not know the sumptuary regulations are exempt from criticism.

On such occasions Chao, it seems, is lenient about an outsider's lack of insight into Chinese protocol. Lack of familiarity with Chinese conventions is understandable. Yet when it comes to family gatherings, Chao's tolerance of difference wanes. In a comparison of Chinese and American meals, the latter does not get a favorable review:

> Many visitors to China or even long-time residents who never eat a Chinese meal except when invited to a formal dinner with "courses" have no idea what a totally different affair a Chinese family meal is. The typical family meal has several dishes all served at the same time. In families, in shops, and on the farm, people eat together, and share a little of several different dishes, and never have one dish belonging to one person. . . . The result is you feel you are all the time carrying on a friendly conversation with each other, even though nobody says anything. I wonder if it is because the American way of each eating his own meal is so unsociable that you have to keep on talking to make it more like good manners.[108]

Commensality in China, then, represents a profoundly different decorum from American etiquette. The intimate and intense *sharing* of food that marks family borders in China is absent from the American conventions, Chao concludes negatively. Food and its proper distribution during meals is the medium of this message. Speech merely interferes with proper conduct, which is focused on the manner of ingestion itself. The integrity of the family unit is symbolized by partaking of a collective meal from communal bowls. Talk is cheap. It cannot replace the solidarity that is engendered by sharing food from a single bowl.

Chao's description of eating at home and eating outside the home, how, when, and with whom, is a masterful ethnographic account of food consumption in Chinese society. In these descriptions her focus is more than food content; it covers customs and manners. She points to each culture's share of seemingly odd behaviors and then, with rhetorical elegance, mocks Western conceptions of appropriate demeanor. On differences in the techniques of eating, Chao offers the following advice:

> Certain hot foods are best when very hot. The technique for eating them is to draw in air over a narrow opening so as to hasten evaporation and diffuse the flavor. This is most effective when the air roughens the surface of the liquid. That is why hot soup, hot soup-noodles, hot congee, etc. are best when sucked in with as loud a noise as possible. Here again, I feel an inner conflict when I remember how I was taught that in foreign countries one must drink soup as quietly as possible. On the other hand, I can never bring myself to blowing my nose in public, as people do in America, since this operation tends to be much louder than eating noodles and sounds much less inviting.[109]

Chao turns the world upside down to make nonsense out of our understandings of proper conduct. By contrasting American health habits with the logic of Chinese eating strategies, she refocuses her social lens on Americans and Europeans.[110] Perhaps we can see ourselves as equally, if not less, "civilized" than the culture with which Americans are compared.

Chao's sensitivity to the differences between Chinese and American commensal patterns reflects her own reminiscences of a childhood in both cultures. The experience of growing up among missionaries left a bitter aftertaste:

Americans who have lived long in China, especially those who have mixed with the Chinese, like to shovel-eat their rice even when they have returned and eat in American-Chinese restaurants. On the other hand, missionary-educated Chinese students hesitate to go Chinese before Americans because when they learned American manners of eating American food, they acquired the feeling that they are also good manners for eating any food. I share some of this feeling myself, because I was partly missionary-educated myself.[111]

Chao recognizes what anthropologists have called "going native." When westerners eat Chinese food in American settings using Chinese manners, they show off their erudition, sophistication, and expertise in cultural matters. How well traveled they are! What prestige accrues to those who have lived in far-off lands and can adroitly maneuver in several cultures. However, unlike their Western counterparts, Chinese, inculcated in Anglo decorum by colonizing missionaries, do not enjoy the same reputation. They learned painfully how much better the manners of the white world are, for they are used everywhere. Missionary teachers imparted not only a sense of cultural difference but of cultural superiority. The westerners who traveled widely were not immigrants; they were adventurers and were acknowledged for their competencies in several cultures. What is most contradictory in this view is that foreign-born "immigrants" who adapt to multiple cultural settings and move comfortably among them are not counted as competent by their adopted country. Consequently, Chao, as do many immigrants, lives in two worlds—her adopted country and the China of her memory and of her research and reconstruction—and not fully in one or the other.

Her collection of recipes is an evocation of the past, a nostalgic representation of regional cuisine. Although some foods have vanished in the trauma of the war and postwar period, her culinary repertoire is an account of war and its hardships on a people, the circumstances contemporary Chinese in China now face. Chao expresses the misery of her compatriots in the Proustian reminiscence of a meal of which she is deprived by relocation and that the Chinese themselves no longer have:

Hearing from friends and relatives about hardships at home and meeting those who have only recently come abroad make me feel how unreal some of those nice-eating things of the good old days seem to be. What's the use of talking about drinking golden, hot millet congee when you cannot get enough gray, gritty rice to eat?[112]

In a culinary mnemonic, she traverses a landscape and recaptures a pristine past. In her narrative account of war through recipes, we learn the new names given to familiar and traditional regional recipes: "Bomb Tokyo" is the title of a recipe—recently renamed in Chungking—for rice toast in soup, a variety of Mongolian Pot; "Depth Charging," the retitled "dropped eggs," consists of a couple of raw eggs poached in a "big pot" of hot soup.[113] What terror and subversion compelled the renaming of such delectable family fare! At the same time, *How to Cook and Eat in Chinese* wants to evoke a way of life that no longer endures, a way of life that exists, perhaps, only in the author's imagination, an imagination born of dislocation and memory. Chao recounts folklore and history in her re-creation of Chinese regional cooking. "In the time of the Emperor Hsuan Tsung [eighth century A.D.], litchi 'nuts' had to be relayed by fast horses from Szechwan to Chang-an in modern Shensi to please his favorite courtesan. Recently, they have been flown from Canton to Shanghai. But on the whole, even in peacetime, most of the juicy peaches of Hopeh or Shantung are known only in their small locality, at least so far as knowledge of the juice trickling up your wrist is concerned."[114] Since the sensate world re-created in cookbooks begs recovery or discovery, it is at best only imitative. As with other memoirs and reminiscences "cookbooks appear to belong to the literature of exile, of nostalgia and loss."[115]

Still, Chao's book is more than a memoir. It is also an anatomy of culinary, cultural, and linguistic patterns. Both author Chao, and the foreword writer, Hu Shih, view the book as a grammar of techniques and methods. Linguistic analogies are profuse and pervasive. Hu Shih praises Chao's abilities as a linguist to surmount cultural borders with the creation of a terminology American women can understand in order to teach them how to prepare Chinese cuisine. Yet, interestingly, and perhaps with particular Chinese modesty, Chao claims not to have written the text; it was written for her, in this case by her daughter and husband. The tensions of writing the book also refer as well to this family's transition to another cultural and social world, an experience similar to other emigrating families. Chao explains, "You know I speak little English and write less. So I cooked my dishes in Chinese, my daughter Rulan put my Chinese into English, and my husband, finding the English dull, put much of it back into Chinese again."[116] "Mushrooms Stir Shrimps" was changed to "Shrimps Fried with Mushrooms" and then changed back again to sound more Chinese. The "Salted Stews the Fresh," a favorite dish in Shanghai consisting of salted and fresh pork clear-simmered together,[117] was finally left in its original Chinese form. Perhaps world-famous philologist Professor Chao thought that the recipes would appear more authentic and quaint to American readers if their titles were literal translations of the Chinese. Rulan, it seems, would have preferred adapted—more modern—titles for the book's English-speaking audience to signal her family's successful acculturation to American society.

Chao credits Rulan with writing the book—but not without cost. "I don't know how many scoldings and answering-backs and quarrels Rulan and I went through."[118] In her critique of the generational strains caused by writing the book, Chao is also speaking to the strains and stresses to which generational relationships are subject in a new country. She says, "if kind friends—too many, who helped too much, to thank adequately here—if they had not come to the rescue to get the book done in a last midnight rush, the strained relations between mother and daughter would certainly have been broken. You know how it is with modern daughters and mothers who think we are modern."[119]

The fictional works of Amy Tan, Gish Jen, Denise Chong, and Maxine Hong Kingston[120] describe the trials of the mother-and-daughter relationship in detail, but the few words Chao uses to describe her situation are, in some ways, adequate. "And it is even more delicate with a mother and daughter, both having had mixed experiences of eating, cooking, and speaking and writing."[121] Multiculturalism, acculturation, and assimilation become issues troubling mother and daughter. In Chao's book, the older woman recounts some of her journeys to different countries as proof of her sophistication and modernity, while, according to her mother, the younger woman views her parent, in this new milieu, as traditional and unworldly. Yet despite their cultural differences and the stresses of writing the book, the bond between mother and daughter is affirmed. Their identities are confounded in the text at least on one occasion. One wonders if the following reminiscence, which is a footnote to the recipe for "Steamed Rice: Changsha Style . . . often used as a drink served individually, like thin congee," belongs to mother or daughter.[122] "This was my favorite drink when I lunched at school in Changsha, because all dishes in Changsha tasted so hot— Rulan."[123] Has Rulan taken the opportunity to share—in her mother's book—her *own* memories of China with the reader in this recipe, or is she embellishing the directions with stories of Chao's childhood told to her by her mother? In her role as translator Rulan may have decided to use her editorial prerogative to add a personal touch to the recipe with this memory. Perhaps she signed it as her contribution to her mother's book rather than as her own reminiscence.

As do many children of immigrant parents, daughter Rulan acts as a cultural mediator/translator for her mother in the larger society and as such assumes an authoritative position vis-à-vis her parent. In this case, the mother-daughter relationship is complicated by several border experiences, not the least of which is generational, culinary, and linguistic. Chao, the mother, knows how to cook; Rulan, the daughter, knows how to write. The enterprise requires negotiating authority within the boundaries of the household as well as outside it.

If writing the book created tension between Chao and her daughter, about her husband's contribution she has this to say: "Next, I must blame my husband for all the negative contributions he has made toward the making of the book. In many places, he has changed Rulan's good English into bad, which he thinks Americans like better. His greatest contribution is even more negative. . . . The only recipe that is really his own is Number 13.1, Stirred Eggs, which I let him write out himself. But he was so long-winded about it that I had to stop him from trying any other dish."[124]

He begins his recipe with unprecedented formality in this list of ingredients. "Obtain: 6 average-sized fresh eggs (for this is the maximum number of eggs I have cooked at one time); 50 c.c. fresh lard, which will approximately equal the content of 4 level tablespoonfuls; 1 plant of Chinese ts'ung (substitute scallion if ts'ung is unobtainable) about 30 cm. long by 7 mm. in average diameter."[125] Professor Chao writes out, with extraordinary scientific accuracy, a recipe that Chao claims is the simplest and most basic of Chinese dishes. The procedural directions are equally precise. "Either shell or unshell the eggs by knocking one against the another in any order."[126] The footnote Professor Chao adds to his text belabors—almost comically—the process of breaking the eggs: "Since, when two eggs collide, only one of them will break, it will be necessary to use a seventh egg with which to break the sixth. If, as it may very well happen, the seventh egg breaks first instead of the sixth, an expedient will be simply to use the seventh one and put away the sixth. An alternate procedure is to delay your numbering system and define that egg as the sixth egg which breaks after the fifth egg."[127]

He continues his rules for making eggs by warning the reader about the obvious next step.

> Be sure to have a bowl below to catch the contents. With a pair of chopsticks, strike the same with a quick, vigorous motion known as "beating the eggs." This motion should, however, be made repeatedly and not just once. Automatic machines, aptly named as "egg-beaters," have been invented for this purpose. Make cross sections of the ts'ung at intervals of about 7.5 mm., making 40 sections altogether. Throw in the ts'ung and the measured amount of salt during the final phase of the beating.[128]

Professor Chao's cookery instructions resemble the analytic parsing of a sentence more than the writing of a recipe. However, we realize that there is some tongue-in-cheek humor embedded in the recipe text when Professor Chao volunteers evidence of his linguistic expertise to the reader: "To test whether the cooking has been done properly, observe the person served. If he utters a voiced bilabial nasal consonant with a slow falling intonation, it is good. If he utters the syllable *yum* in reduplicated form, it is very good—Y. R. C."[129]

Her husband's efforts as a communicator of cooking techniques simply confirm Chao's sensibility that gender domains are sacrosanct. Men should not be in the kitchen. Even a professional woman such as she is better placed there than a man. Of her decision to use a particular orthographic and phonetic system for transliterating Chinese words, she says: "Chinese words are given in the Wade system to which my husband is opposed."[130] If her husband, a world-famous philologist, can intrude upon her kitchen *and* try to determine the language used in her cookbook, then she, in her role as the family's cook, can be an interloper in the realm of linguistics. In the very act of writing about the tension between them, however, she challenges her husband's authority in his domain of expertise and inverts the norm of women's subordination and deference to their husbands.[131]

Postscript

It was not only "celebrity-reformers"[132] like the Beecher sisters who self-consciously published their views on society in their cookbooks, but ordinary women who in their own charitable enterprises scripted a social world that accepted no intruders. Employing their culture's elite literature in the service of their everyday cookbook gives weight and authority both to their kitchen practices and to their beliefs about social and cultural differences. The Presbyterian ladies' selection of speech in a different register—a poem—that eulogizes a New England agrarian past also marks the limits of culinary, and thus cultural, acceptability.

Like many others, immigrant women used what was close at hand as a way of crossing borders or patrolling them. Buwei Yang Chao's book is as obviously an account of difference as it is an attempt to re-create a cuisine and a culture. In all of these instances, women from various classes, cultural origins, and political persuasions found the cookbook a place to circumscribe or cross social and cultural borders, to martial the persuasive force of the kitchen to gain support for their beliefs and causes. In each case, the author evoked a sense of "place" as an ideal with which to conform, whether "place" was a physical locale, a memorialized past, or a social location. The regional China of Chao's memory and the glorified New England of the Presbyterian ladies' poem each commemorate a place, a time, and the genius of a people.

In the process of memorializing a place through its food, women codify cookery and kitchen practices. For this reason, in the writing of a recipe book the author is able to embed status, rank, and power in the book's rules. Because it is born of memory, the food—and the place—is matchless in its re-creation. Cookbook writers are able to claim expertise whether the audience is reading about how to prepare "Sizzling Rice Soup" or "Boston

Baked Beans." Explicitly about disseminating knowledge, the texts, depending on the reader, may as often create a gap as a bond. The very act of inscribing cultural and social differences in food preparation may link author and reader or create a wedge in the form of an "us" and a "them" or a "we" and a "you."

If cookbooks are about the losses of exile and the trauma of expulsion, they are also opportunities for nostalgia, travel, voyeurism, and emulation. They are subtle ways of marking insider and outsider status in social and cultural life. If all of these books are about exile in its broadest sense, they are about exclusion and inclusion. They are about the ways women write a place into being: to defy, delimit, manipulate, and infiltrate social, cultural, and geographical boundaries. And they do so in everyday places like the homely cookbook.

Epilogue

In the late twentieth and early twenty-first centuries, no less than in other historical periods, our fascination with food and cooking remains steadfast. Privately, women continue the practice of compiling recipes from friends and family. They keep their writings in albums, on 3 by 5 cards, in notebooks, and on slips of paper inserted between the pages of their cookbooks. Some women now arrange their cookery compilations electronically on the computer, gathering recipes from websites that facilitate international exchange. A woman's recipe collection may reflect her special interests in health, lifestyle, ethnic, regional, haute or fusion cuisine, and other possibilities with limitless combinations.

These innumerable interests also are embraced by cookbook writers, for whom food remains muse, reverie, intellectual pursuit, commercial venture, passion, art, and vocation. Are the themes we have explored in cookbooks thus far—from the seventeenth through twentieth centuries—still valid for today's world? Are we still in search of cultural roots, family, and a sense of community in which we enjoy reciprocal relations? Do cookbook authors still write about their lives, proffer opinions about how we as citizens should conduct ourselves? Do they wish to instill these values and ideals in the next generation?

If so, how do cookbooks reflect the late modern world and its concerns, its questions, and hopes? In what form will we find the themes elaborated by earlier cookbook writers: community, collective memory and identity, legacy, autobiography, authorship, and social and political commentary?

The genre of the cookbook is as fluid and eclectic as ever, embodying an array of knowledge in its disquisition on food. Now as in the past, cookbooks often merge the distinct themes we have examined in this book. I have separated them only for the purpose of investigation. Here I briefly review several books that demonstrate how cookbook authors have used twentieth-century printed cookbooks to tackle some of the social and political issues of our times.

A few lauded cookbooks of the late twentieth century have embedded different emphases in their explorations through food of history, of region, of memory, of self, and of different lifestyles. There are those that celebrate various cultural heritages. Some entice with trend-setting restaurant cuisines that thrive on ingenuity and invention. One of the more recent fashions is fusion cuisine, which revels in combining often vastly different culinary traditions. Others flaunt time-consuming and labor-intensive haute cuisine while some advocate the preparation of thrifty meals in fifteen minutes. What do they have in common? Each cookbook puts forward its author's vision of the good life, one predicated on an aesthetic of fresh food that is well prepared, hospitality, family, and building community through the sharing of food. If cookbook authors are impassioned in their writing about different cuisines and the lifestyles they conjure, their readers are equally enchanted by them.

Many cookbook writers strike a balance between the sensual pleasures of the table and social responsibility; they write fervently about the need to alter our taken-for-granted habits of eating and preparing food. Despite cookbooks' distinctive historical manifestations and subsequent transformations, authors still explore the quest for health, beauty, and life's meaning through food. Moreover, the explosion of food magazines, restaurants, and cooking shows on television that feature an array of cuisines reveal our delight with food.

We may link our societal preoccupation with culinary matters with class structures, conspicuous consumption, global economies, commercialization and marketing, the heritage and tourist industries, environmental issues, and even, ironically, with a renewed awareness of hunger and food shortages.[1] Many cookbook writers and their commercial enterprises link themselves with agencies and efforts on behalf of those excluded from the bounty: Share Our Strength,[2] the Hunger Site (www.thehungersite.com), food banks across the United States, the World Health Organization, and many local groups too numerous to mention. Despite their efforts, their work has not begun to eradicate the growing numbers of people who go to sleep hungry each night. While we may delude ourselves that famines are the result of food shortages in particular places at particular times, economists such as Amartya Sen argue that "nobody need starve." Famines, she argues, are the result of poverty and indifference.[3]

The distance between rich and poor permit the former to enjoy food as an entertainment while the latter confront scarcity and want. According to Sen and others, hunger can be eliminated. It takes a socially conscious citizenry to monitor and lobby for everyone's right to equal access to food supplies, whether they are imported or locally grown. It means ensuring that those who are hungry have the economic means to buy food; it means that they must have jobs.[4] Thus, some cookbook writers bind their culinary projects to a larger goal—feeding the hungry.[5]

Similarly, some cookbook writers want to save the planet. They advocate for changes in the ways in which we procure our food. Motivated by the Green Revolution of the latter part of the twentieth century, these authors promote sound agricultural and husbandry practices in order to stop despoiling our earth and contaminating our food.

Others want to preserve a way of life, a heritage, and a cultural or regional identity through food. Fearful that time and a global economy are rapidly eroding cultural distinctiveness, some food writers are trying to salvage a group's past by preserving their culinary heritage. While some food writers are not explicitly proselytizing for social change, their culinary tributes to particular cuisines—Italian, French, Thai, Mexican, Russian, and Chinese, for example—are paeans to the good life, a life in which family, community, and mutual responsibility have been idealized. Thus, the delectable dishes of a region or culture symbolize the older values of a more "natural" way of life, expressed as sustenance for both the individual and the social body. The authors of regional or ethnic cookbooks describe food procurement and preparation practices that look back to another era, one that (the author believes) is threatened by or persists in the face of social and cultural change.

If reading a cookbook is like following a sensate trail to another place remote from us in space and time, it is also a path to the present. Although we cannot recapture the gastronomic experience depicted by the recipe, we can approximate it. The recipe is a copy of its original (a dish that could not be duplicated exactly even in its own time) and each subsequent attempt to reconstruct it, a copy of the copy. It is the closest we can come to another world. By its reading we are momentarily transformed. Thus, for some, eating the words of a recipe book is a nourishing act.[6] Cookbooks are literature rather than instructional guides for these people.[7] They frame a fictional world as surely as novels do. Critic Anthony Lane said, "great cookbooks are more like novels than like home-improvement manuals. What these culinary bibles tell you to do is far less beguiling than the thought of a world in which such things might be done."[8] Without ever preparing a dish, reading with one's imagination is a satisfying act.

One genre of cookbooks is transmuted ethnography, history, memoir, travelogue, and fiction. Through the kitchens, food, and meals of other cultures we are introduced to exotic worlds, a form of traveling I call tabletop tourism. Reading cookbooks enables us to travel to distant countries without leaving home. For some people this imaginative form of travel, sparked by flavors, aromas, and novel ingredients blended perhaps in unfamiliar ways, is an affordable way to explore other territories. Immersing oneself in the sensory experiences of another cuisine through reading and cooking allows us to travel and experience the foreign while still feeling the security of home.

Ethnographic writing disguised as cookbooks and memoirs is a popular structure for encapsulating recipes. And vice versa: Recipe books are popular forms for encapsulating ethnographies and memoirs. Outsiders who would like to know other cultures voyage there through cookbooks that enable them to discover or recover a national or regional cuisine and its past, often depicted nostalgically as timeless.[9]

In *Savoie: The Land, People, and Food of the French Alps,* cookbook author Madeleine Kamman has recorded—and rescued—a way of life for herself and her readers. Her cookbook is memoir, ethnography, history, natural history, and culinary archive with drawings of native costumes, hairstyles, and photographs of Savoyard faces and traditional activities. Kamman wrote the book as a remembrance of her childhood trips to Annecy in the Savoie. Her experiences and memories of time spent in this region are so compelling that it is the Savoie that she calls home.[10] Through her cookbook, she recounts the adventures of her youth and her love for a people and a region.

The book is an act of homage and celebration. Kamman opts simultaneously to present and preserve a Savoie born of her experience: the farm where she lived with other children and a community that was "a microcosm of pre–World War II French society (which, fundamentally, has not changed all that much), and the summer was one long and interesting blending of our lives, with that of a very small Savoie village."[11] For those who have never been to the Savoie, it is an introduction: "a general picture of how a people, lived, worked, and cooked, and how they have succeeded in transforming their lives and surroundings to live happily at the end of the twentieth century."[12] Kamman concludes that despite modernity, the Savoie has managed to protect and retain its identity.

As we move from one alpine area to another, to *A Taste of Switzerland* (1992) by Sue Style, we are introduced to another type of cookbook, this one more of a tourist's history and culinary guide than an attempt at reclamation. Photographs of traditional architecture, chocolate logs, and fondue pots by candlelight embellish the pages and offer picturesque glimpses of the country known for recipes such as "Appezöller Rösti," "Birchermuesli," "Chocolate Truffles," and "White Chocolate Mousse in Dark Chocolate Boxes." It opens with a history and closes with the names of small hotels and inns, each of which serves exquisite meals at tables with glorious mountain views. The sensory pleasures of the table suggested by the cookbook are an incentive to tour this country literally if one can, or to enjoy it at a distance through eating.

The cookbook cum guide depicting Switzerland differs from traditional travel narratives that explore the writer's adventures while journeying in remote and exotic countries. Lynne Kasper's *The Splendid Table: Recipes from Emilia-Romagna, the Heartland of Northern Italian Food*, differs from both travel literature and the guidelike quality of Style's cookbook. It draws the reader to the distinctiveness of the region of Emilia-Romagna not through sight, which is the usual way of touring new places,[13] but through the modality of taste and culinary skill.

Replete with folklore, linguistic variations, and a discussion of the origins of many of the dishes, Kasper's volume is a culinary monument to the region. In its author's words, "the book is about five centuries of that culinary heritage."[14] Kasper's volume is a tribute to Emilia-Romagna: "her hospitality, the way the light moves across her plain and her deep passion for her own culinary heritage."[15] Kasper's enthusiasm for this region of Italy is captured in the detail of her historical and folkloristic frames for each recipe: an anecdote describing its creator and its provenance. The recipe for chicken called "Il Pollo in Tegame di Maria Bertuzzi" begins with a description of the setting: "Maria Bertuzzi shared this recipe at her Ristorante Grande in Rivergaro, along the Trebbia River in Piacenza province. She called it good *contadina,* or farm food. I like the way fresh lemon finishes the dish's tomato sauce and the way the chicken easily reheats."[16] It is not just authors like Kasper who romanticize the past, native-born Italians like Bertuzzi also have reclaimed their idealized agrarian roots.[17] By depicting her chicken dish as good farm food, Bertuzzi is as adept at evoking an image of an agrarian past as any cookbook writer. Restaurant owner Bertuzzi has done just that as she selects an image to represent her culinary style.

Although authenticity[18] is her goal, Kasper is candid about the adaptations she has made to re-create the recipes in another time and setting: "When I translated recipes from Emilia-Romagna to America, often products that seemed the same were not."[19] Kasper then lists the ingredients that cannot be reproduced on American soil or that offer more healthful alternatives. In her own practice (as well as some of the region's cooks), "I use olive oil as the actual cooking medium, with reduced quantities of pancetta, prosciutto, and mortadella as flavorings. Although this changes some old recipes, with their generous quantities of pork and butter, it makes them available to a whole new public in Emilia-Romagna and here."[20] Recent trends in nutrition and health motivate Kasper to reshape the ancient cucina of Italy.

Still, if forced to choose between authenticity and adaptation, Kasper wants her cookbook to be a repository of an authentic cuisine. "Wherever I felt a dish's authenticity and quality would be lost with these changes, I left it in its original state, just as it is preserved in Emilia-Romagna."[21] Her choice implies that the region remains, to some degree, an enduring and changeless world, free from the pressures that propel other regions into new forms of thinking, behaving, and eating. Yet she is not unaware of variations: "It is tempting to say that there is only one way to cook a dish. But the most important thing I learned in my years in Emilia-Romagna is one way of preparing a dish was always countered with varying renditions from down the block, down the road, or across the province."[22]

Nor is Kasper unaware of social strata and historical transformations: "The range [of dishes] is broad and deep, from the stews of pasta and beans that sustained field hands and laborers to the grand gilded pies that crowded the tables of counts, dukes, and princes. You will find dishes created centuries ago and modern innovations on those old themes."[23] Kasper depicts Emilia-Romagna in all of its culinary complexity, cultural change, and variation while attempting to delineate its essence.

Kasper's cookbook moves the reader through the region, depicting its local color and scenery and its people. It takes us back into the past and forward to the present, showing us old customs and modern innovations. The artfully composed photographs with their hazy golden-brown hues suggest not only the warmth of a fireside hearth and soil but the vintage daguerreotypes of the late nineteenth century, which lead the reader into the depth and to the "rich . . . dishes of deep, layered tastes" of Emilia-Romagnan culture.

In her volume, Kasper offers readers a tribute to Italian regional culture and identity. She has captured and compiled recipes, myths, and legends—stories that animate Emilia-Romagna's past and present—and that, importantly, help us to imagine its culinary and physical landscape.

Other cultures have used cookbooks in similar ways. In the 1970s in Iran, cookbooks published for the middle class, for example, contained sections on Western cuisine. However, at that time, middle-class Iranian families were still preparing and eating only Persian food in their homes. Thus, the sections on Western cuisine formed a literature of the imagination, rarely, if ever, realized through its creation but archived in the realm of fantasy.[24]

This form of culinary ethnography is as much for insiders living away from their native country as for outsiders. In these instances, cookbooks reputedly offer an authentic cuisine written by natives. Such is the case with

Najmieh Batmanglij's *Food of Life* (1986), a book written in English for fellow Iranians living in disparate parts of the world. As Islamic scholar Bert Fragner has noted, "this cookbook conjures up an idealized, almost ahistorical Iranian cultural setting, represented by a culinarily refined community of eaters, creating the image of an unbroken continuity of Iranian civilization, practised as far away as Los Angeles or Vancouver."[25] Often diaspora communities adhere to customs that have long since changed in their homelands.

Once published, cookbooks do not continue to change. They do so only in the hands of their practitioners (either through editorializing the recipes within the book or through actual practice). Thus, cookbooks portray a culture at a particular moment in time, thus freezing it for posterity. Such a portrait of culture enhances a sense of kinship between the reader and the society with which she is trying to connect.

What do heritage cookbooks and volumes on trend-setting cuisine share? It may appear that the two types of cookbooks are worlds apart: The former seeks to preserve a culinary tradition in a written record, the way a museum curator may seek to conserve a precious object.[26] The latter prides itself on inventiveness and the elaboration of an art form by an artist/chef. In spite of these differences, both types of books are predicated on the love of good food, the implications of cuisine for different lifestyles, and the celebration of community, whether it is tied to an ancient culture, such as Kasper's, or a utopian vision, such as that of restaurateur Alice Waters.

We might expect that when we read Waters's *Chez Panisse Café Cookbook,* we will be introduced to the world of a pioneering restaurateur and to a culinary style lauded for its novelty and ingenuity. Yet Waters, known for her "distinctly American style of cooking,"[27] has not merely created and managed a restaurant; she and her colleagues advance a set of values that underlie her enterprise, a philosophy of social change that supports her entrepreneurial venture:

> I want this book to be an inspiration as well as a reference, each chapter has an introduction describing the sources of the foods we cook—farmers, foragers, and artisans, who care deeply about what they are doing, and who are constantly opening new avenues in our work and giving us ways of seeing things. Our search for fresh and pure ingredients is a work in progress and by

the year 2000, we want all of our ingredients to be certifiable as organically grown. We hope our descriptions of some of our suppliers will inspire you to seek out similarly dedicated farmers, foragers, fisherman, and other purveyors who practice and support the sustainable, ecologically sound harvest of nature's bounty.[28]

Waters uses her cookbook to motivate others to sustain the earth's resources through sound practices: Use locally and organically grown, seasonal foods from trusted and like-minded provisioners. She tells us: "It is not just a list of purveyors, but a community of people who share our goals of providing fresh, perfectly grown food while promoting a sustainable agriculture that takes care of the earth. Like any community, we find ourselves bound together by mutual dependence and a feeling of responsibility for each other."[29] Her friendships are predicated on both a business relationship and a common goal: the provisioning of food in a manner consonant with her activist's philosophy.

If homebound women from the seventeenth through the twentieth centuries celebrated communities in their culinary records, restaurateur Alice Waters does the same. In fact, Waters acknowledges her friends, colleagues, and coworkers by name, giving them the recognition that women have for centuries enumerated in their recipe manuscripts: "Jerry Budrick, maitre d'hotel, Steve Crumley, then bartender, her old college roommate, Eleanor Bertino, journalist Kate Coleman, Fritz Streiff, and tea authority Helen Gustafson."[30] Waters's community is centered on her coworkers, colleagues, and customers, many of whom are also her friends.

With Chez Panisse, Waters attracts people from near and far providing opportunities to celebrate important life events in a setting she and her colleagues have created. How important the restaurant became to diners she learned through a misfortune: a fire that burned the restaurant.

Just two years ago after the Café opened, early one Sunday morning after we had all gone home, a fire started in the downstairs kitchen. No one was hurt, but before it was put out, the Restaurant was gutted and the Café was seriously damaged. We had to close for months to regroup and rebuild, and that time was a turning point for me. As sympathy poured in, I began to understand that

we had, indeed, created a community—not just for ourselves, but one that included our customers.[31]

Waters merges the public commercial world of the restaurant with her personal utopian vision and environmental activism. In her chapter on vegetables Waters acts as an educator who teaches the skills of gardening and
composting, foraging, and harvesting foods at their flavorful peak. She edu-
cates her readers about eggs and cheeses, again opting for locally produced
ones above those bought in supermarkets, where she believes it is difficult to
determine the quality of the produce.

In keeping with her desire to harmonize her business with nature and the
annual cycle, Waters prefers to buy sea and land creatures for her restaurant
from local fisheries and farms where the creatures' natural reproductive cycles are observed. Salmon is served seasonally, appearing on the menu only
from May until October.[32] With the fish and seafood she buys from other
regions, such as Maine lobster and Maryland crabs, Waters buys from purveyors whose values match her own. Her search for perfect poultry means
"serving only healthy animals raised under humane conditions and fed or-
ganic grain."[33] Raising animals in this way ensures not only better-tasting
food but healthier food, food that is safe for the individual who consumes it
and, importantly, safer for the planet.

When we prepare and eat food, we are physically changed. Our bodies
are literally transformed by the substances we ingest. Do we believe that
when we protect our own bodies with healthful, well-prepared food, we are
simultaneously protecting the planet?[34] By "luring us through food to social
activism,"[35] are we really effecting social change? Are we confounding our
economic power to consume quality foods (poison-free, fresh, wholesome,
humanely raised) with political action? Folklorist Kim Lau argues that this
is the artifice of New Age capitalism: We believe that we are making political statements through our consumer choices without realizing that we are
being manipulated by market forces.[36]

However, Waters recognizes that the act of providing good healthful food
to people who have become more than customers entails greater responsibility. After she prepared a meal for President Clinton (and thirty of his top

California contributors) in 1996, she regretted that she did not say something more political when introduced to him. "'He talks about community
all the time,' Waters told interviewer Marian Burros, 'but you can't just demand that of people. The way you have that happen is when you eat and
care about their nourishment around the table, and the bigger table is the
community.'"[37] Waters's community is global. Her restaurant has, according
to Burros, "become a mecca of the culinary world,"[38] and Waters has taken
that duty to heart; she feels responsibility for the world as well.

Waters's political activism has taken several turns: She has helped prison-
ers to create gardens while they are incarcerated and taught them skills they
may use to earn a living when they are released. Recently she worked with a
nearby Berkeley school in an effort to create an "Edible Schoolyard," where
children grow food that they then cook for one another. By yoking farmer
and eater in a harmonious food cycle of mutual benefit, Waters hopes to
provide a model of personal responsibility for sustaining a global community and a local one in a safe environment.

Waters has reproduced these values in a child's cookbook, *Fanny at Chez
Panisse.* Using her daughter's adventures at the restaurant, Waters exposes future generations to the same values that she has inculcated in Fanny. This
cookbook, as are all of Waters's books, is a legacy for her daughter: In the
persona of Fanny, the adult Waters introduces her daughter: "Oh, I almost
forgot! My name is Fanny and Chez Panisse is a restaurant in Berkeley run
by my mom and about a hundred of her friends."[39] Thus the reader is introduced to this child's vision of her mother's large community of people
who we know embrace a common cause.

On a visit to "a friend's boat up the river," Fanny and the book's young
readers are introduced to the natural world, its cycles and rhythms, by ob-
serving the vegetation and creatures of the region: "We go across the river to
a place where fig trees grow. There's two kinds of figs that grow near Bump's
place: green figs that are white inside and purple figs that are red inside. I
can never decide which ones I like the best. It's hard to find good ones because the birds always get there first. They know better than anybody which
figs are the ripest and the sweetest and the best tasting." Fanny is not only
learning about the natural world, she is learning how to be a connoisseur.

She is being schooled in the subtleties of a discriminating palate. Not only does Fanny's exposure to her mother's restaurant and colleagues enable her to become adept in culinary matters, she is also exposed to the values that her mother's community shares with one another. Whereas many children living in cities do not realize that the meat served for dinner comes from a living creature, Fanny knows about humane farming practices. About chicken, Fanny tells her young readers, "You want to eat a chicken that's been eating good things itself. They're usually the ones that come from farms where they take the best care of their birds and give them lots of room."[40]

Yet since she has extended her community to include the thousands of people who visit her restaurant and those she will reach through the publication of her cookbooks, Waters's philosophy and political agenda are not for Fanny alone. Embracing a wider world, Waters's cuisine and the wholesome, sound growing and harvesting practices it implies are a political agenda she wishes to bequeath to the next generation.

This literature of the kitchen obscures the boundaries of past and present, private and public, self and other, cerebral and corporal. Reading a recipe, preparing and consuming it are, in the end, the word and body become one.

We might imagine cookbook author Waters and her counterparts past and present saying: Eat my words. . . . And live by them.

Notes

Chapter 1

1. I use the term "communities" to signify not a territorial or geographic region, large or small, but what some scholars have termed a community of practice. Social scientists Jean Lave and Etienne Wenger who are interested in processes of learning have developed the term "communities of practice" to extend our understanding of communities beyond the usual parameters of space, time, or culture and the homogeneity implied by them. Instead "It does imply participation in an activity system about which participants share understandings concerning what they are doing and what that means in their lives and for their communities." Jean Lave and Etienne Wenger, *Situated Learning: Legitimate Peripheral Participation* (Cambridge: Cambridge University Press, 1991), 98.
2. Jhumpa Lahiri, *Interpreter of Maladies: Stories* (Boston: Houghton Mifflin, 1999), 162.
3. Jane Janviers and others, manuscript receipt book, 1817–1837, Historical Society of Pennsylvania.
4. Janviers and others. The chronology of the book is determined by the dated entries. It is likely that additions followed the last noted date.
5. Ellen Markoe Emlen, manuscript receipt book, 1811–1876, Historical Society of Pennsylvania.
6. Hopestill Brett, manuscript cookery book, 1678, Esther B. Aresty Collection, University of Pennsylvania.
7. I have been unable to discover a place named Horncroft in seventeenth-century England, although a small, twentieth-century Sussex community bears that name.
8. Recipe books varied in size. Some were small to accommodate the fashion for "pocket books" that were kept in apron pockets. Others were grander texts, those that were not carried around by the mistress of the household. The fashion for large or small books varied in different periods and did not always mirror the wealth and station of the family. However, gilded ornamentation and expensive leather do reveal the economic circumstances of a family.

9. Hopestill Brett's book had only a few recipes written in another hand. Several were for medicinals and the formality of the script indicates that perhaps a professional scrivener, physician, or apothecary may have inscribed them into her book. The cookery recipes are predominantly in Brett's hand.

10. I am grateful to Kris Rabberman for raising this question about Brett's literacy.

11. The Esther B. Aresty Collection of Rare Culinary Manuscripts and Books and the Joseph Downs Collection at the Winterthur Library, Museum and Garden provided most of the examples of seventeenth-century materials. However, many monographs and journals, such as those mentioned later in this chapter and throughout the book, were also helpful for examining Brett's manuscript.

12. Sara Mendelson and Patricia Crawford, *Women in Early Modern England, 1550–1720* (Oxford, Clarendon Press, 1998), 271.

13. Mendelson and Crawford, 307.

14. At this time, the gentry class was rising and challenging the power of landed aristocracy.

15. Although Laurel Thatcher Ulrich refers to the good wives of seventeenth-century New England, she points to the usefulness of her descriptions for other regions (xiv). *Goodwives: Image and Reality in the Lives of Women in Northern New England, 1650–1750* (New York: Vintage Books, Random House, 1991), 3.

16. In *Recipes for Reading* (Amherst: University of Massachusetts Press, 1997), Anne Bowers suggests that the women who created community cookbooks in the nineteenth and twentieth centuries did not exclude any woman from participating in the collaborative undertaking. It was important that every woman had an opportunity to contribute to the joint venture as an indication of the cohesiveness of the network and its desire to be inclusive.

17. Hilary Spurling (ed.), *Elinor Fettiplace's Receipt Book: Elizabethan Country House Cooking* (London: Penguin Books, 1986), 40.

18. David Schoonover (ed.), *Ladie Borlase's Receipt Booke* (Iowa City: University of Iowa Press, 1998), 13–15.

19. The abbreviated descriptions—often only a listing of ingredients—indicate a familiarity with combinatory procedures that did not require elaboration but represented shared understandings about basic cookery techniques. This was common enough in all cookbooks of the period, but Brett's hurried penmanship is a sign that she wrote the book herself over the course of her lifetime or at least during the period in which she practiced housewifery.

20. Karen Robertson, "Tracing Women's Connections from a Letter by Elizabeth Ralegh" in Susan Frye and Karen Robertson (eds.), *Maids, Mistresses, Cousins and Queens: Women's Alliances in Early Modern England* (Oxford: Oxford University Press, 1999), 152.

21. The issue of women's alliances in early modern England is brilliantly discussed in Frye and Robertson; see in particular the article by Robertson, 149–174.

22. Robertson, 154.

23. Spellings of names were not consistent but reappeared throughout the book in recognizable forms. Standardized orthographies appeared only in the nineteenth century.

24. Charles Elliott, "The Quaker Connection," *Horticulture* (September/October 2000): 28–30.

25. It is difficult to say whether Hopestill's book contained more scripture than other seventeenth-century cookery books. More than a few recipe books contain biblical verse. Brett devoted the back of her book to her selections.

26. Belinda Peters, review of Sara Mendelson and Patricia Crawford, *Women in Early Modern England 1550–1720.* In H-Net Reviews <books at h-net.ms.edu>. July 26, 2000. H-Review Published by (July 2000), 2. Archived <http://www.h-net.msu.edu>.

27. Mrs. Fred Patterson, recipe commonplace manuscript c. nineteenth century, from the Joseph Downs Collection, Winterthur Museum and Library.

28. Like many women in the period, Patterson designated herself solely by her husband's name.

29. Published community cookbooks most often, but not always, emphasize the place or organization that fostered it. Most manuscript cookbooks neglect geography and chronology, creating a sense of timelessness. Such continuity is, of course, not valid since the recipes themselves are re-created with every making and altered in various eras, in response to different social groups and health trends.

30. Kevin Kenny, *Making Sense of the Molly Maguires* (New York: Oxford University Press, 1998).

31. Johanna L. Stratton, *Pioneer Women: Voices from the Kansas Frontier* (New York: Simon & Schuster, 1981), 62–63.

32. The newspaper clipping was so badly stained that I could not read the byline.

33. Ann Douglas, *The Feminization of American Culture* (New York: Anchor Press, Doubleday, 1988), 200–227; John R. Gillis, *A World of Their Own Making: Myth, Ritual, and the Quest for Family Values* (Cambridge, MA: Harvard University Press, 1996), 201–221; Daniel Pool, *What Jane Austen Ate and Charles Dickens Knew: From Fox Hunting to Whist—the Facts of Daily Life in 19th-Century England* (New York: Simon & Schuster, 1993), 252–255.

34. I was introduced to the concept of the good death when I heard Drew Faust's seminar at the University of Pennsylvania. A revised version of the paper was recently published: See *Journal of Southern History,* Vol. 67, no. 1 (Feb. 2001).

35. For a discussion of the changing concepts of aging and death, see Thomas R. Cole, *The Journey of Life, A Cultural History of Aging in America* (Cambridge: Cambridge University Press, 1992), 137–138.

36. S. L. Louis, *Decorum: A Practical Treatise on Etiquette and Dress of the Best American Society* (Cincinnati: Union Publishing House, 1882), 11.

37. John Kasson, *Rudeness and Civility: Manners in Nineteenth Century America* (New York: Hill and Wang, 1990), 3.

38. Kasson, 36.

39. Kasson, 57.

40. Kasson, 55–56.

41. Elizabeth Emlen Randolph Wister, Recipe book, 1848–1921, Joseph Downs Collection, Winterthur Library.

42. It is not clear who Mrs. W. is. She may be Mrs. Wistar, Louis Wistar's mother, who may have come to live with Elizabeth and her husband, Louis, in her later years. It is as likely that Mrs. W. was a nanny.

43. Another common method of organizing personal recipe books was to categorize recipes according to type of dish, meal, or method and to leave blank pages between categories.

44. Ellen Markoe Emlen, letter, September 9, nineteenth-century manuscript recipe book, Historical Society of Pennsylvania.

45. Regina Bendix has suggested that the blurring of status in recipe exchange may have led to changes in behavior as well.

46. *Nelly Custis' Housekeeping Book,* edited and introduction by Patricia Brady Schmitt (New Orleans: Historic New Orleans Collection, 1982).

47. I am indebted to Gayle Samuels for stressing this point.

48. Susan J. Leonardi, "Recipes for Reading: Summer Pasta, Lobster à la Riseholme, and Key Lime Pie," *Publication of the Modern Language Association of America* 104 (1989): 340–346.

49. Leonardi, 345.

50. Mrs. Downing is the name I have given to this anonymous woman, an early-twentieth-century housekeeper in rural Pennsylvania.

51. I am indebted to Regina Bendix for making this point.

52. Laura Bigelow, nineteenth-century recipe manuscript, Joseph Downs Collection, Winterthur, 45.

53. Quoted in Peggy Hickman, *A Jane Austen Household Book with Martha Lloyd's Recipes* (Newton Abbott: David & Charles, 1977), 96.

54. Anonymous, nineteenth-century recipe book, Joseph Downs Collection, Winterthur Library.

55. The name, which is indecipherable, may be shorthand for a longer name.

56. It is not clear which of these locations was home or if she moved; both of these places are written into her recipe book in the same year.

Chapter 2

1. Anne Michaels, *Fugitive Pieces* (New York: Vintage Books, 1998).

2. Salman Rushdie, *Midnight's Children* (New York: Penguin USA, 1995).

3. The red melange of fruit and spices represents the mortar enslaved Jews used in building the pyramids in Egypt.

4. Rochester Chapter of Hadassah, *Rochester Hadassah Cookbook* (Rochester, NY: Great Lakes Press, 1972), Esther B. Aresty Collection, University of Pennsylvania.

5. Cara De Silva (ed.), *In Memory's Kitchen: A Legacy from the Women of Terezín* (Northvale, NJ: Jason Aronson Inc, 1996).

6. Freda De Knight, *A Date with a Dish: A Cookbook of American Negro Recipes* (New York: Hermitage Press, 1948), Esther B. Aresty Collection, University of Pennsylvania.

7. De Knight, xiii.

8. For a discussion of the African influence on Southern cooking, see Margaret Jones Bolsterli, "The Very Food We Eat: A Speculation on the Nature of Southern Culture," *Southern Humanities Review* 16, no. 2 (1982): 119–126.

9. Alan Grubb, "House and Home in the Victorian South: The Cookbook as Guide," in *In Joy and Sorrow: Women, Family, and Marriage in the Victorian South, 1830–1900.* Carol Bleser (ed.) (New York: Oxford University Press, 1991), 156.

10. F. W. Warren, "Introduction," A. P. Hill, *Mrs. Hill's New Cookbook: A Practical System for Private Families, in Town and Country* (New York: Carleton, Publisher, Madison Square, 1870), 6.

11. F. W. Warren in A. P. Hill, 6–7.

12. Hill, 12.

13. Damon L. Fowler, "Historical Commentary," in a facsimile of *Mrs. Hill's Southern Practical Cookery and Receipt Book* (Columbia: University of South Carolina Press, 1995), xliii.

14. John Egerton, *Southern Food: At Home, On the Road, in History* (Chapel Hill: University of North Carolina Press, 1993), 15.

15. Sidney Mintz, *Tasting Food, Tasting Freedom: Excursions into Eating, Culture, and the Past* (Boston: Beacon Press, 1996), 47–48.

16. Barbara Dianne Savage, *Broadcasting Freedom: Radio, War, and the Politics of Race, 1938–1948.* (Chapel Hill: University of North Carolina Press, 1999), 9.

17. Maxwell Whiteman, editor of the Afro-American History Series (Philadelphia: R Historic Publication no. 235, preface to the reprint of Robert Roberts, *The House Servant's Directory* (originally published in Boston: Munroe and Francis and in New York: Charles S. Francis, 1827).

18. Whiteman, preface.

19. W. E. Burghardt DuBois, *The Philadelphia Negro: A Social Study* (New York: Benjamin Blom, 1899), 32.

20. DuBois, 32–35.

21. Elaine Tait, "Passed-Down Dishes," *The Philadelphia Inquirer,* February 25, 1996. In a recent article, bibliophile and historian Jan Longone discusses Mrs. Fisher and other early African American cookery authors in "Early Black-Authored American Cookbooks," *Gastronomica: The Journal of Food and Culture,* vol. 1, no. 1 (February 2001): 96–99.

22. For another version of Southern food writing and the role of women, see Egerton's insightful analysis.
23. Katharin Bell, *Mammy's Cook Book* (New York: Henry Holt & Co., 1928).
24. Grubb, 162.
25. Grubb, 162.
26. Savage, 21.
27. Savage, 1.
28. De Knight, xiii.
29. De Knight, xiii.
30. Maurice R. Davie, *Negroes in American Society* (New York: McGraw-Hill, 1949), 374.
31. Davie, 374.
32. Jacqueline Jones, *Labor of Love, Labor of Sorrow: Black Women, Work, and the Family from Slavery to the Present* (New York: Basic Books, 1985), 269.
33. De Knight, xiii.
34. Gertrude Blair in De Knight, x.
35. Gertrude Blair in De Knight, x.
36. Gertrude Blair in De Knight, ix.
37. De Knight, xiii.
38. De Knight, 34.
39. De Knight, 34.
40. For a brilliant discussion of the concept of authenticity and its place in folklore studies, see Regina Bendix, *In Search of Authenticity: The Formation of Folklore Studies* (Madison: University of Wisconsin Press, 1997).
41. De Knight, 34.
42. De Knight, 33.
43. De Knight, 33.
44. De Knight, 33.
45. De Knight, 22–23.
46. De Knight, 1.
47. De Knight, 2.
48. De Knight, 2.
49. De Knight, 23.
50. De Knight, back cover.
51. In the United States, many different cultures contributed different culinary ideas to the basic English cooking on which American is founded. Early twentieth-century versions of American food consisted of a fairly bland and unseasoned palate. See Laura Shapiro, *Perfection Salad: Women and Cooking at the Turn of the Century* (New York: Henry Holt and Company, 1986), for a description of home economics cooking.
52. De Knight, 2.
53. De Knight, 23.
54. De Knight, 24.
55. De Knight, 148–49.

56. De Knight, 77–78.
57. De Knight, 29.
58. De Knight, 31–32.
59. De Knight, 292.
60. De Knight, 292.
61. Gunnar Myrdal, *An American Dilemma: The Negro Problem and Modern Democracy* (New York: Harper & Row, 1968), Twentieth Anniversary Edition, first published in 1948, 409–411.
62. For the sake of consistency I use the term "Negro" as it is used in the primary references.
63. De Knight, 63.
64. De Knight, 66.
65. De Knight, 71–72.
66. DuBois does not mention Holland in his section on the Caterers' Guild, but the apex of the period DuBois described waned in 1870, perhaps much earlier than the establishment of Holland's business.
67. De Knight, 73–74.
68. Myrdal, chapter 14, in particular, "The Negro in Business, the Professions, Public Service and Other White Collar Occupations," 304–333.
69. Myrdal, as cited in Davie, 365–366.
70. Jones, 258–259.
71. De Knight, 179.
72. De Knight, 230–231.
73. De Knight, 230.
74. De Knight, 230.
75. De Knight, 227.
76. De Knight, 184.
77. De Knight, 184.
78. Davie, 374.
79. In her work on collective memory, *Recovered Roots* (Chicago: University of Chicago Press, 1995), Yael Zerubavel has described the ways in which groups of people shape their pasts through "multiple forms of commemoration: the celebration of a communal festival, the reading of a tale, the participation in a memorial service, or the observance of a holiday," 5.
80. Kashrut is a system of dietary prescriptions and proscriptions that emphasize culinary purity. Above all, it requires the separation of meat and milk and the prohibition of particular foods, such as shellfish, pork, and certain types of game. For a discussion of the origins of kashrut, see the seminal work by Mary Douglas, "The Abominations of Leviticus," in *Purity and Danger: An Analysis of Concepts of Pollution and Taboo* (Harmondsworth: Penguin Books, 1966), 54–72. For a discussion of the system's complexity, see Barbara Kirshenblatt-Gimblett, "Kitchen Judaism," in Susan L. Braunstein and Jenna Weissman Joselit (eds.), *Getting Comfortable in New York: the American Jewish Home, 1880–1950,* (New York: The Jewish Museum, 1990), 75–105.

81. Hadassah, 11.
82. Hadassah, 16.
83. Kirshenblatt-Gimblet, 77.
84. For a discussion of community cookbooks in the early twentieth century, see Anne. L. Bowers, *Recipes for Reading: Histories, Stories, Communities* (Amherst: University of Massachusetts, 1996); for Jewish communities in particular, see Kirshenblatt-Gimblett.
85. Noted anthropologist Clifford Geertz's phrase quoted in Sherry Ortner, *Sherpas Through Their Rituals* (Cambridge: Cambridge University Press, 1978), 5.
86. Zerubavel, 5. See also Eric Hobsbawm and Terence Ranger, (eds.), *The Invention of Tradition* (Cambridge: Cambridge University Press, 1983), 2. Hobsbawm and Ranger define traditions as "real or invented."
87. Zerubavel, 4.
88. Hadassah, 3.
89. Hadassah, preface.
90. Thanks to Kim Lau for raising this point.
91. Shalach Manot literally means "sharing of portions." Chava Weissler, personal communication.
92. Hadassah, 14. According to Chava Weissler, this is a fairly common conjecture about the origin of Hamantaschen, which literally means "Haman's pockets."
93. Hadassah, 10.
94. Hadassah, 10.
95. Hadassah, 10.
96. Hadassah, 10.
97. Anthropologist Mary Douglas has considered the biblical text of Leviticus as the origin of the Jewish food prohibitions. Jews may eat those foods that are classified according to their mode of locomotion and what and how they eat. Flying, swimming, and perambulating are acceptable forms of movement. Animals that chew the cud are also permitted. Carrion eaters are forbidden. See "The Abominations of Leviticus."
98. Thanks to Kris Rabberman for emphasizing this point.
99. Hadassah, 309.
100. Hadassah, 291.
101. Hadassah, 260.
102. Hadassah, 95.
103. Hadassah, 186.
104. Weissman Joselit, 61.
105. Weissman Joselit, 42–43.
106. Weissman Joselit, 59–68.
107. Weissman Joselit, 59.
108. Both Weissman Joselit and Kirshenblatt-Gimblet demonstrate the ways in which culture change was fostered in and by domestic life.

109. Hadassah, 274.
110. Hadassah, 274.
111. Hadassah, 274.
112. It is not clear from the cookbook whether the Rochester Chapter of Hadassah comprised only one synagogue or several. Therefore, it is difficult to determine whether Sephardic women were part of the editorial board and made decisions about which recipes to include.
113. Details of the story that follows are unrecoverable because most of the principals have died.
114. Although the cookbook actually was compiled by the women during their years of internment during World War II, it was not published until 1996 by Jason Aronson Inc. under De Silva's editorship.
115. *In Memory's Kitchen*, xxxv.
116. Michael Berenbaum, director of the United States Holocaust Research Institute in Washington, writes in his foreword to the book: "Of the 144,000 Jews who were sent to Theresienstadt, 33,000 died there and 88,000 were deported to Auschwitz. Only 19,000 were alive at the end of the war," x.
117. *In Memory's Kitchen*, 24.
118. *In Memory's Kitchen*, 15.
119. Along with the cookbook, Mina Pachter authored several poems on separate sheets of paper. One of the poems refers to "cooking platonically," which her grandson, David Peter Stern believes may be a reference to the cookbook. Perhaps Mina Pachter used the term to refer to the entire community's obsession with cooking with the mind.
120. *In Memory's Kitchen*, xxviii.
121. *In Memory's Kitchen*, xxviii.
122. In keeping with editor De Silva's feelings that the recipes should be rendered in the language they were written, I have kept the original versions with the translations.
123. Beit Theresienstadt is the cultural center, library, and archive of Givat Chaim, at Kibbutz Ichud, Israel, founded by survivors of the ghetto.
124. *In Memory's Kitchen*, xxx.
125. *In Memory's Kitchen*, xxxv.
126. *In Memory's Kitchen*, xli.
127. *In Memory's Kitchen*, xli.
128. *In Memory's Kitchen*, xxxiv.
129. *In Memory's Kitchen*, xxxii.
130. *In Memory's Kitchen*, xxv.
131. These relationships encompass folks who are members of the cultural group and those who are not.
132. Zerubavel, 10.
133. Zerubavel, 5.

Chapter 3

1. Anne Michaels, *Fugitive Pieces* (New York: Vintage Books, 1998), 40.
2. Linda Berzok Murray, "My Mother's Recipes," in Sherrie Inness, (ed.) *Pilaf, Pozole, and Pad Thai: American Women and Ethnic Food* (Amherst: University of Massachusetts Press, 2001).
3. Lucy Emerson, *The New England Cookery Book* (Montpelier, VT: Printed for Josiah Parks, 1808).
4. Some men produced these texts for women who could not write or whose presence in a recipe or scrapbook indicated affection and intimacy. See chapter 5.
5. See Nancy Armstrong, *Desire and Domestic Fiction: A Political History of the Novel* (New York: Oxford University Press, 1987), 3; and Sara Mendelson and Patricia Crawford, *Women in Early Modern England, 1550–1720* (Oxford: Clarendon Press, 1998), 202–212.
6. In, among others, Karen Hess, *Martha Washington's Book of Cookery* (New York: Columbia University Press, 1981).
7. C. Anne Wilson, "A Cookery Book and Its Context," *Petits Propos Culinaires* 25 (1987): 14.
8. Wilson, 16.
9. To date, though I have not done an exhaustive study, I have found no last will and testament that explicitly mentions a woman's book of receipts.
10. Marcia Pointon, *Strategies for Showing: Women, Possession, and Representation in English Visual Culture 1665–1800* (Oxford: Oxford University Press, 1997).
11. The care of those in childbed and deathbed were most often women's responsibilities. Toward the end of the seventeenth century, male midwives began to wrest this area from women's control. See Patricia Crawford and Laura Gowing (eds.), *Women's World in Seventeenth Century England: A Source Book* (London: Routledge, 2000), 23; and Mendelson and Crawford, 208–211. See also Londa Schiebinger, *The Mind Has No Sex: Women in the Origins of Modern Science* (Cambridge, MA: Harvard University Press,1989), 104–112.
12. Lynette Hunter, "Cookery Books: A Cabinet of Rare Devices and Conceits," *Petits Propos Culinaires* 5 (1980): 23.
13. Pointon, 43.
14. Pointon, 33.
15. Pointon, 33.
16. William Eamon, *Science and the Secrets of Nature: Books of Secrets in Medieval and Early Modern Culture* (Princeton, NJ: Princeton University Press, 1994), 131.
17. Eamon argues that in the culinary books of secrets that were published in the early modern period, the voice was voided from the text: "Unlike oral instructions, recipes exist independently of the teacher. Once they are recorded in a book, they become depersonalized and acquire a more general, universal quality"(131). These ad hoc rules and general formulas, he continues, un-

derlay the development of and popularization of science (131). Although this may be true of many printed recipe compilations, I contend that in the domestic context, women's culinary manuscripts were not read as "depersonalized" formulae. The recipients of such manuscripts viewed these texts as metonymic representations of a maternal figure.

18. Lewis M. Stark, *The Whitney Cookery Collection* (New York: New York Public Library, 1959).
19. Lady Frescheville, 1669, manuscript receipt book. Joseph Downs Collection, Winterthur Library, Winterthur, Delaware.
20. Hilary Spurling, *Elinor Fettiplace's Receipt Book* (London: Penguin Books, 1987), 13.
21. Elizabeth David, "A True Gentlewoman's Delight," *Petits Propos Culinaires* 1 (1979): 43–53.
22. Schiebinger, 113.
23. See also Lynette Hunter and Sarah Hutton (eds.), *Women, Science and Medicine 1500–1700: Mothers and Sisters of the Royal Society* (Phoenix Mill, England: Sutton Publishing, 1997).
24. Schiebinger, 112.
25. Mendelson and Crawford, 313.
26. W. M., *The Queen's Closet Opened, Incomparable Secrets in Physick, Chirurgery, Preserving and Candying, etc. The Queen's Delight, The Compleat Cook* (London: Printed by J. Winter for Nat. Brooke, 1668).
27. David, 46.
28. David, 44.
29. David, 49.
30. David, 49.
31. David, 49.
32. Quoted in Evelyn Abraham Benson, *Penn Family Recipes: Cooking Recipes of William Penn's Wife Gulielma* (York, PA: George Shumway, Publisher, 1966), 198.
33. Benson, 198.
34. Benson, 1.
35. Penn's recipe manuscript now resides at the Historical Society of Pennsylvania.
36. Karen Hess, *Martha Washington's Booke of Cookery* (New York: Columbia University Press, 1981), 447–463.
37. There is a slight discrepancy in Hess's account. On p. 449 she claims there are seven hands; on p. 456 she asserts that there are six hands.
38. Hess, 460.
39. Patricia Brady Schmitt, *Nelly Custis Lewis's Housekeeping Book* (New Orleans: The Historic New Orleans Collection, 1982), 18.
40. Personal conversation with Patricia Brady Schmitt, August 25, 2000.
41. Brady Schmitt, 18.
42. In this case at least two intermediaries, Frances Parke Custis's husband and son, passed on the book to appropriate female kin.

43. Mary Perkins, nineteenth-century culinary manuscript, Joseph Downs Collection, Winterthur Library, Winterthur, Delaware.
44. Elizabeth (Lizzie) Randolph, front cover.
45. Mary Jane Hall, recipe book 1850s–1890, Joseph Downs Collection, Winterthur Library.
46. Anonymous, nineteenth-century recipe book, Joseph Downs Collection, Winterthur Library.
47. There are strong oral traditions in many cultures, African American and Italian American, for example, with comparatively recent written compilations. For centuries, much domestic cookery was learned by word of mouth, trial and error, and observation of female kin. Likewise, many Anglo-American families did not transcribe their familial culinary heritage, relying instead on oral transmission.
48. Lady Frankland, nineteenth-century culinary manuscript, Esther B. Aresty Collection of Rare Books on the Culinary Arts, University of Pennsylvania.
49. I am grateful to Marc Miller for this point.
50. Margaret MacDonald (ed.), *Whistler's Mother's Cookbook* (London: Paul Elek, 1979), 9.
51. MacDonald, 10.
52. MacDonald, 37.
53. Jane D. L. Kane, nineteenth-century culinary manuscript, Joseph Downs Collection, Winterthur Library, Winterthur, Delaware.
54. Widows and single women did not fall into the category of femme couvert and could enter into contracts, trade, and otherwise engage in legal activities. Women of means or whose parents saw to their daughters' protection by prenuptial agreements were not constrained by femme couvert. There is ample evidence that many women circumvented the restrictions imposed by common law; however, this was the prevailing norm.
55. Pointon, 43.
56. Pointon, 43.
57. Karen Hess calls the first accreted texts and the second collected ones, 451.
58. Bessie Howard, nineteenth-century culinary manuscript, Joseph Downs Collection, Winterthur Library, Winterthur, Delaware.
59. Pointon, 29.
60. Cited in Peter Targett, "Edward Kidder: His Books and His Schools," *Petits Propos Culinaires,* 32 (1989): 35–44.
61. E. Taylor, *The Art of Cookery or The Lady's, Housewife's, and Cookmaid's Assistant* (Berwick upon Tweed: Printed by H. Taylor, 1769).
62. Amelia Simmons, *American Cookery* (New York: Published by William Beastall; S. Marks, printer, 1822).
63. It was the first American-authored and published cookbook using indigenous resources and written in the vernacular. At this time, items celebrating American independence were used to promote patriotism.
64. Nathan Bailey, *Bailey's Dictionarium Domesticum* (London: C. Hitch, 1736).

65. John Middleton, *Five Hundred New Receipts in Cookery, Confectionary, Pastry, Preserving, Conserving, Pickling* (London: Printed for Tho. Astley, 1734).
66. Eliza Smith, *The Compleat Housewife or Accomplish'd Gentlewoman's Companion* (London: J. & J. Pemberton, 1737).
67. I have used a pseudonym for Rosemary's former husband.
68. Unpublished manuscript belonging to Rosemary Ranck.
69. Conversation with Rosemary Ranck, August 19, 2000.
70. Rosemary Ranck's description of the gift.
71. I have kept Lizzie's spelling and punctuation as she wrote it to keep to the original spirit of the document.
72. After Mr. Mitchell died, Mrs. Mitchell continued to support Lizzie.
73. Caroline French Benton, *A Little Cook-Book for a Little Girl* (Boston: Dana Estes, 1905). The inscription is written on the front flyleaf of this book.
74. Benton, v.
75. Benton, vi.
76. Benton, vii.
77. Benton, 124.
78. Benton, 124.

Chapter 4

1. Nora Seton, *The Kitchen Congregation: A Daughter's Story of Wives and Women Friends* (New York: Picador USA, 2000).
2. Hannah Trimble, manuscript cookery book, 1859–1880. Joseph Downs Collection, Winterthur Library, Winterthur, Delaware.
3. Spellings of Mendenhall varied throughout the manuscript.
4. All of the dates, repairs, purchases, and details of the move are listed in Hannah Trimble's cookbook. I have woven the details of her accounts into a story, as Laurel Thatcher Ulrich did in *The Midwife's Tale*. I consulted other primary sources, such as atlases, census records, maps, and histories of Delaware, to place Hannah's accounts and her cookbook in historical and regional context. One secondary source was essential in my portrayal of Hannah Trimble's life: Joan M. Jensen, *Loosening the Bonds: Mid-Atlantic Farm Women, 1750–1850* (New Haven, CT: Yale University Press, 1986).
5. I am indebted to Wendy Woloson, Library Company of Philadelphia, for the following: "A Table of Stamp Duties" in a pocket diary for 1864 geared for merchants and/or bankers archived at The Library Company of Pennsylvania which lists fees for the various kinds of contracts, agreements, and financial instruments (e.g., bank check, bill of sale, bill of lading, mortgage, passage ticket, power of attorney, and so on). Also included in this list is: Deed, or Conveyance of Real Estate. Where the value is over $100 and not over $500, 50 cents. Over 500 and not over $1,000, 1.00. Over 1,000 and not over 2,500, 2.00. Over 2,500 and not over 5,000, $5.00. Over $5,000 and not over $10,000, 10.00. Over

10,000 and not over 20,000, 20.00. for every additional $10,000, or part thereof, $20 more."

6. I am not suggesting that cookbooks were the only form used by women to announce themselves. Nor was a cookbook the only form each woman employed to record her life. Some women wrote letters, worked outside of the home, and had opportunities for articulating political positions, work-related issues, and other concerns. They may have been notable and well-known women in their communities and families. Family members may well have numerous documents relating to these women's lives. However, my point is that many women cannot be traced to any other legal or historical document such as census data, court records, or wills, and that time and space have erased all but this record of their lives. I have tried to find historical and legal records that would provide more tangible evidence of a woman's existence. In most cases I have not been able to locate any public record pertaining to the writer of a recipe book outside of the book itself. In many cases the recipe book is all the evidence that we have that this woman lived.

7. Betty S. Travitsky and Adele F. Seeff (eds.), *Attending to Women in Early Modern Europe* (Newark: University of Delaware Press, 1994), 202. Although this work refers to women's needlework, I found the phrase apt for cookery books as well.

8. Ann E. Goldman, *Take My Word: Autobiographical Innovations of Ethnic American Working Women* (Stanford: University of California Press, 1996). Although Goldman refers to several working-class women's published work, the concept is useful to describe manuscript cookery books of women whose work was never published for a broader audience than self, family, and friends.

9. See Goldman for an innovative study of autobiographical writing in cookbooks, labor movement histories, and other so-called collective documents.

10. Traditional autobiographical writing—usually modeled after a man's life story—follows the life course of an individual, usually in a linear and progressive narrative, beginning with a pivotal moment in that individual's life. For women, autobiographies seem to take many and different shapes. Rather than a clearly delineated passage from childhood to adulthood heralded by a single driving event, women's autobiographies take many forms depending on the woman, her class, race, age, and the historical period in which she lived. Literary theorists have debated the forms of autobiographical writing for women as well as the contrast between men's and women's autobiographies. For descriptions of men's autobiographies, see James Olney, *Autobiography: Essays Theoretical and Critical* (Princeton, NJ: Princeton University Press, 1980). For discussions of the forms women's autobiographies have taken, see Estelle Jelinek, *The Tradition of Women's Autobiography: From Antiquity to the Present* (Boston: Twayne Publishers, 1986); and Shari Benstock (ed.), *The Private Self: Theory and Practice of Women's Autobiographical Writings* (Chapel Hill: University of North Carolina Press, 1988).

11. I will show later how cookery books also resemble commonplace books. In both manuscript and printed forms, cookbooks vary by era, region, individual woman, and purpose.

12. Jane and William Campbell, nineteenth-century culinary manuscript. Collection of the author.

13. The letter addressed to Campbells, 413 School House Lane contained a recipe using "linseed oil and Metalico."

14. Barbara Welter, "The Cult of True Womanhood," cited in Carroll Smith-Rosenberg, *Disorderly Conduct: Visions of Gender in Victorian America* (New York: Oxford University Press, 1985), 178–179, 199; Shirley Samuels (ed.), *The Culture of Sentiment: Race, Gender, and Sentimentality in Nineteenth-Century America* (New York: Oxford University Press, 1992), 295n.

15. Jane Campbell to nephew Will Campbell, Sunday evening, September 13, 1917 (Letter 6), St. Charles's Seminary, Philadelphia, Pennsylvania.

16. For a full discussion of servants' roles in the lives of middle-class women, see Nicole Tonkovich, *Domesticity with a Difference: The Nonfiction of Catharine Beecher, Sarah J. Hale, Fanny Fern, and Margaret Fuller* (Jackson: University Press of Mississippi, 1997), especially chapter 7, "The Difference Between Authors and Servants," 128–147.

17. Mary Ann Leigh, "An Epistolary Portrait: Sarah Jane Campbell, 1844–1928," master's thesis, University of Pennsylvania, 2000.

18. Leigh, 63. During a visit from her niece Elizabeth in Portsmouth, Rhode Island, she wrote a letter to her nephew John on August 10, 1915, with the following request: "*Elizabeth asks me to ask you to ask Francis to send her the recipe for Chocolate roll that Mrs. Tutweiler gave her, that is in Elizabeth's desk. Now my comsion for you are attended to.*"

19. Correspondence of Jane Campbell (loose scrap), St. Charles's Seminary.

20. I am tempted to interpret the meaning of this fragment of speech as an argument for universal suffrage. It may represent the speaker's effort to reconcile those within the movement who advanced black male suffrage and those who continued to believe that "black suffrage and woman suffrage should be equal and inseparable demands." Ellen Carol DuBois, *Feminism & Suffrage: The Emergence of an Independent Women's Movement in America, 1848–1869* (Ithaca, NY: Cornell University Press, 1999), 55.

21. From the *American National Biography,* John Garraty and Mark C. Carnes (eds.), (New York: Oxford University Press, 1999) vol. 19: 736–737, we learn that Shaw was born in England in 1851. She was a resident of Massachusetts for some time and later became the life partner of Anthony's niece, Lucy.

22. We will not go into the issues of household management and servants here. Middle-class women such as Anthony and Shaw were enabled to engage in public, political affairs because of their privileged status. They had servants to carry out their instructions and their labor.

23. DuBois, 125.

24. Working women attempted to establish their own organizations, but differences between working and middle-class women resulted in a middle-class takeover. DuBois, 135.

25. Anonymous, early twentieth-century cookery manuscript. Collection of the author. Because no name is inscribed in this book, I have given this anonymous cookbook writer the name of Mrs. Downing after the locale of her cookery books.

26. See Laura Shapiro's *Perfection Salad: Women and Cooking at the Turn of the Century* (New York: Henry Holt and Company, 1986), for a discussion of the home economics movement; and Glenna Matthews, *Just a Housewife: The Rise & Fall of Domesticity in America* (New York: Oxford University Press, 1987).

27. My mother-in-law, for example, recorded all of the celebratory meals she served guests at life-cycle occasions such as birthdays, bar mitzvahs, and anniversaries. In this way she could avoid serving repeat guests duplicate meals.

28. Most of the newspaper clippings are without title or dates.

29. Ellen Plante, *The American Kitchen: 1700 to the Present, From Hearth to Highrise* (New York: Facts On File, 1995).

30. I have spoken to women who read cookbooks for pleasure and even for inspiration, but in the end they did not cook any of the recipes they had read. They did not depart from their usual culinary repertoire.

31. Barbara Kirshenblatt-Gimblett, "Kitchen Judaism," in Susan L. Braunstein and Jenna Weissman Joselit (eds.), *Getting Comfortable in New York: The American Jewish Home, 1880–1950* (New York: The Jewish Museum, 1990), 79.

32. Ann Ruggles Gere, *Intimate Practices: Literacy and Cultural Work in U.S. Women's Clubs, 1880–1920* (Urbana: University of Illinois Press, 1997).

33. Judith Goode, Janet Theophano, and Karen Curtis, "A Framework for the Analysis of Continuity and Change in Shared Sociocultural Rules for Food Use: The Italian-American Pattern," in Linda Keller Brown and Kay Mussell (eds.), *Ethnic and Regional Foodways in the United States: The Performance of Group Identity,* (Knoxville: University of Tennessee Press, 1984), 66–91.

34. See chapter 6 of this volume for the *Presbyterian Cookbook's* (Dayton, OH: Historical Publishing Co., 1806), Ladies of the Presbyterian Church (eds.), version of Shakespeare.

35. I have used a pseudonym for the author and for everyone else to whom she refers.

36. Magnolia Le Guin, *A Home-Concealed Woman: The Diaries of Magnolia Wynn Le Guin, 1901–1913,* Charles A. Le Guin (ed.) (Athens: University of Georgia Press, 1990), 169.

37. Betty Friedan, *The Feminine Mystique* (New York: Norton, 1963).

38. I have no sense from her recipe book that there were children living at home. Perhaps there were no children in this nuclear family.

39. Arlie Hochschild (with Anne Machung), *The Second Shift* (New York: Avon Books, 1989).

40. Hochschild, iv.

41. It is not clear who this person is or what role he plays in their lives. He is not mentioned again.
42. This is the first and only mention of what appears to be an injured hip.

Chapter 5

1. Magnolia Le Guin, *A Home-Concealed Woman: The Diaries of Magnolia Wynn Le Guin, 1901–1913,* Charles A. Le Guin (ed.) (Athens: University of Georgia Press, 1990).
2. Retha M. Warnicke, *Women of the English Renaissance and Reformation* (Westport, CT.: Greenwood Press, 1983), 154. See also Merry E. Wiesner, *Women and Gender in Early Modern Europe* (Cambridge: Cambridge University Press), 119; Catherine Hobbs (ed.), *Nineteenth-Century Women Learn to Write* (Charlottesville: University Press of Virginia, 1995), 2.
3. Linda Auwers's exemplary essay cautions researchers about the difficulties of assessing female literacy. However, she does note an increase in women's literacy—although still behind men's—in the colonial period. Class, region, paternal support, maternal knowledge, and religious affiliation all played roles in the development of individual literacy. See Linda Auwers, "Reading the Marks of the Past: Exploring Female Literacy in Colonial Windsor, Connecticut," *Historical Methods* 13, no. 4 (Fall 1980): 204–214.
4. Hilda Smith, *Reason's Disciples: Seventeenth Century English Feminists* (Urbana: University of Illinois Press, 1882), 26.
5. Auwers, 204.
6. Weisner, 119. For those women who were literate and educated, there were also fewer chances to use their skills outside of domesticity to achieve occupational and professional advancement.
7. Sara Mendelson and Patricia Crawford, *Women in Early Modern England, 1550–1720* (Oxford: Clarendon Press, 1998), 90.
8. Despite proscriptions against women's public visibility, some defied social norms and wrote, published, and preached publicly. In particular, women were more conspicuous in religious sectarian movements such as Quakerism. See Elaine Hobby for a discussion of women's literature until 1780: *Virtue of Necessity: English Women's Writing 1646–1688* (London: Virago Press, 1988). In post-Revolutionary America, women were taught to read so that they could teach their children. Women of the upper classes learned to read and write because literacy was expected. Thus literacy was meted out according to social value, not as human right. See also Laurel Thatcher Ulrich, *Good Wives: Image and Reality in the Lives of Women in Northern New England 1650–1750* (New York: Random House, 1991); and Linda K. Kerber, *Women of the Republic: Intellect & Ideology in Revolutionary America* (Chapel Hill: University of North Carolina Press, 1980).
9. Kevin Hayes, *The Colonial Woman's Bookshelf* (Knoxville: University of Tennessee Press, 1996).

10. Warnicke, 42. For example, Jane Barker, seventeenth-century poet and writer, benefited from her brother's Oxford and Cambridge education. See Angeline Goreau, *The Whole Duty of a Woman: Female Writers in Seventeenth-Century England* (New York: Doubleday & Co., 1985), 225.

11. Assuredly, women were reading more than cookbooks. Novels, histories, Bibles, magazines, and other genres proliferated in this period, and women were the primary consumers of the popular commercial press. Catherine Hobbs tells us that from the colonial period on, women "were routinely taught how to read" and that the development of the publishing industry required even greater numbers of women readers (since women were becoming authors, and women were the subjects of many genres) (5).

12. Smith, 26.

13. Maddison/Morison receipt book, manuscript cookbook of predominantly seventeenth-century, Esther B. Aresty Collection, University of Pennsylvania. (Inscribed in pencil on the cover are the names of several members of the Morison family. Their relationship to this manuscript is unknown.) Despite the receipts written in the fifteenth and sixteenth centuries that open the manuscript, the majority of recipes were written in the seventeenth century in predominantly two hands using popular seventeenth-century scripts. However, the text was obviously in use—if only for reading—during the early modern period (1600–1800).

14. An Act for Enclosing the fields of St. Ives parish in Huntingdon was presented to Parliament in 1801 and passed in 1808. British Records: 41 rgnal of King George III, 1801. Lincolnshire History Center, Lincoln, England.

15. This age range was proposed by the archivist at Lincolnshire History Center in Lincoln, England. She made this determination based on the handwriting (the archivist was also a paleographer) and the list of clothing, which I discuss in a later section.

16. In Karen Calvert, *Children in the House: The Material Culture of Early Childhood, 1600–1900* (Boston: Northeastern University Press, 1992), we learn that girls did not dress differently from adult women. Thus a wide age range is possible for Mary Madcap. Second, we learn from Phillis Cunnington and Anne Buck that children wore bibs and aprons until adulthood: *Children's Costume in England From the Fourteenth to the End of the Nineteenth Century* (New York: Barnes & Noble, 1965).

17. In their receipt manuscripts women practiced their penmanship and played with their signatures almost as if they were trying on dresses for different occasions. One nineteenth-century housewife, Mrs. E. A. Phelps, practiced her inscription in several formats before signing her name on the front cover of her book (nineteenth-century manuscript, Joseph Downs Collection, Winterthur Library). Phelps, like young Mary Madcap, seemed to be trying on various "hands" to find the one most suitable to her personality and status. Mrs. Jewett Cain, from Kentucky, in her nineteenth-century cookery manuscript (Joseph Downs Collection, Winterthur) similarly wrote her name first

in block letters and then again in an italic or round hand. On another page she carefully wrote the months of the year as well as her name in several styles.

In book after book, the signature of the owner indicates that even this detail was reflected upon and pondered over. Tamara Plakins Thornton, *Handwriting in America: A Cultural History* (New Haven, CT: Yale University Press, 1996). According to Thornton, finding a script that reflected one's own character was not inconsequential, and women spent some time and thought on how their signatures and books—and hence they—would be perceived. Accordingly, a fair hand was likened to other female arts, such as dancing, music, and embroidery (8).

18. Susan Stewart, *On Longing: Narratives of the Miniature, the Gigantic, the Souvenir, the Collection* (Baltimore: Johns Hopkins University Press, 1984), 14.

19. Susan Frye, "Maternal Textualities" (unpublished paper), 17. A shorter version of this paper appears in Naomi J. Miller and Naomi Yavneh (eds.), *Maternal Measures: Figuring Caregiving in the Early Modern Period.* (Aldershot, Burlington, VT: Ashgate, 2000).

20. Laura Bigelow, manuscript cookery book, Waterville, New York, 1854, Joseph Downs Collection, Winterthur Library.

21. The Maddison-Morison manuscript is an exception since most of the seventeenth-century receipt books I have surveyed are inscribed with the owner's name and the explicit statement "Her Book." For example, "Hopestill Brett, Her Book, 1678"; "Catherine Cotton, 1698 Her Book"; "Doro Petrie, Her Book, 1705" (Esther B. Aresty Collection); "Lady Ann Frescheville, Her Book" (Joseph Downs Collection, Winterthur Library). The Whitney Collection of the New York Public Library has twelve manuscripts, most of which bear an inscription with the owner's name and date. Hilary Spurling (ed.), *Elinor Fettiplace's Receipt Book* (London: Penguin, 1986), and David Schoonover (ed.), *Ladie Borlase's Receiptes Booke* (Iowa City: University of Iowa Press, 1998), also bear the names of their owners and the date of presentation.

22. Two hands predominate in the book: the first, an elegant hand, is found on more than half of the pages; the second hand writes "My dater Mary" and "My dater Margaret" as well as other marginal comments. The same hand also keeps accounts and writes the list of clothing and a large proportion of the recipes, albeit in a more rudimentary script and grammatical structure than the former.

23. It is with this sentence that I recognized the handwriting of Mrs. Maddison.

24. Even those who had numeracy and literacy skills may not have been familiar with fashionable scripts and elegant composition.

25. Hobbs, 2.

26. See David Cressy's classic study: *Literacy and the Social Order: Reading and Writing in Tudor and Stuart England* (Cambridge: Cambridge University Press, 1980). See also Auwer: 204–214.

27. One of the few diaries kept by a woman below middle class will be discussed later in this chapter. It is Anne Hughes, *The Diary of a Farmer's Wife, 1796–1797* (London: Countrywise Books, 1964).

28. See Brian V. Street, *Literacy in Theory and Practice* (Cambridge: Cambridge University Press, 1984), and Brian V. Street, *Cross-Cultural Approaches to Literacy* (Cambridge: Cambridge University Press, 1993).

29. Even when public education was anticipated to further a child's learning, women were expected to teach their children to read.

30. For centuries reading and writing were taught sequentially, not in tandem. Many men and women who were educated to read were unable to write. See Thornton for a detailed discussion of pedagogy. See also William Gilmore's *Reading Becomes a Necessity of Life: Material and Cultural Life in Rural New England, 1780–1835* (Knoxville: University of Tennessee Press, 1989).

31. There are several seminal studies of literacy in colonial and national America: Kenneth A. Lockridge, *An Enquiry into the Social Context of Literacy in the Early Modern West* (New York: Norton & Co., 1974); Ulrich; Cathy N. Davidson (ed.) *Reading in America: Literature & Social History* (Baltimore: Johns Hopkins University Press, 1989); Gilmore.

     For studies of English women's literacy, see Josephine Kamm, *Hope Deferred: Girls' Education in English History* (London: Methuen, 1965); Mendelson and Crawford; Deirdre Raftery, *Women and Learning in English Writing, 1600–1900* (Portland, OR: Four Courts Press, 1997); Weisner, 119–126.

32. Weisner, 122–124.

33. Warnicke, 85.

34. For further discussion of the differences between North and South, see Jane H. Pease and William H. Pease, *Ladies, Women, & Wenches: Choice and Constraint in Antebellum Charleston & Boston* (Chapel Hill: University of North Carolina Press, 1990); and Richard Beale Davis, *A Colonial Southern Bookshelf: Reading in the Eighteenth Century* (Athens: University of Georgia Press, 1979). Davis argues that more Southern women were literate than has been previously noted.

35. See Gilmore; G. A. Cranfield, *A Hand-list of English Provincial Newspapers and Periodicals, 1700–1760* (London: Bowes and Bowes, 1961); David Vincent, *Literacy and Popular Culture: England 1750–1914* (Cambridge: Cambridge University Press, 1989); Natalie Zemon Davis, *Society and Culture in Early Modern France* (Stanford, CA: Stanford University Press, 1965). Broadsides were a cheap and accessible form of print in which news and advertisements were carried. Usually printed on cheap paper on one side of the page, they carried a rather sensationalistic account of local events: murders, uprisings, and so on. From these broadsides popular renditions of events were transformed into ballads and songs. Hence the term "broadside ballad."

36. J. Jean Hecht, *The Domestic Servant in Eighteenth-Century England* (London: Routledge & Kegan Paul, 1956, 1980). Hecht discusses the opportunities available to rural migrants in domestic service. Successful relationships with masters could lead to social mobility: 191–199.

37. William J. Gilmore's account of the growth of print media in New England and New England's role in economic growth shows the intersection of these two areas.

38. Street, (1993) *Cross-cultural Approaches to Literacy,* Street (ed.),9. Catherine Hobbs describes "effective literacy" as "the power to act in society, a phrase suggesting both empowerment and transformation" (2).

39. Barbara Sicherman, among others, describes the role of reading and writing in a middle-class family of women: "Sense and Sensibility: A Case Study of Women's Reading in Late Victorian America," in Dorothy O. Kelly and Susan M. Reverby (eds.), *Gendered Domains: Rethinking Public and Private in Women's History* (Ithaca, NY: Cornell University Press, 1992), 71–89.

40. Drew Faust discusses the role of letters, journals, and diaries in Southern women's lives during the Civil War in *Mothers of Invention: Women of the Slaveholding South in the American Civil War* (Chapel Hill: University of North Carolina Press, 1996), 162. Although the time period Faust studies is different from the one under discussion, the value of gaining literacy may transcend different historical periods. As a counterpoint, arguments have been made that writing is a form of social control. But Catherine Hobbs argues that women resisted or subverted practices intended for social control and used them instead for social reform (13).

41. The text I worked with was a facsimile edition of Anne Hughes's diary first published in serial form in the *Farmers Weekly* in 1937. In book form, Suzanne Beedell (ed.), *The Diary of a Farmer's Wife, 1796–1797* (London: Countrywise Books, 1964).

42. Hughes, 29.

43. Hughes, 30.

44. Hughes, 29.

45. Hughes, 14.

46. Hughes, 29.

47. Hughes, 29.

48. Hughes, 60.

49. Dorothy Leigh's *The Mother's Blessing: or, the Godlie Counsaile, of a Gentlewoman, not long deceased, left behind for her children* (London, 1621, seventh printing), quoted in Susan Cahn, *Industry of Devotion: The Transformation of Women's Work in England, 1500–1660* (New York: Columbia University Press, 1987), 97.

50. Nineteenth-century English and American conduct books prescribed such separate spheres of responsibility. However, the practice of separate spheres most likely varied from group to group, by class and race and region as well as by familial and personal differences.

51. Male chefs who worked in aristocratic and royal households and manors authored the earliest receipt manuscripts. (Some were written for them by scribes.) For centuries the domain of public cooking belonged to the professional chef. Likewise, men authored the earliest published cookbooks, even those for domestic use. Until the 1640s women's literature was largely penned by men.

52. I have borrowed the concept of "sponsor" from a recent article: Deborah Brandt, "Literacy Learning and Economic Change," *Harvard Educational Review* 69, no. 4, (Winter 1999): 373–394. Brandt presents "the analytic concept of a 'sponsor' to identify any agent who supports or hampers opportunities for literacy learning in the lives of her subjects" (373).

53. Merry Weisner notes that parents were unwilling to pay for the expensive materials necessary to teach their daughters to write (123).

54. Anonymous, 1699, Esther B. Aresty Collection, University of Pennsylvania.

55. In an article entitled "Eighteenth-Century Women's Autobiographical Commonplaces," in Shari Benstock (ed.), *The Private Self: Theory and Practice of Women's Autobiographical Writings* (Chapel Hill: University of North Carolina Press, 1988), 147–173, Felicity A. Nussbanum writes of the relationship between eighteenth-century diarist Hester Thrale and Samuel Johnson, who encouraged her to keep diaries to ward off depression. Mary Evelyn and her tutor continued a long correspondence in which he acknowledged her intellectual abilities notes (Ann Elizabeth Wiener, unpublished paper, 1999). And in the nineteenth century, Barbara Sicherman mentions that through the Semi-Colon Club, Catherine Beecher and Harriet Beecher Stowe were introduced to literary men and women, known and influential authors who encouraged the Beechers to publish.

56. All of the arts of the stillroom were revealed in Plat's book, *The Delights for Ladies* (1602). The stillroom was a private place, a room within a manor house that contained "a still" for distillation. A common practice of concealing both medicinal and sugar recipes lent an air of secrecy to the early stillroom. There was also a sense of mystery surrounding the preparation of remedies for good health, beauty, and entertainment. The stillroom and its preparations—perfumes, beauty creams, liqueurs, syrups of quince and barbarie, cordials, and other sweet delicacies—as well as remedies for curing the sick were the provenance of the lady of the house. Thus, the earliest printed books for use in the stillroom describe both the methods of distillation and food preparation and the products to emerge from this cloistered part of the manor. As the secrets of the aristocratic stillroom were disclosed in these specialized printed cookery books such as *The Delights for Ladies,* the social boundaries of the great estates were being expanded by an economically rising middle class. Acquiring, among others, the foodstuffs and cooking "secrets" of the rich, middle-class women symbolically helped to reshape the boundaries.

The "delightes" produced within the stillroom were specialties, often made with sugar, and called "banquetting stuffe." These sweet foods were served both as medicinal aids to digestion and sweetmeats to satisfy the taste buds. Considered a treasure of the nobility, "banquetting stuffe" carried clear implications of status and wealth, and were thus all the more desirable to the middle classes. Plat's books were directed primarily to ladies and gentlewomen and ornamented with all of the refinements suitable for such an audience. As much literary entertainments as they were technical manuals, the books were etched with filigreed borders and embroidered with poetry. Compatible with the tenor of the times, Plat wooed his aristocratic readers with seductive poetry.

> . . . now my pen and paper are
> perfum'd,
> Rosewater is the inke I write withall:
> Of sweetes the sweetest I will now
> Command,
> To sweetest creatures that the earth
> Doth beare;
> These are the Saints to whome I
> sacrifice
> Preserves and conserves both of plum
> and peare.

57. It is possible that an aspiring author seeking a patron may have written the manuscript. Such relationships might bring financial assistance or, at the least, the patron's influence with prominent social networks. Generally, the patron was courted with lavish praise and gratitude in dedicatory prefaces. For example, Hannah Wolley begins her 1664 book, *The Cook's Guide,* with the dedication:

> To the Honourable and truly vertuous Lady Anne Wroth, Wife to the Right Worshipful Sir Henry Wroth. Madam, The Duty I owe to your Ladyship and the rest of your Noble Familie commands more than this Booke is able to express; but since ill fate hath made me altogether uncapable of any worthy Return of your Love and bounty, be pleased to accept this as a Signal of what I am obliged to. I would not willingly dye while I live, nor be quite forgotten when I am dead; therefore have I sent forth this book, to testifie to the scandalous World that I do not altogether spend my Time idlely; somewhat of benefit it may be to the young ladies and Gentlewomen; and such I wish it; it may serve to passe away their youth-full time, which otherwaies might be worse employed.
>
> The Honour your Ladyship does me in accepting the Dedication of it, will, I hope, cherish their belief, and encourage their Practice, and assuredly it doth adde very much to the Obligation of, Madam, Your Honours most Faithful, Real, and most Humble Servant, Hannah Wolley.

58. Among others, Fiske Family Receipt Book, nineteenth-century manuscript, Joseph Downs Collection, Winterthur Library. Both men and women contribute recipes to this manuscript; and Lydia Sanborn (1860), cookery manuscript, Joseph Downs Collection, Winterthur Library. Nestor Sanborn Esq. has inscribed the volume. On the recto of the first page (or flyleaf) is in pencil

"Lydia Sanborn Receipt Book Oct. 28th 1846." On this same page are "Nestor Sanborn—London"; "Nestor Sanborn 58 Turner St. Commercial Rd. London," and "Athen No 12 Grand Hotel, Rue de Capucins, Place du Louvre, Paris." The receipt book is written in two hands primarily: Nestor Sanborn's and Lydia Sanborn's, he on the left in pen, she on the right side of the page in pencil.

59. Samuel Pepys and John Evelyn, both men of letters, kept diaries and compiled recipes during their adult lives.

60. Evelyn's wife Mary also kept a volume of medicinal and cookery receipts similar to her husband's. Although Mary was considered an intellectual by several of her contemporaries, she chose not to venture far from the domestic responsibilities that she saw as woman's proper sphere (Wiener).

61. A sermon or lecture also might have been copied out by others for women who could write. One religious woman kept an account of her life on scraps of paper. She had written her autobiography once but destroyed it because she felt it did not show her to be pious enough. After her death, her son wrote an account of his mother's life based on the scraps of paper she had written as mnemonics. From the Watson Family papers (1834), Collection 189, Joseph Downs Collection, Winterthur Library. The book opens "Experience and Incident in the Life of Mrs. Lucy Watson." "(The following 20 pages, have been *copied* from the original in her own hand writing, but which could not be used here, in this book, because of the paper, being of a larger size, than the present.)"

62. Lydia Grofton Jarvis, manuscript receipt book, c. 1750, Joseph Downs Collection, Winterthur Library. Regrettably, little is known about the Grofton Jarvis manuscript. The body of the text is dated c. 1750. The cover was constructed in the mid-nineteenth century. The archivists at the Joseph Downs Collection at Winterthur Library, do not know the provenance of the manuscript.

63. Thornton, 33.

64. Thornton, 61.

65. Thornton, 62.

66. Many receipt books provide few clues beyond a name—and even this is absent from a number of cookery books. Region is mentioned occasionally but not consistently. Identifying provenance most often depends on clues such as recipe titles, paper marks, and so on.

67. See Ann Blair, "Humanist Methods in Natural Philosophy: The Commonplace Book," *Journal of the History of Ideas* 53 (1992): 541–551; and Rebecca W. Bushnell, *A Culture of Teaching: Early Modern Humanism in Theory and Practice* (Ithaca, NY: Cornell University Press), for deeper understanding of the role of commonplace books as an educational philosophy, its methods and history.

68. For this section, I have drawn liberally from the work of Mary Thomas Crane, *Framing Authority: Sayings, Self, and Society in Sixteenth-Century England* (Princeton, NJ: Princeton University Press, 1993) and Blair. For detailed discussion of the humanist educational philosophy, see Bushnell.

69. Blair, 545.

70. As is the case with other forms of education for women, generally it was aristocratic women who had access to schooling and who were introduced to the commonplace method. In earlier historical periods such as the Renaissance, women—again of the upper class—often were educated as men were. Elizabeth I was reputed to have been a brilliant scholar who studied natural history, Latin, other languages, and literature. But the majority of women did not have such education and opportunities.

71. There is tension between ownership and collaboration in many of women's culinary books. On one hand, many of the recipes are in circulation and shared at least by members of an extended family or a social network. These recipes often are attributed to the donor. In other instances, women sometimes withheld their treasured recipes from others for various reasons: family or class secrets, personal dislike, or rivalry. Esoteric knowledge bestowed on the recipient is a powerful claim to equal status. In barring knowledge from crossing social borders, interlopers were kept outside as well. Anne Hughes describes her Sunday evening visit from the parson and his wife. Although she shares food at a common meal with the couple, she will not share her recipe with the parson's wife. Susan Leonardi uses cases from literature to point out the ways in which women rivals deliberately sabotaged each other by omitting critical ingredients from recipes. See "Recipes for Reading: Summer Pasta, Lobster à la Riseholme, and Key Lime Pie," *PMLA* 104 (1989): 340–346. *PMLA: Publications of the Modern Language Association of America.*

72. Kent, Elizabeth Grey, Countess of. *A choice manuall, or, Rare and select secrets in physick and chyrugery collected and practised by the right honourable Countesse of Kent, late deceased; whereto are added several experiments of the virtues of Gascon pouder and lapic contra yarvam by a professor of physick; as also most exquisite waies of preserving, conserving, candying &c.* (London: Printed by G.D. and are to be sold by William Shears, 1654, the fourth edition).

73. This particular example is interesting because it is a double take: an instance of a text using italics to simulate intimacy (see Thornton's description of italics in published works used as a mechanical vehicle for conveying the intimacy of speech [25]) and the printed version, when copied into the writer's manuscript, copies the image of the printed page to achieve verisimilitude with the printed text.

74. The title in the Maddison manuscript omits a few phrases but is nearly word for word the same as the printed book.

75. Kent, 186–187.

76. Hunter and Hutton, 91.

77. Midwifery was a woman's vocation—in many cases, passed on from mother to daughter—until the seventeenth century. With the professionalization of midwifery, women were prohibited from practicing it as a profession. Informally, women still continued the centuries-old custom of caring for their

immediate kin and poorer neighbors in childbirth. Schiebinger, 104–112; Mendelson and Crawford, 153.

78. The phrase "notable woman" is used in the seventeenth-century by such authors as Mary Kettilby in her *A Collection of above 300 Hundred Receipts in Cookery* (London: 1714). It refers to a woman who has refined her talents and skills in culinary and domestic matters, is neighborly (tends to the sick and the poor in her community), and is also competent in household economy. This term was used in Southern colonial America until the nineteenth century. See Julia Spruill, *Women's Life and Work in the Southern Colonies* (Chapel Hill: University of North Carolina Press, 1938).

79. Kevin Hayes notes in his *The Colonial Woman's Bookshelf* (Knoxville: University of Tennessee Press, 1996) that women in the colonies were also engaging in the same practice of keeping commonplace books and borrowing from print culture to augment their own manuscripts. See in particular p. 87–88.

80. This quote is from Hannah Glasse's eighteenth-century book of cookery, *The Art of Cookery Made Plain and Easy* (London: Printed for W. Strahan, J. and F. Rivington, J. Hinton [etc.], 1774). In it Glasse eschews the use of writing in "the high polite style" but presents her recipes in an accessible language. Hannah Glasse is discussed herein in chapter 6.

81. At the end of a day devoted to household responsibilities, Lady Anne Clifford referred to her sewing or writing as "works of mine own inventions" (5). Quoted in Frye.

82. Jane Campbell, nineteenth-century cookery manuscript. Author's collection.

83. There is another interpretation of these two documents: The two different compilations might have belonged to a woman who, as she aged, resorted to print for two reasons: more modern recipes and a declining ability to write.

84. Hannah Widdifield, *Widdifield's new cook book: or, Practical receipts for the housewife* (Philadelphia: T. B. Peterson, 1856).

85. Mrs. Hannah Keen, manuscript cookbook, 1867–1882. Esther B. Aresty Collection, University of Pennsylvania.

86. Widdifield, 390.

87. Mrs. E. Putnam, *Mrs. E. Putnam's Receipt Book & The Young Housekeeper's Assistant* (Boston: Ticknor and Fields, 1854).

88. Putnam, iii.

89. Putnam, 51.

90. Putnam, 51.

Chapter 6

1. Paula R. Backsheider and John J. Richetti, *Popular Fiction by Women, 1660–1730: An Anthology* (Oxford: Clarendon Press, 1996), xv.

2. I use the terms "author" and "writer" interchangeably and do not enter into a discussion of "what is an author" as raised by Michel Foucault, who views the "author function" as one of legal responsibility and "the concept of liter-

ary property" (29). Roger Chartier discusses the emergence of the term author in relation to print publication (39–41). See his discussion of both his and Foucault's concepts in *The Order of Books: Readers, Authors, and Libraries in Europe between the Fourteenth and Eighteenth Centuries,* trans. Lydia G. Cochrane (Stanford, CA: Stanford University Press, 1994).

3. It has been difficult to recover the early literary history of women. Scholars debate whether women were silenced in the early modern period or whether later anthologies and histories expunged them. See Margaret J. M. Ezell, *Writing Women's Literary History* (Baltimore: Johns Hopkins University Press, 1993), in particular, 83–100 for a discussion of historiographic biases in recording women writers for posterity, and Ezell, *The Patriarch's Wife: Literary Evidence and the History of the Family* (Chapel Hill: University of North Carolina Press, 1987).

4. Hannah Glasse, *The Art of Cookery, made Plain and Easy* (London: Printed for Strahan, J. and F. Rivington, J. Hinton [etc.], 1774), from the preface.

5. I use the term developed by Chartier in *The Order of Books.*

6. For example, John Middleton, *Five Hundred New Receipts in Cookery, Confectionery, Pastry, Preserving etc.,* (London: printed for Tho. Astley, 1734); Richard Briggs, *The New Art of Cookery, According to the Present Practice; Being a Complete Guide to all Housekeepers* (Philadelphia: Printed for W. Spotswood, R. Campbell, and B. Johnson, 1792). Both wrote their books for domestic use.

7. According to Elaine Hobby, *Virtue of Necessity: English Women's Writing, 1646–1688* (London: Virago Press, 1988), 166, Hannah Wolley is the first professional cookery writer.

8. For example, Richard Braithwaite, *The English Gentlewoman* (London: Printed by B. Aslop and T. Favcet for Michael Sparke, dwelling in Greene Arbor, 1631). Some of these men confessed that their sources were women, as Karen Hess also notes in her discussion of *Martha Washington's Booke of Cookery:* Authors such as Gervase Markham and Thomas Dawson, among others, published women's writings (453–455). One W. J. Gent published a woman's manuscript posthumously: *The Countess of Kent's A Choice Manuell of Rare and Select Secrets* (1653).

9. Some male authors such as William Rabisha, *The Whole Body of Cookery Dissected* (1661) and Robert May, *The Accomplisht Cook* (London: R.W., 1660) also promised simplicity in language.

10. I am not claiming that cookery literature was the only literature to debate the woman question and deal with woman's nature and proper sphere. A plethora of household advice literature, novels, romances, drama, poetry, pamphlets, and essays dealt with this issue. However, women were claiming the domain of the household, kitchen, and cooking as their own. In this way, they had created their own forum for the debate.

11. As I have shown in chapter 5, manuscript culture flourished alongside print into the nineteenth and early twentieth centuries.

12. In the seventeenth and eighteenth centuries, literate women circulated their manuscripts among their social peers. See Margaret Ezell, *Social Authorship and the Advent of Print* (Baltimore: Johns Hopkins University Press, 1999), for a full description of seventeenth-century manuscript circulation. In the nineteenth century, women wrote manuscripts and read them at either entirely female-centered reading and writing circles or among a mixed and prominent group of writers. See Joan Hedrick, "Parlor Literature: Harriet Beecher Stowe and the Question of 'Great Women Artists,'" *SIGNS*, (Winter 1992): 277–303; and for a description of the origins of Harriet Beecher Stowe's literary career, see Nicole Tonkovich, "Writing in Circles: Harriet Beecher Stowe, the Semi-Colon Club, and the Construction of Women's Authorship," in *Nineteenth Century Women Learn to Write*, ed. Catherine Hobbs, (Charlottesville: University of Virginia Press, 1995), 145–175.

13. Ezell, *The Patriarch's Wife*, 65.

14. Ezell, *Social Authorship and the Advent of Print*, 12.

15. Professional scribes were used only when small numbers of texts were sold. An increase in quantities of a text necessitated print publication, which was less costly than handwritten texts. James Green, Library Company, personal communication, February 16, 2000.

16. I am indebted to Peter Parolin for his insight.

17. David Potter, "Mrs. Eels' Unique Receipts," *Petits Propos Culinaires* 61 (May 1999): 16–19.

18. Only occasionally does a woman's personal manuscript provide an address or geographical location in the inscription.

19. Such prefaces may have been common in manuscripts designated for scribal publication and a wider reading public; I have not seen one in a personal culinary manuscript until Statham's.

20. Anita Pacheco (ed.), *Early Women Writers 1600–1720* (London: Longman, 1998) also Susan Frye and Karen Robertson (eds.), *Maids and Mistresses, Cousins and Queens: Women's Alliances in Early Modern England* (New York: Oxford University Press, 1999). Also see Elspeth Graham, Hilary Hinds, Elaine Hobby, and Helen Wilcox (eds.), *Her Own Life: Autobiographical Writings by Seventeenth Century Englishwomen* (London: Routledge, 1989).

21. An example is Hannah Glasse, author of *The Art of Cookery Made Plain and Easy* (1747). Authorship was attributed as "by a Lady" until a later edition named her as Mrs. Glasse.

22. Eliza Smith, *The Compleat Housewife*, fourteenth edition (London: Printed for S. Ware, R. Birt et al.), preface.

23. Smith, A2.

24. Although I have not found another example of the metaphor, Smith is apparently not entirely original in the use of the petticoat image.

25. Erin Mackie, *Market à la Mode: Fashion, Commodity, and Gender in The Tatler and The Spectator* (Baltimore: Johns Hopkins University Press), 104–143.

26. Smith, preface.
27. Smith, preface.
28. Smith, preface.
29. Elizabeth Tebeaux, "Women and Technical Writing, 1475–1700: Technology, Literacy and Development of a Genre," in *Women, Science, and Medicine, 1500–1700: Mothers and Daughters of the Royal Society*, ed. Lynette Hunter and Sarah Hutton (Thrupp, Stroud, Gloucestershire: Sutton Publishing, 1997), 56–60.
30. Hobby, 166.
31. Hobby, 172–173.
32. If Hobby is correct, this may be an example of the liberties taken by publishers and printers in the early modern period.
33. Quoted in Deirdre Raftery, *Women and Learning in English Writing, 1600–1900* (Dublin: Four Courts Press, 1997), 45.
34. The biographical data on Hannah Wolley is compiled from several sources: Josephine Kamm, *Hope Deferred* (London: Methuen, 1965); Hilda Smith, *Reason's Disciples: Seventeenth-Century English Feminists* (Urbana: University of Illinois Press, 1982); Deirdre Raftery, *Women and Learning in English Writing: 1600–1900* (Dublin; Portland, OR: Four Courts Press, 1997); and, particularly, Hobby's *Virtue of Necessity*. Because Hobby so thoroughly examines Wolley's career and the conventions of writing during the period, I have quoted her extensively.
35. Hobby, 168.
36. Hobby, 168.
37. Hannah Wolley, *The Cook's Guide* (London: Peter Dring at the Sun in the Poultry, next door to the Rose Tavern, 1664. Never Before Printed), Women Writers Project first electronic edition, 1999.
38. Hobby, 172–173.
39. Hobby, 168.
40. Hobby, 169–170.
41. Wolley, quoted in Hobby, 170.
42. The functions of printing, publishing, and book selling often overlapped in the early stages of print publication. These roles frequently blurred and complicated the relationships with authors, itself a term scholars debate. These differences obscure our understanding of the processes of book manufacture/production in this period. Also see Gilly Lehmann's preface to a facsimile edition of *The British Housewife: Or, the Cook, Housekeeper's and Gardiner's Companion* by Martha Bradley, late of Bath, vol. 1, January (1756) (Devon: Prospect Books, 1996), for a discussion of the audience for books.
43. Hobby, 168.
44. Hobby, 169.
45. Quoted in Hobby, 169.
46. It is not entirely clear if defending one's appearance in print was necessary for women in this period and whether women who published were censured

for becoming public figures. Some literary historians such as Margaret Ezell have argued that antiquarians in later historical periods eradicated many early women writers from the records based on their own era's biases. These omissions have been undetected until recently and unfortunately repeated into the twentieth century, thereby distorting our notions of the barriers early women writers faced. Ezell, a revisionist feminist scholar, would argue instead that women were not prevented or discouraged from writing for the public but were judged by a male standard. See Margaret Ezell, *The Patriarch's Wife* and *Writing Women's Literary History.*

47. Hobby, 189.

48. Quoted in Hobby, 168.

49. Hobby claims that subsequent works attributed to Wolley were authored by others but based on Wolley's and other contemporaries' works. If that is the case, then Wolley's well-known defense of women's education is erroneously attributed to her (170).

50. Hobby, 168.

51. Quoted in Hobby, 170.

52. Hugh Plat, *A Closet for Ladies and Gentlewomen, or, the Art of Preserving* (London: Printed for Arthur Johnson, 1608). This book is attributed to Hugh Plat, however, there is some uncertainty about authorship. *The Delightes for Ladies* mentioned in chapter 5 also begins with a lengthy, flattering tribute to his female readers.

53. Hobby, 172.

54. I borrow this phrase from Esther Aresty, *The Delectable Past* (New York: Simon and Schuster, 1964).

55. Sarah Phillips, *The Ladies Handmaid, or, a Compleat System of Cookery; on the principals of Elegance and Frugality wherein the useful art of Cookery is rendered plain, easy* (London: Printed only for I. Coote, 1758). In her "Preface to the ladies," the author describes her receipts as "excellent in their kind." "Most of them are the product of my own experience, and that for the space of above twenty-five years; during which time I have been constantly employed in genteel families, and have always been so happy as to obtain the approbation and encomiums of those who eat of the repast which I sent to table."

56. Elizabeth Raffald, *The Experienced English Housekeeper,* 10th ed. (London: R. Baldwin, 1786).

57. From the introduction by Roy Shipperbottom to the facsimile edition of *The Experienced English Housekeeper* (1769) by Elizabeth Raffald (Lewes, Sussex: Southover Press, 1997), xvi.

58. See, for example, *Angelica's Ladies Library or Parents and Guardians Present* (London: 1794), Rare Book Collection, Winterthur Library; Richard Braithewaite, *The English Gentlewoman* (London: Rare Book Collection, 1631), Winterthur Collection, Rare Book Collection.

59. Shipperbottom, vii.

60. Shipperbottom, xi.

61. Shipperbottom, xiii.

62. J. Jean Hecht, *The Domestic Servant in Eighteenth-Century England* (London: Boston & Henley: Routledge & Kegan Paul, 1980), 196–197.

63. Shipperbottom conjectures that such a text once existed (xiii).

64. I am grateful to Peter Parolin for this insight about intellectual property.

65. Peter Parolin suggests that though Raffald is seeking approbation from Lady Warburton, the fate of the book is not solely in her hands. By writing for readers of even the meanest capacity, others besides Warburton will pass judgment on the text.

66. Southover edition, 1.

67. Southover edition, 3.

68. Southover edition, 2. Also note that others in her period made similar claims. Among them, Elizabeth Moxon, author of *English Housewifery, Exemplified In above Four Hundred and Fifty Receipts Giving Directions in most Parts of Cookery* (Leeds: printed by Griffith Wright, for George Copperthwaite, 1769). One of the first regional cookbook writers in England, Moxon also claims to have written solely to have appeased her many influential friends: "As the compiler of it engaged in the undertaking at the insistence and importunity of many Persons of eminent account and Distinction . . . her ever honour'd Friends, who first excited her to the Publication of her BOOK . . ." from the introduction. (Gilly Lehmann cites Moxon as among the earliest of provincial cookery books (appearing in 1740s) in "Two 'New' Eighteenth-Century Cookery Books," *Petits Propos Culinaires* #53 (1996): 22–23.

69. Raffald, 10th ed., preface.

70. Southover edition, 2.

71. In Jan Fergus's brief but revealing "Women Readers of Prose Fiction in the Midlands, 1746–1800," she argues that prose fiction was not among the most popular and widely read genres in the provinces. She concedes that there are great difficulties in retrieving and interpreting data but points out that married women were less likely to read novels than widows and spinsters. The data may be concealed since books purchased or borrowed from circulating libraries for women may have been gotten under husbands' auspices and names (although she has no record of such sales for any of the women or their husbands). They were attracted to magazines and may have been limited in their purchases of other forms of fiction by a lack of discretionary income. Perhaps publishers and authors of the period understood that prose fiction, despite its popularity, was somewhat limited to both men and women readers of the middle class but not to all. Household advice and cookery texts may have satisfied a broader audience. *Transactions of the Eighth International Congress on the Enlightenment II* (Oxford: The Voltaire Foundation at the Taylor Institution, 1992): 1108–1112.

72. Magazines with serialized stories were also cheaper sources of fiction and nonfiction.

73. Glasse, 3.

74. Moreover, many working-class families believed that a good position might also have social advantages for their daughters who could find husbands of a suitable rank. The same theme occurs in eighteenth-century fiction. This belief was widely held despite its lack of confirmation in reality. Hecht describes the servant hierarchy and the salary inequities based on gender. Though their training was expected to be the same, women cooks were simply not paid as much as their male counterparts (65).

75. *Madam Johnson's Present Or, the best Instructions for Young Women in Useful and Universal Knowledge with a Summary of the Late Marriage Act and Instructions how to marry pursuant thereto, Digested Under the following Heads* (London: Printed for M. Cooper, Paternoster-Row; and C. Sympson, at the Bible, Chancery-Lane, 1754)

76. Peter Parolin points out that "there would be nothing stopping a servant girl who had a copy of the book from reading it from front to back" (personal communication).

77. Kevin Hayes, *The Colonial Woman's Bookshelf* (Knoxville: University of Tennessee Press, 1996), 86, claims it one of the leading reads in colonial America.

78. Johnson, 1.

79. Johnson, 1.

80. M. Dorothy George, *London Life in the Eighteenth Century* (Chicago: Academy Chicago Publishers, 1984, reprint ed.), 246. First published by Kegan Paul, Trench and Tubner Co., 1925.

81. Johnson, 61.

82. Johnson, 62.

83. Johnson, 61.

84. Johnson, B2.

85. Johnson, B2.

86. Johnson, 9.

87. Johnson, 11.

88. Johnson, 11.

89. Johnson, 8–9.

90. It is beyond the scope of this chapter to discuss the reading practices of the period. From what we know, it is conceivable that servants might as easily have read this section as their mistresses. What Johnson's intentions were we can only guess.

91. Johnson, 13.

92. Johnson, 63.

93. Johnson, 11.

94. Johnson, 12.

95. Virginia Maclean, *A Short-title Catalogue of Household and Cookery Books Published in the English Tongue, 1701–1800* (London: Prospect Books, 1981) 77.

96. Johnson, 217.

97. Johnson, 217.

98. Backscheider and Richetti, xx.

99. Eliza Haywood, *A Present for the Servant-Maid or, The Sure Means of gaining Love and Esteem, The Whole Calculated for making both the Mistress and the Maid happy* (London: Printed and published by T. Gardner at *Cowley's* Head, without *Temple*-Bar; and sold by the Book-sellers of town and country, 1743).

100. Quoted in Mary Anne Schofield, *Eliza Haywood* (Boston: Twayne Publishers, 1985), 1.

101. Schofield, 4.

102. Schofield, 5.

103. Katherine Levin, *Representing the Female Reader: Gender on the Market in Eighteenth-Century England,* Ph.D. thesis, University of Pennsylvania, 1995.

104. Schofield, 82.

105. Schofield claims that Haywood retired from writing under her own name for a decade. Alison Adburgham claims she disappeared from public view for "some sixteen years" (95). One of the biographies of Eliza Haywood from which I draw is that from Mary R. Mahl and Helene Koon (eds.), *The Female Spectator: English Women Writers Before 1800* (Bloomington: Indiana University Press, 1977), 223. More material is drawn from Alison Adburgham, *Women in Print: Writing Women and Women's Magazines from the Restoration to the Accession of Victoria* (London: George Allen and Unwin Ltd., 1972), 95–109; and Schofield's *Eliza Haywood* (1–9).

106. Levin, 84.

107. Levin, 84.

108. Levin, 85.

109. Levin's analysis is rendered here briefly. Levin argues that Haywood's career is marked by an unbroken concern with warning women about the dangers of love. She does so by introducing them to a fictional world in which they may vicariously—and in a protected frame—experience, understand, and thus control love (86).

110. Schofield, 5.

111. Schofield, 5, quoting Nancy K. Miller, "Emphasis Added: Plots and Plausibilities in Women's Fiction" *Publications of the Modern Language Association* 96 (January 1981): 46.

112. Schofield, 117.

113. Toni Bowers, *The Politics of Motherhood: British Writing and Culture 1680–1760* (Cambridge: Cambridge University Press, 1996), 124–147.

114. Backscheider and Richetti point out: "As J. Paul Hunter has recently observed, the eighteenth-century novel is directed at problems or dilemmas that are specific to particular persons and social circumstances, and these fictions are often attentive to such situations. Hunter poses some typical questions that novels of the time seek to answer: 'How is an innocent servant girl to act when her wicked master decides it is his right to seduce her? [Pamela].' Such practical and specific questions (and ostensibly cautionary purposes) are at the heart of these fictions" (xvi).

115. Hecht points out that tracts were published for servants in hopes of indoctrinating them in proper deportment. It is not clear that these volumes supported the servant maid's position as Haywood's does (87).

116. Hecht, 10.

117. Haywood, 2.

118. Haywood, 21–22.

119. The subject of English puddings has generated polemical discussion; about these desserts one cannot be indifferent. One either loves them or hates them.

120. Sidney Mintz, *Sweetness and Power: The Place of Sugar in Modern History* (New York: Viking, 1985).

121. Hecht, 223.

122. Hecht points out that while "splendidly accoutered servants" signaled the wealth and refinement of their employers, it countered the belief that servants "ought to dress in strict accordance with their social status" (122).

123. Haywood, contents, page 48. Among them, *Anti-Pamela* (1741), in which prostitute Syrena, the heroine, engages with different men (Master, son of Master, single and married, male lodgers, giving opinions too freely) in the same scenes as portrayed in *A Present for a Servant-maid.*

124. Haywood, *Present for a Servant-maid,* 48.

125. Schofield, 108.

126. Quoted in Schofield, 108.

127. Both Eliza Haywood and Madam Johnson (as well as others) denigrate "eye-servants."

128. Haywood, 12.

129. *Bailey's Dictionarium* (London: printed for C. Hitch, 1736) and Mrs. Elizabeth Price's *A New Universal and Complete Confectioner, Being the Whole Art of Confectionary Made Perfectly Plain and Easy* (London: printed for A. Hogg, 1780).

Chapter 7

1. Lydia Maria Child, *The Frugal Housewife* (Boston: Marsh and Capen, 1829), 7.

2. Catharine Beecher and Harriet Beecher Stowe, *The New Housekeeper's Manual* (New York: J. B. Ford, 1873).

3. Amelia Simmons, *American Cookery* (Walpole, NH: Printed for Elijah Brooks, 1812).

4. Anne E. Goldman, *Take My Word, Autobiographical Innovations of Ethnic American Working Women* (Berkeley: University of California Press, 1996), 6.

5. Catharine Cotton, manuscript cookery book, 1698, Esther B. Aresty Collection, University of Pennsylvania. See Elaine Hobby, *Virtue of Necessity,* among others, for a list and description of women's spiritual and religious writings during the early to late seventeenth century.

6. Sara Mendelson and Patricia Crawford, *Women in Early Modern England, 1550–1720* (Oxford: Clarendon Press, 1998), 418.

7. For an account of the Presbyterian movement in England and Scotland, see Christopher Hill, *The Century of Revolution: A History of England, 1603–1714*, vol. 5 (Edinburgh: Thomas Nelson and Sons Ltd., 1961); Conrad Russell, *The Causes of the English Civil War: The Ford Lectures Delivered in the University of Oxford, 1987–1988* (Oxford: Clarendon Press, 1990; and J. D. Mackie, *A History of Scotland* (Baltimore: Penguin Books, 1964). In *Religion and the Decline of Magic* (New York: Charles Scribner's Sons, 1971), Keith Thomas points out that interest in investigating reputedly magical acts declined after the Reformation (260).

8. Lynette Hunter, "Cookery Books: A Cabinet of Rare Devices and Conceits," *Petits Propos Culinaires* 5 (May 1980): 21.

9. See Elizabeth Tebeaux, "Women and Technical Writing, 1475–1700: Technology, Literacy, and Development of a Genre," Hunter and Hutton (eds.), *Women, Science and Medicine, 1500–1700*, 29–62.

10. See Mary Douglas, *Purity and Danger: An Analysis of Concepts of Pollution and Taboo* (Harmondsworth: Penguin, 1966), for an analysis of the role of witchcraft in an African society. Since its publication, Douglas's analysis has been accepted widely by historians and other scholars for its usefulness as a concept beyond her African example.

11. Jan Longone, "Amelia Simmons and the First American Cookbook," in *American Bookseller*, August 12, 1996, 449.

12. Arjun Appadurai, "How to Make a National Cuisine: Cookbooks in Contemporary India," *Comparative Studies in Society and History*, vol. 30, no. 1 (January 1988): 5.

13. Mary Beth Norton, *Liberty's Daughters: The Revolutionary Experience of American Women, 1750–1800* (Boston: Little, Brown and Company, 1980), 228. See also Linda K. Kerber, *Women of the Republic: Intellect and Ideology in Revolutionary America* (Chapel Hill: University of North Carolina Press, 1980), 228.

14. Ann Fairfax Witherington, "Manufacturing and Selling the American Revolution," in Catherine E. Hutchins (ed.), *Everyday Life in the Early Republic* (Winterthur, DE: Henry Francis Du Pont Winterthur Museum, 1994), 286.

15. Simmons, iv.

16. Witherington, 286–288.

17. See Kerber; William Gilmore, *Reading Becomes a Necessity of Life: Material and Cultural Life in Rural New England, 1780–1835* (Knoxville: University of Tennessee Press, 1989); and Joan R. Gunderson, *Women in Revolutionary America, 1740–1790* (New York: Twayne Publishers, 1996).

18. Kerber, 54–60, 73–74.

19. Kerber, 11–12.

20. Simmons, iii. Kerber's book helps to contextualize Simmons's rhetoric by noting that "schemes for educating the 'rising generation' proliferated. The need for literate workers would translate into heightened economic, as well as intellectual, opportunities for teachers, who found their skills in demand" (189).

316 EAT MY WORDS

21. English cookery books prior to Simmons's *American Cookery* also gave recipes for American foodstuffs but did so in terms familiar to English housekeepers. Simmons's innovation in this text is the use of vernacular speech on food and cookery.
22. Longone, 449.
23. Cited in Longone, 450.
24. Late in my research I discovered an article by Glynis Ridley entitled "The First American Cookbook." It appeared in a special issue of *Eighteenth Century Life, The Cultural Topography of Food,* Beatrice Fink, ed., 23, no. 52, (May 1999): 114–123. Ridley's analysis of the cookbook's author, Amelia Simmons, as a trope for the new republic is similar to my own. Further, Ridley argues that American cookery was an assertion of nationalism and "anti-British sentiment" (114).
25. Simmons, 1.
26. Simmons, iii.
27. Simmons, iii.
28. Simmons, iii.
29. Kerber, 205.
30. Kerber, 209.
31. Simmons, iii.
32. Simmons, iv.
33. Nancy Cott, *The Bonds of Womanhood* (New Haven, CT: Yale University Press, 1977), 29.
34. Cott, 29–30.
35. Simmons, iii., emphasis in original.
36. Simmons, 3.
37. Please see Elaine Hobby, *Virtue of Necessity,* and Margaret Ezell, *Writing Women's Literary History.*
38. Authors frequently gave as their reasons for publishing to be helpful to their sex and country. See particularly Margaret J. M. Ezell, *The Patriarch's Wife, Literary Evidence and the History of the Family* (Chapel Hill: University of North Carolina Press,1987*).*
39. Simmons, 3.
40. See, for example, Wendy Wall, *The Imprint of Gender: Authorship and Publication in the English Renaissance* (Ithaca, NY: Cornell University Press, 1993), 173. Wall discusses the strategies used by male and female authors during the Renaissance transition from manuscript to print. Considering print culture to be threatening to the social order, the elite denigrated it because it opened class structures to permeability. Authors quickly invented ways of couching their engagement with print by professing modesty, virtue, or theft.
41. Simmons, iv.
42. Gilmore, 40.
43. Gilmore, 40–41.

44. Kerber, 206.
45. Kerber, 204–206.
46. Kerber, 231.
47. Gunderson, 89.
48. I would like to thank Monique Bourque for raising this point.
49. Catharine was first and primary author.
50. Kathryn Kish Sklar, *Catharine Beecher: A Study in American Domesticity* (New York: W. W. Norton & Company, 1973), 151–169.
51. Jeanne Boydston, Mary Kelley, and Anne Margolis, *The Limits of Sisterhood: The Beecher Sisters on Women's Rights and Woman's Sphere* (Chapel Hill: University of North Carolina Press, 1988), 122.
52. For a thorough discussion of this, see Barbara Kirshenblatt-Gimblett and Jenna Weissman Joselit, *Getting Comfortable in New York, The American Jewish Home, 1880–1950*.
53. Change is a continuous feature of most cuisines. Obviously, impoverished people do not have access to the variety of foods available to the middle and upper classes. However, the introduction of new foods and people as well as economic and political fluctuations inevitably alter the composition of dietary patterns. Limited access to foods as a consequence of war, famine, and natural disaster also will affect food choices. Even during "uneventful" historical periods, food patterns undergo transformations and are simultaneously reinvented in an effort to impede social change.
54. Kish Sklar, 265.
55. Kish Sklar, 165.
56. It is not my intention in this chapter to narrate the entire Beecher family story. Each of the sisters (and other family members) had her own vision of American society and of the women who inhabited it; moreover, it was a vision that changed over time. For the definitive biography of Catharine Beecher, see Kish Sklar. A discussion of the Beecher sisters' views on women may be found in Boydston, Kelley, and Margolis. My purpose is to demonstrate the role of printed household cookery books in commenting on contemporary social issues. Later I examine how women used various printed sources to engage in similar social commentary in their private culinary writings. I have chosen only one chapter from *The New Housekeeper's Manual* to demonstrate how the Beechers' popular advice literature depicted women, both of their class and of others. To do justice to their often dissenting views would require more than I have devoted to it in this chapter.
57. George Stocking, *Victorian Anthropology* (New York: Free Press, 1983), 229.
58. Lawrence J. McCaffrey, *The Irish Diaspora in America*, 2nd ed. (Washington, DC: Catholic University of America Press, 1984), 70.
59. Hasia R. Diner, *Erin's Daughters in America: Irish Immigrant Women in the Nineteenth Century* (Baltimore: Johns Hopkins University Press, 1983), 85–88.
60. Beecher and Stowe, 13.
61. Beecher and Stowe, 316–17.

62. Kish Sklar, 135.
63. Kish Sklar, 137.
64. Before the Civil War, both Harriet and Catharine had supported, hesitantly at first, the abolition of slavery. However, it was Stowe's book, *Uncle Tom's Cabin,* with its rhetorical power conveyed through domestic, moral imagery, that stunned Americans and mobilized a nation's popular sentiment.
65. Beecher and Stowe, 309.
66. Faye Dudden, *Serving Women: Household Service in Nineteenth-Century America* (Middletown, CT: Wesleyan University Press, 1983), 6–7. See also Stocking's discussion of the widening gulf between employers and domestic servants in this period, 215.
67. Beecher and Stowe, 311.
68. Beecher and Stowe, 311–312.
69. Beecher and Stowe, 313.
70. Beecher and Stowe, 313.
71. Beecher and Stowe, 320.
72. Beecher and Stowe, 321.
73. Diner, 85.
74. Dudden, 226–228.
75. Quoted in Dudden, 59.
76. Beecher and Stowe, 314–316.
77. Beecher and Stowe, 316.
78. Beecher and Stowe, 327.
79. Beecher and Stowe, 322.
80. Mary W. Janvrin, "Mrs. Deming's Troubles," *Godey's Lady's Book and Magazine,* 72 (April 1866), 345.
81. Janvrin, 345–346.
82. Janvrin, 346.
83. Janvrin, 345.
84. Elnora Blanchard, nineteenth-century manuscript cookbook, Winterthur Collection.
85. Jan Longone, "'Tried Receipts': An Overview of America's Charitable Cookbooks" in Anne L. Bower (ed.), *Recipes for Reading: Community Cookbooks, Stories, Histories,* (Amherst: University of Massachusetts Press, 1997), 18.
86. Goldman, xxvii.
87. Ladies of the First Presbyterian Church, *Presbyterian Cookbook* (Dayton, OH: Historical Publishing Company, 1886), 7.
88. Ladies, 7.
89. Ladies, 53–54.
90. I am using the category of "race" to define Jewish cultural and ethnic identity in keeping with nineteenth-century ideology and usage.
91. Buwei Yang Chao, *How to Cook and Eat in Chinese* (New York: The John Day and Company, 1945).

92. Paper presented at Food: Nature/Culture, a social research conference at the New School University, New York, November 5–7, 1998.
93. See, for example, Maxine Hong Kingston, *The Woman Warrior* (New York: Vintage Books, 1977).
94. Chao, xii.
95. Chao, xii.
96. Chao, xii.
97. Chao, xiv.
98. Chao, xiii.
99. Chao, xi.
100. Chao, x.
101. Chao, book jacket excerpt of review by Clementine Paddleford.
102. Chao, book jacket excerpt of review by Literary Guild.
103. Chao, book jacket.
104. Chao, 228.
105. Chao, xiv.
106. Chao, 3.
107. Chao, 6.
108. Chao, 5.
109. Chao, 12–13.
110. Chao tells us quite early on in the book that she uses the term "American" to denote Americans and Europeans (xv).
111. Chao, 13.
112. Chao, xiv.
113. Chao, xiv.
114. Chao, 19.
115. Appadurai, 18.
116. Chao, xii.
117. Chao, 19.
118. Chao, xiii.
119. Chao, xiii-xiv.
120. Amy Tan, *The Joy Luck Club* (New York: Ivy Books, 1989); Gish Jen, *Mona in the Promised Land* (New York: Vintage Books, 1996); Denise Chong, *The Concubine's Children* (New York: Penguin, 1996); and Hong Kingston.
121. Chao, xiv.
122. Chao, 191.
123. Chao, 191.
124. Chao, xiv.
125. Chao, 133.
126. Chao, 134.
127. Chao, 135.
128. Chao, 135.
129. Chao, 135.
130. Chao, xvi.

131. For this point, see Chong; Hong Kingston; Jen; Pang-Mei Natasha Chang, *Bound Feet and Western Dress* (New York: Doubleday, 1996); for an anthropological perspective, see Margery Wolf and Roxane Witke (eds.), *Women in Chinese Society* (Stanford, CA: Stanford University Press, 1975); Rubie S. Watson, "Named and the Nameless: Gender and Person in Chinese Society," *American Ethnologist* 13, no. 4 (1986): 619–631; Jean Lock, "Effect of Ideology in Gender Role Definition: China as a Case Study," *Journal of Asian and African Studies* 24, nos. 3–4 (1998): 228–38.

132. Thanks to Elisa New, associate professor in the Department of English at Harvard University, for this term.

Epilogue

1. Phyllis Pray Bober's scholarly treatise, *Art, Culture, and Cuisine: Ancient and Medieval Gastronomy* (Chicago: University of Chicago Press, 1999), is not a cookbook—although it contains recipes. In it she points to a political agenda that will "encourage thoughtful participation in conservation practices of a different nature" (13).

2. The proceeds of the *CBS Morning Show*'s cookbook, *Chef on a Shoestring,* are donated to Share Our Strength.

3. Amartya Sen, "Nobody Need Starve," *Granta, Food: The Vital Stuff,* 52: Winter (1995): 215–220.

4. Sen, 219.

5. Judy Wicks and Kevin von Klause of Philadelphia's White Dog Café explicitly discuss their philosophy, "a table for six billion." Wicks and von Klause remark, "The most joyful vision I can imagine is everyone in the world sitting at one big table, sharing in the Earth's abundance and the beauty of each different face." *The White Dog Café Cookbook: Multicultural Recipes and Tales of Adventure from Philadelphia's Revolutionary Restaurant* (Philadelphia: Running Press, 1998), 21.

6. I am grateful to Regina Bendix for this point.

7. I have learned this from discussions with audiences and classes through the years.

8. Anthony Lane, "Look Back in Hunger: Cookbooks, Old and New, and the Perils of the Kitchen," *The New Yorker,* December 18, 1995: 52.

9. Buwei Yang Chao's *How to Cook and Eat in Chinese* is an earlier twentieth-century example.

10. Madeleine Kamman, *Savoie: The Land, People, and Food of the French Alps* (New York: Atheneum, 1989), xi.

11. Kamman, viii.

12. Kamman, xii.

13. John Urry, *The Tourist Gaze: Leisure and Travel in Contemporary Societies* (London: Sage Publications, 1990).

14. Lynne Rosetto Kasper, *The Splendid Table: Recipes from Emilia-Romagna, the Heartland of Northern Italian Food* (New York: William Morrow and Company, 1992), 3.

15. Kasper, vii.

16. Kasper, 273.

17. Although, as Barbara Kirshenblatt-Gimblet (*Destination Culture: Tourism, Museums, and Heritage* [Berkeley: University of California Press, 1998], 150) points out, we never truly reclaim or discover our pasts; we use them as resources to give new meanings to the present.

18. The following adjectives have been used to define the authentic: "original, genuine, natural, naïve, noble, innocent, lively, sensuous, stirring." However, the search for the authentic is a spurious one. See Regina Bendix, *In Search of Authenticity* (Madison: University of Wisconsin Press, 1997), 15. As Bendix describes it: "The search for authenticity is fundamentally an emotional and moral quest" (7).

19. Kasper, 9.

20. Kasper, 10.

21. Kasper, 10.

22. Kasper, 10.

23. Kasper, 7.

24. Bert Fragner, "Social Reality and Culinary Fiction: The Perspective of Cookbooks from Iran and Central Asia," in Sami Zubaida and Richard Tapper (eds.), *Culinary Cultures of the Middle East* (London: I. B. Tauris Publishers), 68.

25. Fragner, 68.

26. I am indebted Regina Bendix for this insight.

27. Paul Mattick, review of *Comfort Me with Apples: More Adventures at the Table* by Ruth Reichl, *The New York Times Book Review*, April 15, 2001, 7.

28. Alice Waters, *Chez Panisse Café Cookbook* (New York: Harper Collins, 1999), xviii.

29. Waters, 2–3.

30. Waters, xi.

31. Waters, xvii.

32. Waters, 63.

33. Waters, 178.

34. Kim Lau, *New Age Capitalism* (Philadelphia: University of Pennsylvania Press, 2000), 9.

35. Wicks and von Klause, 12.

36. Lau, 11.

37. Marian Burros, "Alice Waters: Food Revolutionary," *The New York Times*, April 14, 1996.

38. Burros, 1.

39. Alice Waters, *Fanny at Chez Panisse, A Child's Restaurant Adventures with 46 Recipes* (New York: Harper Perennial, 1992), 4.

40. Waters, 109.

Bibliography

Primary Sources

Abell, L. G., Mrs. *The Skillful Housewife's Book: or Complete Guide to Domestic Cookery, Taste, Comfort, and Economy.* New York: O. Judd & Co., 1852.

Act for Dividing, Allotting and Enclosing the lands within the parish of St. Ives in the county of Huntingdon. British Records: 41 Regnal of King George III, 1801.

Acton, Eliza. *Modern Cookery for Private Families reduced to a system of easy practice, in a series of carefully tested receipts, in which the principles of Baron Liebeg and other eminent writers have been as much as possible applied and explained.* London: Longmans, Green, Reader, & Dyer, 1871.

American Cookery, formerly The Boston Cooking School Magazine of Culinary Science and Domestic Education, 8 vols., June 1914-May 1947. Boston: 1932. The Esther B. Aresty Collection of Rare Books on the Culinary Arts, Van Pelt Library, University of Pennsylvania, Philadelphia, PA.

Angelica's Ladies Library or Parents and Guardians Present. London: Printed for J. Hamiton and Co. at the Shakespeare Library, Beech Street, near Finsbury Square; and Mrs. Harlow, Bookseller to Her Majesty, Pall Mall, 1794.

Ashton family. Household accounts, Ashton Family Papers, 1860. Winterthur Museum and Library, Winterthur, DE.

Aunt Mary. *The Philadelphia Housewife, or Family Receipt Book.* Philadelphia: J.B. Lippincott & Co., 1855.

Aunt Mena's Recipe Book, sold for the benefit of the Baptist Orphanage, Angora, Philadelphia, comp. M. B. Bosson. Philadelphia: The National Baptist, 1888.

Bailey, Ida Cogswell. *The Modern Method of Preparing Delightful Foods.* New York: Corn Products Refining Co., 1926.

Bailey, Nathan. *Bailey's Dictionarium Domesticum.* London: C. Hitch, 1736.

Barnes, Mary Frances. *Feeding the Child from Two to Six.* New York: The Macmillan Co., 1928.

Beddingfield, J. Manuscript cookbook, 1730–1744. The Esther B. Aresty Collection of Rare Books on the Culinary Arts, Van Pelt Library, University of Pennsylvania, Philadelphia, PA.

Beecher, Catharine. *Miss Beecher's Domestic Receipt-Book,* 3rd ed. New York: Harper's, 1857.

————. *Miss Beecher's Housekeeper and Health Keeper Containing Five Hundred Recipes for Economical and Healthful Cooking and Also Many Directions for Securing Health and Happiness Approved by Physicians of All Classes.* New York: Harper & Brothers, Publishers, 1873.

Beecher, Catharine E., and H. B. Stowe. *The New Housekeeper's Manual.* New York: J. B. Ford & Co., 1873.

Beeton, Isabella. *The Book of Household Management.* London: S.O. Beeton, 1861.

Benson, Evelyn Abraham, ed. *Penn Family Recipes: Cooking Recipes of Wm. Penn's Wife, Gulielma, with an Account of the Life of Gulielma Maria Springett Penn, 1644–1694.* York, PA: George Shumway, 1966.

Bell, Katharin. *Mammy's Cook Book.* New York: Henry Holt & Co., 1928.

Benton, Caroline French. *A Little Cook-Book for a Little Girl.* Boston: D. Estes & Co., 1905.

Bethphage Mission Society. *The Mission Cookbook,* 3rd ed. Rock Island, IL: The Tabith Society, 1921.

Better Baking. Winona, MN: The J. R. Watkins Co., n.d.

Bigelow, Laura. Cookbook, ca. 1850-ca. 1870. Winterthur Museum and Library, Winterthur, DE.

Blanchard, Elnora. Cookbook, ca. 1870-ca. 1890. Winterthur Museum and Library, Winterthur, DE.

Borden, E. S. Recipe book, 1873. Joseph Downs Collection of Manuscripts and Printed Ephemera, Winterthur Museum and Library, Winterthur, DE.

Bradley, Alice. *The Alice Bradley Menu-Cook-Book.* New York: Macmillan, 1936.

Bradley, Martha. *The British Housewife: Or, The Cook, Housekeeper's, and Gardiner's Companion.* Facsimile of 1756 edition, ed. Gilly Lehmann. Blackawton, Totnes, Devon: Prospect Books, 1996.

Bradley, Richard. *The Country Housewife and Lady's Director, Parts I & II.* London: Printed for Woodman and Lyon, 1727.

Bradley, Rose. *The English Housewife in the 17th and 18th Centuries.* London: Edward Arnold, 1912.

Braithwaite, Richard. *The English Gentlewoman.* London: Printed by B. Alsop and T. Favcet for Michaell Sparke, dwelling in Greene Arbor, 1631.

Brett, Hopestill. Manuscript recipe book, 1678–1690. The Esther B. Aresty Collection of Rare Books on the Culinary Arts, Van Pelt Library, University of Pennsylvania, Philadelphia, PA.

Briggs, Asa, ed. *How They Lived. Volume III: An Anthology of Original Documents Written Between 1700 and 1815.* New York: Barnes & Noble, 1969.

Briggs, Richard. *The English Art of Cookery, According to the Present Practice; Being a Complete Guide to All Housekeepers.* London: Printed for G. G. J. and J. Robinson, 1788.

Brown, John. *An estimate of the manners and principles of the times.* London: Printed for L. Davis and C. Reymers in Holborn; Printers to the Royal Society, 1757.

Browne, Mrs. A. E., Manuscript cookbook, 1777. The Esther B. Aresty Collection of Rare Books on the Culinary Arts, Van Pelt Library, University of Pennsylvania, Philadelphia, PA.

Buckham, James. "Children and the Servant Problem." *American Kitchen Magazine* 10, no. 4 (January 1899): 113–115.

Byles, Elizabeth. Cookery book, 1759. Winterthur Museum and Library, Winterthur, DE.

Cain, Mrs. Jewett. Recipe book, 1862–1872. Winterthur Library and Museum, Winterthur, DE.

Campbell, Jane, and William Campbell. Culinary manuscript, nineteenth century. Collection of the author.

Carter, Susannah. *The Frugal Housewife, or, Complete Woman Cook.* Philadelphia: Printed for Matthew Carey, 1802.

Chang, Pang-Mei Natasha. *Bound Feet and Western Dress.* New York: Doubleday, 1996.

Chao, Buwai Yang. *How to Cook and Eat in Chinese.* New York: The John Day and Company, 1945.

Chase, Alvin Wood. *Dr. Chase's Recipes, or Information for Everybody.* Ann Arbor, MI: R. A. Beal, 1875.

Chase, Hattie N. Recipe book, 1880–1890. Winterthur Museum and Library, Winterthur, DE.

Child, Lydia Maria. *The American Frugal Housewife,* 12th ed. Boston: Carter, Hendee, and Co., 1832.

Child, Lydia Maria Frances. *The American Frugal Housewife,* 21st ed. New York: Samuel S. & William Wood, 1838.

Chong, Denise. *The Concubine's Children.* New York: Penguin, 1996.

Cleveland's Superior Receipts, Third million—with supplement. New York: Cleveland Baking Powder Co., 1892.

Cole, Mary. *The Lady's complete guide or Cookery in all its branches . . . also the Complete brewer . . . likewise the Family physician, the 3rd edition.* London: Printed for G. Kearsley, No. 46, Fleet Street, 1791.

The Congressional Club Cook Book: Favorite National and International Recipes, 3rd ed. Washington, DC: Congressional Club, 1948.

Cook, Ann. *Professed Cookery: containing boiling, roasting, pastry, preserving, potting, pickling, made-wines, gellies, and part of confectionaries.* Newcastle: Printed for the Author, 1755

Cookery & Domestic Economy for Young Housewives, 25th ed. London: W. and R. Chambers, 1875.

Cookery as It Should Be. Philadelphia: W. P. Hazard, 1853.

Copley, Esther. *The Cook's Complete Guide.* London: George Virtue, 1827.

Corson, Juliet. *The Cooking Manual of Practical Directions for Economical Every-Day Cookery.* New York: Dodd, Mead & Co., 1877.

———. *Fifteen Cent Dinners for Workingmen's Families.* New York: Author, 1877.

———. *Cooking School Text Book and Housekeepers' Guide to Cookery and Kitchen Management.* New York: Orange Judd & Co., 1878.

————. *Miss Corson's Practical American Cookery and Household Management*. New York: Dodd, Mead and Company, 1885.

————. *Twenty-five cent dinners for families of six*. New York: Published by the author at the office of the New York Cooking School, 1878.

Cotton, Catherine. Manuscript recipe book, 1698. The Esther B. Aresty Collection of Rare Books on the Culinary Arts, Van Pelt Library, University of Pennsylvania, Philadelphia, PA.

Coultas, Elizabeth. Recipe book, 1749–1750. Winterthur Museum and Library, Winterthur, DE.

Crawford, Patricia, and Laura Gowing, eds. *Women's Worlds in Seventeenth-Century England: Sourcebook*. London: Routledge, 2000.

Crowfield, Christopher. *House and Home Papers*. Boston: Ticknor & Fields, 1865.

Dainty Desserts for Dainty People—Knox Gelatine. Johnstown, NY: Charles B. Knox. Co.: 1915.

Dawson, Thomas. *The Good Huswife's Jewell*. Facsimile edition, ed. Maggie Black. Lewes, East Sussex: Southover Press, 1996.

De Knight, Freda, *A Date with a Dish: A Cookbook of American Negro Recipes*. New York: Hermitage Press, 1948.

De Silva, Cara, ed. *In Memory's Kitchen: A Legacy from the Women of Terezin*. Trans. Bianca Steiner Brown. Northvale, NJ: Jason Aronson Inc., 1996.

Devitt, Charles W., Mrs. Recipe book, ca. 1871. Winterthur Museum and Library, Winterthur, DE.

Domestic Service, by an Old Servant. Boston: Houghton Mifflin Company, 1917.

[Downing, Mrs.] Cookery manuscript, early twentieth century. Collection of the author.

Eales, Mrs. Mary. *The Compleat Confectioner: or The Art of Candying & Preserving in Its Utmost Perfection*, 5th edition. London: R. Montagu, 1753.

Emerson, Lucy. *The New England Cookery*. Montpelier: Printed for Josiah Parks, 1808.

Evans, Philip. Receipt book, 1793. Winterthur Museum and Library, Winterthur, DE.

Experiences Lady. *The American Housewife*. New York: Newman & Ivison, 1853.

Farmer, Marina. Inventory of estates, 1788. Marina Farmer (New York) Collection. Winterthur Museum and Library, Winterthur, DE.

The Farmer's Wife or Complete Country Housewife. London: Alex. Hogg, No. 16, in Paternoster-row, 1780.

Fisher, Mrs. *The Prudent Housewife, or Complete English Cook for Town and Country*. London: Printed by T. Sabine, 1750.

Fisher, Sarah Logan. Journal, 1816. Winterthur Museum and Library, Winterthur, DE.

Fiske family. Cookbook, ca. 1810-ca. 1890. Winterthur Museum and Library, Winterthur, DE.

Frankland, Lady. Recipe book, 1750–1825. Esther B. Aresty Collection of Rare Books on the Culinary Arts, Van Pelt Library, University of Pennsylvania, Philadelphia, PA.

Frescheville, Lady. Recipe book, 1669. Winterthur Museum and Library, Winterthur, DE.

"From Real Life." *The American Kitchen Magazine* 6, no. 1 (January 1898): 159.

General Foods Cook Book, New York: Consumer Services Dept., General Foods Corp., 1932.

Giger, Frederick Sidney, Mrs. *Colonial Receipt Book: Celebrated Old Receipts Used a Century Ago by Mrs. Goodfellow's Cooking School.* Philadelphia: J. C. Winston, 1907.

Glasse, Hannah. *The Art of Cookery, Made Plain and Easy.* London: Printed for W. Strahan. J. & F. Rivington, J. Hinton, etc., 1774.

"Godey's Arm-Chair." *Godey's Lady's Book and Magazine* (January 1866).

Gold Medal Flour Cook Book. Minneapolis, MN: Washburn-Crosby Co., 1910.

Good Samaritan. *The American Family Keepsake, or People's Practical Cyclopedia.* Boston: Published at 66 Cornhill, 1848.

Grant, Bartle, ed. *The Receipt Book—Elizabeth Raper and a Portion of Her Cipher Journal.* Soho, England: The Nonesuch Press, 1924.

Growden, Hannah. Inventory of her estate, 1783. Winterthur Museum and Library, Winterthur, DE.

Hall, Mary J. Receipt book, ca. 1851–1927. Wistar Family Papers, Winterthur Museum and Library, Winterthur, DE.

Hammond, Mrs. Ericsson. *The Swedish, French, American Cook Book.* New York: Printed for the author, 1918.

Harland, Marion. *Breakfast, Luncheon and Tea.* New York: Scribner, Armstrong & Co., 1875.

———. *Common Sense in the Household: A Manual of Practical Housewifery.* New York: Scribner, Armstrong & Co., 1876.

———. *Cookery for Beginners.* Boston: D. Lothrop & Co., 1893.

Harrison, Mrs. Sarah. *The Housekeeper's Pocket-Book, and Compleat Family Cook, Containing Above Three Hundred Curious and Uncommon Receipts in Cookery, Pastry, Preserving, Pickling, Candying, Collaring, &c.* London: T. Worrall, at Judge Coke's Head, Fleet Street, 1733.

———. *The House-keeper's Pocket Book,* 2nd ed. London: Printed for R. Ware, 1739.

Harwood, Diadema. Account book, 1823–1825. Winterthur Museum and Library, Winterthur, DE.

Haywood, Eliza. *Anti-Pamela.* London: Printed for J. Huggonson, 1741. Brown University: Women Writers Project, first electronic edition, 1999. www.wwp.brown.edu.

———. *A Present for a Servant-Maid: or, The Sure Means of Gaining Love and Esteem, The Whole Calculated for Making Both the Mistress and the Maid Happy.* London: Printed and Published by T. Gardner, at Cowley's Head, without Temple-Bar; and sold by the Book Sellers of Town and Country, 1743.

———. *A New Present for a Servant Maid: containing rules for her moral conduct both with respect to herself and her superiors: the whole art of cooking.* London: Printed for G. Pearch [etc.], 1771.

Hess, Karen, ed. *Martha Washington's Booke of Cookery.* New York: Columbia University Press, 1981.

Hickman, Peggy, ed. *A Jane Austen Household Book with Martha Lloyd's Recipes.* Newton Abbott: David & Charles, 1977.

Hill, A. P. *Mrs. Hill's New Cook Book: A Practical System for Private Families, in Town and Country.* New York: Carleton, Publisher, Madison Square, 1870.

Howard, Bessie. Recipe book, 1888. Joseph Downs Collection, Winterthur Museum and Library, Winterthur, DE.

Howard, Mrs. B. C. *Fifty Years in a Maryland Kitchen,* 3rd ed. Baltimore: Turnbull Bros., 1877.

Hughes, Anne. *Diary of a Farmer's Wife, 1796–1797,* facsimile ed. Fleet Street, London: Countrywise Books, the Farmer's Weekly, 1964.

Huntington, Emily. *The Cooking Garden.* New York: Press of J.J. Little & Co., 1885.

Huthwaite, Hannah. Recipe book, ca. 1720. Winterthur Museum and Library, Winterthur, DE.

Janviers, Jane, and others. Manuscript receipt book, 1817–1837. Historical Society of Pennsylvania, Philadelphia, PA.

Janvrin, Mary W. "Mrs. Deming's Troubles." *Godey's Lady's Book and Magazine* 72 (April 1866): 345–351.

Jarvis, Lydia Grofton. Recipe book, ca. 1840. Winterthur Museum and Library, Winterthur, DE.

Jell-O: America's Most Famous Dessert. Le Roy, NY: Genesse Pure Food Co., 1916.

Jen, Gish. *Mona in the Promised Land.* New York: Vintage, 1996.

Jocelyn, Robert, Viscount of. Dinner book, 1740–1751. Winterthur Museum and Library, Winterthur, DE.

Jones, Kenneth W., ed. *Marconi Senior Citizens' Club: Recipes from South Philadelphia Kitchens.* Philadelphia: South Philadelphia Community Center, 1980.

Kamman, Madeleine. *Savoie: The Land, People, and Food of the French Alps.* New York: Atheneum, 1989.

Kander, Mrs. Simon (comp.). *The Settlement Cook Book,* 4th ed. Milwaukee, WI: J. H. Yewdale & Sons Co., 1910.

Kane, Jane D. L. Recipe book, n.d. Winterthur Museum and Library, Winterthur, DE.

Kasper, Lynne Rosetto. *The Splendid Table: Recipes from Emilia-Romagna, the Heartland of Northern Italian Food.* New York: William Morrow and Company, 1992.

Keen, Mrs. Hannah. Manuscript cookery book, 1867–1882. The Esther B. Aresty Collection of Rare Books on the Culinary Arts, Van Pelt Library, University of Pennsylvania, Philadelphia, PA.

Kellet, Susanna, Elizabeth Kellett, and Mary Kellett. *A Complete Collection of Cookery Receipts (Consisting of near Four Hundred) Which have been Taught upwards of Fifty Years, with great Reputation.* Newcastle: Printed by T. Saint, 1780.

Kent, Elizabeth Grey, Countess of. *A Choice Manuall, or Rare and select secrets in physick and chyrurgery collected and practised by the right honourable the Countesse of Kent, late deceased; whereto are added several experiments of the virtues of Gascon pouder and lapis contra yarvam by a professor of physick; as also most exquisite waies of preserving, conserving, candying, &c.* 4th ed. London: Printed by G. D. and are to be sold by William Shears, 1654.

Kettilby, Mary. *A Collection of Above Three Hundred Receipts in Cookery, Physick and Surgery, Part I.* London: Printed for Richard Wilkin, 1714.

————. *A Collection of Receipts in Cookery, Physick and Surgery, Part II.* London: Printed for Richard Wilkin, 1719.

Keyworth, T., Mrs. Cookbook, 1820–1870. Winterthur Museum and Library, Winterthur, DE.

Kidder, E. D. *Receipts of Pastry and Cookery for the Use of His Scholars.* London, 1720.

Kingston, Maxine Hong. *The Woman Warrior: Memoirs of a Girlhood Among Ghosts.* New York: Vintage, 1975.

Ladies of the First Presbyterian Church. *Presbyterian Cookbook.* Dayton, OH: Historical Publishing Company, 1886.

Ladies of the Grand Army of the Republic in Portland, Maine. "Hints to Housekeepers. Presented by Bosworth Circle, No. 1." Winterthur Museum and Library, Winterthur, DE.

The Lady's Companion, Containing Upwards of Three Thousand different Receipts in every kind of Cookery; and those the best and most fashionable; Being Four Times the Quantity of any Book of this Sort. London: Printed for T. Read, 1751.

Lahiri, Jhumpa. *Interpreter of Maladies: Stories.* Boston: Houghton Mifflin, 1999.

Lawrance, Miss Ann. Manuscript cookbook, 1737. The Esther B. Aresty Collection of Rare Books on the Culinary Arts, Van Pelt Library, University of Pennsylvania, Philadelphia, PA.

LeGuin, Charles A., ed. *A Home-Concealed Woman: The Diaries of Magnolia Wynn Le Guin, 1901–1913.* Athens: University of Georgia Press, 1990.

Lee, Mrs. N. K. M. *The Cook's Own Book.* New York: Oliver S. Felt, 1865.

Leslie, Eliza. *New Receipts for Cooking.* Philadelphia: T. B. Peterson, 1854.

Lincoln, Mrs. D. A. *Boston School Kitchen Text-Book Lessons in Cooking for the Use of Classes in Public and Industrial Schools.* Boston: Roberts Brothers, 1887.

Lincoln, Mrs. D. A. Carrie Dearborn, and Anna Barrows. *Dainty Desserts.* Portland, ME: Schlotterbeck & Foss Co., n.d.

Lincoln, Mary Johnson. *Mrs. Lincoln's Boston Cook Book: What to Do and What Not to Do in Cooking.* Boston: Little, Brown, 1883.

Lloyd, Grace. Will, 1765. Winterthur Museum and Library, Winterthur, DE.

Louis, S. L. *Decorum: A Practical Treatise on Etiquette and Dress of the Best American Society.* Cincinnati: Union Publishing House, 1882.

MacDonald, Margaret, ed. *Whistler's Mother's Cookbook.* London: Paul Elek, 1979.

Madam Johnson's Present: Or, the Best Instructions for Young Women in Useful and Universal Knowledge, with a Summary of the Late Marriage Act and Instructions how to marry pursuant thereto. London: M. Cooper, Paternoster-row, and C. Sympson, at the Boble, Chancery Lane, 1754.

Maddison & Morison families. Maddison family receipt book, manuscript cookbook, predominantly seventeenth century. The Esther B. Aresty Collection of

Rare Books on the Culinary Arts, Van Pelt Library, University of Pennsylvania, Philadelphia, PA.

Mann, Mary Tayler Peabody. *Christianity in the Kitchen. A Physiological Cook Book.* Boston: Ticknor & Fields, 1857.

Manuscript cookbook, 1699. The Esther B. Aresty Collection of Rare Books on the Culinary Arts, Van Pelt Library, University of Pennsylvania, Philadelphia, PA.

Markoe, Ellen. Letter in manuscript recipe book, nineteenth century. Historical Society of Pennsylvania, Philadelphia, PA.

May, Robert. *The Accomplisht Cook.* London: R. W., 1660.

Middleton, John. *Five Hundred New Receipts in Cookery, Confectionary, Pastry, Preserving, Conserving, Pickling.* London: Printed for Tho. Astley, 1734.

Milhous, Sarah. Commonplace Book, 1786. Winterthur Museum and Library, Winterthur, DE.

Mora, Pat. *House of Houses.* Boston: Beacon Press, 1997.

More Nurses in Training. *The Cook Book of Left-Overs.* Rochelle, IL: The Movement, 1920.

Moxon, Elizabeth. *English Housewifery, Exemplified in above Four Hundred and Fifty Receipts Giving Directions in Most Parts of Cookery.* 10th ed. Leeds: Printed by Griffith Wright, for George Copperthwaite, 1769.

Parloa, Maria. *Choice Receipts. Specially Prepared for Walter Baker & Company.* Dorchester, MA: The Company, 1892.

————. *Miss Parloa's Kitchen Companion, A Guide for All Who Would Be Good Housekeepers,* 20th ed. Boston: Estes and Lauriat, 1887.

Parloa, Maria, and Elizabeth K. Burr. *Choice Recipes, By Miss Maria Parloa and Miss Elizabeth K. Burr, Specially Prepared for Walter Baker & Company.* Dorchester, MA: The Company, 1901.

Partridge, John. *The Treasurie of Hidden Secrets: Commonly Called, the Good-Husewiues Closet of Prouision for the Health of her Household.* London: Printed for E. B. & R. B., 1627.

Patterson, Mrs. Fred. Recipe book, ca. 1870-ca. 1879. Winterthur Museum and Library, Winterthur, DE.

[Peabody, Mrs.? A. J.] Account and recipe book, 1837–1894. Winterthur Museum and Library, Winterthur, DE.

Pennell, Elizabeth Robins. *My Cookery Books.* Boston: Houghton Mifflin, 1903.

Perkins, Mary. Recipe book, nineteenth century. Winterthur Museum and Library, Winterthur, DE.

Petrie [Pettee?], Doro. Manuscript cookbook, 1705. The Esther B. Aresty Collection of Rare Books on the Culinary Arts, Van Pelt Library, University of Pennsylvania, Philadelphia, PA.

Phelps, Mrs. E. A. Receipt book, 1919. Winterthur Museum and Library, Winterthur, DE.

Phillips, Sarah. *The Ladies Handmaid, or, a Compleat System of Cookery; on the principals of Elegance and Frugality wherein the useful art of Cookery is rendered plain, easy.* London: Printed for J. Coote, 1758.

Pilsbury, H. N. Recipe book, 1847. Winterthur Museum and Library, Winterthur, DE.

Plat, Hugh. *A Closet for Ladies and Gentlewomen, or, The Art of Preserving.* London: Printed for Arthur Johnson, 1608.

———. *Delights for Ladies, Written originally by Sir Hugh Plat, first printed in 1602, London, England, Reprinted from the edition of 1627.* Herrin, IL: Trovillion Private Press, 1939.

Polly Put the Kettle on, We'll All Make Jell-O. Le Roy, NY: Genesee Pure Food Co., 1924.

Powell, Mabella. "The Delights for Ladys to adorne there Persons, Beautyes, Stillyris, Banquits, Perfumes, Waters," 1655. The Esther B. Aresty Collection of Rare Books on the Culinary Arts, Van Pelt Library, University of Pennsylvania, Philadelphia, PA.

Price, Mrs. Elizabeth. *The New, Universal, and Complete Confectioner,* 1st ed. London: Printed for A. Hogg, 1781.

Putnam, Mrs. E. *Mrs. Putnam's Receipt Book & The Young Housekeeper's Assistant,* new and enlarged ed. Boston: Ticknor & Fields, 1854.

Rabisha, William. *The Whole Body of Cookery Dissected.* London: Printed by R.W. for Giles Calvert, 1661.

Raffald, Elizabeth. *The Experienced English Housekeeper,* 10th edition. London: R. Baldwin, 1786.

Randolph, Mary. *The Virginia Housewife.* Oxmoor House, Birmingham, AL: Antique American Cookbooks, 1984.

Rappe family. Recipe book, ca. 1810-ca. 1840. Winterthur Museum and Library, Winterthur, DE.

Recipe book, includes recipe for scripture cake, nineteenth century. Winterthur Museum and Library, Winterthur, DE.

Recipe book, many recipes copied from Mary Hall's, ca. 1850s–1890s. Winterthur Museum and Library, Winterthur, DE.

Recipe book, Pennsylvania German recipe book, 1750–1830. Winterthur Museum and Library, Winterthur, DE.

Recipes and menus, 1822–1829. Winterthur Museum and Library, Winterthur, DE.

Recipes for the Use of Huyler's Cocoa and Chocolate. New York: Huyler's, 1913.

Reynolds, Catherine. Letters, Ashton Family Papers, 1810. Winterthur Museum and Library, Winterthur, DE.

Richardson, Francis. Account book, 1729. Winterthur Museum and Library, Winterthur, DE.

Roberts, Robert. *The House Servant's Directory, or A Monitor for Private Families,* 2nd ed. Boston: Munroe & Francis, 1828.

Rochester Chapter of Hadassah. *Rochester Hadassah Cook Book,* 2nd ed. Rochester, NY: Great Lakes Press, 1972.

Rogers, Mary Anne, ed. *Favorite Recipes of Home Economics Teachers: Casseroles Including Breads.* Montgomery, AL: Favorite Recipes Press, 1965.

Rorer, Sarah Tyson. *Mrs. Rorer's New Cook Book: A Manual of Housekeeping.* Philadelphia: Arnold, 1902.

Rundell, Maria Eliza Ketelby. *A New System of Domestic Cookery.* London: Printed for J. Murray, 1807.

Rushdie, Salman. *Midnight's Children.* New York: Penguin, 1995.

Salmon. *The Family Dictionary, or Household Companion.* London: Printed for H. Rhoades, 1710.

Sanborn, Lydia. Recipe book, 1860. Winterthur Museum and Library, Winterthur, DE.

Schmitt, Patricia Brady, ed. *Nelly Custis Lewis's Housekeeping Book.* New Orleans, LA: The Historic New Orleans Collection, 1982.

Schoonover, David E., ed. *Ladie Borlase's Receiptes Booke.* Iowa City: University of Iowa Press, 1998.

Scott, Sarah E. *Every-Day Cookery, for Every Family.* Philadelphia: Porter & Coates, 1866.

Seton, Nora. *The Kitchen Congregation: A Daughter's Story of Wives and Women Friends.* New York: Picador USA, 2000.

Shailer, Mrs. M. V. "The Practical Solution of the Domestic Service Problem." *The American Kitchen Magazine* 7 no. 2 (February 1898): 175–177.

Shirley, John. *The Accomplished Ladies' Rich Closet of Rarities, or The Ingenious Gentlewoman and Servant Maids Delightfull Companion.* 2nd ed. London: Printed by W. W. for Nicholas Boddington . . . and Josiah Blare . . . , 1687.

Shuman, Carrie V., comp. *Favorite Dishes: A Columbian Autograph Souvenir Cookery Book.* Chicago: R. R. Donnelley, Printers, 1893.

Simmons, Amelia. *American Cookery: A facsimile of the first edition, 1796.* New York: Oxford University Press, 1958.

———. *American Cookery by an American orphan.* Walpole, NH: 1812.

———. *American Cookery.* New York: Published by William Beastall; S. Marks, printer, 1822.

Smedley, Emma. *The School Lunch; Its Organization and Management in Philadelphia,* 2nd ed. Media, PA: Emma Smedley, 1930.

Smith, Eliza. *The Compleat Housewife.* London: J. & J. Pemberton, 1737.

———. *The Compleat Housewife: or Accomplish'd Gentlewoman's Companion.* Williamsburg, VA: William Parks, 1742.

———. *The Compleat Housewife or Accomplish'd Gentlewoman's Companion.* London: Printed for R. Ware, S. Birt, T. Longman. C. Hitch, J. Hodges, and 4 others, 1750.

Smith, Mrs. *The Female Economist,* 2nd ed. London: Printed for Mathews & Leigh, 1810.

Spaulding, Lily May, and John Spaulding, comps. and eds. *Civil War Recipes: Receipts from the Pages of Godey's Lady's Book.* Lexington: University Press of Kentucky, 1999.

Spurling, Hilary, ed. *Elinor Fettiplace's Receipt Book: Elizabethan Country House Cooking.* London: Penguin Books, 1986.

Statham, Mary. Manuscript cookbook, "The great and Rare art of candying, cooking, distilling, Preserving, Pickling and Physick containing 2 Hundred thirty six

Receipts or above never before this made publick now made publick thro the intercession of some friends for the use good & Benefit of the Country," 1724. The Esther B. Aresty Collection of Rare Books on the Culinary Arts, Van Pelt Library, University of Pennsylvania, Philadelphia, PA.

Stevenson family. Receipt and recipe book, ca. 1850-ca. 1890. Winterthur Museum and Library, Winterthur, DE.

St. Luke's United Church of Christ Cookbook. Hills, MN: Crescent Publishing, Inc., 1989.

Tan, Amy. *The Joy Luck Club.* New York: Ivy Books, 1989.

Tarleton, Margaret. Notebooks, 1740–1761. Photocopy from microfilm 226, Tarleton papers in Liverpool Record office. Read at Winterthur Museum and Library, Winterthur, DE.

Taylor, E. *The Art of Cookery of The Lady's, Housewife's, and Cookmaid's Assistant.* Berwick upon Tweed: Printed by H. Taylor, 1769.

Tillinghast, Mary. *The True Way of Preserving & Candying.* London: Printed for the author, 1695.

Trimble, Hannah. Account and recipe book, 1859–1880. Winterthur Museum and Library, Winterthur, DE.

"Useful Receipts." *Saturday Chronicle,* February 25, 1837.

W. M. *The Queen's Closet Opened, Incomparable Secrets in Physick, Chirurgery, Preserving and Candying, etc. The Queen's Delight, The Compleat Cook.* London: Printed by J. Winter for Nat Brooke, 1668.

War-Time Cook and Health Book. Lynn, MA: Lydia E. Pinkham Medicine Co., 1917.

Waters, Alice. *Fanny at Chez Panisse: A Child's Restaurant Adventures with 46 Recipes.* New York: Harper Perennial, 1992.

———. *Chez Panisse Café Cookbook.* New York: Harper Collins, 1999.

Watson, Lucy Fanning. Watson family papers, 1834. Winterthur Museum and Library, Winterthur, DE.

Wecker, Anna. *Ein köstlich new Kochbuch von allerhand Speisen an Gemüsen, Obs, Fleisch, Geflügel, Wildpret, Fischen vnd Gebachens: nicht allein für Gesunde, sondern auch vnd fürnemlich für Krancke, in allerley Kranckheiten vnd Gebresten . . .* Basel: Ludwig Koenigs, 1605.

White, Anne Louise Hadley. Collection with album, recipe book, and scrapbook, ca. 1880-ca. 1890. Winterthur Museum and Library, Winterthur, DE.

Wicks, Judy, and Kevin von Klause. *White Dog Café Cookbook.* Philadelphia: Running Press, 1998.

Widdifield, Hannah. *Widdifield's new cook book: or, Practical receipts for the housewife.* Philadelphia: T. B. Peterson, 1856.

Wilcox, Estelle Woods. *Buckeye Cookery and Practical Housekeeping,* 2nd edition. Marysville, OH: Buckeye Publishing Co., 1877.

Williamson, Mrs. M. E. Recipe book, 1847. Winterthur Museum and Library, Winterthur, DE.

Wister, Elizabeth (Lizzie) Emlen Randolph. Receipt book, ca. 1848–1921. Winterthur Museum and Library, Winterthur, DE.

Wister, Sarah Logan (Fisher). Commonplace book, 1831. Winterthur Museum and Library, Winterthur, DE.

Wolley, Hannah. *The Cook's Guide.* London: Peter Dring at the Sun in the Poultry, next door to the Rose Tavern, 1664. Women Writers Project, Brown University, first electronic edition, 1999. www.wwp.brown.edu.

Zelickson, Sue, ed. *Minnesota Heritage Cookbook: Hand-Me-Down Recipes for the Benefit of the American Cancer Society, Minnesota Division, Inc.* Minneapolis, MN: The Division, 1979.

Secondary Sources

Adburgham, Alison. *Women in Print: Writing Women and Women's Magazines from the Restoration to the Accession of Victoria.* London: George Allen and Unwin Ltd., 1972.

Altick, Richard D. *The English Common Reader: A Social History of the Mass Reading Public, 1800–1900.* Chicago: University of Chicago Press, 1957.

———. *The English Common Reader: A Social History of the Mass Reading Public, 1800–1900,* 2nd ed. Columbus: Ohio State University Press, 1998.

Armory, Hugh, and David D. Hall, eds. *The Colonial Book in the Atlantic World.* Cambridge: Cambridge University Press, 2000.

Anderson, Linda. *At the Threshold of the Self: Women and Autobiography.* Brighton: Harvester Press, 1986.

Andrea, Bernadette Diane. *Properly Speaking: Publishing Women in 17th-Century England.* Ph.D. diss., Cornell University, 1996.

Appadurai, Arjun. "How to Make a National Cuisine: Cookbooks in Contemporary India." *Journal of the Society for the Comparative Study of Society and History* (1988): 3–24.

Aresty, Esther B. *The Delectable Past.* New York: Simon & Schuster, 1964.

Armstrong, Nancy. *Desire and Domestic Fiction: A Political History of the Novel.* New York: Oxford University Press, 1987.

———. "The Rise of Domestic Women." In *Ideology of Conduct: Essays on Literature and the History of Sexuality,* ed. Nancy Armstrong and Leonard Tennenhouse. New York: Methuen, 1987.

Armstrong, Nancy, and Leonard Tennenhouse, eds. *Ideology of Conduct: Essays on Literature and the History of Sexuality.* New York: Methuen, 1987.

Auwers, Linda. "Reading the Marks of the Past: Exploring Female Literacy in Colonial Windsor, Connecticut." *Historical Methods* 13, no. 4 (September 1980): 204–214.

Backscheider, Paula R., and John J. Richetti, eds. *Popular Fiction by Women: 1660–1730: An Anthology.* Oxford: Clarendon Press, 1996.

Barker, Francis, ed. *1642: Literature and Power in the 17th Century: Proceedings of the Essex Conference on the Sociology of Literature, July 1980.* Colchester: University of Essex, 1981.

Barker, Hannah. "Women, Work and the Industrial Revolution: Female Involvement in the English Printing Trades, c. 1700–1840." In *Gender in Eighteenth Century England: Roles, Representations and Responsibilities*, eds. Hannah Barker and Elaine Chalus. London: Longman, 1997.

Barker, Hannah, and Elaine Chalus, eds. *Gender in Eighteenth Century England: Roles, Representations and Responsibilities*. London: Longman, 1997.

Baym, Nina. *Woman's Fiction: A Guide to Novels by and about Women in America, 1820–1870.* Ithaca, NY: Cornell University Press, 1978.

Bayne-Powell, Rosamond. *Housekeeping in the Eighteenth Century.* London: John Murray, 1956.

Beilin, Elaine. *Redeeming Eve.* Princeton, NJ: Princeton University Press, 1987.

Bendix, Regina. *In Search of Authenticity: The Formation of Folklore Studies.* Madison: Wisconsin: University of Wisconsin Press, 1997.

Bennett, Judith M. *Ale, Beer, and Brewsters in England: Women's Work in a Changing World, 1300–1600.* Oxford: Oxford University Press, 1996.

Benstock, Shari. "Authorizing the Autobiographical." In *The Private Self: Theory and Practice of Women's Autobiographical Writings,* ed. Shari Benstock. Chapel Hill: University of North Carolina Press, 1988.

Benstock, Shari, ed. *The Private Self: Theory and Practice of Women's Autobiographical Writings.* Chapel Hill: University of North Carolina Press, 1988.

Berkin, Carol. *First Generations: Women in Colonial America.* New York: Hill & Wang, 1996.

Bermingham, Ann, and John Brewer, eds. *The Consumption of Culture, 1600–1800: Image, Object, Text.* London: Routledge, 1995.

Blair, Ann. "Humanist Methods in Natural Philosophy: the Commonplace Book." *Journal of the History of Ideas* 53 (October 1992): 541–551.

Bober, Phyllis Pray. *Art, Culture, and Cuisine: Ancient and Medieval Gastronomy.* Chicago: University of Chicago Press, 1999.

Bolsterli, Margaret Jones. "The Very Food We Eat: A Speculation on the Nature of Southern Culture." *Southern Humanities Review* 16, no. 2 (1982): 119–126.

Bower, Anne L., ed. *Recipes for Reading: Community Cookbooks, Stories, Histories.* Amherst: University of Massachusetts Press, 1997.

Bowers, Toni. *The Politics of Motherhood: British Writing and Culture 1680–1760.* Cambridge: Cambridge University Press, 1996.

Boydston, Jeanne, Mary Kelley, and Anne Margolis. *The Limits of Sisterhood: The Beecher Sisters on Women's Rights and Woman's Sphere.* Chapel Hill: University of North Carolina Press, 1988.

Branca, Patricia. *Silent Sisterhood: Middle-Class Women in the Victorian Home.* London: Croomhelm, 1975.

Brandt, Deborah. "Literacy Learning and Economic Change." *Harvard Educational Review* 69, no. 4 (December 1999): 373–394.

Braunstein, Susan L., and Jenna Weissman Joselit, eds. *Getting Comfortable in New York: The American Jewish Home, 1880–1950.* New York: The Jewish Museum, 1990.

Bridenthal, Renate, and Claudia Koonz, eds. *Becoming Visible: Women in European History.* Boston: Houghton Mifflin, 1977.

Brown, Kathleen M. *Good Wives, Nasty Wenches, and Anxious Patriarchs: Gender, Race, and Power in Colonial Virginia.* Chapel Hill: University of North Carolina Press, 1996.

Burman, Sandra. *Fit Work for Women.* New York: St. Martin's Press, 1979.

Burros, Marian. "Alice Waters: Food Revolutionary." *The New York Times,* April 14, 1996.

Bushnell, Rebecca. *A Culture of Teaching: Early Modern Humanism in Theory and Practice.* Ithaca, NY: Cornell University Press, 1996.

Cagle, William R. *A Matter of Taste: A Bibliographic Catalogue of the Gernon Collection of Books on Food and Drink.* New York: Garland Publishing Inc., 1990.

Cagle, William R., and Lisa Killion Stafford. *American Books on Food and Drink: A Bibliographical Catalog of the Cookbook Collection Housed in the Lilly Library at the Indiana University.* New Castle, DE: Oak Knoll Press, 1998.

Cahn, Susan. *Industry of Devotion: The Transformation of Women's Work in England, 1500–1660.* New York: Columbia University Press, 1987.

Calvert, Karin. *Children in the House: The Material Culture of Early Childhood.* Boston: Northeastern University Press, 1992.

Camitta, Miriam. "Vernacular Writing: Varieties of Literacy among Philadelphia High School Students." In *Cross-cultural Approaches to Literacy,* ed. Brian V. Street. Cambridge: Cambridge University Press, 1993.

Campbell, Mildred. *The English Yeoman Under Elizabeth and the Early Stuarts.* New York: Barnes & Noble, 1960.

Capp, Bernard. *English Almanacs 1500–1800: Astrology and the Popular Press.* Ithaca, NY: Cornell University Press, 1979.

Carr, Lois Green, and Lorena S. Walsh. "The Planter's Wife: The Experience of White Women in Seventeenth-Century Maryland." In *A Heritage of Her Own,* ed. Nancy Cott and Elizabeth H. Pleck. New York: Simon & Schuster, 1979.

Cavallo, Guglielmo, and Roger Chartier, eds. *A History of Reading in the West.* Trans. Lydia G. Cochrane. Amherst: University of Massachusetts Press, 1999.

Chartier, Roger. *Forms and Meanings: Texts, Performances, and Audiences from Codex to Computer.* Philadelphia: University of Pennsylvania Press, 1995.

———. *The Order of Books: Readers, Authors, and Libraries in Europe between the Fourteenth and Eighteenth Centuries.* Stanford, CA: Stanford University Press, 1994.

———. ed. *The Culture of Print: Power and the Uses of Print in Early Modern Europe.* Trans. Lydia G. Cochrane. Princeton, NJ: Princeton University Press, 1989.

Clark, Alice. *Working Life of Women in the 17th Century.* London: Routledge & Kegan Paul, 1982.

Cogan, Frances B. *All-American Girl: The Ideal of Real Womanhood in Mid-Nineteenth-Century America.* Athens: University of Georgia Press, 1989.

Cole, Thomas R. *The Journey of Life, a Cultural History of Aging in America.* Cambridge: Cambridge University Press, 1992.

Cott, Nancy. *Root of Bitterness: Documents of the Social History of American Women.* New York: Dutton, 1972.

———. *The Bonds of Womanhood: Woman's Sphere in New England, 1780–1835.* New Haven, CT: Yale University Press, 1977.

Cott, Nancy, and Elizabeth H. Pleck. *A Heritage of Her Own: Families, Work and Feminism in America.* New York: Simon & Schuster, 1979.

Cowan, Ruth Schwartz. *More Work for Mother: The Ironies of Household Technology from the Open Hearth to the Microwave.* New York: Basic Books, 1983.

Crane, Mary Thomas. *Framing Authority: Sayings, Self, and Society in 16th-Century England.* Princeton, NJ: Princeton University Press, 1993.

Cranfield, G. A. *A Hand-list of English Provincial Newspapers and Periodicals, 1700–1760.* London: Bowes and Bowes, 1961.

Crawford, Patricia. "Women's Published Writings, 1600–1700." In *Women in English Society, 1500–1800,* ed. Maddy Prior. London: Methuen, 1985.

Cressy, David. *Literacy and the Social Order: Reading and Writing in Tudor England.* New York: Cambridge University Press, 1980.

Cunnington, Phillis, and Anne Buck. *Children's Costume in England from the Fourteenth to the End of the Nineteenth Century.* New York: Barnes & Noble, 1965.

David, Elizabeth. "A True Gentlewoman's Delight." *Petits Propos Culinaires* 1 (1979): 43–53.

Davidoff, Leonore. "Class and Gender in Victorian England: The Diaries of Arthur J. Munby and Hannah Cullwick." In *Sex and Class in Women's History,* ed. J. L. Newton, M. Ryan, and J. Walkowitz. London: Routledge & Kegan Paul, 1983.

———. *Family Fortunes: Men and Women of the English Middle Class, 1780–1850.* Chicago: University of Chicago Press, 1987.

Davidson, Caroline. *A Woman's Work Is Never Done: A History of Housework in the British Isles, 1650–1950.* London: Chatto & Windus, 1982.

Davidson, Cathy N., ed. *Reading in America: Literature and Social History.* Baltimore: Johns Hopkins University Press, 1989.

Davie, Maurice R. *Negroes in American Society.* New York: McGraw-Hill Book Company, 1949.

Davis, Natalie Zemon. *Society and Culture in Early Modern France.* Stanford, CA: Stanford University Press, 1975.

Davis, Richard Beale. *A Southern Colonial Bookshelf: Reading in the Eighteenth Century.* Athens: University of Georgia Press, 1979.

de Certeau, Michel. "Reading as Poaching." In *Readers and Reading,* ed. Andrew Bennett. London: Longman, 1995.

Deetz, James. *In Small Things Forgotten: An Archaeology of Early American Life.* New York: Doubleday, 1996.

Degler, Carl. *At Odds: Women and the Family from the Revolution to the Present.* New York: Oxford University Press, 1980.

Delany, Paul. *British Autobiography in the 17th Century.* London: Routledge & Kegan Paul, 1969.

Dimock, Wai-Chee. "Feminism, New Historicism, and the Reader." *American Literature* 63, no. 4 (1991): 601–622.

Diner, Hasia R. *Erin's Daughters in America: Irish Immigrant Women in the Nineteenth Century.* Baltimore: Johns Hopkins University Press, 1983.

Dodds, Madeleine Hope. "The Rival Cooks: Hannah Glasse and Ann Cook." *Archaeologia Aeliana,* Series 4, vol. 15 (n.d.): 43–68.

Donnelly, Mabel Collins. *The American Victorian Woman: The Myth and Reality.* New York: Greenwood Press, 1986.

Douglas, Ann. *The Feminization of American Culture.* New York: Anchor Press, 1988.

Douglas, Mary. *Purity and Danger: An Analysis of Concepts of Pollution and Taboo.* Harmondsworth: Penguin Books, 1966.

Douglas, Mary, and Baron Isherwood. *The World of Goods.* New York: W. W. Norton, 1979.

DuBois, Ellen Carol. *Feminism and Suffrage: The Emergence of an Independent Women's Movement in America, 1848–1869.* Ithaca, NY: Cornell University Press, 1999.

DuBois, W. E. B. *The Philadelphia Negro: A Social Study.* New York: Benjamin Blom, 1967 [reprint].

Dudden, Faye E. *Serving Women: Household Service in Nineteenth-Century America.* Middletown, NY: Wesleyan University Press, 1983.

DuSablon, Mary Anne. *America's Collectible Cookbooks: The History, the Politics, the Recipes.* Athens: Ohio University Press, 1994.

Eamon, William. *Science and the Secrets of Nature: Books of Secrets in Medieval and Early Modern Culture.* Princeton, NJ: Princeton University Press, 1994.

Egerton, John. *Southern Food: At Home, on the Road, in History.* Chapel Hill: University of North Carolina Press, 1993.

Elias, Norbert. *The Civilizing Process.* Oxford: Blackwell, 1994 [reprint].

Elliott, Charles. "The Quaker Connection." *Horticulture* (September/October 2000): 28–30.

Ezell, Margaret J. M. *The Patriarch's Wife: Literary Evidence and the History of the Family.* Chapel Hill: University of North Carolina Press, 1987.

———. *Writing Women's Literary History.* Baltimore: Johns Hopkins University Press, 1993.

———. *Social Authorship and the Advent of Print.* Baltimore: Johns Hopkins University Press, 1999.

Fairbank, Alfred. *A Book of Scripts.* Harmondsworth: Penguin Books, 1949.

Faragher, Johnny, and Christine Stansell. "Women and Their Families on the Overland Trail to California and Oregon, 1842–1867." In *A Heritage of Her Own,* ed. Nancy Cott and Elizabeth H. Pleck. New York: Simon & Schuster, 1979.

Faust, Drew Gilpin. *Mothers of Invention: Women of the Slaveholding South in the American Civil War.* Chapel Hill: University of North Carolina Press, 1996.

Fergus, Jan. "Women Readers of Prose Fiction in the Midlands, 1746–1800." *Transactions of the Eighth International Congress on the Enlightenment,* July 21, 1991: 1108–1112.

Findlen, Paula. "Science as a Career in Enlightenment Italy: The Strategies of Laura Bassi." *Isis* 84 (1993): 441–469.

Flint, Christopher. *Family Fictions: Narrative and Domestic Relations in Britain, 1688–1798.* Stanford, CA: Stanford University Press, 1998.

Flint, Kate. *The Woman Reader, 1837–1914.* Oxford: Clarendon Press, 1993.

Fowler, Damon L. "Historical Commentary." In *Mrs. Hill's Southern Practical Cookery and Receipt Book,* facsimile edition. Columbia: University of South Carolina Press, 1995.

Fox-Genovese, Elizabeth. *Within the Plantation Household: Black and White Women of the Old South.* Chapel Hill and London: University of North Carolina Press, 1988.

Fragner, Bert. "Social Reality and Culinary Fiction: The Perspective of Cookbooks from Iran and Central Asia." In *Culinary Cultures of the Middle East,* ed. Sami Zubaida and Richard Tapper. London: I. B. Tauris Publishers, 1994.

Fraser, Antonia. *The Weaker Vessel.* New York: Knopf, 1984.

Frey, Sylvia R. *New World, New Roles: A Documentary History of Women in Pre-Industrial America.* New York: Greenwood Press, 1986.

Friedan, Betty. *The Feminine Mystique.* New York: Norton, 1963.

Frye, Susan. "Maternal Textualities." In *Maternal Measures: Figuring Caregiving in the Early Modern Period,* ed. Naomi Miller and Naomi Yavneh. Aldershot, Burlington, VT: Ashgate, c. 2000.

Frye, Susan, and Karen Robertson, eds. *Maids and Mistresses, Cousins and Queens: Women's Alliances in Early Modern England.* Oxford: Oxford University Press, 1999.

Gallagher, Catherine. *Nobody's Story: The Vanishing Acts of Women Writers in the Marketplace, 1670–1820.* Berkeley: University of California Press, 1994.

Gardner, Kevin J. "The Aesthetics of Intimacy: Lady Mary Wortley Montagu and Her Readers." *Papers on Language & Literature; A Journal for Scholars and Critics of Language and Literature* 34, no. 2 (March 1998): 113–133.

Garraty, John A., and Mark C. Carnes, gen. eds. *American National Biography,* vol. 19. New York: Oxford University Press, 1999.

George, M. Dorothy. *London Life in the Eighteenth Century.* Chicago: Academy Chicago, Publishers, 1925.

———. *London Life in the Eighteenth Century.* Harmondsworth: Peregrine Books, 1966.

Gere, Ann Ruggles. *Intimate Practices: Literacy and Cultural Work in U.S. Women's Clubs, 1880–1920.* Urbana: University of Illinois Press, 1997.

Gernes, Todd Steven. Recasting the Culture of Ephemera: Young Women's Literary Culture in Nineteenth-Century America. Ph.D. dissertation. Brown University, 1992.

Gillis, John R. *A World of Their Own Making: Myth, Ritual, and the Quest for Family Values.* Cambridge, MA: Harvard University Press, 1996.

Gilmore, William J. *Reading Becomes a Necessity of Life: Material and Cultural Life in Rural New England, 1780–1835.* Knoxville: University of Tennessee Press, 1989.

Gleason, Philip. "Crevecoeur's Question: Historical Writing on Immigration, Ethnicity, and National Identity." In *Imagined Histories,* ed. Anthony Molho and Gordon S. Wood. Princeton, NJ: Princeton University Press, 1998.

Goldman, Anne E. *Take My Word: Autobiographical Innovations of Ethnic American Working Woman.* Berkeley: University of California Press, 1996.

Gonda, Caroline. *Readings Daughters' Fictions, 1709–1834: Novels and Society from Manley to Edgeworth.* Cambridge: Cambridge University Press, 1996.

Goode, Judith, Janet Theophano, and Karen Curtis. "A Framework for the Analysis of Continuity and Change in Shared Sociocultural Rules for Food Use: The Italian-American Pattern." In *Ethnic and Regional Foodways in the United States: The Performance of Group Identity,* ed. Linda Brown and Kay Mussell. Knoxville: University of Tennessee Press, 1984.

Goreau, Angeline. *The Whole Duty of Woman: Female Writers in Seventeenth-Century England.* Garden City, NY: Dial Press, 1985.

Graham, Elspeth, Hilary Hinds, Elaine Hobby, and Helen Wilcox, eds. *Her Own Life, Autobiographical Writings by Seventeenth-Century Women.* London: Routledge, 1989.

Granfield, G. A. *A Hand-list of English Provincial Newspapers and Periodicals, 1700–1760.* London: Bowes & Bowes, 1961.

Green, Harvey. *The Light of the Home: An Intimate View of the Lives of Women in Victorian America.* New York: Pantheon Books, 1983.

Green, James. "Author-Publisher Relations in America up to 1825." Ms., 1994.

Grubb, Alan. "House and Home in the Victorian South: The Cookbook as Guide." In *In Joy and In Sorrow: Women, Family, and Marriage in the Victorian South, 1830–1900,* ed. Carol Bleser. New York: Oxford University Press, 1991.

Gunderson, Joan R. *To Be Useful to the World: Women in Revolutionary America, 1740–1790.* New York: Twayne Publishers, 1996.

Hall, David D. *Cultures of Print: Essays in the History of the Book.* Amherst: University of Massachusetts Press, 1996.

Hall, Kim F. "Culinary Spaces, Colonial Spaces: The Gendering of Sugar in the Seventeenth Century." In *Feminist Readings of Early Modern Culture,* ed. Valerie Traub, M. Lindsey Kaplan, and Dympna Callaghan. Cambridge: Cambridge University Press, 1996.

Hanawalt, Barbara A. *Growing Up in Medieval London: The Experience of Childhood in History.* New York: Oxford University Press, 1993.

Hartley, Dorothy. *Food in England.* London: MacDonald and Jane's, 1954.

Hartman, Mary S., and Lois Banner, eds. *Clio's Consciousness Raised: New Perspectives on the History of Women.* New York: Harper & Row, 1974.

Hayes, Kevin. *A Colonial Woman's Bookshelf.* Knoxville: University of Tennessee Press, 1996.

Hecht, J. Jean. *The Domestic Servant in Eighteenth-Century England.* London: Routledge & egan Paul, 1980.

Hendrick, Joan. "Parlor Literature: Harriet Beecher Stowe and the Question of 'Great Women Artists.'" *Signs* (Winter 1992): 277–303.

Hess, Karen. "The Carolina Rice Kitchen and Creole Culture of New Orleans." *Petits Propos Culinaires* 41 (1992): 24–29.

Hill, Bridget. *Women, Work, and Sexual Politics in 18th-Century England.* New York: Blackwell, 1989.

Hill, Christopher. *The Century of Revolution: A History of England, 1603–1714,* vol. 5. Edinburgh: Thomas Nelson and Sons Ltd., 1961.

Hobbs, Catherine. *Nineteenth-Century Women Learn to Write.* Charlottesville: University Press of Virginia, 1995.

Hobby, Elaine. *Virtue of Necessity: English Women's Writing 1649–1688.* London: Virago Press, 1988. Ann Arbor: University of Michigan Press, 1989.

Hobsbawm, Eric, and Terence Ranger, eds. *The Invention of Tradition.* Cambridge: Cambridge University Press, 1983.

Hochschild, Arlie (with Anne Machung). *The Second Shift.* New York: Avon Books, 1989.

Hole, Christina. *English Home-life, 1500 to 1800.* London: B. T. Batsford Ltd., 1947.
———. *The English Housewife in the 17th Century.* London: Chatto & Windus, 1953.

Homans, Margaret. *Bearing the Word: Language and Female Experience in Nineteenth-Century Women's Writing.* Chicago: University of Chicago Press, 1986.

Hueston, Robert Francis. *The Catholic Press and Nativism, 1840–1860.* New York: Arno Press, 1976.

Hull, Suzanne. *Chaste, Silent and Obedient: English Books for Women, 1475–1640.* San Marino, CA: Huntington Library, 1982.

Hunter, Lynette. "Cookery Books: A Cabinet of Rare Devices and Conceits." *Petits Propos Culinaires* 5 (May 1980): 19–34.
———. "Women and Domestic Medicine: Lady Experimenters, 1570–1620." In *Women, Science and Medicine 1500–1700: Mothers and Sisters of the Royal Society,* ed. Lynette Hunter and Sarah Hutton. Thrupp, Stroud, Gloucestershire: Sutton Pub., 1997.

Hunter, Lynette, and Sarah Hutton, eds. *Women, Science and Medicine 1500–1700: Mothers and Sisters of the Royal Society.* Thrupp, Stroud, Gloucestershire: Sutton Pub., 1997.

Iser, Wolfgang. "Interaction Between Text and Reader." In *The Reader in the Text: Essays on Audience and Interpretation,* ed. Susan R. Suleiman and Inge Crosman. Princeton, NJ: Princeton University Press, 1980.

Jelinek, Estelle C., ed. *Women's Autobiography: Essays in Criticism.* Bloomington: University of Indiana Press, 1980.
———. *The Tradition of Women's Autobiography from Antiquity to the Present.* Boston: Twayne Publishers, 1986.

Jensen, Joan M. *Loosening the Bonds: Mid-Atlantic Farm Women, 1750–1850.* New Haven, CT: Yale University Press, 1986.

Johns, Elizabeth. "Science, Art & Literature in Federal America: Their Prospects in the Republic." In *Everyday Life in the Early Republic,* ed. Catherine Hutchins. Winterthur, DE: Henry Francis Du Pont Winterthur Museum, 1994.

Jones, Jacqueline. *Labor of Love, Labor of Sorrow: Black Women, Work, and the Family from Slavery to the Present.* New York: Basic Books, 1985.

Jordan, Constance. *Renaissance Feminism: Literary Texts and Political Models.* Ithaca, NY: Cornell University Press, 1990.

Joselit, Jenna Weissman. "A Set Table: Jewish Domestic Culture in the New World, 1890–1950." In *Getting Comfortable in New York: The American Jewish Home, 1880–1950,* ed. Susan L. Braunstein and Jenna Weissman Joselit. New York: The Jewish Museum, 1990.

Joyce, William L., David D. Hall, Richard D. Brown, and John B. Hench, eds. *Printing and Society in Early America.* Worcester, MA: American Antiquarian Society, 1983.

Kafalenos, Emma. "Reading to Cook, Cooking to Read." *Southwest Review* 73, no. 2 (1988).

Kamm, Josephine. *Hope Deferred: Girls' Education in English History.* London: Methuen, 1965.

Karcher, Carolyn L. *The First Woman in the Republic: A Cultural Biography of Lydia Maria Child.* Durham, NC: Duke University Press, 1994.

Kasson, John F. *Rudeness & Civility: Manners in Nineteenth-Century Urban America.* New York: Hill and Wang, 1990.

Keeble, N. H., comp. & ed. *The Cultural Identity of Seventeenth Century Women.* London: Routledge, 1994.

Kelley, Mary. *Private Woman, Public Stage: Literary Domesticity in Nineteenth-Century America.* New York: Oxford University Press, 1984.

Kelso, Ruth. *Doctrine for the Lady of the Renaissance.* Urbana: University of Illinois Press, 1956.

Kenny, Kevin. *Making Sense of the Molly Mcguires.* New York: Oxford University Press, 1998.

Kerber, Linda K. "Gender." In *Imagined Histories,* ed. Anthony Molho and Gordon S. Wood. Princeton, NJ: Princeton University Press, 1998.

———. *Women of the Republic: Intellect and Ideology in Revolutionary America.* Chapel Hill: University of North Carolina Press, 1980.

Kirshenblatt-Gimblett, Barbara. *Destination Culture: Tourism, Museums, and Heritage.* Berkeley: CA: University of California Press, 1998.

———. "Kitchen Judaism." In *Getting Comfortable in New York: The American Jewish Home, 1880–1950,* ed. Susan L. Braunstein and Jenna Weissman Joselit. New York: The Jewish Museum, 1990.

Knight, Kate Brannon. *History of the Work of Connecticut Women at the World's Columbian Exposition, Chicago 1893.* Hartford, CT: The Hartford Press, 1898.

Koehler, Lyle. *A Search for Power: The "Weaker Sex" in 17th-Century New England.* Urbana: University of Illinois Press, 1980.

Lane, Anthony. "Annals of Gastronomy: Look Back in Hunger." *The New Yorker* (December 1995): 50–66.

Langland, Elizabeth. *Nobody's Angels: Middle-Class Women and Domestic Ideology in Victorian Culture.* Ithaca, NY: Cornell University Press, 1995.

Lau, Kimberly. *New Age Capitalism*. Philadelphia: University of Pennsylvania Press, 2000.

Lave, Jean, and Etienne Wenger. *Situated Learning: Legitimate Peripheral Participation*. Cambridge: Cambridge University Press, 1991.

Lehman, Gilly. "Preface." In *The British Housewife: Or, the Cook, Housekeeper's, and Gardiner's Companion*, by Martha Bradley,. vol. 1, 1756 ed. Devon: Prospect Books, 1996.

———. "Two 'New' Eighteenth-Century Cookery Books." *Petits Propos Culinaires* 53 (1996): 22–24.

Leigh, Mary Ann. "An Epistolary Portrait: Sarah Jane Campbell, 1844–1928." Master's thesis, University of Pennsylvania, 2000.

Leonardi, Susan J. "Recipes for Reading: Summer Pasta, Lobster a la Riseholme, and Key Lime Pie," *PMLA* 104 (1989): 340–346.

Lerner, Gerda. "The Lady and the Mill Girl: Changes in the Status of Women in the Age of Jacksonian America, 1800–1840." In *A Heritage of Her Own*, ed. Nancy Cott.

Levenstein, Harvey. *Revolution at the Table: The Transformation of the American Diet*. New York: Oxford University Press, 1988.

Levin, Katherine. *Representing the Female Reader: Gender on the Market in Eighteenth-Century England*. Ph.D. diss., University of Pennsylvania, 1995.

Levine, David. "Illiteracy and Family Life During the First Industrial Revolution." *Journal of Social History* 14, no. 1 (September 1980): 25–44.

Lewis, Benjamin M. *A Register of Editors, Printers, and Publishers of American Magazines, 1741–1810*. New York: New York Public Library, 1957.

Lockridge, Kenneth A. *Literacy in Colonial New England: An Enquiry into the Social Context of Literacy in the Early Modern West*. New York: W. W. Norton & Co., 1974.

Longone, Jan. "Amelia Simmons and the First American Cookbook." *American Bookseller*, August 12, 1996.

———. "Introduction." In *The Good Housekeeper* by Sara Josepha Hale, 1841 ed. Mineola, NY: Dover, 1996.

———. "'Tried Receipts': An Overview of America's Charitable Cookbooks." In *Recipes for Reading: Community Cookbooks, Stories, Histories*, ed. Anne L. Bower. Amherst: University of Massachusetts Press, 1997.

Lowenstein, Eleanor. *Bibliography of American Cookery Books, 1742–1860*. New York: American Antiquarian Society, 1972.

Macfarlane, Alan. *The Origins of English Individualism: The Family, Property and Social Transition*. Oxford: Blackwell, 1978.

Mackie, Erin. *Market a la Mode: Fashion, Commodity, and Gender in The Tatler and The Spectator*. Baltimore: Johns Hopkins University Press, 1997.

Mackie, J. D. *A History of Scotland*. Baltimore: Penguin Books, 1964.

Mahl, Mary R., and Helene Koon, eds. *The Female Spectator: English Women Writers Before 1800*. Bloomington: Indiana University Press/the Feminist Press, 1977.

Main, Gloria L. "Gender, Work, and Wages in Colonial New England." *The William and Mary Quarterly*, 3d series, 51, no. 1 (January 1994): 39–66.

Matthews, Glenna. *'Just a Housewife': The Rise and Fall of Domesticity in America.* New York: Oxford University Press, 1987.

Mattick, Paul. Review of *Comfort Me with Apples: More Adventures at the Table* by Ruth Reichl. *The New York Times Book Review,* April 15, 2001, 7.

McCaffrey, Lawrence J. *The Irish Diaspora in America.* Bloomington: Indiana University Press, 1976.

———. *The Irish Diaspora in America,* 2nd ed. Washington, D.C.: The Catholic University of America Press, 1984.

McKinstrey, E. Richard. *Personal Accounts of Events, Travels, and Everyday Life in America: An Annotated Bibliography.* Winterthur, DE: A Winterthur Book, 1997.

McMahon, Sarah Frances. "'A Comfortable Subsistence': Changing Composition of Diet in Rural New England, 1620–1840." *William and Mary Quarterly* 3:42, no. 1 (January 1985): 26.

———. "Laying Foods By: Gender, Dietary Decisions, and the Technology of Food Preservation in New England Households, 1750–1850." In *Early American Technology: Making and Doing Things from the Colonial Era to 1850,* ed. Judith A. McGaw. Published for the Institute of Early American History and Culture, Williamsburg, VA: University of North Carolina Press, 1994.

Megson, Barbara. *English Homes and Housekeeping, 1700–1960.* London: Routledge & Kegan Paul, 1968.

Mendelson, Anne. *Stand Facing the Stove: The Story of the Women Who Gave America the Joy of Cooking.* New York: Henry Holt, 1996.

Mendelson, Sara Heller. "Stuart Women's Diaries and Occasional Memoirs." In *Women in English Society,* ed. Maddy Prior. London: Methuen, 1985.

Mendelson, Sara, and Patricia Crawford. *Women in Early Modern England, 1550–1720.* Oxford: Clarendon Press, 1998.

Michaels, Anne. *Fugitive Pieces.* New York: Vintage, 1998.

Mills, Bruce. *Cultural Reformations: Lydia Maria Child and the Literature of Reform.* Athens: University of Georgia Press, 1994.

Mintz, Sidney. *Sweetness and Power: The Place of Sugar in Modern History.* New York: Viking, 1985.

———. *Tasting Food: Tasting Freedom: Excursions into Eating, Culture, and the Past.* Boston: Beacon Press, 1996.

Monaghan, E. Jennifer. "Literacy Instruction and Gender in Colonial New England." In *Reading in America: Literature & Social History,* ed. Cathy N. Davidson. Baltimore: Johns Hopkins University Press, 1989.

Morgan, Marjorie. *Manners, Morals and Class in England, 1774–1858.* New York: St. Martin's Press, 1994.

Murray, Linda Berzok. "My Mother's Recipes." In *Pilaf, Pozole, and Pad Thai: American Women and Ethnic Food,* ed. Sherrie A. Inness. Amherst: University of Massachusetts Press, 2001.

Myers, Robin, and Michael Harris, eds. *Serials and their Readers 1620–1914.* New Castle, DE: Oak Knoll Press, 1993.

Myers, Sylvia Harstark. *The Bluestocking Circle: Women, Friendship, and the Life of the Mind in 18th-Century England.* Oxford: Clarendon Press, 1990.

Myrdal, Gunnar. *An American Dilemma: The Negro Problem and Modern Democracy.* New York: Harper & Row, 1944.

Newton, Judith L., Mary P. Ryan, and Judith R. Walkowitz, eds. *Sex and Class in Women's History.* Boston: Routledge and Kegan Paul, 1983.

Norton, Mary Beth. *Liberty's Daughters: The Revolutionary Experience of Women 1750–1800.* Boston: Little, Brown & Co., 1980.

Nussbaum, Felicity. "Eighteenth-Century Women's Autobiographical Common-places." In *The Private Self: Theory and Practice of Women's Autobiographical Writings,* ed. Shari Benstock. Chapel Hill: University of North Carolina Press, 1988.

Olney, James. *Autobiography: Essays Theoretical and Critical.* Princeton, NJ: Princeton University Press, 1980.

Ortner, Sherry. *Sherpas Through Their Rituals.* Cambridge: Cambridge University Press, 1978.

Pacheco, Anita ed. *Early Women Writers: 1600–1720.* London: Longman, 1998.

Pease, Jane H., and William H. Pease. *Ladies, Women, & Wenches: Choice & Constraint in Antebellum Charleston and Boston.* Chapel Hill: University of North Carolina Press, 1990.

Peiss, Kathy. *Hope in a Jar: The Making of America's Beauty Culture.* New York: Henry Holt & Co., 1998.

Peters, Belinda. Review of Sara Mendelson and Patricia Crawford, *Women in Early Modern England 1550–1720.* H-Review published by H-Albion@h-net.msu.edu, July 2000.

Plante, Ellen M. *The American Kitchen 1700 to the Present: From Hearth to Highrise.* New York: Facts On File, 1995.

Pointon, Marcia. *Strategies for Showing: Women, Possession, and Representation in English Visual Culture, 1665–1800.* Oxford: Oxford University Press, 1997.

Pool, Daniel. *What Jane Austen Ate and Charles Dickens Knew: From Fox Hunting to Whist—the Facts of Daily Life in 19th-Century England.* New York: Simon & Schuster, 1993.

Poovey, Mary. *The Proper Lady and the Woman Writer: Ideology as Style in the Works of Mary Wollstonecraft, Mary Shelley, and Jane Austen.* Chicago: University of Chicago Press, 1984.

Porter, Roy. *English Society in the Eighteenth Century.* New York: Penguin Books, 1982.

Potter, David. "Mrs. Eels' Unique Receipts." *Petits Propos Culinaires* 61 (May 1999): 16–19.

Prettyman, Quandra. "Come Eat at My Table: Lives with Recipes." *Southern Quarterly* 30, no. 2–3 (March 1992): 131–140.

Prince, Gerald. "Recipes." *Studies in 20th Century Literature* 9, no. 2 (1985): 207–212.

Prior, Mary. "Women and the Urban Economy: Oxford, 1500–1800." In *Women in English Society, 1500–1800,* ed. Maddy Prior. London: Methuen, 1985.

Prior, Mary, ed. *Women in English Society, 1500–1800.* New York: Methuen, 1984.

Radway, Janice A. *A Feeling for Books: The Book-of-the-Month Club, Literary Taste, and Middle-Class Desire.* Chapel Hill: University of North Carolina Press, 1997.

———. *Reading the Romance: Women, Patriarchy, and Popular Literature.* Chapel Hill: University of North Carolina Press, 1984.

Raftery, Deirdre. *Women and Learning in English Writing, 1600–1900.* Portland, OR: Four Courts Press, 1997.

Raven, James. *Judging New Wealth: Popular Publishing and Responses to Commerce in England, 1750–1800.* Oxford: Clarendon Press, 1992.

Richetti, John. *The English Novel in History 1700–1780.* London: Routledge, 1999.

Ridley, Glynis. "The First American Cookbook." *Eighteenth Century Life* 23 n.s., no. 2 (May 1999): 114–123.

Roberson, Susan L. "Matriarchy and the Rhetoric of Domesticity." In *The Stowe Debate: Rhetorical Strategies in Uncle Tom's Cabin,* ed. Mason I. Lowrance Jr., Ellen E. Westbrook, and R. C. De Prospo. Amherst: University of Massachusetts Press, 1994.

Robertson, Karen, "Tracing Women's Connections from a Letter by Elizabeth Ralegh." In *Maids, Mistresses, Cousins and Queens: Women's Alliances in Early Modern England,* ed. Susan Frye and Karen Robertson. Oxford: Oxford University Press, 1999.

Romero, Lora. *Home Fronts: Domesticity and Its Critics in the Antebellum United States.* Durham, NC: Duke University Press, 1997.

Romines, Ann. *The Home Plot: Women, Writing, and Domestic Ritual.* Amherst: University of Massachusetts Press, 1992.

Rose, Mary Beth, ed. *Women in the Middle Ages and the Renaissance: Literary and Historical Perspectives.* Syracuse, NY: Syracuse University Press, 1986.

Russell, Conrad. *The Causes of the English Civil War: The Ford Lectures Delivered in the University of Oxford, 1987–1988.* Oxford: Clarendon Press, 1990.

Ryan, Mary P. *The Empire of the Mother: American Writing about Domesticity 1830–1860.* New York: Harrington Park Press, 1982.

Samuels, Shirley, ed. *The Culture of Sentiment: Race, Gender, and Sentimentality in Nineteenth-Century America.* New York: Oxford University Press, 1992.

Sanders, Valerie. *The Private Lives of Victorian Women: Autobiography in Nineteenth-Century England.* New York: St Martin's Press, 1989.

Savage, Barbara Dianne. *Broadcasting Freedom: Radio, War, and the Politics of Race, 1938–1948.* Chapel Hill: University of North Carolina Press, 1999.

Schiebinger, Londa. *The Mind Has No Sex? Women in the Origins of Modern Science.* Cambridge, MA: Harvard University Press, 1989.

Schofield, Mary Anne. *Quiet Rebellion: The Fictional Heroines of Eliza Haywood.* Washington, D.C.: University Press of America, 1982.

———. *Eliza Haywood.* Boston: Twayne Publishers, 1985.

Sen, Amartya. "Nobody Need Starve." *Granta, Food: The Vital Stuff* 52 (Winter 1995): 215–220.

Shammas, Carole. "The Domestic Environment in Early Modern England and America." *Journal of Social History* 14 (September 1980): 4–24.

Shapiro, Laura. *Perfection Salad: Women and Cooking at the Turn of the Century.* New York: Henry Holt & Co., 1986.

Shaw, S. Bradley. "The Pliable Rhetoric of Domesticity." In *The Stowe Debate: Rhetorical Strategies in Uncle Tom's Cabin,* ed. Mason I. Lowrance Jr., Ellen E. Westbrook, and R. C. De Prospo. Amherst: University of Massachusetts Press, 1994.

Shipperbottom, Roy. "Introduction." In *The Experienced English Housekeeper,* by Elizabeth Raffald. Facsimile ed., ed. Ann Bagnall. Lewes, East Sussex: Southover Press, 1997.

Sicherman, Barbara. "Sense and Sensibility: A Case Study of Women's Reading in Late Victorian America." In *Gendered Domains: Rethinking Public and Private and Women's History,* ed. Dorothy O. Kelly and Susan M. Reverby. Ithaca, NY: Cornell University Press, 1992.

Sklar, Kathryn Kish. *Catharine Beecher: A Study in American Domesticity.* New York: W. W. Norton & Co., 1973.

Smith, Barbara Clark. "Food Rioters and the American Revolution." *William and Mary Quarterly* 51, no. 1 (January 1994): 3–38.

Smith, Hilda L. *Reason's Disciples: Seventeenth-Century English Feminists.* Urbana: University of Illinois Press, 1987.

Smith, Karen Manners. Marion Harland: The Making of a Household World. Ph.D. diss., University of Massachusetts, February 1990.

Smith, Alice, and Elizabeth David. "The John Trot Fault: An English Dinner Table in the 1750's." *Petits Propres Culinaires* 15 (1983): 55–59.

Smith, Sidonie. *A Poetics of Women's Autobiography: Marginality and the Fictions and Self-Representation.* Bloomington: Indiana University Press, 1987.

Smith-Rosenberg, Carroll. *Disorderly Conduct: Visions of Gender in Victorian America.* New York: Oxford University Press, 1985.

Spender, Dale. *Mothers of the Novel: One Hundred Good Women Writers before Jane Austen.* London: Pandora, 1986.

Spruill, Julia. *Women's Life and Work in the Southern Colonies.* Chapel Hill: University of North Carolina Press, 1938.

Stanton, Donna C., and Jeanine Parisier Plottel, eds. *Female Autograph.* New York: New York Literary Forum, 1984.

Stark, Louis M. *The Whitney Cookery Collection.* New York: New York Public Library, 1959.

Stewart, Susan. *On Longing: Narratives of the Miniature, the Gigantic, the Souvenir, the Collection.* Baltimore: Johns Hopkins University Press, 1984.

———. *Crimes of Writing: Problems in the Containment of Representation.* New York: Oxford University Press, 1991.

Stocking, George. *Victorian Anthropology.* New York: Free Press, 1983.

Stone, Lawrence. *The Family, Sex, and Marriage in England, 1500–1800,* abridged ed. New York: Harper, 1979.

Stratton, Johanna L. *Pioneer Women: Voices from the Kansas Frontier.* New York: Simon & Schuster, 1981.

Street, Brian V., ed. *Literacy in Theory and Practice.* Cambridge: Cambridge University Press, 1984.

———. *Cross-Cultural Approaches to Literacy.* Cambridge: Cambridge University Press, 1993.

Stryker-Rodda, Harriet. *Understanding Colonial Handwriting.* Baltimore: Genealogical Publishing Co., 1986.

Suleiman, Susan R., and Inge Crosman, eds. *The Reader in the Text.* Princeton, NJ: Princeton University Press, 1980.

Swindells, Julia. *Victorian Writing and Working Women: The Other Side of Silence.* Cambridge: Polity Press, 1985.

Tait, Elaine. "Passed-Down Dishes," *The Philadelphia Inquirer,* February 25, 1996: S1 & S4.

Targett, Peter. "Edward Kidder: His Book & His Schools." *Petits Props Culinaries* 32 (1989): 35–44.

Taylor, Charles. *Sources of the Self: The Making of the Modern Identity.* Cambridge, MA: Harvard University Press, 1989.

Tebeaux, Elizabeth. "Women and Technical Writing, 1475–1700: Technology, Literacy, and Development of a Genre." In *Women, Science and Medicine 1500–1700: Mothers and Sisters of the Royal Society,* ed. Lynette Hunter, and Sarah Hutton. Thrupp, Shroud, Gloucestershire: Sutton, 1997.

Temple, Judy Nolte, and Suzanne L. Bunkers. "Mothers, Daughters, Diaries: Literacy, Relationship, and Cultural Context." In *Nineteenth-Century Women Learn to Write,* ed. Catherine Hobbs. Charlottesville: University Press of Virginia, 1995.

Theophano, Janet. "A Life's Work: Women Writing from the Kitchen." In *Fields of Folklore: Essays in Honor of Kenneth S. Goldstein,* ed. Roger D. Abrahams. Bloomington, IN: Trickster Press, 1995.

———. *Household Words: Women Write from and for the Kitchen.* Philadelphia: University of Pennsylvania, 1996.

Thick, Malcolm. "Sir Hugh Plat's Promotion of Pasta as a Victual for Seamean." *Petits Propos Culinaires* 40 (1992): 43–50.

Thomas, Keith. *Religion and the Decline of Magic.* New York: Charles Scribner's Sons, 1971.

Thomson, Gladys Scott. *Life in a Noble Household, 1641–1700.* London: Jonathan Cape, 1950.

Thornton, Tamara Plakins. *Handwriting in America: A Cultural History.* New Haven, CT: Yale University Press, 1996.

Tilly, Louise. *Women, Work, and Family.* New York: Holt, Rinehart & Winston, 1978.

Tobias, Steven. "Early American Cookbooks as Cultural Artifacts." *Papers on Language and Literature* 34, no. 1 (December 1998): 3.

Tonkovich, Nicole. *Domesticity with a Difference: The Nonfiction of Catharine Beecher, Sarah J. Hale, Fanny Fern, and Margaret Fuller.* Jackson: University Press of Mississippi, 1997.

Towner, Lawrence William. *A Good Master Well Served, Masters and Servants in Colonial Massachusetts, 1620–1750.* New York: Garland Press, 1998.

Travitsky, Betty S., and Adele F. Seeff, eds. *Attending to Women in Early Modern England.* Newark: University of Delaware Press, 1994.

Tuchman, Gaye. *Edging Women Out: Victorian Novelists, Publishers, and Social Change.* New Haven, CT: Yale University Press, 1989.

Turner, Cheryl. *Living by the Pen: Women Writers in the Eighteenth Century.* London: Routledge, 1992.

Ulrich, Laurel Thatcher. *Good Wives: Image and Reality in the Lives of Women in Northern New England, 1650–1750.* New York: Vintage Books, 1982.

———. *A Midwife's Tale: The Life of Martha Ballard, Based on Her Diary, 1785–1812.* New York: Alfred A. Knopf, 1990.

Updike, John. "Books Unbound, Life Unraveled." *The New York Times on the Web,* June 18, 2000.

Urry, John. *The Tourist Gaze: Leisure and Travel in Contemporary Societies.* London: Sage Publications, 1990.

Vickery, Amanda. "Women and the World of Goods: a Lancashire Consumer and Her Possessions, 1751–1781." In *Consumption and the World of Goods,* ed. John Brewer and Roy Porter. London: Routledge, 1993.

Vincent, David. *Literacy and Popular Culture, England 1750–1914.* Cambridge: Cambridge University Press, 1993.

Wall, Wendy. *The Imprint of Gender: Authorship and Publication in the English Renaissance.* Ithaca, NY: Cornell University Press, 1993.

Wallas, Ada Radford. *Before the Bluestockings.* Folcroft, PA: Folcroft Library Editions, 1977.

Warnicke, Ruth M. *Women of the English Renaissance and Reformation.* Westport, CT: Greenwood Press, 1983.

Watson, Rubie S. "Named and the Nameless: Gender and Person in Chinese Society." *American Ethnologist* 13, no. 4 (1986): 619–631.

Watt, Ian. *The Rise of the Novel: Studies in Defoe, Richardson and Fielding.* Berkeley, CA: University of California Press, 1964.

Waugh, Nora. *The Cut of Women's Clothes 1600–1930.* New York: Theatre Arts Books, 1968.

White, Cynthia L. *Women's Magazines 1693–1968.* London: M. Joseph, 1970.

White, Isabelle. "Sentimentality and the Uses of Death." In *The Stowe Debate: Rhetorical Strategies in Uncle Tom's Cabin,* eds. Mason I. Lawrence Jr., Ellen E. Westbrook, and R. C. De Prospo. Amherst: University of Massachusetts Press, 1994.

Whiteman, Maxwell. "Robert Roberts: Pioneer Author and Abolitionist." In *The House Servant's Directory, or A Monitor for Private Families,* reprint ed., ed. Maxwell Whiteman. Philadelphia: Rhistoric Publications, 1969.

Wiesner, Merry E. *Women and Gender in Early Modern Europe.* Cambridge: Cambridge University Press, 1993.

Williams, Julie Hedgepeth. *The Significance of the Printed Word in Early America: Colonists' Thoughts on the Role of the Press.* Westport, CT: Greenwood Press, 1999.

Wilson, C. Anne. "A Cookery Book and Its Context: Elizabethan Cookery and Lady Fettiplace." *Petits Propos Culinaires* 25 (1987): 7–26.

Wilson, C. Anne, ed. *Luncheon, Nuncheon, and Other Meals: Eating with the Victorians.* Dover, NH: Alan Sutton Publishing Inc., 1994.

Wilson, Mary Tolford. "Essay." In *American Cookery: A Facsimile of the First Edition, 1796,* by Amelia Simmons. New York: Oxford University Press, 1958.

Witherington, Ann Fairfax. *Everyday Life in the Early Republic.* Winterthur, DE: Henry Francis Du Pont Winterthur Museum, 1994.

Wolf, Edwin. "The Textual Importance of Manuscript Commonplace Books of 1620–1660." Address before the Bibliographic Society of the University of Virginia, January 14, 1949.

Wolf, Margery, and Roxanne Witke, eds. *Women in Chinese Society.* Stanford, CA: Stanford University Press, 1975.

Wood, James Playsted. *Magazines in the United States: Their Social and Economic Influence.* New York: Ronald Press Co., 1949.

Wostroff, Nancy J. *Grame Park: An Eighteenth-Century Country Estate in Horsham, Pennsylvania.* Ph.D. diss., Winterthur, June 1958.

Yoshioka, Barbara. *Imaginal Worlds: Woman as Witch and Preacher in 17th-Century England.* Ph.D. diss., University Microfilms, 1991.

Zerubavel, Yael. *Recovered Roots: Collective Memory and the Making of Israeli National Tradition.* Chicago: University of Chicago Press, 1995.

Zlotnick, S. "Domestic Imperialism." *Frontiers* 16, no. 2–3 (1996): 51–68.

Index